Forging a Multinational State

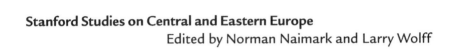

**Stanford Studies on Central and Eastern Europe**
Edited by Norman Naimark and Larry Wolff

# Forging a Multinational State

*State Making in Imperial Austria*
*from the Enlightenment to the First World War*

## John Deak

Stanford University Press

Stanford, California

Stanford University Press
Stanford, California

This book has been published with the assistance of the Institute for Scholarship in the Liberal Arts, College of Arts and Letters, University of Notre Dame.

Printed in the United States of America on acid-free, archival-quality paper

Library of Congress Cataloging-in-Publication Data

Deák, John (John David), author.
  Forging a multinational state : state making in imperial Austria from the Enlightenment to the First World War / John Deak.
      pages cm--(Stanford studies on Central and Eastern Europe)
  Includes bibliographical references and index.
  ISBN 978-0-8047-9557-9 (cloth : alk. paper)
  1. Austria--Politics and government--1848-1918. 2. Austria--Politics and govern-ment--1740-1848. 3. Habsburg, House of. I. Title. II. Series: Stanford studies on Central and Eastern Europe.
  DB86.D43 2015
  943.6'04--dc23

                                    2015019551

  ISBN 978-0-8047-9593-7 (electronic)

Typeset by Bruce Lundquist in 11/13.5 Adobe Garamond

*To Karen Deak, fellow traveler*

# Contents

# Illustrations

## Maps

## Tables

## Figures

# Acknowledgments

Writing this book has been like going on a long pilgrimage. It has taken me many places and introduced me to many wonderful people, whom my introversion and fear of the unknown otherwise never would have allowed me to meet. It has not always been pleasurable and some lessons on the journey I was disinclined to learn. But others' grace and generosity have always saved me from myself. It is with great pleasure that I share these experiences with you here.

My journey began in the Department of History at the University of Chicago, where I benefited from the direction and mentorship of John W. Boyer. Despite his busy schedule as the Dean of the College, he always gave me as much time and patience as I needed. His meticulousness, his energy and vitality, and above all his generousness, model a scholar I still hope to become. Michael Geyer and Jan E. Goldstein were equally generous with time, advice, and concern. I could not ask for a better start to my own journey than what these scholars gave me. Cam Hawkins, Derek Hastings, Jonathan Gumz, Thomas Grischany, and Ke-chin Hsia became companions along this book's journey. I benefitted from many informal discussions with them, their camaraderie, their great advice, and their time.

My journey changed in 2009 when I joined the History Department at the University of Notre Dame. My colleagues at Notre Dame have, once again, provided what money could not: camaraderie, attention, and friendship. There is not a better, more collegial department anywhere in the world and I feel fortunate to be a part of it. I am especially grateful to Patrick Griffin for reading the whole draft of the manuscript and for buying me breakfast more times than I can remember. Ted Beatty bought me a pint (or two), read and commented on several chapters, and gave me the confidence to keep walking. Tom Kselman took me under his wing and offered not only his good advice, but his friendship. Alex Martin likewise was always there to listen and help me refine my ideas. My fellow junior professors, Catherine Cangany, Rebecca McKenna, and Paul Ocobock read several chapter drafts, and helped improve the manuscript substantially. Fr. Robert Sullivan and Chris Hamlin read drafts of early chapters and helped put me on the right track as I put the manuscript together. Finally, in the department and out, I have been boosted by the kindness of the people around me. Sebastian Rosato in the Political Science Department has been my constant interlocutor since the day I arrived on campus. If I explain anything well, it is because he has helped me take Occam's razor to my ideas.

My journey has often led me to Austria, where I have benefited equally from camaraderie, support, and help. Much of the early research was done with a Fulbright Fellowship, sponsored by the Austrian-American Education Commission. Grants from the Notre Dame Office of Research, the Institute for Scholarship in the Liberal Arts, and the Nanovic Institute for European Studies allowed me to return to the archives for research between 2010 and 2014. A Richard Plaschka Scholarship in 2012, from the Bundesministerium für Wissenschaft und Forschung (BMWF), provided a much-needed sabbatical from teaching and allowed me to re-engage with this book manuscript. While I was there, the Österreichischer Austauschdienst (OeAD) provided me with stimulating programming, a friendly and capable support network, and, finally, housing. In one of the odder moments of my journey, I found myself living with three nineteen-year-old college students in a shared apartment. Simon Gerstmann, Marko Gregurić, and Bastian Stemer took good care of the strange American college professor in their apartment, and accepted me, despite the fact that I was nearly twice their age. The staff of Austrian State Archives, especially Dr. Roman-Hans Gröger, provided friendly help navigating through carton after carton of burnt, musty, dirty documents. I am likewise grateful to the staff of the Austrian National Library for their aid in locating sources for this project. Dr. Meggi Grandner kindly volunteered to act as my sponsor during the fellowship, despite the hyperactivity at her new job in the Institut für Internationale Entwicklung at the University of Vienna.

Research in Vienna allowed me to reconnect with my friends in Vienna who have fed me, served as a springboard for my ideas, and shared their lives with me. Daniela and Barry O'Shea count as my friends of longest standing. As I was writing this book, they would drag me away from my books for quiz nights at the pub, card games, and World Cup matches on television. Dr. Richard Germann and his wife, Karin, fed me, gave me too much to drink, and kept me up way too late for my own good. Toni and Michael Siegmund got me out to enjoy the cafés and restaurants of Vienna. Katharina Schneider has been an all-around colleague and friend. She read chapter drafts, introduced me to her favorite *Heurigen*, and took me out to the theater. Dr. Julie Thorpe read the first two chapters, helped me reformulate my ideas, and led me on a few memorable adventures. Dr. Jonathan Kwan read and commented on Chapter 5. Together, my Viennese crew reminded me—when I caught up on my sleep—that I have some of the best friends in the world.

As this journey has neared its end, Larry Wolff emerged as an advocate and mentor. At Stanford University Press, Eric Brandt, Friederike Sundaram, and Kate Wahl have provided patient guidance and helped me to reach the end. Andrew Frisardi has been an excellent, patient, and meticulous copy editor. My readers, including Jeremy King and Nancy Wingfield, stepped in to provide helpful and timely suggestions. Patrick McGraw provided early help in developing the manuscript. Matthew Sisk, a postdoctoral fellow at the Center for Digital Scholarship at the University of Notre Dame, produced maps on short notice and with good cheer. Julie Tanaka, Western European History Librarian, has bought many books on "eastern and central" European history to keep my shelves full.

This pilgrimage has not been without its harder moments and sloughs of despond. Several of my colleagues and friends did not live to see me complete my journey. Professor Sabine McCormack welcomed me to Notre Dame and provided a constant source of encouragement and stimulation in my first three years at Notre Dame. Professor Remie Constable likewise always stopped for conversation and provided a model of scholarship and collegiality. Finally, my father died within two hours of my submitting this manuscript to Stanford University Press. I miss him, but am so grateful for the time, attention, and love he gave me, to the very end.

My family has stood by me for this entire journey. To my brother and sister, their spouses and children, to my mother, and to my wife, I know how much your love sustains me. Thank you. Thank you.

## A Note on Nomenclature and the Perils of Habsburg History

One of the results of the state-building project over the course of the eighteenth, nineteenth, and twentieth centuries is that the names, titles, and nomenclature of the parts of the Habsburg monarchy and its institutions evolved. In the eighteenth century, the state could be referred to only as the Habsburg's lands. In 1804, the entirety of the Habsburg's possessions became officially known as the Austrian Empire. Hungary was constitutionally part of this empire until 1867, when the entire polity became Austria-Hungary. At that point in time, Hungary entered into its own state-building process, while the non-Hungarian parts of the monarchy continued on the trajectory that began in the eighteenth century. The non-Hungarian part of the monarchy was officially called the "Kingdom and Lands represented in the *Reichsrat*"—but I have chosen to call it Austria, or Cisleithania, as a matter of convenience. In addition, cities and towns carried multiple names, depending on the language in which they were referred. When there was an English equivalent for a place or city (Vienna, Prague, Transylvania), I have sought to use that name. For places without an equivalent, I have privileged the German name, since that was the dominant language of the administration. I list the German name, followed by the other possible names when these places first appear in the text.

Forging a Multinational State

# Introduction

IN 1910, Emperor Francis Joseph, as an example to all his peoples, filled out that year's Austrian census form. Under the rubric for occupation, the eighty-year-old emperor could have put down any number of titles: Emperor of Austria; Apostolic King of Hungary; King of Bohemia; Archduke of Austria; Duke of Styria, Carinthia, and Carniola. If he felt ironic—which he rarely did—he could have put down King of Jerusalem, a title he inherited from his crusading ancestors from Lorraine. Instead of trotting out these ancient titles, however, Francis Joseph thought for a moment and wrote "self-employed chief official."[1] Historians often recount Francis Joseph's many titles as they open their accounts of the late imperial monarchy. The titles make the monarchy seem old and obsolete—a product of medieval times; and they make Francis Joseph's sovereignty seem broken and antiquated. Francis Joseph, when considering how he fit into the colorful mosaic of his multinational, diverse empire, was at heart a bureaucrat. In this book, I will also argue that Francis Joseph was also a state builder who followed the lead of the tens of thousands of civil servants whose mantle he wore.

Francis Joseph was a state builder insofar as he sat as the head of a state that had shared in the larger process of modernization and state building with the other states of Europe. So, when historians recount his titles, his kingdoms and lands, they hide or obscure the modern state that Francis Joseph ruled. That modern state was the result of a process which began with his great-great grandmother, Maria Theresia, in the eighteenth century, and culminated in Francis Joseph's Imperial Commission for

Administrative Reform on the eve of the First World War. This book is the story of this state-building process and the state that came from it.

What is state building? State building is a historically grounded concept, describing long-term structural changes in temporal power. State building, or "state making," has framed our understanding of early modern Europe. It encompassed the processes and features of building the apparatuses of the state as well as the formal and informal institutions that make up a state: building and organizing armies, taxing the populace, policing citizens, and controlling the food supply. Finally, building a state means creating "technical personnel" to coordinate all of the above. It meant creating a bureaucracy, building a bigger army, and therefore fighting more successful wars. Early in the modern period, these innovations in the reach and the technologies of statecraft snowballed, accumulating more and more objects, tools of knowledge, and aspects of society as it formed. After the eighteenth century, the state increasingly took over education from the Church and private institutions, determining the curriculum to create obedient subjects and potential state agents.[2] It would acquire knowledge in road and bridge building, it would fund railroads and build canals to create greater networks of transportation for its armies and in order to speed the flow of taxable commercial goods.[3] States broke down the intertwined economic, social, and political authority of guilds in the towns and the nobility in the countryside.[4] Citizenship and public law ultimately were set at the state level; people's rights and obligations as citizens were no longer dependent fully on their belonging to a town, a *civitas*, but to the state.

The Habsburg monarchy from Maria Theresia to Francis Joseph offers us a rich multinational and multicultural history. But it typically has not been the subject of books that approach it from the standpoint of state building. Positive assessments of the Habsburg monarchy, ones that put the monarchy squarely in the middle of European history, are few and far between. For a long time, the history of imperial Austria in the modern era has been a story of backwardness, a failure to innovate, and thus a story of decline and fall.[5] If anything, the Habsburg monarchy has typically been seen as a failed state which could not and did not provide an adequate army to survive the First World War or the proper democratic outlets for its many national movements.[6]

The idea that the Habsburg Empire was not a state, or was a failed one, has long and deep roots. Its seeds were planted by the philosopher Georg Wilhelm Friedrich Hegel in his *Lectures on the Philosophy of History*, first published by his students in 1837. Hegel taught that progress happens in a complicated process, but that it could be understood linearly, through the rise and fall of successive civilizations. Hegel's contribution to a holistic understanding of the past came from looking at pinnacle civilizations at any given time. At the time of his writing, this was Prussia. The modern form of society in his own time became the nation-state, and it would be Prussia's historical raison d'être to unite Germany under its tutelage. Austria was not a pinnacle civilization. It contributed little to the forward movement and progress of European civilization. If anything, Austria served as an obstacle to European development. It was a hindrance and therefore a topic for antiquarians but not for true historians who sought to understand the progress of humanity as a whole.[7]

Following Hegel, historians, historical sociologists, economists, and political scientists have seen the Austrian state as an anachronism. As the rest of western Europe developed into "modern" nation-states, between the Renaissance and the First World War, Austria remained bound by a supposedly medieval organization of formerly independent kingdoms and lands. The persistence of this view is striking and its place in modern history texts is pernicious. By the twentieth century Austria was, according to a recent volume on the First World War, a "medieval holdover."[8] For Hegel, the diverging historic paths of Prussia and Austria showcased where the "world-spirit" was at work and where it was wholly absent. In courses on German history, we often see and hear the phrase, "While Prussia innovated, Austria incubated."[9] Prussia acquired legitimacy as a European power through a thorough reform of its institutions while Austria clung to its legitimacy through the loose unification of its historic parts. One was destined to rise, to become a state, while the other was doomed to decline and fall as a rickety old empire and a monument to a bygone age.

Historical studies of state building, the way we understand the emergence of modern states on the map of Europe, have largely followed Hegel's lead. In the works of Tilly and his fellow scholars in comparative politics of the Social Science Research Council, the long-term structural changes that Europe underwent between 1500 and 1900 favored the development of nation-states. Tilly wrote in the introduction to his landmark edited volume of 1975, that "the relative homogeneity of the European population facilitated the emergence of the national state" because it made it "easy to divide the continent up into mutually exclusive territories."[10] As subsequent authors wrote on the state-building aspects of military, police, and taxation, for all their erudition and sophistication, the nation-state was still the endpoint; they wrote in the universe that Hegel created in the second decade of the nineteenth century. Within European history at large and in western civilization courses (even if less so than when I attended college in the late 1990s), we still follow Hegel's narrative of the rise of the nation-state.

This is a major mistake. State building needs to come to Habsburg central Europe and be read by historians, sociologists, and political scientists, because the state was utterly transformative there. Moreover, historians of Europe have done something Tilly probably never intended: we have written large parts of Europe out of the narrative of European history. Nonnational narratives—narratives that do not arrive at the establishment of nation-states—have been ignored. The Habsburg monarchy, for instance, appears as an imposing or great blotch of a single color on the European map, but it is rarely covered in our textbooks or in our courses on western civilization. The story of western Europe's rise has for a long time been taken as the story of Europe. The story of the less fortunate east—whether as economically backward or the "bloodlands" between Hitler and Stalin—has long been the story of pathology and misery. It is also, now, a story of the nation-state.

This book presents a new history of the Austrian state-building project, a history which is also a deeply European one. Standing at the center of Europe, the Austrian monarchy was home to a multitude of established and emerging national movements.[11] A largely peasant society in 1740, it was industrialized in many places by the First World War, and was establishing robust trading and economic links all over the world. Moreover, it developed strong state institutions that constantly had to negotiate with regional and local interests, interests that became increasingly shaped by nationalist ideas. In a very real sense, the Habsburg monarchy offers many lessons to the multinational, global present. Particularly relevant is the story that historians have largely ignored—that of the central state.

Recent studies which look beyond the nation-state paradigm for understanding the past—for Europe's past offers the present more than just the story of emerging nation-states—have offered much in the way of subverting a larger and overly simplistic narrative of East and West, modern and anachronistic, democratic and despotic.[12] The Hegelian narrative of Europe loses its primacy through the ever-evolving European Union and by the influence of postcolonial history. Nation-states no longer seem like the "natural" endpoint of state building. Now we can pose the question of how nations will fit into the new Europe? Are regions like Catalonia or Bavaria better units than nation-states? During a talk at the Johns Hopkins University Center in Bologna, Italy, in 1995, Tony Judt asked his audience to consider the Habsburg Empire as a multinational antecedent of the EU: "For what is 'Brussels' after all, if not a renewed attempt to achieve that ideal of efficient, universal administration, shorn of particularisms and driven by rational calculation and the rule of law?"[13] It is time we begin to consider, twenty years after Judt's lecture, just what the Habsburg monarchy can tell us about the emergence of states and about the possibilities and challenges of multinationalism, or transnationalism, in Europe.

The story of the Habsburg state has become relevant once again, and the nation-state histories which have underpinned our understanding of progress now seem less natural and absolute. But we still have far to go. We need new narratives of central-European history that take account of historical change divorced from narratives that privilege political decline and the rise of the nation-state. It is imperative that we look at what kind of state the Habsburg monarchy was, how it developed over the nineteenth century, and in what ways its structures answered and did not answer the challenges of exercising sovereignty in a diverse space with many languages and a variety of social, legal, and economic systems. The real challenge is that state-building and political developments make for large, sweeping narratives, while telling the story of the Habsburg monarchy calls for qualifications, exceptions, and complexity. From Barrington Moore to Theda Skocpol, writing about how states develop, and how political participation emerges within states, has required comparative history and a broader view: the "big structures, large processes, and huge comparisons," to borrow a phrase from Charles Tilly.[14] These works have provided historians and social scientists with broad outlines and an incredibly broad view of institutional change over the centuries; but they have also—unintentionally—created large gaps in our knowledge of states by focusing on paradigmatic cases. Moreover, the trend has been to write about state building and the larger social and economic processes that accompany the emergence and solidification of states as divorced from context, from contingency, and from people. This did not have to be the case.

Applying the knowledge and questions of state building to the problem of the Habsburg Empire has traditionally meant telling the story of what the Habsburg Empire failed to do:[15] it failed to become a highly centralized nation-state; to adapt to modernity; and, eventually, to survive the First World War. It missed out on the key developments of strong states, including the mobilization of nationalism, rapid industrialization, and the maintenance of its great power status.[16] But such stories miss what actually happened in the monarchy; they miss the intentions of the rulers, the dynamics of compromise that characterized Habsburg rule, and they miss the fundamental groundwork for central European political culture that was forged under the Habsburg rulers. To tell this story, I focus on the intentions of Vienna and its central reformers, who continually sought to refine the Austrian state between 1740 and 1914.

## The Bureaucrats

In telling the story of the Austrian state-building project, I have invariably told the story of imperial Austria's officials and bureaucrats. The word *bureaucracy*, and by extension *bureaucrat*, carry a pejorative meaning. Literally, bureaucracy means "rule of the office" and is often used as a foil to democracy, "rule by the people." Bureaucracy therefore signifies larger problems of complex societies, like red tape, bean counting, and, of course, the arbitrary use of authority. But democracy and bureaucracy are false antonyms. Administration, to use a less pejorative term, in the twenty-first century is inherent to modern democratic societies. Bureaucracy is the instrument of parliaments, presidents, and elected representatives to "accomplish the complex social tasks" that the people charge their elected representatives to do.[17] Bureaucratic power seems like a boring thing, filled with tedium and routine. But the very act of collecting papers and selecting cases and files produced norms—norms that would build routines in bureaucratic policy making in the far corners of the monarchy. These routines extended and concentrated authority in the state and its officials, and structured how the Habsburg monarchy developed, in terms of infrastructure and institutions of political representation, over the course of the nineteenth century.[18]

Telling such stories is not without its challenges. The Austrian writer Robert Musil (1880–1942), one of the greats of twentieth-century modernism, peppered his unfinished magnum opus, *The Man Without Qualities*, with casual observations on imperial Austrian politics and the bureaucracy. One such passage evokes the cultural capital and yet mystique of Austrian bureaucratic culture. The protagonist, Ulrich, while listening to proposals on "the Parallel Campaign" to celebrate Francis Joseph's seventy-year jubilee (which would have occurred in 1918), told an impertinent joke. His interlocutor, Diotima, ignored him and continued speaking. Ulrich "searched involuntarily between her words for the yellow and black strings, which punctured and bound together the leaves of paper in the ministries." Doderer tells us that Diotima continued speaking and Ulrich tried to interrupt, but somehow "in that moment, the vestral incense of the high bureaucracy gently clouded over his interruption and gently veiled its tactlessness. Ulrich was astounded. He stood up, his visit had obviously come to an end."[19]

Ulrich lost his sense of time, and his ability to speak or even to think, in the incense cloud of Austria's gentle bureaucracy. Bureaucratic organization, red tape, laws in legalese—all of these things combine to cloud our vision of the past. How can we grasp the essence of change when we cannot see its center? How can we find our own way through? The bureaucracy produced all the pages that fill the files of the General Administrative Archives in Vienna and its papers fill up mountains of files in provincial and national archives across central Europe. Its reports, drafts, and documents, fastened together with "the yellow and black strings" that Musil mentions, are the single largest evidence of their existence. And yet the authors of these reports remain hidden behind the cloud of incense, evading our grasp. Waltraud Heindl, the master of the history of Austria's imperial civil service, writes of the inherent "secrecy" that impedes study of the bureaucracy. The scholar encounters anonymity and "the intangible . . . that which is meaningful and that which resists meaning."[20] The bureaucracy produces mountains of paper, but these papers offer no direct account of its own history. The names on the reports are scribbled at the bottom, often illegible. One can cross check them with the names printed in the *Court and State Handbook of the Austro-Hungarian Monarchy*, published yearly between 1874 and 1918, but names can tell us only so much. As the Austrian state expanded and the volumes of paper increased, crowding the bureaucrats out of their own offices, the bureaucrats systematically pulped the paper, thus shredding the vestiges of their own recent past. Finally, the Austrian bureaucracy hid its own numbers. For large periods of time, we do not know with any certainty how many people the state employed. The incense cloud sits over large swathes of state building, veiling our inquiries.

Nevertheless, pockets of clarity appear now and then. Bureaucrats left behind discernible traces of themselves and their careers. My sources include memoirs, handbooks, reports, private letters, statistical handbooks, and

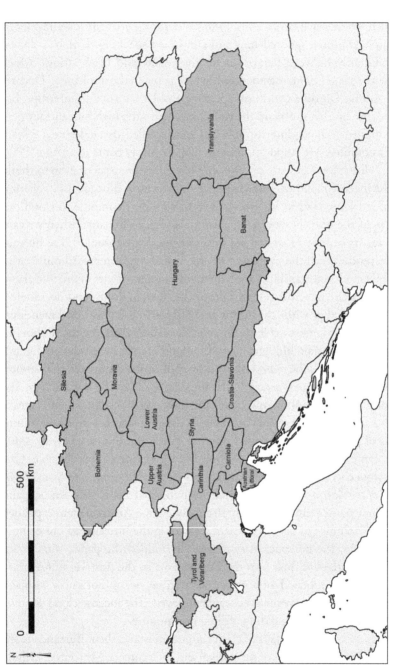

MAP I.1. Lands of the House of Habsburg in 1740

manuals on regulations and comportment of the bureaucrats themselves. In many ways, the state-building project is their story: the reformation of the bureaucracy under Maria Theresia; Joseph II's infusion of the civil service with a particular statist ethos; the reforming impulse of the bureaucracy in bloom after the revolutions of 1848; and the struggle to maintain the bureaucracy as a cohesive force in the monarchy after the systematic expansion of suffrage after 1860. But I am well aware that, though the story I tell is particular, it is also the story of the central, imperial state. This, at least on the surface, goes against the grain of recent work in the field of empire and bureaucracy studies. In particular, relatively recent work on colonial bureaucracies has emphasized how regional and local bureaucrats implemented their own ideas and followed their own interests independent of the metropole.[21] Bureaucrats frequently changed their orders on the ground in order to negotiate the differences between the grand ideas in the central offices and the realities of their local situation. Bureaucrats had to and did form their own tools of knowledge, their own methods of administration, and their own strategies for state building. Habsburg bureaucrats did this as well, proving to be a flexible instrument that navigated the linguistic, legal, and social diversity of the Habsburg lands. The late imperial period of the Habsburg Empire (roughly from 1867 to 1918) has been widely criticized for its "bureaucratic absolutism," but absolutism in the monarchy was always negotiated. Officials were the negotiators. How this bureaucracy formed, the constitutional structures on which it grew, and finally, how the bureaucracy came to be both the glue which held the state together and the lubricant which ameliorated its natural friction, is the story of this book.

## Maria Theresia and State Building

The story of the Austrian state is therefore a story of becoming—a process—which started both with war, defeat, and—ironically—a family document. Charles VI, after he became the head of the House of Habsburg in 1711, drew up the Pragmatic Sanction. Charles, in order to maintain his family's inheritance and ensure that his lands would not be divided among his descendants, declared that the lands of the Habsburgs were "indivisible and inseparable," and, in so doing, imagined their lands as a single entity.[22] When Maria Theresia ascended the Habsburg throne on the basis of the Pragmatic Sanction in 1740, however, she had to defend both her lands and the idea of an "indivisible and inseparable" monarchy (see Map I.1). She found herself beset on all sides by powerful princes who hoped to pick apart her patrimony. The most daring of these princes was Frederick II of Prussia, who invaded the Habsburg province of Silesia in December 1740. Smelling blood in the water, the Bavarian Duke Charles Albert—her cousin by marriage—had declared himself "Archduke of Austria" and threatened to march on Vienna. By November 1741, she was surrounded by enemies: the Bavarians had taken Linz and occupied Upper Austria and Prague had fallen to a Franco-Bavarian army. Saxony also invaded Bohemia. The War of Austrian Succession (1740–48) threatened to tear apart the House of Austria, rending it from almost all its possessions in but a few years.[23] Maria Theresia survived the war and was able to defeat the Bavarian challenge to her house's reign. She maintained most all of her patrimony, reclaiming her lands from Bavarian, Saxon, and French armies. In spite of her victories, she could not unseat Frederick II of Prussia from Silesia, which he held for the remainder of the war and incorporated into his growing Prussian kingdom.

The War of Austrian Succession strained Maria Theresia's resources to their limit, deepening her debt, and stretched her abilities to field armies to defend her lands. Many historians see this war as a turning point for the venerable Habsburg family—a significant step down the road of decline that paralleled the rise of Prussia. In reality it marked a moment of change and restoration. Defeats have a way of making change more acceptable, easier; they often can pave the way for reform. Maria Theresia now began a search for a bigger and better army, an army that would crush Frederick's and that would be commensurate with the defense of the realm.

To build a bigger and better army and maintain it for action at any moment to defend her lands, Maria Theresia would have to reorganize her state. As a result of the War of Austrian Succession, as a result of her search for new ways to protect her patrimony, Maria Theresia began a state-making process that would flourish during her reign and that of her successor and son, Joseph II. Considering the need to change the structure of her government, in 1749 Maria Theresia began to write down her political testament. She begins her story by drawing attention to how far she had come: "When the unexpected and lamentable death of my father of blessed memory occurred . . . [I] was at the time the more devoid of the experience and knowledge needful to rule dominions so extensive and so various because my father had never been pleased to initiate or inform me in the conduct of either internal or foreign affairs, I found myself suddenly without either money, troops, or counsel."[24] Under Maria Theresia, the

Habsburgs became more assertive of their prerogatives and powers. But the story does not end there; in fact, it is only the beginning.

From the War of Austrian Succession to her death in 1780, Maria Theresia, her son Joseph II, and their advisors created a new state. This occurred in two discrete steps. First, Maria Theresia created new structures for her patrimony and increased the number of officials to staff them. After the structures were in place, Habsburg public officials were infused with an ethos and given a mission to serve and transform the lands under the Habsburg scepter. This second process would not end, but would evolve over the course of the nineteenth century as Austria's state evolved and the work of public administration expanded and changed. This book is a story of this process—a state-building process that offers up confirmation, variation, and alternatives to the larger structural history of modern Europe.

In the wake of the war, as Maria Theresia studied the structures which supported her authority, she saw a tangled mess of reforms and inherited tradition. Indeed, it was, in Maria Theresia's own words, "dominions so extensive and so various" that posed her problem—a difficulty that the Habsburgs had traditionally solved through a certain flexibility and willingness to rule all their kingdoms and lands according to local customs and through compromise with the local nobility. Her many lands and provinces were administered from Vienna by four distinct chancelleries. Each chancellery was responsible for a group of provinces. The Bohemian chancellery was responsible for communicating and coordinating the wishes of the crown with the three lands of the Bohemian crown (Bohemia, Moravia, and Silesia). An Austrian chancellery did the same for the "hereditary lands"—lands that the Habsburgs had ruled in one form or another since the days of Rudolf I in the thirteenth century. Separate chancelleries also administered the crown's prerogatives for Hungary and Transylvania. Fighting the War of Austrian Succession forced Maria Theresia to negotiate with the nobility in each of her disparate kingdoms and lands through these four separate chancelleries over taxes and soldier contingents. Austria's war with Prussia proved the woeful inefficiency of such a system. The crown administered four different groups of provinces separately, negotiated with them for revenues separately, and—most importantly—depended on administrative bodies to implement its wishes. It was not always possible to find four capable chancellors, ready to represent the wishes of the crown over the vested interests of the noble estates. Often Maria Theresia's chancelleries represented the rights and prerogatives of the nobility at the expense of her own.

The "big picture" arguments of Charles Tilly have emphasized that the extreme fiscal costs of war meant that only strong states capable of raising enough taxes to field armies would survive. The constant pressure for bigger and better-equipped armies then forged state institutions, as monarchs searched for more efficient ways to extract tax revenues and people from their lands. The early reforms of Maria Theresia followed this pattern. Following the War of Austrian Succession, Maria Theresia's government undertook a series of administrative and fiscal reforms that reorganized the way in which Vienna related to its provinces. Maria Theresia responded to defeat by cleaning her house of old nobles who defended their own social interests at the expense of her own. She quickly found advisors who would rectify her patrimony's finances and restore her position as a leading monarch of Europe. These men would ruffle feathers, alienate the old guard, and suggest new ways of creating a steady income. Such changes, sudden and brutal, set in motion deep-reaching reforms that would pull the disparate Habsburg kingdoms, counties, and lands toward Vienna. Over time, fiscal policies built up new structures and institutions that would come to form the backbone of an imperial state.

These early structural and fiscal policies emerged under Friedrich Wilhelm von Haugwitz in the 1740s and gained their fullest expression in the following decade. Haugwitz may have been "ugly, unrefined, and colorless" to the high nobles at the Habsburg's court,[25] but he was just the shade of man Maria Theresia needed to reform the fiscal situation of the Habsburg's public coffers, which were even uglier. He sought to intervene in Austria's provinces and local administration and to flip the structures of power in the crown's favor—away from the nobility who collected taxes, maintained law and order, and served as the crown's local administrators. Haugwitz's interventions concentrated on the fiscal techniques of the Habsburg state. Haugwitz proposed financial and, above all, structural reforms to wrest financial control from the nobles and the chancelleries in Vienna, which were staffed by the nobles who administered the provinces on behalf of the empress.[26] The basis of Haugwitz's system came out of an emergent discourse on state sovereignty and fiscal power, which meant that state finances had to reflect the sovereignty of the state—which they did not, at least not yet. Haugwitz argued "that the Monarchy's defective system of finance and government constituted an internal enemy fully as dangerous to the Crown as the more obvious enemies without."[27] The problem would be imposing the power of the sovereign onto the estates and breaking the latter's will to resist the former's fiscal claims. If the crown could not raise revenue as it saw fit, the realm would be indefensible.

It was here, in the negotiation of fiscal prerogatives between the crown and the estates, that the Austrian state-building project started to outgrow the mere "war makes the state" paradigm.[28] State building quickly became a public good, an ideology that freed itself from bigger armies and steady supplies of troops. After a series of reforms led by Haugwitz met with the intransigence of the chancelleries in 1748, Maria Theresia was even more determined to change the entire structure of government, because the intransigence represented the system of particularism and privilege that Haugwitz convinced her needed to be overcome. In the chancelleries, nobles—Maria Theresia's own advisors—pursued their interests with a fierceness that Haugwitz had to overcome. They fought Haugwitz's reforms and principles, which included the regular taxation of noble land in peacetime.[29] Maria Theresia responded decisively. She dissolved the Bohemian and Austrian chancelleries, put the administration of justice under the supervision of a supreme court (a slight to patrimonial justice), and united the fiscal and administrative power of the crown under a new central administration, the *Directorium in Publicis et Cameralibus*, with Haugwitz as president.[30] All of this she did by fiat, not consulting with the noble estates—who were not inclined willingly to grant assent to such a turning of the tables.

Revolutions in Austria have a habit of being silent administrative revolutions—but that makes them no less disruptive when viewed from a longer-term perspective. Haugwitz's reforms in the center quickly affected the provinces and the local levels of government. The *Directorium* served a new crown council—the *Conferenz in Internis*, which would enable the crown to enforce its will in the provinces regarding all aspects of social and political life in the hereditary lands and in the lands of the Bohemian crown. For these reforms to succeed, Haugwitz needed new agents and officials and new offices to "represent" the will of the crown in the lands and countryside. The provincial offices came in the form of *Repraesentationen und Cammern* to represent the crown—not the people nor the nobles. These offices were intended to replace the officers of the estates in the provinces in all local matters, from army provisioning to tax assessment and collection, from administration to executive matters. More locally, royal power seeped into the countryside through "circle offices" (*Kreisämter*), which functioned as intermediary offices between the crown's provincial governments and the local authorities dominated by the local lords and town magistrates. These counties were led by a circle, or better put, county prefect who was to watch over the implementation of royal edicts in the localities and to ensure that the local lords did not abuse the authority that was left to them. Local clergy, school officials, and above all the nobility would see the crown's county prefects as a thorn in their side.[31]

Throughout the 1750s, Haugwitz's reforms showed the power of structural change. Within ten years, he had broken the authority of the estates in more than half of the Habsburg's kingdoms and lands by simply changing the structures of central government and installing new administrative organs—loyal to Vienna—in the provinces. Additionally, fruits of Haugwitz's reforms had already increased the annual contribution of the various lands, leading to plans for a standing army of 108,000 men. Moreover, Haugwitz's reforms stirred a veritable stew of injured economic and political interests, because the reforms sought to strengthen the authority of the crown, to strip the estates of their abilities to skim tax revenue and maintain their own interests through the provincial administration, and to establish local offices to supervise the rural nobles and oversee the implementation of Maria Theresia's edicts.

But when these structural changes failed to secure a complete victory over Frederick II's Prussia in the Seven Years' War (1756–63), Maria Theresia turned her ear to the reform proposals of her foreign minister, Anton Wenzel Kaunitz (1711–94). Haugwitz's sacking tells us a few things about the Austrian state-building project. For his demotion indicated that the building of a central state apparatus would engage multiple thinkers, reformers, and planners over the course of more than a century and a half. The torch had passed for the moment to Kaunitz. It would be taken up again and again, as servants of the crown became servants of the state and sought not only to consolidate that state but to adapt it to a growing and changing empire.

What Kaunitz had in mind, however, was to use the structures of taxation and supervision, which Haugwitz had created, to transform society. Haugwitz had made a bureaucracy that reached into the provinces and reported back to Vienna, with both information and money. Kaunitz wanted to make it a two-way street. After 1761, Kaunitz transformed the administration and the very structures that Haugwitz created in the provinces to do more than oversee taxes and represent the interests of the ruling prince. Instead, they were vessels for new ideas, new methods of farming, promotion of healthy bodies (which in turn made a more productive labor force and soldiery), industry, and commerce. Kaunitz laid down these ideas in a memorandum on "founding principles," which he presented to the Council of State in January 1761.[32] The memo exhibited many of the larger ideas regarding enlightened statecraft in the eighteenth century. Kaunitz wrote that the state should act as a "sensible warden," which sees its population not merely as "contributors to the needs of the state, but should see to it that their sustenance and physical strength is expanded and increased."[33] For Kaunitz, then, the bureaucracy could be the channel for new social projects that contributed to the general prosperity of society.[34]

By the end of Maria Theresia's reign, the bureaucracy not only had a structure but a mission. Haugwitz had sought to change the structures of princely authority. Kaunitz saw an opportunity to use the new structures of state that Haugwitz had created as a foundation for new relationships between ruler and ruled. In the six decades that followed Maria Theresia's reign, the bureaucrats would deepen their roots into the lands of the Habsburgs and weave themselves into the fabric of greater Habsburg society. Thus, what began as a war in which Maria Theresia defended her patrimony and the right to rule her diverse lands would emerge as a major reform project that would continue under her son, eventual co-regent and successor, Joseph II. This reform project would transform, in the five decades of Maria Theresia and Joseph II's combined rule, the relationship between temporal authority and the various levels of political, social, and spiritual authority in the lands of the Habsburgs. With taxes and changes to the framework of governance came new ideas of governance: rationality and secular grounding of authority in natural law, which expressed itself in service to the common good through service to the state, replaced rule by the grace of God.[35] And as the basis of authority changed, how that authority was exercised was transformed as well.

This process of state building can be understood on many different levels, from the theoretical basis of authority to actually building and staffing new state offices. Suffice it to say for now that Maria Theresia created new state institutions, which would have lasting significance for central Europe. These new institutions and the new bureaucracy they necessitated had the immediate effect of suppressing the traditional political rights of the provincial nobility and replacing many provincial institutions, which had allowed the nobility to resist the growing budgetary and military needs of the crown. Thus, the process of state building in the era of enlightened absolutism radically altered the structure of social and political life in central Europe; traditional rights of nations, provinces, cities, and the noble estates were abrogated, annulled, or ignored as Maria Theresia, and later Joseph II, sought to create unity and conformity out of the mixture of kingdoms and lands that the imperial house controlled.[36] Although her reforms created a state that does not fit the ideal-typical mold of a modern European nation-state à la Charles Tilly, the Habsburg state that Maria Theresia forged would have a lasting impact in the economic, social, and political development of Habsburg central Europe over the next two centuries and beyond. Moreover these state reforms set other reforms in motion, which would gradually transform Austrian society from one based on privilege and hierarchy to one based on equality under the law.[37]

Between 1740 and 1790, from the beginning of Maria Theresia's reign to the end of Joseph II's, the Habsburg monarchs attempted in a concerted effort to solve the perennial problem of the Habsburg Empire—that is, how to rule "dominions so extensive and so various" in the most efficient and efficacious way possible. Their efforts restructured the Habsburg state and changed the entire nature of Habsburg rule, which would be based on a new attitude and call upon its servants to exhibit a new ethos. But their efforts did not necessarily reflect a steady process. Each monarch brought her and his own concept to crack the Habsburg nut: diversity, particularism, breadth. Maria Theresia responded to crisis with structural reforms. Joseph II would build upon these structures and his contribution would be as equally great: it was one of attitude. By 1790, Maria Theresia and Joseph's combined reforms had far surpassed the fiscal and cameralist theories out of which their first steps originated;[38] they had created a whole new pillar of the state—a bureaucracy. This bureaucracy would become a pillar of Austrian statecraft. Eventually, the bureaucracy would work to build new pillars: representative government, the rule of law, judicial review, which would complicate the nature of rule in Austria and expand participation in governance. That is the story of Austria's long nineteenth century and the story that is the subject of this book.

What I hope to show in this book about imperial Austria are its many possibilities. Between 1740 and 1914 it was not a state in decline, but rather a continually evolving polity. In many ways it offers models and warnings for multinational polities like the European Union whose education, legal, and infrastructure- and state-building policies the Habsburg monarchy resembled. That the monarchy fell and its multinational project fell, can be considered a European tragedy. And yet, it took steps, especially after 1914, to bring about its own destruction. If I can convince you that this was not the only possibility for the monarchy in 1914, than I can be assured that we have come a long way from seeing its history as just one long narrative of decline. Maybe, after all these years, Hegel, who said that this multinational Empire was a thing unto itself and therefore not worth historical study, owes us all an apology.

# 1

## The Dynamics of Austrian Governance, 1780–1848

JOSEPH II suffered grievously at the end of his short life. He suffered from tuberculosis and was too weak to fight political battles anymore. His illness and his recent military and political failures soon led to depression. As he wrote to his brother and successor, Leopold, in lines that have become associated with his reign: "I confess that, brought low by what has happened to me, seeing that I am unfortunate in everything I undertake, the appalling ingratitude with which my good arrangements are viewed and I am treated . . . all this fills me with doubt."[1] Joseph died February 20, 1790, less than a month later. He had ordered a simple, unadorned sarcophagus for himself, befitting the emperor's taste for the simple, functional, and miserly.

Traditionally, historians have seen the death of Joseph and the rise of Emperor Francis as the beginning of the end—the moment in which the monarchy sets down the road toward decline.[2] This is especially the case within the grand narrative of German history, which seeks to explain why Prussia would eventually unite Germany. In the widely accepted narrative, Austria stood still while Prussia was forced to reform itself and become a modern state.[3] But such ideas suggest that Joseph's reforms and the institutions he created did not continue after his rule came to an end. This was not the case, however. First, the institutions that Joseph's successors inherited, especially the administration and the legions of officials who staffed it, continued the work of state building. Second, Joseph's most revolutionary action as monarch was the implementation of a new attitude—both toward rule and toward the Austrian state. This attitude would, over the course of his reign, permeate the imperial public administration and become a new ethos of state service. Joseph conceived the very concept of the Pragmatic Sanction and the indivisible and inseparable monarchy as depending on the networks of officials and public servants whom Vienna sent out into the hinterland. Joseph was able to imagine a centralized, unified monarchy and he worked to pound his lands into a mold that fit his preconceived ideas. It would be this attitude, "Josephinism," or Joseph's reformist, state-centered ethos, which would continue well after his death and shape the Austrian state-building project in the nineteenth century.[4] In fact, Joseph's departure from the scene in 1790 allowed his officials the freedom and independence to develop these ideas further and adapt them to the rapid changes of the nineteenth century, which brought with them not only new forms of industry and social change, but an increasing call for public participation in governance.

Joseph's legacy is an important one, but it was not the only ethos which permeated the Austrian state in the nineteenth century. Joseph's radical changes, his relentless drive to reform, was exhausting to some and struck others as dangerous. "Change" increasingly became something to fear, a slippery slope that would lead to revolution, social unrest, and anarchy. Fear of change only intensified with the outbreak of the French Revolution, which was held up as the possible outcome of state policies that sought to displace the nobility and alter the structures of social and economic life. Joseph's successors increasingly turned away from reform and political change in order to maintain stability. Joseph's state-reforming ethos quickly fell out of favor at court, even if it was preserved in the offices of Habsburg administrators.[5]

In essence, the period between Joseph II and the revolutions of 1848 established the modern Austrian dynamic: an interplay between storm and tranquility—between reform and its opposite, a desire to hold onto tradition and leave things as they are. This dynamic would structure political and social developments in the Habsburg monarchy from the late eighteenth century to the monarchy's entry into the First World War in July 1914. For it was this interplay, not reaction, retrenchment, or incubation, that produced both Austria's political frustrations and its flexibility in organizing and administering a multinational space in the center of Europe. Both forces, reform and resistance, were forged in the era of Joseph II and the French Revolution.

## The Dynamic of Movement: Change and Reform

How should a monarch handle a body of civilian officials? What are they capable of doing? Joseph had been pondering these questions since his twentieth birthday. When he became co-regent in 1765 upon the death of his father, he could finally put many of his ideas into action.[6] If Friedrich Wilhelm Haugwitz had made the argument under Maria Theresia that the presence of the crown's officials in the provinces was necessary to enforce the crown's will, Joseph II wanted these officials to be capable of much more. He wanted to instill them with a spirit that would match the system.[7] In fact, he showed a deep—if sometimes harsh—interest in Austria's corps of civil servants from his early involvement in the Council of State and throughout his co-regency with Maria Theresia (1765–80) and years of his sole rule (1780–90). Joseph II's legacy, despite many of the reforms he attempted, would turn out to be the bureaucracy he left behind, "which held together the socially complex multinational empire until its fall."[8]

Joseph's attitude and his revisioning of the work of the state were his greatest and most consequential innovations. He imagined a state that was an entity in itself, a public good, which extended far beyond his own person. Joseph believed that the role of the state should be to benefit the largest number of people possible. Under Joseph, the state—this abstract entity that provides and encapsulates the common good—eclipsed the ruler and his dynasty. Joseph imbued his civil servants with these views, founding their self-conception as the guardians of the state. For them, self-sacrifice and service to the state—which took the form of the primary progressive agent in society—were the highest calling, a secular priesthood.

The drive for centralization, uniformity, and control brought Joseph again and again to devote his attention to his imperial civil servants, the officials who enacted his decrees and represented his authority outside the walls of Vienna. All of this imperial attention—imbued with the same principles of rationality, uniformity, and the value of efficiency—created a modern, professional civil service in the Weberian sense.[9] Additionally, however, Joseph believed in the transformative power of good government; this would become the staple of Josephinism, to be adhered to by his intellectual heirs well into the nineteenth century. Joseph desired to create an administration that shared his ideas and ethos, and which would serve the common good. These officials would act as his instrument to create a simplified, efficient, and powerful state. Thus, the ten years he spent as the sole ruler of the Habsburg lands, after his mother's death in 1780, were directed toward expanding the state apparatus, unifying territories, eliminating traditional privileges and constitutional exceptions, and combining the separate administrative systems and regimes. In terms of the general education and the restructuring of norms, regulations, and even language, we can see that for Joseph, state officials were to be ideal citizens, the very model of the new person Joseph wanted to create. They were to put aside their personal interests, their egos, and their own will, and conform to the general will of the state. Joseph wanted his authority to be handed down to every province, every county, and every town and village in the same way.

Max Weber's sociology of statecraft captures how the drive for uniformity and centralization necessitates a restructuring of power. The creation of a loyal, hierarchically organized body of officials to carry out orders needs a corresponding body of professional and administrative norms. Body and spirit—or bureaucracy and law—worked together in the Habsburg lands to smooth out the rugged terrain of constitutional differences in the provinces. The Austrian state passed ordinance after ordinance relating to the conduct and the ideal behavior of state officials.[10] Court decrees addressed discipline and punishments for officials if they embezzled, mistreated the local populace, or did not keep their assigned working hours.[11] Bureaus were established to maintain the secrecy of state affairs. In these bureaus the officials could be supervised and disciplined. Maria Theresia and Joseph II's decrees also established a standard system of salaries; norms for how the state offered employment and what qualifications were required for various positions; what age officials should be at the time of first employment (it was between eighteen and forty years); when they would be promoted and given a pay raise; as well as how their children and widows would be cared for after they died. These reforms were important, but they were just the beginning.[12]

Education and competence joined rank and standing in imperial service. Maria Theresia worked to establish Vienna as a center of cameralism, an emerging discipline in the German-speaking world which focused on the study of statecraft and the "science of governing."[13] Cameralists believed that good government meant paying attention to the treasury, the *Kammer*, and for coming up with ways to stimulate growth in state revenues without taxing subjects into debtors' prison. Habsburg institutions of learning sought out prominent cameralists to teach and brought in leading scholars like Johann Heinrich Gottlob von Justi, who took up a post at the Theresianum. The Theresianum itself was a testament to the new educational program. Maria Theresia founded this secondary school in 1746 with a curriculum which prepared nobles and burgher alike for posts in her state.[14] Joseph von Sonnenfels likewise accepted a professorship in 1763 in *Polizei*,[15] and political economics, at the University of Vienna.[16] Both Justi and Sonnenfels would publish books and texts based on their lectures, making Vienna, in the process, a center of cameralist thought.[17]

Building on the work of his mother, Joseph again deepened the state's commitment to educating officials in the sciences of state. He expected his "political officials," those responsible for local or provincial policy and administrative matters, to be university-educated jurists.[18] Better training and education would serve as a reliable foundation for a state that would expand into areas where it previously feared to tread. These included matters of public welfare, sanitation, and economic development (agriculture and trade), forestry, water regulation, bridges and roads, and veterinary medicine. He and his successors would continually engage in efforts to establish and refine the education for civil servants to make them capable of carrying his ideas, his reforms, or even "the enlightenment" to the far corners of the monarchy.[19]

As Joseph expanded his reach, he needed officials who understood his regulations and could put his ideas and laws into action. Joseph worked to animate the spirit of the bureaucracy, not just create new offices and structures. As such, Joseph made his officials' education, their attitudes and ethos, a primary concern. Under Joseph, universities became seminaries for the servants of the state. Their primary purpose became the training of civil servants, who received *the* elite education of the monarchy.[20] Universities under Joseph were reformed so that the practical knowledge of the law received a pride of place. In the Juridicum, natural law, constitutional law, canon law were supplemented by coursework on administrative writing, political economy and cameralism, and legal praxis in the courts.[21] Additionally, technical institutes filled the need for a new crop of "technical" officials: as the monarchy took a greater interest in its economic infrastructure and the welfare of its citizens as economic producers, it needed more officials to serve as building, sanitation, agricultural, forest, or even mine inspectors.[22]

Joseph's insistence on practical knowledge required changes in the university and technical academies' curricula. Knowledge of foreign languages and the semester abroad were written out of the university curriculum for juridical students. Chairs of French, Spanish, and even Latin were eliminated in favor of "Bohemian" and other Slavic languages, which were more practical for the administration of the Habsburg lands. The refinement of German was also emphasized. As government was formalized by moving into bureaus and out of the rooms and apartments of the local notables, so too was writing and communication standardized. Josef von Sonnenfels covered proper German grammar in his course on administrative writing.[23] His text for the course, *On Office Style* (*Über den Geschäftsstil*), reached its fourth edition by 1820 and was vastly important for instilling a cultural and linguistic component to the Josephinist bureaucratic ethos.[24] Requiring precision in language and grammar, use of simple phrases, and the reduction of foreign words, served to rationalize further the work of state. Sonnenfels not only taught his students how to write reports with precision, his book and lectures contained information on how to number, file, and later, find documents. Sonnenfels's ideas on office management combined and emphasized clarity of style with clarity of government. Through the standardization of the written word, knowledge could be standardized. A local official could be promoted or let go and replaced, and his successor could quickly understand local conditions by looking into the files. The state's expanded activity necessitated a more standard and widened communication network. Naturally, the written word would connect center and periphery, monarch and official. In the process, the "bureaucratic gaze" in the core lands of the Habsburgs became standardized.[25] Knowledge was power, not in the abstract, but in praxis.

The curriculum in formal university training instilled both a belief in progress and the sense that state service not only represented the crown but also reason and enlightenment.[26] Such a reformulation of the bureaucracy's self-conception imbued the civil service down to its core with a sense of self-criticism and shaped it into an ideological army of enlightened absolutism. Under Emperor Joseph, the civil servant was trained in a statist atmosphere, in which public officials were taught that the greatest good came from their subordination to the state and the office. This too, is part of Max Weber's description of the development of modern bureaucracy: "It is decisive for the modern loyalty to an office that, in the pure type, it does not establish a relationship to a person, like the vassal's or disciple's faith under feudal or patrimonial authority, but rather is devoted to *impersonal* and *functional* purposes."[27] Joseph was establishing a bureaucracy that would not be the servants of the prince, but of the state. Through these twin processes, one of the administration's function and another of its ethos and self-conception, civil servants became more than just local overseers and tax collectors, and even more than just the executors of the monarchy's authority. Rather, state officials and employees, from the simple doorman to the lord-lieutenants in the provinces, were made into servants of a greater, more abstract, and more powerful entity: the state. These transformations raised the framework of a modern state in the nineteenth century, when representation would come to mean something more than the representation of the crown's interests.

Education, training, and refinement aided Joseph to raise the "totality" of his lands to an abstract whole. These qualities provided him with an objective, obedient, and efficient administration which could help him forge a framework of unity that would provide the model and the course for the entire state. Within this framework the state adopted a common, *bürgerlich*, and German cultural basis.[28] Joseph saw efficiency and utility in the common use of the German language and he recognized the value of civil servants identifying—no matter what their background—with German *Kultur*. Germanization, carried out through the *Volksschulen*, was followed by the implementation of German as the language of Austria's entire administration and supplemented by Sonnenfels's work at the university, training future civil servants in how to write in the new, Austrian, bureaucratic German.[29] Joseph pinned his hopes on the German language both as a force and as a tool for bringing the disparate parts of his monarchy together, just as he also hoped to use his administrators to raise the power and status of the central state both among his diverse lands and abroad.[30] In the end, Joseph's reforms and Sonnenfels's lectures on *Geschäftsstyl* combined the principles of Germanization and a professional officialdom to create a German-speaking and even Germanophile bureaucracy.[31]

In addition to the social and career aspects of the administrators' work, Joseph devoted his attention to the comportment and ethos of the officials themselves. Joseph applied his austerity measures at court in brutal fashion to the civil service. They had to be efficient, do more with less, and—above all—work hard to earn their meager pay. As Joseph attended the Council of State, he gained a perch from which he could observe and criticize, although his most vociferous writings were always turned in privately to his mother.[32] In 1761, Joseph penned a memo to Maria Theresia, which, in addition to expressing a desire to "humble and impoverish" the nobility, also stated a hope to instill discipline and a culture of merit among state officials.[33] Joseph attacked what he saw as indecisiveness and complacency among the officials who staffed the Habsburgs' new bureaus. He hoped to purge the ranks of officials who showed themselves less fit for such an important task as service to the state, "removing the inefficient without regard to rank, and the lazy."[34] "With me there would be few people employed," Joseph wrote to his mother. "None who were lazy, negligent, incapable would have anything to hope for." Joseph claimed that those officials who purposefully committed errors or did not follow the rules "would be punished with maximum severity, with no account taken of birth." Joseph's railings contained an egalitarianism that showed that both noble and commoner were equal before the law and the state. Errors, negligence, and personal gain would be punished the same way whether one had the "scraps of paper" to claim nobility or not.[35] Although Joseph was just twenty years old when he penned these *Rêveries*, his focus on the work, ethos, and efficiency of the administration remained a central theme of his efforts to strengthen the Habsburg state. At times his attention resulted in a brutal, sarcastic assessment of the Habsburgs' officials. In a memorandum to his mother on the conditions of the state in 1765, Joseph wrote, "Among the 100 reams of paper that are easily used within eight days in the offices of Vienna, there is not four pages that contain spirit, new concepts or original ideas." Joseph's impatience with his officials' lack of original thinking is apparent in his description of a ministerial report as containing "an introduction, a long summary, and two words of an individual standpoint."[36] Moreover, in the midst of his criticism, Joseph complained in his memorandum about the culture of authority (mutual distrust between superiors and subordinates), a culture of laziness, a lack of decisiveness stemming from the structural organization of the entire system, and an "unbelievable enormous wastefulness, negligence, and laziness" among the councilors and ministers. "To get these people to work is both right and necessary."[37]

In the midst of Joseph's rather biting assessment of his own officials, there is, however, a sense that his ire stemmed from the high expectations that he had for the Habsburg state and its ministers and officials. Joseph wanted an administration to which he could delegate authority and therefore trust to act decisively "without partisanship" or "chicanery."

His officials would be the state's executors, promoting the health, wealth, and prosperity of his subjects. From 1765, when he became co-regent with his mother, until his death as emperor and sole ruler in 1790, Joseph and a series of advisors, academics, and fellow admirers of the Enlightenment tweaked education policies, university curriculum, the hierarchy of the administration and its organization. They also experimented with new codes of discipline, supervision, and ways of improving the bureaucracy's technical abilities and efficiency. Especially after 1780, when Joseph became sole ruler, the pace of reforms increased. Structurally, this meant administrative and organizational reforms, judicial and fiscal reorganizations, further efforts at centralization of monarchical authority, and attempts to bring his Hungarian and Transylvanian lands under a common administration with the Bohemian and Austrian territories, now the core of the monarchy.[38] Joseph pushed for efficiency with a ruthlessness that came from a desire to make the complicated central European realities fit into a rational, schematic elegance born of abstract principles of governance. Joseph forced rational principles onto a milieu permeated with the historical and constitutional entanglements resulting from centuries of settlements, compromise, and adherence to tradition.[39]

Joseph's reform impulses found their most succinct crystallization in the emperor's "pastoral letter" of 1783. The epithet itself is important, for Joseph issued this circular as a bishop would to the priests in his diocese. For Joseph, officials had their own pastoral mission: bringing the state to the people. The letter which also bore the title "Principles for Every Servant of the State," encapsulated the spirit of the administration that came to be part of its unique ethos—an ethos that would endure.[40] Joseph reminds his civil servants that they derive their authority from the emperor himself, who also trusts them to commit themselves wholly to their work and to apply their faculties to serve their Austrian fatherland and their fellow citizens. Joseph's officials were to be efficient, to eliminate waste both of time and money; they were to read all of the emperor's orders and instructions; and finally, they were to deny their own selfish interests for the sake of the state and the good of all. Joseph railed against what he termed *Eigennuz*—selfish interest—with the most capacious definition of what it entailed and meant. In his administration, there was no room for the personal, for putting oneself before others, or for putting one's wealth, happiness, or aspirations before those of the state—the common good. "Self-interest," Joseph wrote, "is not only to be understood as involving money, but rather as all side-interests, which darken, cloud, conceal, delay or enfeeble that which is singularly true and best, the assigned duty, truthfulness in reporting and exactitude in following orders." Moreover, Joseph used language that suggested the duty of the civil servant to serve the state, and through it to serve one's fellow man, was something almost holy and pure. Self-interestedness, following putting oneself above the state, then, was a form of pollution, which was "dangerous and damaging" and the "bespoilment of all work," resting an "unforgivable burden" on the civil servant.[41]

A common refrain in Joseph's pastoral letter is that a civil servant must serve the state entirely. Every personal or official matter that interferes with this purpose must be cut out, root and branch. "No side matter, no personal business, no form of distraction must keep him or remove him from his main task." Moreover, state service eclipsed issues of courtly rank, ceremony, and deference. Burgher and noble were to have no real distinctions when it came to service to the state, because such additional differentiation could work against the hierarchy and the efficiency of state service. "No authority contest, no ceremony, courtesy, or rank, must get in his way in the least." Joseph wanted the state's civil servants to—like he himself—put work first and to do that with the utmost eagerness, with one's entirety. The civil servant must "motivate himself, he must not ignore any means to make progress, he must look after the weak and infirm, he must bear with patience his subordinates, he must know how to win their trust."[42]

Commentators on the pastoral letter have either praised it as a statement of Joseph's enlightened principles of statecraft or they have focused instead on its imperious tone and the insensitivity with which it handled the bureaucracy.[43] Joseph's exasperation, his official expression of displeasure at the failure of his civil servants to implement his reforms without delay and in more than just a mechanical manner, was meant as the sternest form of rebuke for his civil servants. But the pastoral letter was more than just an imperial tongue lashing, because in it we can see the further formation of new principles of Habsburg statecraft. The letter paralleled Maria Theresia's and Joseph's institutional and financial separation of the princely court from the state, the building of central offices to manage and oversee the provinces, the concomitant removal of local authority from the nobles and estates and fiscal reforms, and the establishment of tax offices and state tax collectors.[44] These trends gave impetus to the centralization of authority in the prince and, later, in the state. Moreover, these general trends are part of the larger development of all-powerful, western nation-states. Joseph presents us with a significant collateral example of this development, for Joseph is seeking, not only to solidify his power and the uniformity of his authority as the ruling prince, but to unify his collection of provinces, which under the Habsburgs had no name, into a centralized state. To create this centralized state, Joseph had to start with the bureaucracy. But here the body of public administrators was not merely the by-product of a state-building and state-making process; it was the motor, the exemplar, and the vanguard of that process.

The success of Joseph's administrative reforms required a new type of citizen who saw the world much differently than a patrimonial official of the previous generations who worked for the estates or for a local lord. Education reforms would lay a foundation for this new outlook, which Joseph needed to develop partners in the collective reimagining of his lands as an organic totality—and the bureaucracy would be those partners. Joseph tied this new ethos to the selfless service to the state. He linked the common good to the whole of the Habsburgs' dominions, writing in his pastoral letter that "since the good can only be namely that which touches the generality and the largest number and likewise all provinces of the Monarchy only make a totality [ganzes] . . . so it must be necessary that all jealousy, or prejudice, which is often present between provinces and nations, which then causes so much worthless paperwork between departments, cease; and it must be made right again because in the state-body, as in the human body, when not every part is healthy, all suffer and must contribute the least evil to recovery."[45] In reimagining the Habsburg state as a coherent, standardized whole, Joseph reimagined an ideal citizenry of people committed to it.

The era of Maria Theresia and Joseph II thus saw the emergence of a professional, objective bureaucracy. Joseph ensured that his officials followed administrative procedures that functioned according to written norms; that they divided their labor for maximum efficiency; that they displayed—for the power of the state was always on display—jurisdictional competence. His attention to the comportment and training of officials, his maintenance of a culture of merit—or at least of equal disparagement—worked alongside the creation of a rational organizational hierarchy and strict lines of monocratic (instead of collegial) authority. Finally, civil service emerged as a vocation; it became a profession that could not be held in conjunction with other functions or jobs that might affect the objectivity of the official.[46]

## The Forces of Inertia: Idea, State, and Society

Joseph hoped to transform the lands of the Habsburgs into a unified and coherent state. His imperial officials, educated at universities, trained in modern languages, and in many ways constituting a new caste of Austrian society, were to be the executors of his plans. But by 1790, Joseph despaired at his unfinished reforms. He and his mother were able to unify many of their lands under a single central government but not all of them—particularly not the largest and most powerful of them, Hungary. They created provincial and regional offices, which brought the central state closer to the populace, but they could not completely supersede the institutions of the local nobility. Moreover, many of Joseph II's more drastic reforms had to be rescinded for the sake of domestic stability. By the end of Joseph's reign, Belgium stood in open revolt and would never return to the Habsburg's patrimony. In the meantime, the French Revolution engulfed France and loomed as a great unknown across the Rhine. Joseph's immediate successor, Leopold II (1790–92), and his advisors backed away from Joseph's conception of an Austrian *Gesamtstaat*, or "complete-state," to forestall revolution and preserve stability. Retreating from Joseph's vision also meant backing away from many of Joseph's centralizing reforms and his attempts to supplant and undermine the authority of the local nobility by taking away their administrative and legal functions. But Emperor Leopold died less than three years after assuming the head of the House of Habsburg. After Leopold's short reign, Leopold's son Francis (r. 1792–1835) became emperor.

Between 1790 and 1815, "Austria" fought off revolution at home and revolutionary armies abroad. Francis's Austria participated in nearly all of the coalitions against revolutionary France and the armies of Napoleon. Over the course of these twenty-five years, the Austrian Empire would lose some territories and, eventually, gain them back or acquire new ones altogether. The state's finances were stretched to the limit and broken. State bankruptcy came in 1811. After the defeat of Napoleon in 1815, the Congress of Vienna put Austria in the important role of stabilizer. It had gained a great degree of international prestige under its shrewd and calculating state chancellor, Prince Klemens von Metternich—a Rhine émigré who had fled the invading French armies to Vienna. Under Metternich, Austria was able to aggrandize itself by the acquisition of new territories, such as the archbishopric of Salzburg, and former territories from the Venetian

Republic, including the coast of Dalmatia. Austria also exerted itself as a conservative power in the German states and on the Italian peninsula, propping up smaller monarchies and coordinating antirevolutionary policies among the various principalities and states. But territorial acquisitions only made the Habsburg Empire more linguistically and legally diverse and spun it further away from Joseph's reforming trajectory.

The wars had other repercussions as well, not least because they were so expensive. The almost fantastic increase in the size of armies and the costs of war between 1792 and 1815 meant that the fiscal innovations of the eighteenth century could provide only a rudimentary foundation for war. Austria's military campaigns depended less and less on the taxes that the state collected ever more efficiently after the era of great reforms. Now that techniques of maintaining an army were increasingly financial, Austria had to finance its wars through loans. It lessened its resulting debts by printing money, thus devaluing its currency.[47] Moreover, Austria, despite its great fiscal innovations in the eighteenth century, did not have the financial-technical capacity to repay its debts quickly. As the economic historian Harm-Hinrich Brandt tells us, "Only a state which has at its disposal the fully mature institutions and necessary technologies of taxation," and which can count on decision-making bodies that integrate state with society—that is, some kind of representative control—"is capable of coping with the emergency of war."[48] Reliance on pre-Josephine social and constitutional traditions meant that Austria did not have the administrative capabilities for leveling income taxes. So how would Austria cope with the continuous strain of war?

If we consider Austria's coping strategy for a moment, we see how the French Revolution and Napoleonic Wars could have strengthened the state-building project of Maria Theresia and Joseph II. Indeed, how historians think about state building is process-oriented: war and financial strain provides the impetus for building state institutions, the centralization of authority in the hands of the monarchy and his officials, and new techniques of wealth extraction and state financing. In fact, implicit in the state-building project is the modernization of governmental institutions and the eventual expansion of political life. Thus, the next step in the state-building process, according to economic history, would be representative institutions that exercise financial control over state budgets and further the capacity of the state to extract wealth, promote business, and thus increase the financial strength of the state.[49] But though this might lead us to conjecture that the Austrian state then embarked on these new elements of state building, in fact it did not. All the wars with France had taken a psychological toll on Josephinism and state building. The young emperor, Joseph's nephew Francis, turned away from Joseph's drive to standardize, tax, and build for the survival of the empire. Instead, Francis and Metternich would call upon tradition and monarchial legitimacy to buttress the right of the Habsburgs to rule. In practice, this meant turning away from the centralizing, state-building impulses of Joseph and instead upholding the traditional rights and privileges of the individual lands and kingdoms.

The early years of Francis's reign thus were dominated by the events of the French Revolution and the fear of revolutionary ideas spreading throughout Europe. These fears would become the basis for policy for the next two generations, as Joseph's reform impulses continued to lay the foundations of the bureaucracy's education—their conception of the Austrian state and their self-awareness of the role they were to play. Just as Joseph's ideas animated the state-building project and Austria's new emerging class of officials, the quest for tranquility, the fear of unrest, brought the Habsburgs to turn away sharply from their state-building project.

The consequences of the wars and the financial problems they brought were substantial. Austria declared a partial bankruptcy in 1811 which—while creating a large deficit in financial trust—nonetheless failed to wipe out an enormous debt that Austria would continue to pay back for decades. There were constitutional and institutional issues of stability as well. The strains of fighting, the territorial loss and acquisitions, and rapid changes in constitution and public law in many of the territories during the Napoleonic Wars reinforced the traditional Habsburg statecraft of compromise with local and regional elites and the promotion of autonomy and regional difference. That was, after all, how the Habsburgs kept the peace for centuries. In addition, Napoleon had brought major administrative and legal changes to the territories he conquered. As these territories entered the fold of the Habsburgs after 1815, they furthered administrative and social differences among the Habsburgs' lands. Joseph's centralization and standardization project seemingly stretched further out of reach. The territories of Lombardy and Venetia, for instance, which were part of Napoleon's Kingdom of Italy, came to the Austrian Empire with a system of laws that allowed the state much greater central control at the local level at the expense of the nobles. Conversely, the Galician territories, which Austria first acquired during the Partitions of Poland and then reacquired in 1815, depended greatly on the local lords for local administration.[50] With such diversity of legal statutes and traditions under its roof, Austria was still the Noah's ark of public law.[51]

After 1790, the reform impulses seemed to lose their momentum and tradition seemed to gather mass, adding to its inertial weight. The French Revolution, fears of revolution at home, war, bankruptcy, and institutional stagnation brought the government of Joseph II—which resembled a machine in perpetual motion—to a snail's pace under his successors. Emperor Francis II, who laid down the crown of the Holy Roman Empire only to forge himself a new one as "Francis I, Emperor of Austria" between 1803 and 1806, would be the opposite of Joseph II. Kind where Joseph was boorish, soft where Joseph was tough, and fearful where Joseph was impetuous, Francis "the Good" was determined to fight the evils of the nineteenth century by clinging to the forms of the eighteenth. First and foremost would be the resistance to change for its own sake. He advised his son, the future Emperor Ferdinand I, in his political testament, "Do not change any of the foundations of the State; rule and do not alter; stand firm and unwavering on the principles, through the continued observance of which I not only led the monarchy through the storms of hard times, but also through which I secured the high point in the world which it now occupies."[52] Although Francis dictated this testament in the last weeks of his life, his fear of revolution, the experience of wars, bankruptcy, and territorial dismemberment at the hands of France, led him to distrust the Josephinian ethos and the state institutions that remained. He feared the slippery slope of political and social "progress."

With a desire to avoid tumult, whether as revolution from above or from below, Francis had quickly decided upon assuming the throne in 1792 that he needed to make peace with the very element of society whose power his uncle Joseph had fought to destroy: the nobility. An alliance with the nobles in each province could bring an end to the subversion in his lands, which he feared so much.[53] The discovery of a "Jacobin plot" by an overly energetic secret police in 1794 did little to help the tightening of the circle and the end of a reformist spirit. In reality, the more than thirty "Jacobin conspirators" were little more than pamphleteers, admirers of Joseph II and the French Revolution, and general bunglers. Yet, they were tried and some of them were even executed.[54] Their imprint on the political culture of Vienna may have been more important than whatever revolution these conspirators pursued over cigarettes and coffee. Francis became more paranoid and more determined to resist the waves of revolution.

Joseph II's legacy and the central state idea would be more concretely acknowledged in at least one respect under Francis: the Habsburg patrimony now had a name, the Austrian Empire. Contingency played a role in this to be sure, because Francis II—his name as "Holy Roman Emperor"—was forced to set aside this crown after suffering defeat at the hands of Napoleon's France. To maintain his imperial dignity, a new title was created for him: "Emperor of Austria." As emperor of this state with a name, Francis became Francis I. This is not unimportant—the name "Austria" signified a unified way of thinking about the lands that stretched from Vorarlberg to the Subcarpathian Basin.[55] The name represented the idea that all the lands of the Habsburgs formed one body, one state. Francis nonetheless found that the imperial idea lacked the stability he needed to protect his patrimony during the years of war and revolution because it was an idea, an abstraction. For Francis, loyalty to ideas was a path to revolution, which led him to attack how this imperial idea was transmuted to the civil service—the juridical education at university. Francis removed the historical and statist emphasis from legal training, which had been used to inculcate jurists with a state-serving ethos.[56] Francis intended this "reform" as an assault on the Josephinist ethos of the bureaucracy, which encouraged service to the abstract notion of the state through an education with a strong sense of history and an ideology of "love for the fatherland." Waltraud Heindl found that most historically grounded legal courses had fallen off the curriculum by 1810; even church history and world history would be removed by 1824. General-law subjects had also been reduced under Francis, while subjects like German constitutional law, which had been a two-semester required course in the 1780s, had been eliminated altogether by 1810.[57]

If we are to understand early nineteenth-century Austrian history, we must confront a certain paradox. As the civil service continued to develop into a professional body under Joseph II, as in Max Weber's historical sociology, Emperor Francis attempted to break the very ethos-instilling educational aspects that taught the civil servants to serve the state as an abstraction and as a larger ideal, while he also strengthened the curricular requirements for entering imperial service. In a supreme cabinet decree from December 1806, the emperor demanded that his officials show "subordination, submissiveness, and obedience" toward their superiors, and he expected the "precise following of orders" along with unfaltering understanding and knowledge of the business of the office. Officials were not to question decrees; they were not to criticize directives, for those present an "alarming evil" in the state. Francis demanded personal loyalty ahead of the service to the state and to the following of general principles.[58] Francis hoped personally to command the loyalty of his officials, thereby loosening the ties that bound officials to abstract ideals or utopian visions, which Francis believed led down the path to revolution.

Distrusting his officials and fearing revolution, Emperor Francis often personally took over both the supervisory and coordinating roles of the central authorities and often would not convene the Council of State, preferring to meet with his high officials individually. The civil servant Karl Friedrich Kübeck, the later architect of neoabsolutism in the 1850s, noted in his diary in the first decade of the nineteenth century how a senior colleague observed the reign of Francis in terms of "reactionism":

Emperor Joseph recognized the State as an end in itself and [he saw] the good of the people as the object of such a supreme dignity as himself, [and so] he recognized himself as the first official of the *Reich*. The French Revolution went even further and made the *Volk* the sovereign, what was extreme and therefore absurd. [After all,] Emperor Napoleon ruled. He went from being the first official of the realm—as Consul—to being the sovereign of the people (des Francais and not de la France); in this way he was less progressive than [our] Emperor Joseph. [Nowadays] We have gone a large step further backward. The new form of our organization restored the sovereign as an end in itself, made the court a participant, and the state as a means. The state is a dominion, in which the sovereign divided with the court (the nobility) and which is administered for them by the officials. We are on the straight path back to chivalric feudalism—and that is also extreme—and therefore absurd.[59]

Officials who possessed independence of thought or creativity were dangerous to Francis, and therefore he prized blind obedience and loyalty in his civil service. He replaced the abstraction of the greater good and the state, which commanded the loyalty of civil servants under Joseph, with the person of the emperor. Under Joseph, officials were expected to be dynamic servants of the state, but Francis had changed the rules of the game.[60] In this context, the ability of civil servants to maintain their loyalty to higher ideals, abstract principles, and to the idea of a larger Austrian state became a form of resistance.[61]

As Francis turned away from Joseph's reform ideas, he sought to make his public officials more dependent on his own person. Francis, like Joseph, sought to rule personally and exert a level of complete control over his officials. However, Joseph's personal despotism was a means to change the nature of Austria's state system and organization, so that the state would eventually follow his ethos of service for the greater good of its own accord. In contrast, for Francis, personal rule was not a means but an end in itself. Francis believed his control and fatherly care for his realm would be the best guarantor of stability and order, and could forestall the perils and excesses of French-style revolution. Francis issued edict after edict, in the early years of his reign, that were intended to increase his ability to control the civil service.[62] He promised to hire and promote only the best and brightest of his servants, and issued edicts that promised punishment or release from duty for civil servants who committed crimes or who were "under suspicion of questionable behavior."[63] The difference between the meritorious officials and officials under suspicion, however, depended wholly on the perspective of an official's immediate supervisor as discussed in detail later in this chapter.

An unintended effect of Francis's distrust and fear of his administration may actually have been to reinforce the bureaucracy's statist ethos. Josephinism became a more powerful force when the forces of inertia emerged to challenge the state-reformist ethos of the administration.[64] It became the underlying ethos of a century of reformers, a book of ideas that could be pulled off the shelf at any moment in the next century. And, increasingly, under Francis the state-reforming culture of Josephinism became detached from the person of the monarch himself. In essence, when Francis distrusted the bureaucracy and its lingering service to Joseph's ideals of state, he set the bureaucracy free to chart its own course and to produce its own ideas of what form the Habsburg state should take.[65]

Although Francis would resist change as a matter of principle, for his eldest son, Ferdinand (emperor, 1835–48), resistance to change was more a matter of the hand dealt him. Ferdinand's ability to rule is not quite clear and he has yet to receive a modern academic biography.[66] While some historians have labeled Ferdinand "mentally retarded" (Alan Sked) or, more mean-spiritedly, a "noodle" (A. J. P. Taylor),[67] it is clear that Ferdinand was an epileptic and suffered developmental and mental disabilities as a result of hydrocephaly.[68] Despite these obstacles, Ferdinand took over as the head of the House upon Francis's death in 1835. Good-natured but incapable of ruling alone, Ferdinand possessed a diverse monarchy, which Metternich showcased through a series of coronation ceremonies. Ferdinand was crowned as the king of Hungary even before his father's death in 1830. In 1835 the archbishop of Prague laid the Bohemian crown upon Ferdinand's head.[69] The third and last coronation occurred in Milan in 1838. These coronations were lavish, exorbitantly expensive ceremonies: for the final ceremony in Milan, the court set aside the astronomical sum of three million gulden. It involved intricate planning, from the design of the uniforms for all the footmen to the robes and insignia of Lombardy-Venetia's "king," Ferdinand.

Why all the fuss? Ferdinand's advisors hoped, at least, to express to the residents of Lombardy-Venetia that they belonged to a province as important as Hungary or the Lands of Bohemia.[70] Strictly speaking, the coronation in Milan was a performance for the benefit of the audience. But it also reflects how far Austria had returned to its federalist governmental traditions by 1838, and how much the monarchy's leadership had abandoned the state-conceptions of Joseph II. Ferdinand had become the figurehead of a dynasty that held firmly onto the principle of legitimacy, even if his sickly frame sometimes cut a sharply unvirile figure. The coronations may have done little to alter the relationship between Vienna and its provinces, but they reflect the view Ferdinand's advisors in Vienna held of the monarchy in the 1830s: the monarchy was the sum of its parts, not a whole in and of itself. The artifice of the coronations also silenced the Josephinian concept of the central state. Ferdinand's three coronations and numerous homage ceremonies were not accompanied by a coronation with the crown that encompassed them all: the imperial crown of Austria.

Although the idea of the central state was silenced in the spectacle of coronations, it still existed and was kept alive in the institutions Joseph II had created: the imperial civil service. Though this institution had suffered neglect in the hard years of war and inflation leading up to 1815. The years of stability that followed offered little in the way of innovation or improvement. But discontent would make the bureaucracy into a more vocal and more steeled institution. The result of this dysfunctional system was that change was on the lips of everyone from the loyal opposition in the bureaucracy to aristocrats who wanted to resurrect the good old days of unfettered patrimonial rule. The stagnation of Austrian government and administration, which was neither fish nor fowl, not fully centralized or wholly old-regime, pleased no one.

## The Two Meanings of Bureaucracy:
## Storm and Tranquility at Work in Austria Before 1848

Austria's foremost scholar of the Habsburg imperial civil service reminds us that the word *bureaucracy* actually papers over two meanings: the administrative apparatus and the officials themselves.[71] These separate aspects of bureaucracy were filled with the tensions of the period. The number of civil servants increased, while their chances of advancement diminished. The number of "political officials"—of university-educated civil servants—grew from about twenty-six thousand to nearly thirty thousand between 1828 and 1846, an increase of 14 percent. At the same time the number of interns—*Praktikanten*—often unpaid, doubled from 3,212 to 6,363 during the same period.[72] The structures of Austria's administration, held in stasis by Francis's search for tranquility and his mission to change as little as possible, became a source of frustration for Austria's officials. The dynamic of reform and tranquility, movement and inertia, thus replicated itself in the two aspects of bureaucracy: the inert structures of state and the Josephinist civil service, who wanted, expected, and needed change.

During the forty-five years following Joseph's death, new forms of authority emerged that catered to Austria's conservative, antirevolutionary stance in Europe. These forms harkened back to Austria's heritage as a collection of independent kingdoms and lands, held together by the person of the monarch. Joseph's successors, however, possessed neither the energy nor the wherewithal to be the central and decisive feature of government to hold the lands together. The realities of imperial Austria are a useful reminder that Austrian history should be understood as an evolving dialectic between plans and reality. The tension between the drive for reform and the search for tranquility often manifested itself in the gulf between plans for a unified state and the reality of Austria's administrative, constitutional, social, and—lest we forget—linguistic diversity. These tensions emerged during Joseph's quest for reform, but persisted and matured after his death. Joseph had built a bureaucracy that was to help him create a unified state, but that state had not been completed before his death.[73] The bureaucracy was intended to carry on his project, but his death and the sheer diversity of lands would stand in the way of the fulfillment of Joseph's project. Joseph had instilled a state-serving ethos in his civil service to push his officers toward the fulfillment of his vision for a unified state that was powerful, efficient, and promoted the common good. Joseph left his successors with an unfinished project and with a juristically educated imperial civil service—an army of counting, surveying, and reporting myrmidons, whose job was to push the project onward.[74] But the dynamic that this tension created between tradition and reform, between administrative plans and social and political realities, would frame the political landscape of central Europe in the long nineteenth century.

The thirteen-year reign of Ferdinand (1835–48) followed the same course that Francis laid down over his forty-two years on the throne. Ferdinand inherited a government that had been largely constructed for him. It enabled him to take the throne as a figurehead monarch, while his advisors made the important decisions and kept the ship of state on an even keel, maintaining the system of Emperor Francis that focused on stability. The complete continuation of Francis's system, however, presented the state with a unique problem. Francis had built his government on the foundations of Joseph II's enlightened absolutism. But Francis had transformed Joseph's system, in which all laws, institutions, and subjects were subsumed to the purpose of the state, into a system in which everything centered on the person of the emperor.[75] This personal absolutism was affirmed and at the same time crippled by the ascension of Ferdinand to the throne. Weakened mentally and physically, Ferdinand did not have the energy, will, or the capacity to rule personally over the wide expanses of the Austrian state. The long-serving official Karl Friedrich Kübeck described Ferdinand in his memoirs as "unable to understand one word of what was laid in front of him, but willing to sign off on anything."[76] Austria was ruled, in fact, by committee in the 1830s and 1840s.

Rule-by-committee had taken the form of the State-Conference, or *Staatskonferenz*, an advisory body created by Emperor Francis in 1815. With Ferdinand's ascension, this advisory body had morphed into regency. The State-Conference was a collegial body where resolutions were made by majority vote of the five members. The members of the State-Conference included the two top government officials of the Austrian Empire: Prince Klemens von Metternich and Franz Anton Kolowrat-Liebsteinsky. These two men were interminably locked in a feud in which personal battles played out on the field of Austria's administration. Metternich was the state chancellor (*Staatskanzler*), and in charge of Austria's foreign policy and diplomatic service, while Kolowrat was minister of state and the State-Conference (*Staats- und Konferenzminister*), and in charge of the domestic administration.[77] In addition to Metternich and Kolowrat, two members of the imperial family also had permanent seats on the committee: Francis's youngest brother, Archduke Ludwig, who was good-natured but lacked real political experience in Austria; and Ferdinand's younger brother, Archduke Francis Karl, who was neither exceptionally gifted nor had the desire or acumen for governing Austria.[78] The State-Conference had the awkward task of advising an absolute monarch who was unfit to make decisions while perpetuating the appearance of absolute monarchy. One historian called this delicate situation "the tragic comedy of an absolute monarchy without a monarch."[79] Apart from his highly public coronations, Ferdinand's frequent bouts of illness generally kept him out of the public eye. The Habsburg penchant for theater and spectacle had temporarily, at least, moved from public ceremonies to the theater of government in which the bureaucracy played the role of the supporting cast and the stage hands.

While rule by committee was cumbersome and precluded any real change implemented from the top of the administrative hierarchy, Austria's confusing entanglement of administrative structures further slowed the turning cogs of government. In several cases, the lines of hierarchy and supervision expressed the personal and informal domination that Emperor Francis cultivated—and which the unlucky Ferdinand inherited. For one, the State-Conference had neither firm rules for its operation nor any prescribed executive powers.[80] Ostensibly, the work of the State-Conference was to make resolutions on decisions that were passed in the Council of State (*Staatsrat*), the central office of the domestic administration in the empire which Prince Anton Wenzel von Kaunitz had established in 1761. The head of this Council of State was now none other than the *Staats- und Konferenzminister*, Count Kolowrat. The Council of State's administrative role encompassed supervisory and coordinating powers over the entire administration, except, of course, for Metternich's foreign service. Like the State-Conference, the Council of State had no executive powers, nor did it have a clearly defined administrative role. Rather, Kaunitz in 1761 had intended the council to act as a central institution of the bureaucracy that created both a central supervisory body and a means for the different branches of government to communicate with one another.[81] Kaunitz could make such a system work because he, as its head, had the ear of Maria Theresia and to a lesser extent, that of Joseph II. By the 1830s, however, this administrative structure was no longer fully effective, as Kolowrat had to battle Metternich for influence.

The informal and improvised central government rested on the more established, rigid, hierarchical administrative apparatus that Maria Theresia and Joseph II created in the eighteenth century. But the Austrian state-building project was unfinished when Francis took it over and left everything as it was. Reforms had been stopped in midstep. The Austrian bureaucratic apparatus stretched from Vienna into the provinces, but it was truncated, unfinished, and not yet uniform. There were still gaps in the structures of the state through which the power of the center could be subverted and undermined.

Below the emperor's advisory councils, the Austrian administration was not divided into specialty sections, or ministries, which covered qualitative aspects of governance (domestic administration, finances, justice, education, and the military). Instead, Austria still was organized into three geographically defined *Hofstellen*, or court offices, which supervised all areas of government in the provinces, resulting in legal and administrative unevenness. The first of these court offices, the United Imperial-Royal Court Chancellery (*Vereinigte k.k. Hofkanzlei*), encompassed much of the monarchy, including the Austrian hereditary lands, the lands of the Bohemian crown, Galicia, Dalmatia, and the Italian lands. A second Court Chancellery served as the central administration for Hungary; the third Court Chancellery did the same for Transylvania (see Map 1.1). These three chancelleries encompassed geographic areas that differed vastly in size and population as well as in the laws, rights, and obligations that were compiled in their constitutions. A contemporary description of the Habsburg monarchy by a professor of law at the University of Vienna shows how the centralizing efforts of Joseph II and his bureaucrats had been partially successful, but also awkwardly cut short by the 1840s:

Austria is a hereditary Monarchy, consisting of lands that indeed do not share the same fundamental laws throughout, but rather, irrespective of their peculiarities, form a single political power to a common purpose under one overlord. The emperor unifies all imperial rights [Majestätsrechte] in his hand, and exercises these rights in all lands, with the exception of Hungary and Transylvania. Austria is therefore a pure or unlimited Monarchy; Hungary and Transylvania are therefore limited monarchies.[82]

Although the United Imperial-Royal Court Chancellery consolidated the core Austrian and Bohemian lands, the Italian and Polish lands, and Dalmatia under one administrative roof, even this core group of the empire was still far from being a unified state. This Court Chancellery, with

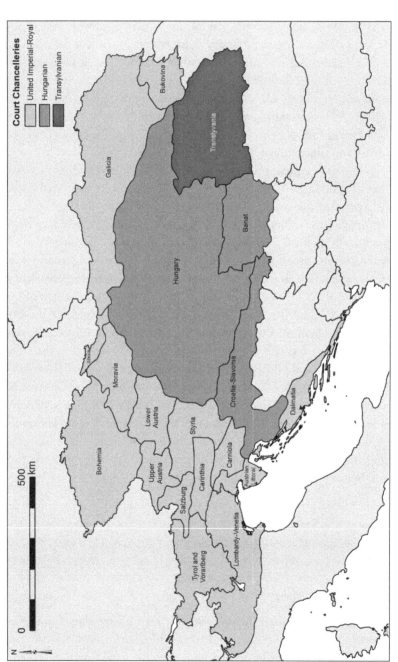

MAP 1.1. Map of Austrian Court Chancelleries in 1840

its widely dispersed territory, acted as a superministry, controlling what would later be divided into several separate ministries: Church and confessional matters, streets and waterways (and by the 1840s, railways), military matters (including conscription and recruitment), agriculture, building and sanitation inspectorates, emigration, public welfare institutions, land taxation, and the relationships between peasants and their local lords.[83] The Unified Imperial-Royal Court Chancellery consisted of a chairman (*oberster Kanzler*), a court chancellor, a chancellor, a vice-chancellor, and thirteen court counselors (*Hofräte*).[84]

The three Court Chancelleries were also collegial bodies, which meant that decisions were reached through a simple majority vote among the chancellery's members. The opinions of experts in specific matters could be drowned out by other voices. As the business of administration steadily increased under Ferdinand, the means of decision making increasingly became a problem. The three Court Chancelleries simply had neither the time nor the resources to take up every matter for discussion. Franz Hartig, in his classic contemporary work *Genesis der Revolution in Oesterreich im Jahre 1848*, observed that the increased work had the "double disadvantage" of delaying decisions as they awaited discussion and also consuming so much of the chancellors' time that they could not devote a watchful eye to the officials under them. This double disadvantage, in turn, led to "rule by officials without personal responsibility."[85] Nonetheless, the Court Chancelleries reported directly to Emperor Francis during his reign. The Council of State did not intervene in this direct link, but rather stood available to the emperor to advise him on matters which the Court Chancelleries put before him. The emperor made his decision on the matter—or often ignored the matter entirely. Once he rendered a decision, it was given to the Council of State for review; the Council of State then communicated the emperor's decision to the Court Chancellery, which then had to implement the decision.[86] Under Emperor Francis's successor, the mentally handicapped Ferdinand, the State-Conference took over the decision making of the emperor, adding yet another collegial organ and rule by committee to the top of Austria's administration (see Figure 1.1).

The central executive power in Vienna, ruled by the emperor through the different collegial committees, extended its power into the far reaches of the empire through provincial and regional administrative units. Under the Unified Imperial-Royal Court Chancellery stood no less than twelve provincial offices, which were called Land-Governments (*Landesregierung*

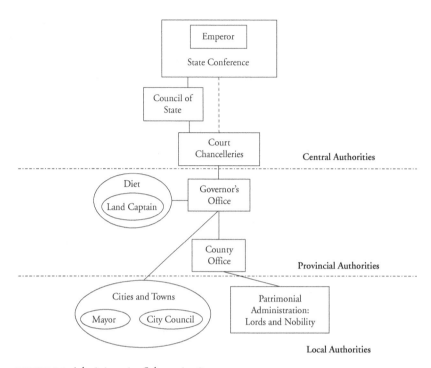

FIGURE 1.1. Administrative Schema in 1840

or *Landgubernium*).[87] These provincial governments dated back to administrative reforms carried out under Maria Theresia by Prince Kaunitz.[88] A governor at the head of each provincial government,[89] and his administration was generally responsible for a wide range of policy making in his province.[90] Special bureaus complemented the work of the governor's office and included the offices of the police and censor.[91] Hungary proper and Transylvania stood completely outside this system. They each had their own Court Chancellery in Vienna, which communicated with the provincial governments (*consilium regium locumtenentiale* in Buda for Hungary, and *Gubernium* in Kolosvár for Transylvania). Members of provincial councils were drawn from the estates, which also elected the officials to the county governments, or *Comitaten*. These county governments stood under the provincial governments and were the local seats of representation. County officials were not always elected either—the system of merit had not yet penetrated into some parts of Hungary and Transylvania; rather, the local county prefects (the *Obergespan*) were sometimes still inherited through families, dating from a time when special service to the crown was awarded with a permanent paid position.[92] In other words imperial Austria did not possess an independent, technical bureaucracy in all of its lands. In Hungary and Transylvania, the Habsburg king or grand duke (for he was not the "emperor" here) relied on the local nobles and gentry to administer these lands, make policy, collect taxes, and preserve law and order at all levels of the administration. In the other provinces, the nobility served only as the first level of local administration.

The governors of the Land-Governments represented the person and exercised the power of the emperor in the provinces. However, this did not mean that they were given a free hand to rule as they saw fit. Emperor Francis was not like Joseph. Joseph emphasized the freedom of action by his civil servants, because he believed their training in natural law and political economy would make their ethos and actions correspond to his own, rational statecraft.[93] In contrast, Francis, jealous of his power, had concentrated decision making in his own person and in the Court Chancelleries in Vienna, which reported to him.[94] Francis excluded his governors from having a free hand to direct policy or make laws in their own provinces. After Francis died, Kolowrat and Metternich directed policy from the State-Conference.

In addition to the entanglements of the central government, provincial conditions further limited the governors' exercise of authority. The vestiges of feudal autonomy—the provincial diet and its *ständisch* administration—still existed alongside the more recent offices of the central government in the provinces. The diet, a provincial assembly dominated by the *Grundherren*,[95] the noble lords, still had the power to propose, distribute and levy direct taxes in addition to managing the funds of the province, which had traditionally belonged to the estates. And yet, Maria Theresia and Joseph II had curbed the diet's real power to influence policy. With the exception of Hungary, the dynasty achieved an almost complete liquidation of the power of the noble lords at the provincial level.[96] Joseph II went as far as abolishing the provincial diets altogether, although his brother and successor Leopold reinstated them to forestall a revolt of the nobility against the crown.[97] By the 1840s the diets represented another state theater enacted at the provincial level, but here one found not a provincial legislative body, but a traditional play reenacted for the sake of its players. Heinrich Börnstein, a German radical who emigrated to St. Louis, Missouri (and later returned to Austria), described the Upper

Austrian diet with both a flair and derision that came from his position as director of the *Landestheater*, which incidentally belonged to the Upper Austrian estates:

Here these landed estates [Landstände], whose provincial diet was the bitterest mockery of a representative institution [Verfassung], assembled themselves once every year and "dieted" for one day from nine to twelve in the morning. A high mass—consisting of ceremonial arrivals and departures—took away two of the three hours, and finally in the third hour the President read out the imperial postulate on account of approving the tax levy. The estates then, *secundum ordinem*, nodded their heads, said *ja*, and with that the diet came to an end.[98]

The *Stände* and their diets had merely become the rubber stamp of the central authorities. Nonetheless, the provinces, or *Länder*, were maintained as administrative units along with their legislatures, the diets. The members of the diet even received standard stipulations for a uniform in 1807. It consisted of a red tailcoat with a black and gold collar, gold epaulettes with the coat of arms of the land, and an épée with a Moroccan-leather sheaf. The members of the estates wore them with pomp and pride, but could not escape the very real fact that the state was dressing them in full subservience.[99]

If the provincial diets were little more than theaters of pomp and places where the provincial nobility could sport their social status, the local administration in Austria—with the same cast of characters—featured much more substance.[100] In fact, Austria's administration relied on these same members of the diet, who came overwhelmingly from the ruling estates of prelates, lords, and knights, to serve as local magistrates and judges.[101] Essentially, the central government had never étatized the local administration, but rather left it in the hands of the *Grundherren*, the local lords. These local lords not only did much of the local work of the central government, but had to pay the cost of running the local administrations out of their own pockets.[102]

The fiscal and administrative reforms of Maria Theresia and Joseph's centralizing ethos had attacked and truncated the nobles' absolute power, as well as their service as tax collectors in the countryside, but the nobles were not completely removed from their public role. In many parts of the monarchy—those places that did not fall under the control of Napoleon's favorites in Italy, Illyria, or Bavaria during the Napoleonic Wars—the local landed nobility formed the foundation of the social, economic, and political order.[103] Fear of revolution meant that Emperor Francis was loathe to displace them with state authorities. The patrimonial administration of the

landed nobility had become the base of "the pyramid of Austria's administrative structure."[104] The local noble as official owed his office both to his
social status, which was handed down by the whim of tradition, and to the
central state authority, which provided the laws and norms to which he had
to conform.[105] The *Grundherren* provided the first level of local administration and civil justice and a litany of other services that had been assigned
to them by the central state. These included such diverse functions as the
responsibility for public order; regulating land and forest according to state
mandates; acting as local hunting, sanitation, and market officials; supervising the care for the indigent, communal finances, schools, and churches;
as well as serving as the local justice of the peace, tax official, and military
representative.[106]

Although this system of provincial administration allowed for the
smooth continuance of local customs and forms of public law, it also translated into a lack of administrative uniformity and a complexity in the way
the parts related to the whole—precisely what Emperor Joseph tried to
change. Austria's local, patrimonial administration also varied according
to the structure of landholding by the nobility in each of the provinces.
This in turn affected, to different degrees, the ability of these administrations to keep pace with the growing obligations that the central government
required of it.[107] In the Bohemian lands and Galicia, where large magnates
dominated the landscape, a single seigneur could and often did hold all the
territory in an administrative district. The continuance of local "patrimonial administration" placed in his hands a veritable "administrative monopoly" in addition to all his inherited economic and social rights as a feudal
lord.[108] A peasant who looked at his lord would see not only his landlord,
but his local justice, his local government official, his local military recruiter
and draft officer, his school superintendent, his tax collector, sanitation official, and whatever else was remotely governmental. On the other hand, the
patrimonial administration in Inner Austria (Styria, Carinthia, Carniola)
and the two archduchies of Upper and Lower Austria allowed no such
concentration of local power. Rather, administration dissolved at the local
level into a confused overlapping of jurisdictions and responsibilities that
were seemingly impossible to untangle and rationalize. Lordships were scattered and noncontiguous: peasants had multiple lords to whom they owed
different rents and services. In contrast to the administrative monopoly
Bohemian nobles held, the nobles in the hereditary lands had economic,
social, and administrative jurisdictions that could hardly be disentangled

from their neighbors' jurisdictions. Thus, although the magnates of Bohemia and Galicia could often adapt to new and more numerous tasks and regulations assigned by a growing central authority, the *Grundherren* of the Alpine lands could hardly keep up.[109] State administration simply could not modernize and grow with so many entangled jurisdictions at the local level.

In the 1830s and 1840s, the Austrian state-building project, the drive for reform and uniformity, did not yet reach into the real diversity of local life, local hierarchies, and local customs. Rather, it sat on top of them, watching the nobles' patrimonial administration. Officials of the central state continually undermined the power of the landed nobility through the state's administrative offices in the hinterland. These offices were called the county offices (*Kreisämter*) and reported to the governors.[110] County offices had a long history in central Europe, dating to the reign of Ottokar II (king of Bohemia, 1253–78) in parts of Bohemia; in their current form, however, they were introduced by Maria Theresia as part of her state reforms of 1749. The counties varied widely in size and population: the smallest country was Cattaro at 11 km² and the largest (seventeen times larger in fact) was Bukovina at 189 km². Despite their variety, they lent uniformity to the monarchy at the regional—at least in the provinces outside of Hungary and Transylvania—dividing it into 102 administrative units.[111] A county prefect, or *Kreishauptmann*, chaired the administration in each county. Unlike the central offices in Vienna, which were collegial organs whose decisions resulted from committee voting, the county prefect had exclusive authority to make decisions.[112] His job was to carry out the domestic administrative responsibilities at the regional level and thus had a similar purview to that of the governor. To carry out his functions, which included supervision of the local administration conducted by the landed nobility, the county prefect had a modest supporting staff, which included several commissars, university-trained lower officials (*Konzeptsbeamte*), office secretaries and service staff, as well as medical and technical experts.[113]

Despite its humble position as the lowest rung on the central and absolutist state's administrative ladder, the county offices played an important role in the undermining of *Grundherrschaft*, or the landowning nobility's legal and administrative control of the subjects under his lordship. Otto Brunner noted in his *Adeliges Landleben* that the modern bureaucratic state of Maria Theresia and Joseph II destroyed the social, economic, and administrative dominance of the local *Grundherrschaft* "through its very existence."[114] In particular the county offices allowed the central state "to reach into the inner life of lord-subject relations" (*Herrschaften*) and "erect a wide network of local administrative authorities."[115] If by chance a peasant could not make a claim against his lord, because his lord was simultaneously his local magistrate, he now at least had recourse to his local county seat, where the officials may give his matter a fair hearing. With the county offices, the state was able to intervene in the traditional order and alter the relationship between lord and peasant. If the governments in the 1830s and 1840s appeared static and undynamic, they had however perpetuated the institutions of Maria Theresia and Joseph II, which continued to undermine the authority of the nobility.

### Homo Magistratus Austriacus

If the imperial civil servants who staffed the imperial public administration, from the county offices and *Gubernia* in the provinces, to the central bureaus of Vienna's Court Chancelleries had been harangued by Joseph II's meddling, they became neglected under Francis and Ferdinand. Underpaid, understaffed, overworked, the bureaucracy that Joseph created began to disengage from Emperor Francis and his stability system. They began, more and more, to be attached to Joseph, his memory, and his ideals. They became Austria's Josephinists, its educated, reform-oriented elite. The active suppression of the state ethos by Francis I and the regime of Ferdinand I combined with a lack of investment in the day-to-day operations of the administration to demoralize Austria's officials. Francis's fatherly care for his realm often meant critical neglect of the legions of men whose personal loyalty he demanded. The everyday material neglect of the administration and its officials came to present a serious threat to its social prestige and the strength of its administrative ethos.

Neglect, then, can be a powerful force for change. As Francis and Ferdinand ignored the needs and ideas of the civil service, the Josephinist ethos of the bureaucracy evolved essentially without imperial input. And just as before, officials still educated under the eighteenth-century principles of state science were sent out into the countryside as missionaries for progress, enlightenment, and citizenship. The larger trend of Francis and Ferdinand's neglect of the bureaucracy created an ideological divorce between crown and bureaucracy. The bureaucracy was established under Joseph to be an educated elite, infused with the ideas of public service for the greater good. But the "greater good" of Austria's imperial officials and bureaucrats was grounded and understood as service to the state. Francis's cultivation of personal loyalty to his own program could not overcome the ideas of cameralist education and the ever-evolving ideals of state service that had originated with Joseph. Josephinism, this attitude that the state should serve as the greatest motor of social progress, was shaped just as much from the state of hibernation under Ferdinand as by the ideas of its namesake. Over time, its ideals became even more deeply ingrained into the state service.[116]

How neglect was received differed among Austria's legions of servants. Some protested in their writings and turned into oppositional celebrities. A leading voice of opposition in the 1840s emerged from the depths of the bureaucracy in the form of a thirty-six-year-old *Kreiskommissär*, Victor von Andrian-Werburg, an aristocrat of small means and grandiose dreams. Born in Görz in 1813, Andrian-Werburg finished his studies at the University of Vienna and entered the civil service at the *Gubernium* office of Venice in 1833 as an unpaid intern.[117] A scion of an old noble family of Lombardy, Andrian-Werburg felt entitled to rise quickly through the ranks of bureaucracy and became deeply frustrated when the reality of service in Austria's administration confronted his high hopes with a rather ordinary and slow-moving career.[118] After years of setbacks and refusals by his superiors to promote him out of his unpaid status and into the leagues of officials proper, Andrian-Werburg decided to strike out on an oppositional course against Austria's government. On December 15, 1839, he noted in his diary his fateful decision to begin writing what came to be the most famous political tract of Austria's *Vormärz*, the period preceding the revolutions of 1848: *Oesterreich und dessen Zukunft* (Austria and Its Future).

Already for a long time, and even before I had to give up on the idea of (entering) the diplomatic corps, I carried a plan around with me that excites me powerfully and decisively; and this is to launch an anonymous work into the world, which will describe Austria's current situation and its probable future, truly and without rancor, but rather with love and attachment to the land &etc.—and also to the dynasty—since I truly love both as an enlightened friend, looking with care into the future.[119]

Andrian-Werburg egotistically saw his own stunted career as a metaphor for Austrian society as a whole. The administration strangled innovation and progress, just like it throttled his own aspirations to become a court counselor or ambassador. In the little book that resulted from Andrian-Werburg's career frustrations, Andrian-Werburg painted a portrait of the Austrian administration that, in his own estimation, laid bare its real existence as a "tangled vine, a purely negative force, without any roots in the *Volk*, without any cultivation, without any other ethos than that of egoism, without the strength and the will to topple the government at the decisive moment."[120]

Andrian-Werburg thus spoke for resurgent conservatism, one that recalled the estates in their resistance to Joseph's state reforms in the 1780s. In a very real way, then, Joseph's reforms and his creation of a state-loyal administration changed not only the Austrian state, but what counted as political discussions, the party in power, and the opposition.[121] For Andrian-Werburg, and for generations of critics and reformers who followed him, reforming the bureaucracy was wholly wrapped up with calls to reform the greater structures of Austria's administration. Andrian-Werburg did not address the administrative frustrations of officials or their dissatisfaction with their working conditions. Instead, Andrian-Werburg believed the administrative structures of the state were a root cause of Austria's "backwardness," and its slow, cumbersome steps toward progress. Tellingly, for Andrian-Werburg and later for the Lower Austrian estates, who took the second volume of his *Oesterreich und dessen Zukunft* and turned it into their political program, reform of the Austrian state had to begin with an administrative reform that unfettered modernization from the central bureaucracy.[122] Andrian-Werburg's argument that Austrian society could be liberated from the oppressive bureaucratic central state meant that some historians have thought that Andrian-Werburg was a liberal,[123] but this mistakenly confuses his reception in Germany and Austria with his actual intentions.[124] Andrian-Werburg's idea of freedom from the bureaucracy meant more freedom for the landed nobility at the level of local government. This included the landed nobility's "liberation" from the increasingly onerous and expensive obligations to run the local, patrimonial administration.[125]

Andrian-Werburg was increasingly frustrated by his own stifled career. It is telling that his response to his lack of success was to suggest that Austria wipe out the entire apparatus of his oppression. Though Andrian-Werburg thought the grace given him by his nobility entitled him to a fast-tracked career, his colleague in the judicial administration—Ignaz Beidtel—complained that after 1815, the imperial bureaucracy increasingly was dominated by the nobility.[126] The actual social situation was more complex, as Waltraud Heindl admirably shows in her 1990 study on the imperial civil service before 1848.[127] The problem, though, was the way in which only people of means could really afford to join the civil service after 1815. In the years following the upheaval and financial ruin of Austria's wars against Napoleon, inflation greatly reduced the value of officials' salaries. Social and political status deteriorated in tandem. Ignaz Beidtel, the justice official who provides us with so much rich detail of the central bureaucracy in the early nineteenth century, complained that the social status of the bureaucracy had significantly declined since the days when the ruler provided for his officials to live "with a means commensurate with their class."[128] In the years preceding 1848, the financial situation of Austria's state officials deteriorated further. Lower officials became "half-beggars" who had to petition the provincial offices (*Gubernia*) for emergency support, while regular salary increases were prohibited.[129] The bureaucracy keenly felt the shocks to the monarchy's finances during the Napoleonic Wars, when their salaries remained fixed in the face of drastic inflation.[130] Josef Karl Mayr describes the lifestyle of officials after the Napoleonic Wars as a "great withdrawal into the insularity of duty."[131] There was nothing else for them to enjoy. The Austrian state neglected its civil service as a matter of necessity as it fought both France and, later, impending bankruptcy. However, the "neglect" also represents a continuity of policy since Joseph II in public administration, where low pay and overwork had become endemic matters of policy.

If Joseph II paid officials less and expected them to work more, he was trying to give the state the most for its money. The inflation that set in during the Napoleonic Wars and afterward, on the other hand, reduced the lower rungs of the bureaucracy to a less than middle-class existence. The state under Francis or Ferdinand did little to combat the decline in pay. Middle-class entrants into the bureaucracy were being pushed out through material want. Between 1811 and 1831, the percentage of the middle class and the lower aristocracy (the lower nobility were often families ennobled for service to the crown in the military or in the bureaucracy) in the central offices in Vienna fell more than 5 percent. During the same period the percentage of high nobility, who presumably had the wealth necessary to cover the expenses not met by an official's salary, rose by 5 percent.[132] Emperor Francis, by failing to pay his civil servants a wage that had kept pace with rampant inflation, slowly but surely made entrance to civil service less accessible to the middle classes—the core of the Josephinist bureaucracy.

Culturally and socially, the legions of civil servants who staffed the central offices in Vienna, the *Gubernia* in the provincial capitals, and the county offices in provincial towns and cities were divided by education.

The entry level for officials with university degrees was higher than for those who did not have a degree; for promotion into the upper ranks of the bureaucracy a university decree was an absolute necessity. This social fact permeated the internal hierarchy of the civil service, and it determined the type of work and the type of positions that officials could fill. In the parlance of Austria's bureaucracy, education rendered one as a member of the *Konzeptspersonal* or the *Kanzleipersonal;* that is, one capable of drafting documents versus a lesser, office worker.[133] The differentiation caused by holding a university degree would remain a constant in the imperial civil service until the end of the monarchy. University-educated officials could be promoted through the ranks of the bureaucracy to serve as county prefects, in the ranks of the provincial offices (*Gubernia*), or in the ministerial elite in Vienna. The ranks of the more prestigious *Konzeptsbeamte* and their superiors formed a separate social class in society, a caste that built upon an elevated social status and buttressed by special privileges (*Sonderrechte*) accorded to the civil service.[134]

However, these class divisions do not adequately describe the hierarchy of the bureaucracy. The educational division had become one of tradition, so deeply imprinted into the culture of the administration that it was largely unwritten but perceptible everywhere. The civil service was regulated according to a unified classification or ranking system in every land that stood under the United Imperial-Royal Court Chancellery—that is, everywhere under the Habsburgs except Hungary and Transylvania. This system divided the civil service into twelve ranks, or *Diäten-Classe* (literally, daily pay classes), to which every court counselor in Vienna and every doorman in Bukovina could be assigned. Despite this underlying unity, the Austrian Empire's civil service sprawled out over these twelve classes in amazingly complex ways. Johann Georg Megerle von Mühlfeld's handbook for civil servants, published in an expanded edition in 1824, requires forty-seven pages to catalog all the different positions and posts according to their *Diäten-Classe.*[135] Moreover, these salary classes did not absolutely mirror the social and education differences that already existed in the bureaucracy and therefore did not necessarily reinforce them. But these salary classes did reflect in some ways the difference between the center and the provinces. A university-educated young man entering the civil service as a drafting intern (*Concepts-Pratikant*) would be assigned to the eleventh *Diäten-Classe,* as would a doorman to the Court Chancellery. In the provinces, the same drafting intern would belong to the lowest rank, the twelfth.

To understand this rather complex hierarchy of the Austrian civil service, it is helpful to consider the civil service in the shape of a diamond, having three levels.[136] The highest level of the civil service was formed by the crème de la crème of Austria's bureaucracy, who staffed the leadership roles of Austria's Chancelleries in policy-making supporting roles. These councilors, presidents, section heads, and their secretaries who were called by various titles, headed the Chancelleries and their suboffices in Vienna, and the *Gubernia* in the provinces. These men comprised the entirety of the first five ranks of the civil service. Inversely, at the bottom of the bureaucratic diamond were the groups of people almost permanently assigned to the twelfth and lowest rank, the doormen, stokers, *portiers*, and servants who looked after the physical spaces that the bureaucracy occupied. All of them were interconnected in Austria's bureaucratic world, but climbing to the top was easier for those with education and birth (see Table 1.1).

The bulk of the Habsburg imperial civil service, like its Prussian counterpart, could be found in the middle ranks. Here the two spheres of Austria's bureaucratic world, the university-educated civil servants (*Konzeptspersonal*) and the non-elite clerks (*Kanzleipersonal*) rubbed shoulders in the ranks from the sixth class down to roughly the eleventh. Though integrated into the same pay scale and rank, the two spheres of bureaucracy were still separated by the gulf of education, which widened over the course of one's career (see Table 1.2). Education and distinguished service allowed a juridically educated civil servant to climb the ranks of the bureau. A clerk, on the other hand, had little chance of rising higher than the personnel director, the *Hilfsämterdirektor*—the lower official in charge of all the clerks in a section or office. Despite the incredible responsibility of this position, it would take a lifetime of service by a clerk to achieve this rank. Clerks worked on routine tasks and served as copyists, stenographers, and kept the catalogs of the correspondence coming in and going out of the office. The work of a historian of nineteenth-century Austria is dependent on the good records and legible handwriting of these largely forgotten *Kanzleipersonal*. Unlike civil servants, clerks had no contractual relationship to the government. They were hired and let go at the discretion of the office chairman, be he the minister, the governor, the county prefect, or the archive director.[137]

By contrast, a university-educated official could begin his official career in the civil service in Vienna in the ninth class and be promoted into the eighth rather quickly. In such cases, Vienna's gravity and prestige mattered: officials beginning their careers in the countryside, in the county

**TABLE 1.1.** The Highest Ranks of the Civil Service Before 1848

| Diäten-Classe | Positions |
|---|---|
| 1 | minister of state / State-Conference minister (Metternich, Kolowrat) |
| 2 | president of a Court Chancellery |
| 3 | second president of a Court Chancellery, provincial governor |
| 4 | state counselor, *Conferenz-Counselor*, vice-president of a Court Chancellery |
| 5 | court counselor (*Hofrat*), vice-president of a *Gubernia* |

SOURCE: See note 137.


**TABLE 1.2.** Middle and Lower Ranks of the Civil Service Before 1848

| Rank or Diäten-Classe | drafting personnel Konzeptsdienst | office personnel Kanzleidienst | service personnel |
|---|---|---|---|
| 6 | *Sektionsrat* *Gubernial-Rat* county prefect | | |
| 7 | *Hof-Sekretär* *Ministerial-Sekretär* *Archiv Director* | *Hilfsämter-Direktor* court pay master | |
| 8 | ministerial drafting official provincial Regierungs-rat county vice-prefect | *Hilfsämter-Direktor*, second class *Bibliothekar* *Adjunkt* | |
| 9 | drafting adjunct (in Vienna) provincial drafting official | *Kanzleiofficial* court treasury cashier | |
| 10 | county secretary Vienna city secretary | stenographer-adjunct (Court War Council) Provincial Court of Audit official | |
| 11 | ministerial drafting intern (in Vienna) | *Kanzlist* (clerk) | ministerial doorman |
| 12 | drafting intern (provincial) | *Kanzleiassistent* county *Kanzlist* (clerk) court treasury scribe | various watchmen, craftsmen, and office servants |

SOURCE: See note 137.

offices for instance, were slower to be promoted and the ranks were correspondingly lower.[138] These university-educated civil servants formed the backbone of the Habsburg state, a state that during the reigns of Francis and Ferdinand combined Josephinian centralism and traditional federalism, as neither Francis nor Ferdinand could do without a central bureaucracy that improved the finances of the state. These men—and they were exclusively men, for women were not admitted to Austria's universities until the end of the nineteenth century—finished their studies in one of Austria's major education centers: Vienna, Innsbruck, Prague, or Graz (later Lemberg or Bukovina). In many cases, their career aspirations would carry them far from home. For example, Johann Neopmuk Eder joined the city prefecture of Vienna as a drafting intern (twelfth *Diäten-Classe*) after finishing his studies in Vienna in 1814. He received a transfer to Cilli/Celje in Styria, where he hoped to rise through the ranks faster. Nine years later he was the second county commissar, in the ninth class.[139] Eder dreamed of returning to Vienna, the metropolis, where life was better and the pay higher.

The Austrian provinces offered opportunity, but they could also be a form of banishment and a source of torment. The Austrian playwright and public intellectual Hermann Bahr produced a novel that touched exactly on the allure and dangers of making a career in the countryside. This work, *Drut*, first published in 1909, opens with an ambitious civil servant leaving the central ministry for a resort town in Upper Austria, where he will serve as the local administrator. The administrator felt himself to be free in his life for the first time, away from the watchful eyes of his superiors, his father, and his fellow civil servants. But soon the district administrator fell prey to a *Drut* (more commonly known as a *Drude*), a witch from Alpine lore who creeps into her victims' homes at night, sits on their chests while they sleep, and then possesses them. This *Drude* took the form of a baroness who lured the administrator into marriage, only to force him to the brink of despair through a public scandal and the exposure of immorality.[140] The administrator in *Drut*, much like Eder, thought he had been freed to make his career, but he had been sent out from Vienna into the great unknown of the hinterland, where the witches of folklore still roamed and careers were stalled or even ended.

Professional and social pitfalls aside, the administration formed a recognizable educated elite in larger Austrian society. They were the carriers of the Austrian state idea and a substantial part of the *Bildungsbürgertum*—the educated strata of Austria's middle class. Like the priesthood from former times, *Konzeptsarbeit*—the policy-making work of these educated officials—also offered a form of social mobility. Officials who distinguished themselves through length of service were regularly granted a title of nobility. They formed Austria's "second society," "the wide strata that in the epoch of Maria Theresia directly thrust itself between the aristocracy and the common *Volk*."[141] They were active in the cultural and artistic circles in Austria's administrative centers, and often they contributed to Austria's artistic life as artists themselves or consumers of art.[142] Moreover, bureaucrats as specialists in political economy and economics often used their time outside their offices to produce academic works. Carl Freiherr von Hock, who earned a doctorate in law and spent a career rising to high rank in the financial administration, published numerous works on national economy and trade, histories of the Austrian merchant marine, and even a history of the finances of the United States.[143]

Moreover, facets of Joseph's state project—particularly facets of his administration—remained, because Francis and later Ferdinand could not do without the central bureaucracy of Joseph II. The central bureaucracy helped the crown to raise taxes, field armies, and strengthen the authority of the monarch. Neither Francis nor Ferdinand was willing to destroy a pillar of their power; Francis continued the emphasis on education and training of bureaucrats that Joseph had started. Francis required that officials receive a law degree before entering the state service.[144] In so doing, he raised the status of the bureaucracy and took a firm step toward modernizing it. Nobles in the state service were also required to attend university, where they mixed with the middle-class aspirants to public service. Waltraud Heindl notes that after 1800 there was hardly an official in the Austrian bureaucracy who did not hold a university degree.[145] Francis also attempted to increase the status of his officials by putting them in an official uniform in 1814. The dark green uniform advertised the higher caste of the civil service, while velvet accents of different colors on the uniform told an observer to what branch of the government the servant-in-uniform belonged; golden embroidery on the uniform allowed a further differentiation of ranks in the hierarchy of officialdom.[146] Although Francis introduced the uniform with the intention of raising the social status of and morale in the civil service, it found acceptance with neither the nobility nor officials. The nobility wanted the sole right to wear uniforms, and the officials found them stiff and uncomfortable. In the end, the uniform became something to be worn at parades and left in the wardrobe at other times.[147]

Educational achievements or artistic and literary involvement did not offer solace to all disquieted souls in the bureaucracy. Professional frustration, impossible expectations, and despair at the underfunded and undersupported system dominated the attitudes of many in the civil service. Under Francis and Ferdinand, dissatisfaction for some officials began from the moment they left university and began a career in the bureaucracy, because it took time—sometimes many years—before a university graduate could reach a post with a fixed salary in the bureaucracy. Typically, an aspiring official, fresh with his legal degree, would not be given a post immediately but instead would be taken on as an unpaid intern. Although the chancelleries in Vienna and the provincial and county offices were expected to have two or three interns who would be groomed for eventual employment, Beidtel observed rampant abuse of this system between 1814 and 1848. The number of interns increased three- or four-fold, with the result that some poor souls remained in unpaid internships for seventeen years![148]

The situation worsened during in the 1830s and 1840s as the governmental authorities took on more and more work but did not receive the financial support to hire new staff and expand the bureaucracy. Interns were taken on to provide the additional workforce; the price for their service came at virtually no cost to the government.[149] One fiscal office in Graz hired eight new interns in the course of two years to supplement the four it already had.[150] Without the obligation to pay or even promote these interns, the state could eventually hire the best and leave the rest to work in unpaid positions until they gave up and entered another career.[151] Members of the high nobility again had an advantage in the bureaucracy of Emperor Francis: their independent wealth could be used to help remain in the service without pay for an extended period of time.[152]

In addition to the lack of financial remuneration, these interns, called *Pratikanten* or *Konzeptspratikanten*, had no legal claim for a promotion into the official service; they could work as unpaid interns indefinitely.[153] These conditions, according to Beidtel, brought much resentment and ridicule. The long-serving intern, gray and stooped with overwork and age, became the object of comedy in Vienna's theaters and the subject of intermittent emergency financial support from Vienna's treasury. Under the financial straits of the monarchy, which never seemed to recover from the Napoleonic Wars, the glory of state service had begun to lose its shine.

There were exceptions to the long and long-suffering career in state service. Karl Friedrich Kübeck entered the Austrian administration in

1801 as an intern in the Olmütz/Olomouc county office and was made a *Konzeptsbeamte* five years later.[154] His promotion into the ranks of the officially employed was slow despite the excellent reputation he earned by working late into the evening and mastering the files, the regulations, and the precedents and norms of the administration. His patience paid off. Though from simple origins (his father was a tailor), Kübeck was ennobled in 1816—after ten years of official employment. Nine years later he was promoted into the baronage.[155] Kübeck, however, was the great exception. Most interns remained in their unpaid positions for at least six years. To last this long in an unpaid position, interns needed to be independently wealthy or have a steady source of outside income; moreover, they had to prove—through official documentation—that they financially could support themselves.[156]

Julius Bunzel's 1911 study of treasury official (*Hofkammerprokurator*) Josef von Varena, who took control of the Styrian treasury office in 1804 and served there until 1839, presents a reasonably representative picture of how the bureaucracy operated among the lower ranks and away from Vienna's crème de la crème like Kübeck.[157] Varena's career exemplifies the Austrian state's call to its midlevel bureaucrats to work under extraordinary conditions and to keep the state running despite its many growing pains—including a growing mountain of files. The course of Varena's career, his everyday reports and complaints, showcase the gulf that stretched between the continued efforts to increase the role of the Austrian state in the everyday life of its citizens and the state's continued incapacity to invest the resources or hire the personnel necessary to take on these growing administrative tasks. In other words, midlevel officials like Varena had to carry on the increasing work of state largely on their own backs and, surprisingly, often paid for additional expenditures out of their own pockets.

Varena's career offers us some striking figures. Upon taking over the treasury office in 1804, Varena inherited no less than 329 files that had not been dispatched—including eighteen of which had been waiting for more than four years! Thereafter the work seemed to increase exponentially for Varena's office while Varena himself rarely received approval, despite his frequent protestations, to hire additional staff.[158] In 1825, a year in which the office dispatched over 5,000 files, but also had a backlog of 671 files (over 10 percent), Varena's superiors in the Styrian governor's office declared that the backlog was completely normal and appropriate. Despite the lack of concern among his superiors, Varena continued to beg for the funds to hire more office staff; when his request was denied, he hired literate day laborers to serve as copyists with his own money. Varena's efforts to alleviate the backlog came at the price of his and his underlings' health: he recounts in a report to Graz how long hours in the office, in an effort to stay on top of new files and chip away at the office's backlog, had led to the early deaths of two of his assistants (*Kanzleibeamte*).[159]

Adding insult to injury was the dreaded *Conduit-* or *Qualifikationsliste*, the secret evaluation that comprised each official's dossier. These evaluations were introduced by Joseph II, suspended under Leopold II, and reintroduced by Francis I.[160] Beidtel, ever our guide through the bureaucratic world before 1848, complains about one of Emperor Francis's several court decrees on the form and content of these evaluations, that "the basis that the most qualified and most worthy should receive promotions, was left to the subjective judgment of the superiors . . . a large and carefully exploited leeway."[161] Every official had a personnel file in which an ongoing evaluation was kept by his immediate superior. An official had no right to see what was written in his file, nor was he allowed any opportunity to contest or appeal any information therein. No official could be promoted, transferred, or pensioned without submitting his *Conduiteliste*. It was a bureaucratic passport whose owner could not look inside.

Beidtel's complaints summed up the general dissatisfaction in the middle ranks of the bureaucracy that supposedly objective decisions for transfers and promotions were actually based on wholly subjective evaluations by superiors. Compounding this complaint was the subjective nature of the material in the personal dossiers kept for each official. These *Conduitelisten* contained much more than simple evaluations of performance. Rather, a *Conduiteliste* also contained a superior's account of a civil servant's public comportment, his appearance, as well as assessments of character and any rumors of scandal. A superior was expected to include among his evaluations whether his underlings gambled too much, whether and where they owed money, if they were sickly, or if their choice of public company did not conform to the elevated social position of a public official.[162] In a sense, the Austrian evaluation system took the whole person into account and as such it embodied an attempt to, in Weber's terms, reinforce an "elevated social standing" of the bureaucracy in the minds of those they governed or dominated.[163] Joseph, of course, intended such supervision to ensure that his civil servants served the state with their entire being and it was part of the way he conceived state service as sacred work (recall his "pastoral letter").

But Joseph's state had stagnated. His reforms were interventions, but he expected them to be improved upon over time. Mostly, however, they were left in place to evolve without the emperor's direction. Over time these confidential dossiers perverted the very objectivity and impartiality that civil servants were expected to exercise in making official decisions and judgments. *Conduitelisten* made "superiors into despots, subordinates into sycophants," and made colleagues within an office distrustful of one another.[164] And what is more, this system of evaluations permeated the entire hierarchy of the administration from the Court Chancelleries to the county offices. Given that the *Conduitelisten* provided the foundation for the bureaucracy's promotion system, it is no wonder that the procedures which governed promotions developed into an informal yet pervasive system of patronage—*Protektion*. Under *Protektion* officials with connections, the nobility in the civil service naturally had more of these, could bypass what one contemporary official described as a "tedious and cumbersome" career path.[165] *Protektion* promoted officials into the higher ranks of the bureaucracy who possessed more connections than talent. It also therefore encouraged servility vis-à-vis one's superiors and a longing for harmony that often clashed with the rationalizing reform-absolutist roots of the institution itself.[166] Among officials like Varena, or Beidtel, who battled with low pay and little support far from the chancelleries in Vienna, changes would have to be made. Staying the course, whatever that course was, seemed impossible. These captains of the bureaucracy could no longer keep grasp of their ship's wheel, the current was too strong, their ship seemed on the verge of breaking. They were ready for change.

## To 1848

Joseph II's successors did not maintain or cultivate the momentum of state building that flourished in the Enlightenment. The dynamism of state-sponsored change was suppressed and a vigorous approach to statecraft during the French Revolution was set aside in favor of a traditional reliance on the estates. But while Francis and Ferdinand ruled under the banner of reaction, they were not reactionaries. They did not dismantle the structures of the central state, and they certainly did not want to rock ship of state with more change, whether backward- or forward-looking. Moreover, they could hardly dispense with the central bureaucracy that Maria Theresia and Joseph II had created. Francis and Ferdinand were not able to reconcile their need for the bureaucracy's ability to collect taxes and its potential to strengthen the crown's authority with their desire to steer it away from policies which promoted social and political change. The result was a state locked in midstep. It was held in place by the competing forces of inertia and momentum, forming a delicate balance that was finally broken by the revolutions of 1848.

The five decades that had passed since the funeral of Joseph II had seen the retreat of centralism, multiple coronation ceremonies, and lip service to noble elites and traditional cooperation between throne and the noble estates. The taxes raised, the armies fielded, the personal strength and authority of the monarch, all depended on the legions of bean counters, minute takers, building inspectors, and—of course—censors and police officials. The reforms of Joseph and Maria Theresia had created a third pillar of central authority that took a place beside the army and the Church. Their successors would not willingly destroy a pillar of their power. This was a silent viewpoint in the central chancelleries, but the prevailing view nonetheless.

It would be wrong to think that the period between the Napoleonic Wars and the revolutions of 1848 was a period of total stasis or a prelude to revolution. For all the lack of change, the world of government silently and subtlety evolved. Most importantly, the bureaucracy developed an ideology separate from the crown. Faced with lack of support and neglect, especially when they saw the state's once-transformative power in Austrian society sitting idle, this new caste of Austria's officials—its educated elite— took the reins from its master. The bureaucracy, despite its lagging pay, the confusing entanglement of the central administration, and the stultifying behavior of the emperor and his advisors, held firm to the ethos of Josephinism and the faith in its role as the motor of progress and development. Progress and reform, from the time of Maria Theresia through the early era of constitutionalism, centered on the activity of the absolutist state. The transformation of the Austrian state from a conglomerate to a unified *Reich*—incomplete though it was—embodied Austria's attempts to modernize and to meet the challenges of the modern world. This modernization was led and carried out by the Josephinist bureaucracy. Moreover, both conservatives and liberals/Josephinists called for reform of the Austrian state and wanted first and foremost to reform the structure of the administration. Calls for administrative reform qua structural reform would become the administration's own tradition, one that would accompany the monarchy into the twentieth century. The revolutions of 1848 would bring several parties of change to the fore. It was the bureaucracy's own party of change that would win out.

# 2

## The Madness of Count Stadion; or,
## Austria Between Revolution and Reaction

**WITHIN DAYS** of the promulgation of the Provisional Municipalities Law on March 17, 1849, interior minister Count Franz Stadion suffered a nervous breakdown. Stadion had not only written this new law, which had granted newfound freedoms to municipalities and rural townships, but he also wrote the new Imperial Constitution, of March 4, 1849, upon which the Provisional Municipalities Law was based. Stadion clearly had been overworked, but exhaustion had given over to madness. By April, much like the revolution, which Stadion himself had sought to capture, harness, and tame, Stadion was gone.

Little is known about the gifted interior minister after April 1849. By April, Stadion had to escape Vienna, the court, the ministry. He first made his way to Baden, a spa town southwest of the city. As he sat at a restaurant and tried to regain his senses, he discovered he could no longer read. Days later, he could no longer speak German. He chose to remain silent. His friends hoped he would regain his mental equilibrium, but he never did. He ceased to recognize faces of old friends and his own mouth began to hang wider and wider, a result of dementia. Precious few of Stadion's letters have survived; those that date from this period are written with an unsure and weak hand. The letters are gnarled and bodiless, the content of their juxtaposition empty and tired. His sole biographer, Rudolph Hirsch, wrote in 1861 that Stadion's mind broke at the high point of his career. "This dear leader," according to Hirsch, mentally "collapsed under the weight of the days' events."[1] What had weighed Stadion down so much? What had finally broken his mind?

Count Franz Stadion thoroughly exemplified the talent and energy of the ideal Austrian civil servant.[2] He came from a bureaucratic family, the third son of Count Phillip Stadion. The elder Stadion had served Emperor Francis as foreign minister—before Metternich—and later as minister of finance. This status of double birth, into the status of nobility and the caste of the ministerial bureaucracy, certainly helped the younger Stadion rise through the ranks, but not before he spent several years as an unpaid intern in the Austrian provinces. He entered the civil service in 1828 after receiving a law degree at the University of Vienna. Spending much of his career in regional and provincial offices, first in Galicia and then in the Tyrol, he worked for several years without pay—hoping for quick promotion into the higher ranks. He was promoted to *Hofrat*—court counselor—at the young age of twenty-eight and was brought to Vienna to work in the General Court Chamber. In 1841, Stadion's time to show his talent had arrived—he took the post of governor of the Coastal Provinces of the Austrian Littoral—Görz, Gradiska, and the city of Trieste. Helfert, the conservative chronicler of the revolution, called Stadion's tenure in Trieste the "most brilliant period of his life."[3] His work in the province gave him the reputation as a reformer and an enlightened minister—a Joseph II on a smaller stage.[4] For certain, his career as an official in the civil service also provided Stadion with an unsurpassed knowledge of Austria's domestic situation and the condition of the administration in the provinces. Such abilities as a bureaucrat did not go unnoticed. In 1848 he stood for election to the new Austrian parliament, the Reichstag, representing Galicia, and won. He would be one of many officials elected to parliament, joining the loose political grouping of the moderates.[5] Like the German National Assembly, which met in Frankfurt, the Constitutional Assembly in Vienna was an opportunity for bureaucrats to use their knowledge and educational level to serve the state. They received leave from their superiors and trekked to Vienna to join the proceedings in the assembly.

An 1849 biographical sketch of Stadion as a parliamentary deputy called Stadion one of "the greatest revolutionaries in Austria." The anonymous author followed this provocative statement with a command not to laugh at his proclamation.[6] But Stadion, as minister of the interior under Schwarzenberg, would revolutionize Austria, from the top down and the inside out. His influence was so great that Heinrich Friedjung would call him the "leading personality of the Schwarzenberg ministry."[7] What Stadion represented was the importance of the administration, not only as the workers who built the Austrian state, but the thinkers who would transform it. When revolution hit Austria in 1848, Austria's officials were ready to contribute. They stood for election, they wrote new laws and constitutions, and they joined in, now and again, in the revelry of victory. But, like Stadion, they shied away from revolutionary violence.

During the revolutionary year, Stadion's challenge had been one of balance. The stakes had been incredibly high. Revolution had overtaken Vienna—indeed, it had overtaken large urban centers all over the monarchy. Milan and Venice declared independence in the spring of 1848. Hungary's diet, flush with ideas for reform, had called for far-reaching autonomy and even their own government. By the end of 1848, reform had turned into a full-scale war of independence. Violence spread throughout the monarchy. Riots in Vienna in March and May 1848 were just a prelude to October's full-scale revolution, when a mob lynched the Austrian minister of war, Count Theodor von Latour, in the ministerial offices. Stadion's colleague, the minister of justice, Alexander Bach, witnessed Latour hounded down by the angry mob. Within minutes the crowd had killed Latour with heavy blows. They stripped the clothes from his body, hung it from a lamppost, and then continued to torture and mutilate his corpse while others stormed the Vienna armory, preparing themselves to defend the city from a counterstrike.

As extreme as the mob's actions were, Stadion equally feared the reaction, which came draped in general's epaulettes. Since March 1848, when Metternich had fled Vienna, Alfred Windisch-Graetz, prince and field marshall lieutenant, had tried to provide the regime with the backbone that it lacked.[8] With the regime seeming to buckle under the pressure from protesting burgher, students, and workers, Windisch-Graetz made his own rules. He ignored civilian authorities to pursue his own course of counter-revolution. As the military commander of the armed forces in Bohemia, Windisch-Graetz paraded his soldiers through Prague. When crowds there decided to harangue him with charivaris, he responded to their cat songs by withdrawing from the city and bombarding it with cannon. The mill in the old town caught fire and the fire from the bombardment rained down on the students and burgher like apocalyptic brimstone. Windisch-Graetz proclaimed martial law over the city and brought Prague's autonomy movement—a full revolution it certainly was not—to its knees.[9]

One of his biographers likened Windisch-Graetz to a man of the sixteenth century, living uncomfortably in the nineteenth. Albrecht Wallenstein, a commander of Habsburg armies during the Thirty Years' War, had been equally pitiless, but this was a new era. Windisch-Graetz cared not for public opinion. He had no fear of being portrayed as a butcher in the freer, looser revolutionary press. He crusaded for counterrevolution and mercilessly attacked Vienna. By the time Latour hung on a lamppost in Am Hof, the largest square in Vienna's inner city, Windisch-Graetz had moved his army to the outskirts of Vienna. Vienna would suffer an even bloodier fate than Prague. Over two thousand died in the bombardment and street fighting as the revolutionary city collapsed. Windisch-Graetz shot twenty-five ringleaders after the fight was over, including a representative of the Frankfurt parliament. He then turned his attention to influencing the emperor's retinue in Olmütz/Olomouc, two hundred kilometers north of the imperial capital.

Stadion did not know what kind of counterrevolution the sixty-one-year old Windisch-Graetz would insist upon, but he knew that the field marshal possessed enormous influence at court. Karl Kübeck even suggested that Prince Windisch-Graetz, now prince of the counterrevolution, be made dictator and be responsible for building a government and restoring general order. The title of dictator seemed extreme, even to someone like Windisch-Graetz's stone-hard sensibilities. Instead, Windisch-Graetz insisted that his brother-in-law, career diplomat Prince Felix Schwarzenberg, become prime minister. Schwarzenberg had moved quickly to form a government, and as a compromise between the two brothers-in-law, Count Franz von Stadion became the minister of the interior. This was the second-most influential member of the cabinet, behind the prime minister himself. The minister of the interior held the reins of government in his hands. He was responsible for law, order, and oversaw the entire public administration.[10]

Stadion, a career civil servant and a product of the Josephinist ethos that had hibernated through the long years of Francis and Metternich, fought the violence of the mob and the equally disturbing violence of Windisch-Graetz's counterrevolution the only way he knew how. He sat at his minister's desk and wrote a constitution for the regime. Revolution had not only awakened students, burgher, and workers who marched through the streets proclaiming their rights as citizens; it had also awakened bureaucrats. Stadion's March Constitution of 1849 reflected the bureaucratic compromise on Austria's revolution because it reflected a worry that revolution would teeter out of balance and into the destruction of the regime. Too much rule by the people and too much repression went hand in hand. Stadion's constitutional ideas were about steering a middle course, and a difficult one at that, because he had to search for ways to organize public participation in a multinational state. In the end, he produced a series of laws and a constitution that would shape the organization of the state, the growth of public participation, and the eventual establishment of universal male suffrage.

What then emerged out of the revolutionary year was not only tales of grapeshot, barricades, national guards, and streets filled with blood; 1848 forged a compromise between Joseph's absolutist administration and representatives of the people. Sealed with blood, it was the compromise between two ideas: a powerful central state and the idea of "state-free" autonomous towns and townships. It sought the balance between the mob and the generals, to avoid rousing the bear of counterrevolution while keeping the wolves of revolution at bay.

Stadion's constitution would speak for him long after he fell silent. His constitution called for an administrative restructuring of the monarchy and the integration of political participation in government. It was a retooling of the centralism of the Josephinian state, and it required a renewal of the administration's ethos and mission to be Austria's leaders and its missionaries for progress in the hinterland. The year 1848 was not a missed turn that led Austria down the road to dissolution, but it did open up the monarchy to include participatory politics. The imperial administration, which was forged in an era of enlightened, reform absolutism and imbued with an ethos that emphasized service to the state as serving the common good, constantly nurtured and managed this new participatory politics. For the imperial administration to take on this role, the old regime—the regime that kept its people silent and its officials locked up under mounds of paperwork—had to fall. A revolution, even Stadion's silently constitutional one, needs a spark.

## The Revolutions of 1848
### Revolution and Constitution: Pillersdorf's Constitution of April 1848

A year before Stadion fled Vienna, the city had become obsessed with politics. Following the news of the overthrow of the French king in late February 1848, Vienna's coffeehouses filled with burgher who wanted to read the latest news from abroad.[11] Liberal movements—for there was never just one—were actively engaged in debating Austria's political questions and its economic and legal development. These liberal movements sought the opening up of governmental institutions to representative bodies. Farther from Vienna, liberal questions about economic and individual freedoms were answered by plans for national independence or national autonomy. As revolutionary fever infiltrated the Austrian Empire, Hungary was the first to develop a cough. On March 3, Louis Kossuth, who would become the political leader of a massive Hungarian revolt, gave a speech in the Hungarian diet that set the wheels of revolution in motion. His speech was immediately translated into German and began to circulate in the streets, newspapers, and coffeehouses in Vienna.[12] In addition to demanding that the Hungarian diet receive its own ministry of finances, Kossuth proclaimed the necessity of a constitutional government, both for Hungary and for all of the empire. He also took a page out of Victor Andrian-Werburg's book and blamed the "bureaucratic governmental system" for the repression of the Austrian peoples and the backwardness of the empire. Kossuth, given over to dramatic effect, described the unlucky situation of the Austria peoples living under the "bureaucratic stagnation" of Austria's stability-system, the long-fossilized policies that emphasized stability and repressed change: "Yes, honorable colleagues, an accursed and stifling wind weighs heavy on our fatherland; out of the charnel house of the Viennese cabinet comes an all-consuming puff of wind to us over here, which paralyzes our nerves and lames the flight of our souls."[13]

The revolutions of 1848, which would engulf the Habsburg Empire in a fight for its dominance in the German-speaking world and for its very survival, began as movements for constitutional autonomy and independence from Vienna. But these movements quickly became—in a dynamic that even Alexis de Tocqueville could admire—a moment for a centralization, administrative evenness, and homogenization that would in turn deliver a major social and economic transformation of Austrian society. Thus, the great puffs of wind that emerged from the revolutionary speech makers brought change to Austria's governmental systems through the politics of the street. The revolutionaries, by overturning tradition, by ending the vestiges of patrimonial rule and noble dominance in the countryside, hoped to clear a path for rule by the people. In doing so, they would strengthen the state by defeating its traditional enemy. Thus, the revolution broke apart the ossified cartilage of Austria's stability-system, which had been in place since the days of the French Revolution. Ministerial officials came to the fore and supplanted the old guard of Metternich and Kolowrat. These new statesmen at first followed the tone set by liberal journalists and speech makers, planning a thorough reshaping of Austria's governmental system. Later, however, once the rhetoric of revolution and its mouth-pieces were slowly swept aside, Austria's ministers would erect an absolutist system that was even stronger than before—and one that depended even more so on a trained and loyal bureaucratic apparatus.

In early 1848, however, all of this remained unclear, as revolutionaries erected street barricades and called for a constitution. Metternich, al-though not the only architect of the governmental system, received much of the early blame and fled Vienna on the night of March 13. Ferdinand's advisors had hoped to placate the revolutionaries with an assembly of es-tates to advise the monarch on "legislative and administrative questions." During the night of March 14, it quickly became clear that this attempt to forestall the revolution by promising administrative reform would not quiet the calls for change. On March 15, Ferdinand issued a proclama-tion that promised the revolutionaries what the old guard least wanted to concede: a constitution.[14] The emperor's proclamation, in addition to granting freedom of the press and a national guard, called delegates of the estates to form a central commission to draft a constitution. Further de-crees followed, abolishing the Court Chancellery and establishing central ministries—along with cabinet ministers who were to be held responsible for all the work done by the administration underneath them. Ministries were created for the portfolios of foreign affairs, domestic affairs (Ministry of the Interior), education, justice, war, and finances.[15]

Change was in the air, but how much change was under debate. Em-peror Ferdinand's first prime minister was none other than Metternich's rival, Count Franz Anton Kolowrat. Kolowrat had little intention of re-forming himself out of a job, or devolving any policy making to a body of elected officials. His policy was therefore to preserve the personal control of the monarch and to control the damage brought on by the street riots and the expectations of political change.[16] Even after he resigned on April 3, 1848, the emperor's ministers did not change from his course. As such, the drafting of a constitution did not fall as promised to a meeting of the estates but to the minister of the interior, Baron Franz von Pillersdorf. Pillersdorf was the only constitutionally-friendly minister in a cabinet of notables, and set himself fully to the task of drafting a constitution—with the help of *bürgerlich* deputies—in little more than a month.[17]

The April—or Pillersdorf—Constitution, as it came to be known, has avoided close inspection by generations of historians. After all, this constitution received an almost immediate rejection by democrats and students. Nonetheless, the document opened wide the doors of constitutional change. It broke apart much of the monarchy's administrative culture and organization and changed the relationship between Vienna and the provinces.[18] After Pillersdorf, there was no going back to patrimonial administration, feudal privileges, and noble dominance in the countryside. Unity was the order of the day: this constitution clarified the formerly uncertain and medieval relationship between the individual provinces and the throne. Ferdinand was the crowned king of Hungary, Bohemia, and Lombardy-Venetia, and he now ruled—according to the constitution—an "indivisible constitutional monarchy."[19] In addition to invoking once again the language of the Pragmatic Sanction and giving the lands of the monarchy a legal and explicit unity, the Pillersdorf Constitution also established a parliament (Reichstag) that would share legislative powers with the emperor. This representative body had the power and responsibility to approve the size of the army, as well as to regulate the state's finances such as state income and expenditures, how much the state could borrow, and the sum of the taxes it could levy. The emperor, aided by his legions of bureaucrats, would continue to hold the executive power.

The Pillersdorf Constitution de facto altered the administrative culture of the monarchy. In addition to clearing away Metternich's and Kolowrat's unpopular system under the State-Conference, the Pillersdorf Constitution solidified the end of the Court Chancelleries with the implementation of the ministerial system. The constitution mentioned the concept of ministerial responsibility, though it was unclear to whom these ministers were responsible, whether to the future parliamentary assembly, the emperor, or to popular opinion. Each minister, however, was personally accountable for the work, for the cases, and for the policies that were implemented by his subordinates. The old system of collegial organization, where bureaucrats would discuss matters which then would be decided by a majority vote, was swept away.[20] This personal responsibility of ministers also changed the self-conception of Austria's bureaucrats, who were no longer court officials or simply the officials of the emperor—they were now ministerial officials.[21] The ministers now controlled and were responsible for Austria's administration.

The changes that the Pillersdorf constitution brought were structural and important, but they did not satisfy the people on the street. On May 15, 1848, Viennese burgher and students stormed the emperor's residence and demanded a more representative constitution, written by representatives of the people. Their ire also focused on the process of writing the constitution; they found it particularly vexing that the emperor octroyed, or decreed, the Pillersdorf Constitution by imperial patent and provided only a limited version of the suffrage they desired.[22] Ferdinand and his advisors quickly folded, and gave into the crowd's demands. In fact, following this "Storm Petition," Ferdinand issued a proclamation that transformed the lower house of parliament, which Pillersdorf's constitution had called for, into a Constitutional Assembly. Under this proclamation, the members of the Constitutional Assembly would be indirectly elected and charged with drafting a new constitution. This Constitutional Assembly was scheduled to convene in July 1848.[23]

Despite the failure of the Pillersdorf Constitution to satisfy the populace, it effectively ended the old regime in Austria. The administrative changes it called for would be implemented slowly over the course of the revolution, but the conditions for their development happened immediately in the excitement of March and April 1848. The freedoms that the revolutionaries wanted and needed, the freedoms that Pillersdorf's constitution spoke to, but did not fulfill, became increasingly thinkable under a unified central state. The Habsburg's penchant for ruling all the territories as distinct entities, with their own rules and methods of distributing power and privilege, was seen as increasingly incompatible with the individual-based freedoms that revolutionaries had in mind and that liberals wanted. Josephinist centralism had found a new ally against the weight of tradition, particularism, and noble intransigence. Hence liberty—and freedoms of conscience, movement, enterprise, and religion—became increasingly tied to the more distant and abstract idea of a central state authority. As administrative changes from March slid down the administrative ladder, a new system emerged with an ever-increasing pace. Time seemed to quicken too. The state that emerged from the dust cloud of 1848 was markedly different from the one that entered it.

## Parliament and Administration

The failure of Pillersdorf's constitution would be its lasting achievement, for it led to a collective Austrian introspection on the organization of the Austrian state and the integration of public participation in that state. Its failure served to spawn a year that was characterized not just by revolution, but by refashioning and revisioning the Austrian state. First and foremost, this search for new forms brought public participation into Austrian governance. Elections were held to select electors and members of a new parliament, which for now would function as a constitutional assembly. Moreover, this parliamentary body appeared to mean business. At the beginning of August, this assembly elected thirty men from its membership (three members from each governmental district, or *Gubernia*) to a constitutional committee that would be responsible for writing the new constitution. The constitutional committee further divided itself into two subcommittees. The first subcommittee consisted of three members and was charged with drafting a list of fundamental rights, while the second subcommittee consisted of five members and would draft the rest of the constitution.[24] Parliamentary life began in Austria in 1848. Stadion joined the assembly, as did the jurist and future minister Alexander Bach. In fact out of the 383 representatives sent to the Reichstag in Vienna, a full 87, nearly a quarter, were bureaucrats like Stadion. Members of the intelligentsia, jurists like Alexander Bach, numbered 94. It would be these groups, officials steeped in Josephinist state service as well as jurists and liberals who would steer the work of writing a constitution.[25] The two subcommittees immediately began work on a draft of the new constitution and were given a free hand to discuss almost everything. This, to some degree, included even the sacrosanct powers of the emperor in the waning months of 1848.

As the Reichstag debated such issues as fundamental rights, the powers of the emperor and of parliament, and the organization of the Austrian state, their work was interrupted in early October by an uprising of workers and radical democrats in Vienna.[26] The uprising, initially directed by the angry mob in the heat of October 6 against the ministers in the Austrian government, had immediate effects. As the radicals gained control of the city and prepared for its defense against a military siege, three of the ministers resigned, while the remaining ministers fled with the emperor and his court to Olmütz/Olomouc in Moravia. Having abandoned both Vienna and the revolution, Emperor Ferdinand left uncertain the fate of the yet-unwritten constitution. In Moravia, the forces of reaction and counterrevolution gathered to mount their offensive.[27] The reaction then followed in rapid steps, but this was more a reaction against the politics of the street than the politics of change. Hope among the parliamentarians was still alive, but on October 16, Count Alfred Windisch-Graetz took command of all military campaigns outside of Italy. His task was to defeat the revolutionaries. First he needed to retake Vienna; later he would steer his armies against the rebellious Hungarians. Windisch-Graetz proceeded to simply invade the city, allowing his troops to engage in street fights against an undersupplied and hungry enemy—the city's citizens. His troops were able to take the city by the end of the month, leaving thousands of dead and wounded as a result.[28]

In the stormy days of October, not only did the Viennese suffer defeat at the hands of Windisch-Graetz, but the latest government had become isolated and discredited, while Windisch-Graetz was able to gain support for the violent suppression of the politics of the street in Vienna. Moreover, Windisch-Graetz increasingly seemed to gain traction in Austria's high political circles. On October 19, Ferdinand entrusted Prince Felix zu Schwarzenberg, Windisch-Graetz's brother-in-law, to form a new government. Parliament had adjourned on October 22 and was scheduled to reassemble in the Moravian town of Kremsier/Kroměříž on November 15.[29]

In Prince Felix zu Schwarzenberg the imperial family found exactly the right man for the job of restoring order and bringing an end to the political revolution of 1848.[30] War in Venetia and in Hungary still waged on. Moreover, despite the wishes of his brother-in-law, Schwarzenberg had no intention of overturning the gains the revolution had made for the authority of the monarch and the central state. Schwarzenberg belonged to one of the wealthiest and most prestigious noble families of the Habsburg Empire, a family which had distinguished itself in service to the emperors for centuries. Schwarzenberg, born in 1800, combined a career official's absolute loyalty with the flair of a high aristocrat. After a six-year term in the military, the young prince entered the diplomatic corps in 1824, which took him to St. Petersburg, Berlin, London, Lisbon, and even Rio de Janeiro.[31] Since the diplomatic corps kept him out of Austria for so much time, Schwarzenberg had no firm grasp of the domestic political situation in Austria when he took the reins of government. Nevertheless, Schwarzenberg was ever the diplomat, even more so as a leader of government, and he would prove to be a decisive force for harnessing the revolution. Intelligent enough to rely on people smarter than he, he appointed men of talent to cabinet positions who embodied a new era in Austrian government. Two appointments in particular would be initially important for Austria's later constitutional and administrative development: minister of interior Count Franz Stadion and minister of justice Alexander Bach.[32]

A third minister, who would eventually join the cabinet as minister of justice in 1849, was Anton Ritter von Schmerling—the future architect of Austria's constitutional system in the 1860s. Thus, the most important men who, over the course of the next twelve years, would be instrumental in building Austria's foundations for political life and for preparing the administration to once again be Austria's leaders and model citizens, got their start in ministerial politics in Schwarzenberg's ministry.

Flanked by his new ministers, who represented the best and brightest of the Austrian public administration and the Viennese burgher, Schwarzenberg presented his new ministry and his government program to the Austrian Reichstag at Kremsier/Kroměříž on November 27.[33] Schwarzenberg began his speech hesitantly but his words struck the right chord among the Reichstag's delegates and, after reports of the speech extended beyond Kremsier, among the Viennese as well.[34] He had promised strong, principled leadership that would neither follow the swinging temperament of revolution nor usher in an aristocratic reaction. Schwarzenberg spoke of the need for a relationship of trust between the government, which now consisted not of informal councils but of a council of ministers, and the representatives of the people. Together they would work to unify the diverse peoples and lands into a single unified state. He also affirmed the liberal achievements of the revolution, including the equality of all citizens regardless of rank or station before the law, the equality of nationalities in the empire, and the transparency of government. Finally, at the end of an oft-quoted passage, Schwarzenberg affirmed that these liberal achievements would be secured through "the free communes and the free formation of the provinces in all internal affairs."[35] Liberals and aristocrats alike were hopeful after the speech. They wanted to ensure that any reassertion of the heavily centralized bureaucratic absolutism of the prerevolutionary period be checked through local, autonomous institutions. Schwarzenberg paid lip service to these calls for the local government to be free of state interference, but he was careful to add that these institutions would be "enveloped by the common wrappings [gemeinsamen Bande]" of a strong central power.[36] Then, on December 2, Emperor Ferdinand abdicated in favor of his eighteen-year-old nephew, Francis Joseph. There was new life in the emperor's cabinet and on the throne.

Beyond the hills of Moravia, where the court, ministers, and Reichstag had gathered, the future was cloudy. Although Victor von Andrian-Werburg, the former civil servant and perpetual critic of Austria's administration, was pleased with promises of future autonomy and constitutional rule, he could not hide his skepticism of this new regime that was being erected in Vienna. The revolutions of 1848 had promoted him from general critic of the old regime into an ambassador for "Germany" in London. Returning from Great Britain to the provisional government in Frankfurt am Main in December 1848, Andrian-Werburg heard word that Emperor Ferdinand had abdicated in favor of Francis Joseph. When, two days later, he heard that Francis Joseph dropped the title of "constitutional monarch" in favor of "Emperor by the grace of God," he registered his displeasure: "Why do that? In any case, that was a blunder."[37] He wondered silently in his diary, "What was happening in Vienna?" What was happening, in fact, was that Count Franz Stadion was trying to tame both the revolution and counterrevolution.

The key counterweight of Stadion's careful balancing act was Austria's legion of officials, whom Stadion counted on to be flexible managers in a new system, in a new state that had taken the best of the revolution and restored both civility and stability. Stadion began his term as minister by addressing the role and work of the civil service. Stadion released two decrees in December 1848 that were meant to change the culture and practice of the Austrian administration. The first hints that Austria's administration would undergo fundamental change came with the promise of a constitutional government and the introduction of a ministerial system in March 1848. Stadion would bring such change to fruition. Thus, Andrian-Werburg's quizzical unease with what was happening in Vienna was the reestablishment of the central state, one that would adapt to working with and guiding representative institutions. This retooling of the state began with the civil service.

Stadion's first decree, issued to the provincial governors on December 3, 1848, explicitly regulated the relationship between the provinces and the center, plus the relationship of an official to his superior.[38] Stadion prefaced his instructions to the governors with the statement that the promotion of the new constitutional system in Austria, "with the management of the executive power of the government," necessitates the cooperation of the central ministry and the governors. But the "cooperation" (*übereinstimmendes Zusammenwirken*) Stadion had in mind for the governors was one in which the governors rendered unquestioning obedience to the interior minister—that is, to himself. "This unity on the side of the political administration can only be provided through the Minister of the Interior." Stadion continued by "strictly" insisting that his "directives

[Verfügungen] be executed always energetically and exactly with the most possible speed." Stadion was reminding his governors that the collegial system had been replaced and that he was now the sole person responsible for everything in the Ministry of the Interior. Therefore, he "cannot permit" that his "commands be subject to further discussion." Governors had often used "discussion" as a pretext either to delay or avoid the implementation of directives, and as such, according to Stadion, "brought disgrace" to the bureaucracy in the eyes of the populace. As Austria was opening up to representative government, Stadion was pushing the realm of discussion and debate onto the public's representative institutions, while simultaneously ending discussion within the ranks of the administration. The administration, in order to work in a future constitutional monarchy and with the vagaries of an open political life, had to be unified, disciplined, and prepared.

Stadion's loyalty toward the bureaucracy and the state sat easily with an equal commitment to parliamentarism. For him these two institutions of political authority could be combined and integrated. But first, he not only needed to change the way the administration worked within its own hierarchical system, as he attempted in his administrative decree of December 3; he also needed to change the bureaucrats themselves and prepare them for a leadership role in local and regional politics. His second major administrative order to "all civil servants of the Interior Ministry," on December 26, 1848, was intended to do just that. Stadion's second *Verordnung* was like Joseph's II's pastoral letter, but adapted for a new, constitutional age with representative institutions. Constitutionalism demanded a new, more thoroughly committed civil servant.[39] And though Stadion wanted strict obedience from his underlings, he did not want his civil servants executing his commands blindly, but to act as "thinking organs of the government" so that "the populace becomes convinced that all authorities are inhabited by the same spirit." His officials should not only be thoughtful in the application of the law and directives, but remember that they are servants of the state. Stadion writes that he cannot tolerate "a lack of energy [Eifer] or ill will" on the part of his officials. In these directives, Stadion hoped to create a new type of civil servant, one who realized that he is placed in office and provided with a living, not for his own sustenance, but so "he can devote [mitwirke] his energy to the promotion of the purpose of the state."[40] Imperial officials would become more than the obedient agents Emperor Francis expected them to be. This was in essence a return to Joseph II's thinking, independent, model citizens.

In these two decrees, Stadion combined a tightening of the hierarchical structure of the administration on the one hand with increased expectations for the independence and leadership of the bureaucracy on the other. Standardization and devolution of decision making fit into Stadion's larger ideals for constitutional practice and political participation. Strict obedience from the civil service allowed for political dissent and debate outside the walls of the administration. But at the same time, he did not believe that this required the central government to be weak or passive. Part of his purpose in issuing these directives was certainly to shore up his command of the Ministry of the Interior and to instill in his bureaucracy a culture compatible with the ministerial system and the principle of ministerial responsibility. But Stadion, a firm believer in local autonomous government, was also preparing his bureaucrats to think for themselves. In particular, he was preparing them to work in a new system that demanded cooperation between local administrators and the representatives of autonomous municipalities, districts, and county offices. Stadion intended his directives to prepare the civil service for its new and different role in Austrian society—a role that Stadion thought would be dictated by the new constitution being prepared in Kremsier.

### The Reichstag at Kremsier and the Coming of Parliamentary Governance

A common understanding of this period has been that the defeat of the Viennese revolutionaries was a victory for the forces of counter-revolution and reaction, because after the revolution failed, a system of repression and absolutism took its place.[41] This narrative is too facile and fails to recognize that the Austria that emerged from the revolution was fundamentally different than the Austria that entered it. It was not counterrevolution that won in fall of 1848, but a different revolution, a silent one that sought to harness revolutionary change to a stronger and more centralist state apparatus.

Parliament had reconvened in November 1848 in the summer palace of the archbishop in Kremsier, where the two constitutional subcommittees had been working throughout the autumn.[42] Before the October Uprising and the unplanned moved to Kremsier, the work of the two constitution-writing subcommittees had gone slowly; the Reichstag busied itself while it was in Vienna with matters other than the constitution, such as the all-important abolition of feudalism and the emancipation of the peasantry. In Kremsier, however, the various parliamentary committees and the Reichstag focused on writing the constitution. Schwarzenberg, in his address to the Reichstag at Kremsier on November 27, specifically mentioned his intention to lay a constitutional draft before the emperor in the coming months.[43] The Reichstag's favorable impression of Schwarzenberg after his speech at Kremsier gave it the necessary encouragement to finish its work. In the meantime, Stadion prepared the administration to fit into the representative and constitutional framework that the Reichstag was in the process of constructing.

Schwarzenberg may have not expected much from Austria's parliament, but he had been willing to let it work.[44] Stadion had been more sanguine. When the plenary meeting of the Reichstag began to discuss the opening articles of the bill of rights, however, parliament confronted Stadion with renewed claims of sovereignty for itself. Stadion had an increasingly difficult time holding the center line between the Schwarzenberg government and parliamentary authority. The two bodies, which represented different types of authority, one monarchical and executive, the other *bürgerlich* and representative, headed for a showdown. Specifically, Schwarzenberg and his entire ministry took issue with the first article, which stated that "the power of the state proceeds from the people." Stadion had to choose a side. On January 2, 1849, he submitted a draft to his fellow ministers, which laid out the government's position vis-à-vis the first article of the bill of rights. He argued that the idea that the power of government proceeds from the people was completely incompatible with the monarchical principle and therefore the ministry must come out decidedly against it.[45] Stadion presented these arguments two days later before the Reichstag and demanded that the assembly retract the article. The *Wiener Zeitung* reported that as Stadion left the tribune, the parliamentary delegates sat in stunned silence. They agreed to adjourn for two days to let Stadion's words sink in.[46] Thus, in quick succession, the Schwarzenberg ministry's most committed parliamentarian became a target for its ire. Although the Reichstag did agree to retract the first article of the bill of rights, they issued an emergency proclamation on January 8, 1849, which rebuked Stadion for his intervention in the deliberations (*Willensbildung*) of the people's representatives and for impugning the dignity of the assembly.[47]

During this episode, the government quietly held back from deepening this confrontation. Schwarzenberg, along with Stadion, had tried to steer a middle course between his own ministers, who wanted parliament to successfully take its place among Austria's governmental institutions, and a parliament that sought to put itself, as representatives of the people, above the monarch and his executive. The ministerial council broached closing parliament and declaring its own constitution by imperial decree, but not all of the ministers could agree on this course.[48] At first justice minister Alexander Bach, Stadion, and others went against closure, and even Schwarzenberg seemed willing to let the Reichstag continue its work. However, when it became clear that the Reichstag was unified in its stance against the government—when the progovernment parliamentary members joined the left in its censuring of Stadion's speech of January 6—the Schwarzenberg ministry turned its back on Kremsier once and for all.[49]

On January 20, 1849, the Council of Ministers decided that it was necessary to dissolve the Reichstag in Kremsier due to its "recently emerging radical bias [Tendenz] and its antagonistic position toward the government."[50] The council also decided to release its own constitution and entrusted Stadion to draft it. Here Schwarzenberg's acumen as a diplomat rose to the fore. He allowed the Kremsier parliament to continue to meet and deliberate, while Stadion worked on his own constitution, which would prepare for a future Austria without the Constitutional Assembly's hands.[51] As Stadion secretly worked on his own draft of a constitution, the subcommittees at Kremsier did so as well, believing that their work would become the basis for constitutional government in central Europe. On March 2, the members of the Constitutional Committee declared their intention to present their final constitutional draft to the entire Reichstag for a plenary discussion on March 15—the anniversary of Emperor Ferdinand's initial promise to grant a constitution.

However, when the Kremsier delegates assembled on March 7, the doors to the archbishop's palace—their erstwhile meeting place—were locked. Instead of open doors and an open pathway to proclaim their constitution, they found a message from the emperor, thanking them for their service and announcing that he, three days previously, had sanctioned a different constitution "of his own authority." The emperor, tired of "parliamentary negotiations which had stretched on for months" and which had entered into the wild world of "theory," necessitated that he decree a constitution which corresponded to the actual conditions of the monarchy and ended the uncertainty which was clouding the age and weighing heavily on his peoples' minds.[52] The work of the Kremsier parliament had come to an end. They had produced a constitution, destined for historians to read but not for the emperor to sanction.

The Kremsier Constitution, in its afterlife, became the epitome of Austria's failure.[53] Although it never made it out of the Reichstag, the Kremsier Constitution loomed large over the recurring debates on administrative and constitutional reform. It especially began to take on a greater significance among politicians after 1897, when the fissures separating the nationalities in Austria—and thus the possibilities for political compromise among the nationalities—began to divide into deeper, seemingly unbridgeable chasms. By the end of the monarchy, the Kremsier Constitution had acquired a semimythic status as a road to national coexistence that, if taken, would have saved the monarchy from political conflict among the nationalities that had rendered diets and the imperial parliament little more than an arena for throwing inkwells and insults.[54] This line of thinking that Kremsier was a missed opportunity has a long history among German liberals of the monarchy who lamented Austria's loss of supremacy in Germany in the nineteenth century, as well as among German liberals who lamented the fall of the monarchy in the twentieth.[55] But, of course, it puts the discussion of *what could have been* in the forefront, while pushing *what was* into the background.

Beyond its mythical status among old Austria's historians, the Kremsier Constitution proved influential for later constitutional discussions in two important ways: first, it sought to answer the nationalities question through administrative reform, and second, it regulated the relationship between local, regional, and provincial administrative units and the central ministries in Vienna. In the Kremsier Constitution, the Austrian parliament essentially imagined authority in Austria as a pyramid of representative bodies, culminating in itself—the Reichstag. From an administrative-technical standpoint, Kremsier's importance—and its continued resonance at the end of the monarchy—was its channeling of compromise through the gateway of administrative reform. It proposed administrative organization with regional parliaments, which corresponded to Maria Theresia and Haugwitz's counties (*Kreise*). The county organization balanced administrative federalism and centralism with administrative units small enough (both administratively and geographically) to separate Austria's nationalities. Thus, the "missed opportunity" of Kremsier comes from the perspective of the 1890s and early twentieth century, when contemporaries saw Kremsier as the moment when Austrian politics took a turn that led to the stalemate of nationalist politics.[56]

If we take a larger view, and divorce ourselves from the monarchy's twentieth-century critics, however, we can see that Kremsier was only the beginning of attempts to reach a working compromise between centralism and federalism, between German and Slavic politicians, through administrative reform and constitutional change. This search for a compromise through the structure of the empire, its shape and form, along with questions of the expanding electorate, the role of the public in governance, the power of the administration and the monarch in the constitutional system, would frame Austria's political debates for the coming decades. This search for compromise, begun in Kremsier, actually continued in the document that was nailed to the door of the archbishop's palace. That was Stadion's constitution of March 4, promulgated by the emperor for his entire empire, out of his own authority.

## Taming the Revolution: Stadion's Octroyed Constitution of March 4, 1849

While the Constitutional Assembly at Kremsier had been hammering out its constitution draft, Count Franz Stadion was busy—secretly—reimagining the Austrian state in his own constitution. Stadion's reimaging would shape constitutional developments in Habsburg central Europe over the next twenty years. Even more important in the long run was Stadion's approach to the structure and the system of governance in the Habsburg Empire. He saw the future of the Habsburg monarchy working through a hybrid system of political participation *and* bureaucratic leadership. Stadion's vision would guide the expansion of political participation in Austria—and the evolution of the Austrian state over the next *seventy* years. Revolution essentially tore down the old regime, and Stadion could now rebuild. In the new state that Stadion imagined, political participation was deemed necessary for the economic and cultural development of Habsburg central Europe. But, for Stadion, political participation also required that statesmen control and guide the political process. The imperial bureaucracy would provide those statesmen, and Stadion would place them in positions closer to the populace, in smaller cities and towns, where they could act as paragons of virtue and as representatives of the crown and—more importantly—the state.

Just as the Reichstag deputies found themselves locked out of the archbishop's palace, Stadion issued two laws that put forward his conception of the Austrian state. The first of these was a new constitution for the entire empire, announced to the Reichstag deputies in the form of an imperial proclamation, pasted onto the locked doors of the archbishop's palace at Kremsier.[57] The second document was a sweeping new Provisional Municipalities Law. Not only were the deputies' services no longer needed, Stadion beat them to the finish line in drafting a constitution.[58]

Stadion's constitution and Provisional Municipalities Law continued his balancing act between revolution and counterrevolution, between the people and the crown. The constitution preserved the administrative changes that the revolution had brought to Austria and solidified the power of the central government in dried ink on parchment. It spelled out the authority of the emperor and the rights of citizens. It reaffirmed the Pragmatic Sanction and, thus, the unity of the empire. Stadion used the word *Austria* to describe this imperium, emphasizing the importance of the whole over its historic parts. In addition, the emperor was to be crowned once: as emperor of Austria. He was the supreme commander of the armed forces and responsible for the empire's foreign policy with other states.

The constitution also, importantly, created an arena for social change and political involvement. The emperor had to swear an oath to uphold the constitution, which included several articles on the rights of citizens. The rights of citizens were an imperial matter: from the Swiss cantons to Russian and Ottoman borders, all peoples of the empire enjoyed the same rights. People were free to move about the monarchy; they were no longer to be tied to the land. They could practice whatever trade they wished and their property was protected by the law. Seigniorial rights and obligations were abolished once and for all. The liberal individual, with all his economic freedoms and rights, had been born in central Europe.

Stadion's balance between the crown and the crowd was a careful one at first, but his constitution sought to build structures that would hold up both sides permanently. These structures were enumerated in the rest of the constitution and the Provisional Municipalities Law which established a new framework of the monarchy. The bulk of Stadion's March Constitution, after spelling out the rights of the emperor and the monarchy's citizens, described a new framework for the monarchy. The municipalities law filled in many of the details. Together they established an administrative pyramid of localities (cities and rural townships), districts, lands, and empire. At the head of the empire was the emperor, of course. But the empire also received a central legislative body, the Reichstag, which shared legislative and law-making authority with the emperor. Under the unity of the whole, Stadion envisioned the kingdoms and lands of the Habsburgs as "crownlands"—provinces proper. Stadion placed all the crownlands in an equal, subservient position to a newly restored and revitalized central state. In these terms, Stadion was able to do what Joseph II was not—to remove all the vestiges of the rights and privileges of the diets and the ability of the nobles to resist the crown. Underneath the crownlands came two regional authorities, the county and the district. Stadion kept the county, which in its current form went back to Maria Theresia's reforms of 1749, as an administrative unit. But, importantly, Stadion wanted the Habsburg state to penetrate further into local life. After all, the revolutionary year and his constitution had done away with the patrimonial administration of the nobles. For this reason, he wanted to divide each county into approximately three or four districts. Finally, each district would contain a number of municipalities or rural townships, which would form distinct and autonomous political units and allow for public participation at the local level (see Figure 2.1).

Stadion's constitution differed in many ways from the one drafted by the deputies at Kremsier.[59] The key for understanding Stadion's constitution is to view it first and foremost as a push for major imperial and

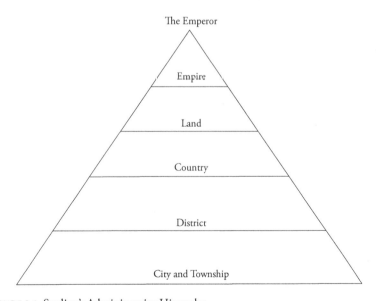

FIGURE 2.1. Stadion's Administrative Hierarchy

administrative reform, not that it was a lesser replacement of the Kremsier draft. Stadion's approach to solve the conundrums of Austrian politics was administrative and structural, an approach he inherited from Joseph II. As such, his constitution and Provisional Municipalities Law completely altered the structures of administration and governance to combine local autonomy with a stronger and more interventionist administration. Stadion intended to harness the achievements of the revolution to a new, stronger central government. He expanded the role of municipalities, rural townships, *and* imperial bureaucrats in the administration at the expense of the nobility and their federalist allies. With the central state's authority stretching deeper into the heart of the hinterland, its civil servants would work closer with local politics to ensure that the state was bringing the greatest benefit to local needs. Stadion envisioned a monarchy that was stronger and more unified than before. Revolution had given him the opportunity to wipe away the institutional memory of the nobles' authority—a feat Joseph II was unable to achieve sixty years earlier. Echoing the language of Pillersdorf's 1848 constitution, Stadion would, mere months later, build a system in which every crownland—even those which held on to the status of semi-independent states under Ferdinand—would be part of a unified and homogenous system in which every territory would be subordinate to the central government.[60]

What made Stadion's constitution and municipalities law a radical administrative reform was its very institutionalization of public involvement. Stadion based his new governmental system on elected citizens working together with the state administration. In this way, the system created unity and stability through the active participation of sectors of the public in Austria's governance. Political participation was meant to be the glue holding Stadion's administrative reform, his restructuring of the empire on a centralist course, together. But public participation would have to be managed and supervised by imperial officials, officials whom—following his two administrative decrees in December 1848—Stadion was grooming for a more active and supervisory role. Stadion's was a complex and unique system, which combined elected councils and bureaucratic supervision at local, regional, and provincial levels of government. Stadion's hybrid administrative system became known as dual-track administration, or *Doppelgeleisigkeit*.[61]

Dual-track administration can be characterized by its system on the one hand and its structure on the other. Dual-track administration reflected the principle that political participation could only be integrated into governance and policy making if guided by an imperial official. Elected representatives who sat on parliamentary bodies at the various levels of government would interact with an official who was responsible for the same jurisdictional territory. In essence, the parliamentary body was responsible for managing the property and funds of a given territory, while the official was responsible for implementing government policy in the same region. This system corresponded to an administrative structure which balanced autonomous councils—elected by voting citizens—on the one hand and state administrative offices led by a prefect on the other (this principle is illustrated in Figure 2.2).

Dual-track administration was certainly the defining feature of Austria's administration and government in the constitutional era, which would stretch from 1867 to the outbreak of the First World War. Its dual-tracks meant that administration was essentially divided between an "autonomous"

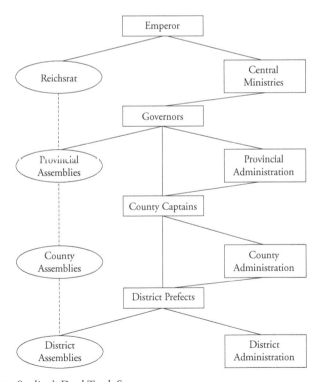

FIGURE 2.2. Stadion's Dual-Track System

administration—the elected parliamentary bodies—and what was termed the "political administration," which was an office, staffed by officials and led by a juridically trained bureaucrat (see Figure 2.2). At the level of the crownlands, policy making was to be determined by a crownland assembly which shared authority with the governor, called a *Statthalter* in the larger crownlands and a *Landespräsident* in the smaller ones. Counties would likewise share this principle. They would be led by a county chairman, a juridically trained official, who supervised a staff of state officials and consulted with an elected county assembly, or *Kreistag*. Likewise, the districts were led by a district-prefect, or district captain (*Bezirkshauptmann*), who consulted with a district assembly or council.

The "political" administration, that is, the central administration of the monarchy, resembled a rationalized, hierarchical bureaucratic pyramid. At the top of this system sat Francis Joseph, the self-employed official, as he called himself in an Austrian census. From him emanated the sinews of power, running through the central ministries in Vienna, the governors in the provincial capitals, and terminating in the local district captains. The autonomous administration, conversely, had only a rudimentary hierarchy whereby the autonomous crownlands could supervise the use of municipal and local assets. This side of Austria's administration consisted of townships, crownland diets, and charter towns, which were responsible for managing the property and funds of their territory.

Autonomy, although now expressly granted, was curtailed by both the structure of the administrative system that Stadion was building and the equalization of all provinces and places in a rational legal framework. The old saying, which encapsulated the glory days of the Habsburg dynasty in the Middle Ages, "Tu felix Austria, nube! [You, happy Austria, marry!]," had referred to the Habsburgs having acquired many different territories through marriages and good fortune—each of which demanded that their ruler abide by their own traditions. Importantly, the constitution Stadion had written would be equally in force in Hungary, which still stood in rebellion in March 1849; in Bohemia, which demanded special rights and privileges; and in Lombardy-Venetia, recently reincorporated into the *Reich* by Field Marshal Radetzky's Italian campaign. Each of these places, which had celebrated their unique status in various coronation ceremonies, and had fostered calls for autonomy or independence from Vienna in their revolutions, would be administratively flattened by Stadion's constitution. Thus, Stadion was able to use the revolution to wash away the mounds of traditions and special privileges that had been built over time.

Jiří Klabouch writes that Stadion conceived the Habsburg monarchy as a potentially "unified, centralized multi-national empire."[62] *How* Stadion intended to unify the monarchy, however, was brilliant and subtle. Stadion constructed a comprehensive system for the reorganization of the monarchy, which combined space for liberal-popular participation in government and for a strong central administration. While both increasing the possibilities for political representation and increasing the responsibilities for the imperial administration, Stadion foresaw a point of contact between the "people" and the administration that happened on local and regional councils. In addition to the two cornerstones of this sweeping reform—the constitution and the municipalities law—Stadion envisioned new constitutions for each of the crownlands, which would forever cement them into the system and sever them from their distinct legal and administrative traditions.[63] With the constitution and the municipalities law, Stadion had created a new system for governing the diverse lands of the Habsburgs, one that stretched from every rural township or market town to the center, Vienna. Stadion thus unified the lands of the monarchy under a single administration and under the same laws. His constitution rationalized the monarchy's government and removed the heavy weight of history, tradition, and precedent that burdened the Austrian state.

By granting a large share of autonomy and opening up Austria's political sphere to participatory politics, Stadion wanted to rebuild the structure of civil society so that it would be dominated by the burgher, the intelligentsia, and also his officials. Socially, Stadion privileged the middle classes with his constitution, his municipalities law and his administrative reform; by doing so—by dealing a blow to the federalist-minded nobility—Stadion attempted to unify the monarchy under crown and bureaucracy like never before. What resulted from Stadion's constitution was a completely reimagined administrative organization of the Austrian state. First and foremost, Stadion sought to integrate popular involvement in local government—a feature of the revolutionary year—and harness it to the Habsburg central state. The emphasis of local autonomy, however, melted away the higher one climbed the administrative and governmental ladder. Josef Redlich, in his classic study of political development in Austria on the eve of the constitutional era, called attention to the larger centralism implicit in Stadion's constitution. First, he wrote, Stadion sought to bring Hungary legally into the Austrian state system, which was made possible through the state of war that existed by March 1849. Secondly, Stadion took the achievements of the revolution, bound them to a strong central government, and created an "organically connected complete-state." Stadion's plan used parliamentarism as a path toward centralism, one that would subjugate, legislatively, administratively, and in its system of laws the "entire system of autonomous lands" under a "radical, strong, centralized imperial authority of the emperor in Vienna."[64]

Of course, as Redlich analyzed Stadion's constitution, it was 1920 and he was looking back from atop the rubble of the collapsed monarchy with a clear memory of its territorial dismemberment by new national states. For him and for many historians who have closely used his analysis, the Stadion Constitution was a wrong turn and the precursor of nationalist politics. But Stadion hoped to found support for the empire on new, firmer footing—in local townships and municipalities. His dual-track administrative system offered a compromise between the Josephinist tradition of centralism and bureaucratic leadership and the pragmatic necessity of governing a large, highly differentiated empire. The brilliance of Stadion's plan also rested on its timeliness—local self-government and liberty were catchphrases of the revolutionary year. Stadion's system worked to make political participation and bureaucratic management mutually palatable. His Provisional Municipalities Law, which supplemented his constitution, opened with the catchphrase of liberalism and municipal autonomy: "The foundation of the free state is the free commune."[65] The free townships or communes were intended to be more than the most local administrative units. In the words of Josef Redlich, "The Austrian commune . . . is an attempt to put into practice the fundamental idea which forms a constituent part of the whole theory of continental liberalism: the idea that the commune . . . is . . . independent of the central Government and that there belongs to it . . . a particular sphere of the political and social life, within which it looks after and promotes its own interests in freedom."[66]

In line with the idea of municipal autonomy, article 33 of Stadion's constitution granted the fundamental rights of local townships to elect officials, govern their own affairs, and, just as important for Austria's liberals, determine who belonged to the municipality and who did not.[67] Stadion's municipalities law further codified the administrative responsibilities of the townships and its legal-administrative position vis-à-vis the central administration, that is, the districts and the counties.

Stadion's conception of the autonomous townships provided for genuine autonomy, in which decisions that affected the township were made by elected officials and thus were free from direct interference from the central state. But this autonomy did not stretch beyond these communes and townships, the *Gemeinde*. Rather Stadion's constitution and municipalities law provided appointed officials to supervise regional government. The administrative reform that Stadion envisioned through his new constitution sought to fill the need for popular participation in government while maintaining a strong state. His plan was to combine autonomy and centralism into a single system. Stadion conceived his system as a totality, consisting of integrated, interlocking institutions.[68] The lower units of the administration were weighted toward autonomous government; however, as one climbed the administrative ladder, autonomy was curtailed in favor of the authority of state officials.[69] Stadion conceived a hierarchy in which local notables contributed to the system at the local level while central officials and judges supervised them. The closer the hierarchy approached the monarch and supreme official, Francis Joseph, the more the decisions rested in the power of the officials themselves.

One of the major reasons that Stadion's 1849 constitution should be understood as a major administrative reform is that it created a new administrative unit: the district or *Bezirk*. For Stadion the guarantee of local autonomy meant bureaucrats had to be more numerous and closer to the ground. To this end, he introduced this new administrative unit, which would be comprised of several townships with roughly ten thousand inhabitants.[70] The district in Stadion's plan would adhere to his dual-track administrative philosophy: a district captain or prefect (*Bezirkshauptmann*), an official appointed by the central government, would serve as the district's head. He would work with representatives elected to the district board (*Bezirksausschuß*), but in matters of executive power, he exercised authority alone.[71] The district also allowed Stadion to bring the central state closer to the populace and supplant the traditional role of the nobility as the leading statesmen of the countryside. Following passage of a law on September 7, 1848, in which the Reichstag abolished both the ancient privileges and the patrimonial administration of the landed nobility, Stadion created the district to replace the patrimonial administration of the nobles. The state's own officials would now serve as the "first instance," the first level of the administration which directly dealt with Austria's citizens.

This new administrative district, which would take over for the old administration of the landed nobility, would make Austria's administration much more expensive, because the nobles had previously borne the costs of the patrimonial administration. But Stadion believed the implementation of these administrative units, and thus closing the door on the feudal order in the countryside, would be worth the expense. Stadion also created the districts to modernize Austria's administration. In Bohemia, for instance, 79 districts would replace 868 patrimonial offices, which had been run and funded by the local nobility.[72] Stadion was confident that his officials, with their juridical education and their commitment to the state, would be more efficient and loyal to the center than the local landlord. Moreover, the districts helped to create a more direct relationship between the central state and Austria's citizens.

Greater than its efficiencies, the district prefecture also served a social function by driving a wedge between traditional and patrimonial forms of state and society. While the local lord could reign as both the lord of the manor and as the local governmental official in pre-revolutionary Austria, under Stadion's constitution his position of prominence depended on the state-appointed official, the district prefect. "Only under the further prerequisite, that he [the local noble] succeeded to come to an agreement with the district prefect, could his social and economic weight fall into the scales of politics."[73] By creating smaller administrative units, putting their offices in small cities and towns, Stadion's state would be brought closer to the populace.

A step up the ladder from the districts was the counties, which provided a representative function—representing the crown—as part of the fiscal reforms of Maria Theresia and Haugwitz. Stadion intended to use the counties to even greater advantage as an intermediate unit in Austria's administration. Administratively, the county would supervise the administration of the districts and render decisions in matters that were appealed or needed review.[74] Its interventionist character under Maria Theresia had been passed down to the districts. An appointed state official, a county prefect, would likewise head the government of the county and would work with a democratically elected county assembly (*Kreistag*), which consisted of between twenty-four and sixty members. Stadion inserted the county into the administration between the districts and the crownlands for discrete political reasons.

On the nationality question, Stadion followed the work of Kremsier. Linguistically delineated counties, erected in the larger crownlands, would

serve to segregate the national movements from one another and limit
the degree to which a linguistic majority in any crownland could oppress
minorities. If Stadion was heavily influenced by ideas of autonomy that
came from western Europe, he most certainly was also impressed by the
strong centralism of France's departmental system. The authority and autonomy granted to the county cut deeply into the power of the crownlands
to function independently of the central government.[75] Together, the political and the administrative functions of the counties served as a regional
filter for problems and crises. Politics were made regional or local matters;
there was little chance for them to boil over into the spheres of provincial
or empire-wide problems. The manageable size of the counties allowed
them to function as miniprovinces, under a central official and therefore
under the full control of the central state.

From Under Stadion, autonomy and bureaucratic authority worked together
in a hybrid system, but the administration was to take the leading role. This
dual-track system, created by Stadion's March Constitution and his municipalities law, established the self-administration of communes and townships
through elected representatives and officials. However, appointed officials at
the district and regional administrative levels could wield executive power to
effectively circumscribe any local autonomy. Article 84 of Stadion's March
Constitution reads: "The executive power is one and indivisible in the entire
*Reich* and in all crownlands. It is the exclusive right of the emperor, who exercises it through responsible ministers and the officials and employees subordinate to them."[76] Since Stadion kept the crownland in his administrative
organization of the monarchy, this executive right of the administration was
therefore also maintained at the level of the crownland. However, unlike in
the Kremsier Constitution, Stadion removed autonomy for its institutions.
Rather, as Joseph Redlich observed in his study, Stadion overcame "all these
ideas, specters, and attempts to create an 'autonomous' provincial administration as completely 'state-free,' [i.e., as an administration] liberated from
the authoritarian power of the imperial central authorities."[77] Moreover,
Stadion envisioned new crownland statutes, or constitutions, for each of
the lands in the monarchy, which would differ little from one another. They
represented Stadion's desire to cut the legs out from under the traditional
locus of the estates' resistance to the central authority.[78]

From an administratively technical point of view, Stadion's constitutional system sought to homogenize Austria's public law. The particularities of the individual provinces often translated into constitutional

arguments for autonomy and privileges, and—in revolutionary times—
independence. Francis Joseph, unlike his predecessor, Ferdinand, would
only be crowned in one ceremony. He would be crowned, not as king of
Bohemia, or king of Hungary, or king of Lombardy-Venetia, but as emperor of Austria. Under these constitutions all crownlands would now be
treated equally by the central government: no province could lay claim on
the basis of historic rights to specialized treatment. Each crownland would
be headed by a state-appointed governor. In addition, each crownland was
permitted an elected diet; each diet selected members out of its own ranks
to form a standing committee (*Landesausschuss*), which served to coordinate crownland-level administration. However, Stadion had stripped
away much of the power and many of the administrative functions that
either traditionally belonged to the crownlands or would have belonged
to them under the Kremsier Constitution. The diets were able to share
legislative authority with the emperor, but executive power belonged to
the emperor and his officials. In addition, Stadion laid the weight of administrative authority at the level of the districts and the counties, cir-
cumventing the crownlands altogether.[79] Thus, important decisions were
made either through bureaucratic fiat or by district and county assemblies,
avoiding the crownland-level of the administration—the traditional locus
of the politics of the estates. Autonomy for Stadion—to the joy of the
liberals—was shifted lower down the ladder to the counties, districts, and
communes, keeping them small enough to be managed by his centralist,
disciplined, reinvigorated body of state officials.

Stadion's March Constitution also redefined concepts of citizenship
in the monarchy. Having already overturned tradition and historical precedent, Stadion had heated up the iron. The rights of citizens were to be
defined not in terms of what they could do, but their equality under the
*Reich*. A Hungarian from Pest had the same status, rights, freedom of enterprise, and freedom of movement as a peasant from Moravia. Stadion's
conception of the unified multinational state naturally drew heavy resistance from the right side of Austria's political spectrum. Federalists and
the landed nobility wanted to channel the revolution's impetus for change
to create a new federal system of government in which the diets, the old
estates, and the crownlands held the most weight.[80] But the right side of
the political spectrum was not dominated exclusively by the federalists.
High-ranking bureaucrats and officials, most notably Karl Kübeck, wanted
to see a return to the bureaucratic absolutism of Emperor Francis.

## Stadion's Legacy

Stadion had fought against both the crownland federalism of the nobility and against the absolutism supported by high officials like Kübeck and military men like Windisch-Graetz by integrating local autonomy and self-government into a centralized administration. Stadion was essentially writing the emperor and his advisors out of their arbitrary authority, pushing decisions down the administrative ladder to bureaucrats who were closer to the people. Thus, his reforms were intended to sweep away the strongholds of the nobility and the old-regime bureaucracy. His failing mental health, however, prevented him from implementing his plans.

The task of interpreting Stadion's system was left to Alexander Bach, who became the interior minister in July. Bach only partially fulfilled the administrative and legal changes that Stadion envisioned. Both Stadion's blueprint and Bach's construction, however, are each decisively important: Stadion's constitution was an enormous model for further centralist reform in the monarchy, while Bach's piecemeal implementation of Stadion's constitution would be equally decisive, if not more so, in the creation of Austria's modern administrative culture, and in the structures and limitations of the Austrian state.

In the five years following 1848, the Austrian administration underwent a complete overhaul that transformed its institutions, and thus Austria, into a highly centralized and absolutist state. The new minister of the interior, Baron Alexander von Bach, began a reorganization of the bureaucracy and administration on a massive scale, which built upon Stadion's conception. Bach used Stadion's institutions to establish central bureaucratic authorities at the local and regional level, and thus brought an end to the control of the nobility over the local administration. This resulted in hundreds of new state offices in regional cities and towns, from the Alpine regions to the forests of Transylvania—places where the central state had never been before. At the same time, however, Bach chose not to create the autonomous institutions that Stadion envisioned to serve as a balance to bureaucratic power. Under Bach, Austria was again under a powerful absolutist system, as before 1848, but the system served a state that was more vigorous. A young monarch sat on the throne and all checks to his central power had been removed. Austria, once "administered" according to norms that the emperor had accepted under the weight of tradition and the power of the nobility, now could be effectively ruled by an energetic bureaucracy that was taught to be flexible, adaptive, obedient to the center, and yet free to do what was necessary for the good of the state and for law and order in the hinterland. This system would comprise the fundament of Austria's era of neoabsolutism, which would last through the 1850s.

In the aftermath of 1848, Alexis de Tocqueville was in the process of composing his own work on the politics of administration and its relationship to revolution. One of Tocqueville's theses in *The Old Regime and the Revolution*, simply put, was that the revolution allowed the French state to overcome the local, aristocratic, and particularist impediments to an ongoing process of centralization. The sound and fury of riots, protests, the Terror, merely hid the underlying features of continuity: "Despite appearances, [the French Revolution] was essentially a social and political revolution, and in comparison with others of its kind it did not at all tend to perpetuate disorder, to make it somehow permanent, to make anarchy into a method, as one of its principal adversaries said, but rather to increase the rights and power of political authority."[81] In Tocqueville's eyes, the revolution severed the ties between social position and political privilege enough to establish a more uniform—in Max Weber's words "rational"—political order in society. Tocqueville would have had to look no further than the Austria during the five years following Stadion's departure from Vienna, to find validation for his thesis. But this was but a step toward a more open society in central Europe; for the revolutions of 1848 renewed the bureaucracy as a leading political institution in Austrian government.

The informal motto of Josephinian reform, "Everything for the people, nothing through the people," fundamentally changed in these seminal years.[82] Under Joseph II, "reform" came through the emperor himself, his energy, and his committed leadership. After Joseph II, the administration he established could no longer count on the leadership of the emperor to push through a course of modernization. For the Austrian state-building project, for the larger project of infrastructure-building and modernization, for all the notions of economic and social progress that were so ingrained in the Europe of the early nineteenth century, the emperor and the court were increasingly less convenient partners. Stadion's constitution, his careful balancing act, put Austria's administration on a course to find a new partner to modernize and make policy. And that partner came in the form of the public and political participation. In a way, Stadion's career and his ideals reflected the transformation of Joseph's administration: it had matured into an institution that was able to carry on Joseph's project as his true heir.

Revolution in March 1848 produced a spark, Stadion's reforms then became a self-sustaining reaction. In broader terms, the revolutions of 1848 opened up a twenty-year period of constitutional and political experimentation in Habsburg central Europe. These experiments eventually produced a unique and intricate system of governance, which relied on an innovative integration of administrative authority and institutions of public representation. What 1848 began, and should be remembered for introducing, was a long-term public discussion about how to integrate political participation into central European governance. Finally, in 1867, the rules of the political game were written in the December Constitution. Less metaphorically, the period of the revolution and its aftermath produced three successive constitutions, two imperial patents, and one imperial diploma. Each of these documents contributed to a general air of constitutional experimentation where fundamental questions about the form and shape of the Austrian Empire intersected with more basic issues revolving around the ground rules for public participation in governance, administration, and policy making—in short, politics.

The two decades between 1848 and 1867 saw the birth of a central parliament, new provincial diets, district councils, town councils, and elected officials. But these developments were slow, stuttering, and layered. The representative institutions, which eventually came about in 1861, were founded on a liberal conception of society that awarded merit, held onto principles of individualism, and made property and wealth the basis for active citizenship. But they were not founded on new, virgin territory. Like ancient cities, they were built upon the foundations of old structures: feudalism, neoabsolutism—ideas of sovereignty that were not fully compatible with rule by the people and for the people. And yet, political participation opened up and mattered a great deal for the stability of the multinational state.

The revolutions of 1848, while clearing the legal and administrative structures of the old regime and allowing the central administration to emerge stronger than ever before, simultaneously opened the path for democracy. On the surface, a paradox still ensued, increased political participation generated a growth, in every sense of the word, of the state administration. As the larger dynamic of central authority and provincial resistance evolved, both politically and constitutionally, the period of constitutional experimentation, of revolution and reaction, served largely to expand—not limit—the power of the central bureaucratic state. The revolutions in Austria wiped away many of the entanglements of old regime administration, both in the center and the aristocratically controlled countryside. The result was innovation in governmental control and economic development.[83] In this brief period, the administration was reborn, retooled, and re-ignited with the fire of a progressive ethos. It would be further challenged by the growth of representative institutions, a process that will be examined in the next chapter.

# 3

## The Reforging of the Habsburg State, 1849–1859

"FEW PEOPLE really know about the Constitution," the Moravian Count Egbert Belcredi wrote in his diary in May 1850, but "the bureaucracy touches everyone."[1] While the new interior minister, Alexander Bach, was busy expanding the state's takeover of justice and implementing Stadion's overhaul of local administration, Belcredi observed the changes from his family estate in Líšeň/Lösch on the outskirts of the Moravian capital of Brno/Brünn. Belcredi was the brother of a future prime minister and the cousin of Victor von Andrian-Werburg, but unlike his relatives—who hoped to make a career in the Habsburg administration—Belcredi stayed at home to manage the family lands. From his manor, he observed a fundamental shift in the landscape of local life. As the local nobles, the Belcredis had been responsible for maintaining law and order, for maintaining local roads, and for taking care of the "greater good" in the lands that belonged to their estate. Earlier, Maria Theresia and Joseph II had already curtailed the Belcredis' authority with administrative supervision in the form of the county offices and with regulations regarding the practice of justice. But the years 1848 and 1849 had wiped every bit of the nobility's official functions off the map. The state displaced Belcredi's traditional role in the Austrian countryside as the state created local judicial and administrative offices that would bring it one step closer to every Austrian citizen.

When Belcredi's cousin Victor von Andrian-Werburg visited Líšeň/Lösch in March 1850, their discussions quickly turned to politics. Belcredi remarked in his diary that they both complained of the incompetence of the "new officials"—the local officials whom Count Franz Stadion had created in his March Constitution and whom Bach was now sending out into the countryside to take over the former duties of the nobles.[2] In the 1850s, Belcredi found himself having to adapt to a new political world, which brought him into frequent contact with peasant farmers, communally elected officials, and the district officials in the imperial bureaucracy. Belcredi also complained of incompetence in the nobles, who were listless and unable to lead; the administration, which was marked by overconfident punctiliousness; and the politicians, who served naked interest rather than the good of all. Scanning the wide horizon of Austria's future, Belcredi saw the 1850s as the age of bureaucracy. "We live," he wrote in 1851, "in an age of systemization, schematization, and the rule of the § [the symbol for a paragraph in an ordinance]." Every organic form of life can expect acceptance only if it follows an official ordinance.[3] In Belcredi's view, bureaucracy meant politics, government, the decline in efficiency— everything that represented the poisonous new spirit of the age. "Everything that does and should come to pass has been delivered over—without resistance—to the bureaucrats, to an organized democracy (or better put, anarchy), to the most dangerous proletariat in uniform, which is these days known as the government."[4]

Although Belcredi and Andrian-Werburg emerged from the revolutions of 1848 seeing the need for change, they lamented the changes the revolution brought, in particular the end of patrimonial (i.e., noble) authority. Belcredi saw his patrimonial authority given over to an "administrative mechanism" that abandoned the monarchy's organic roots and exposed its local life to bureaucratic incompetence and local councils ruled by ignorant peasants.[5] Belcredi was witnessing the fundamental process of the central state's expansion into local society. At the same time, however, politics and political participation emerged at the local level. As townships and communes elected councils, imperial officials moved in to oversee them.

Historians of imperial Austria traditionally have seen the 1850s as the era of "neoabsolutism," but it may be more useful for historians to follow Belcredi and see the 1850s as the era of bureaucracy. This decade provided a pivotal moment in building the structures and the mentalities of the Austrian imperial system and the bureaucracy that staffed and maintained it. For at the same time Belcredi received his political schooling, the Austrian administration did so too. It was a formative period for the reach and scope of bureaucratic authority in the midst of twenty years of constitutional experimentation. Between 1848 and 1867, Austria had no less than three constitutions and three imperial decrees that reworked the larger system of governance. Nestled in these years was a period of great change, of "revolution from above," when the state again became a major force for reform and innovation. Bureaucrats were trained in Vienna and sent out to hundreds of new districts. They oversaw the building of roads, bridges, and canals. They witnessed school reform, the erection of town councils, agricultural societies, and clinics, hospitals, and pharmacies. They participated in the massive expansion of state offices and courts. In Vienna, they saw the city tear down its walls and begin the building of the Ringstrasse. What these bureaucrats witnessed was the transformative capabilities of the state—and their institutional power. The administration would not forget this lesson in transformative power when representative institutions were reestablished in the 1860s.

## Dismantling the Constitution

In 1849 the liberal dream appeared in ruins, shattered by grapeshot and Windisch-Graetz's cannon fire. Subsequent government programs were pilloried at the time and by later generations of historians as absolutist. But what came to be known as neoabsolutism was in many ways the implementation of the liberals' revolutionary program of 1848, and not the failure of progressivism at the hands of a reinvigorated administrative state. Many men of 1848 did in fact throw their shoulders behind the neoabsolutist regime. Alexander Bach had become a minister and traded in his liberal card to implement the revolution by means of administrative absolutism. He became neither a liberal nor a conservative, but a "Man of the State";[6] and generations of men would follow him. But Bach was not the only liberal prime minister that Felix Schwarzenberg appointed. The new finance minister, Baron Karl von Bruck, who was Prussian, a parliamentary member in Frankfurt in 1848, and a founder of the great shipping consortium the Austrian Lloyd, represented the economic aspirations of the grand bourgeoisie. Schwarzenberg tapped him to right Austria's financial ship after a lingering deficit and a very expensive counterrevolution. Anton von Schmerling returned from the Frankfurt parliament to be minister of justice; he would resign his portfolio out of protest, after the now Baron Karl von Kübeck proceeded to gut all the representative provisions of Stadion's 1849 constitution. Francis Joseph could not tolerate representation, but he still wanted the fruits of liberalism. And many liberals held their noses and served the regime, seeing state innovation and reform as better than stagnation, federalism, and the rule of landed elites. Schmerling might have left the imperial cabinet in 1851, but he still served the neoabsolutist regime as the president of the Supreme Provincial Court in Vienna. Liberals were also actively building, judging, and teaching in the neoabsolutist state—especially in newly retooled research universities.[7]

At the same time, our narrative of the period has been subsumed by the Hungarian perspective of neoabsolutism as a form of administrative occupation, complete with the iconic image of "Bach's Hussars," wearing their special uniforms, consisting of the "attila" jacket, a hat, and a sabre. The object of ridicule, these officials became a symbol of neoabsolutism and of the tyranny of a regime that lacked popular support and would eventually fail.[8] Although Hungary provides a dramatic lens, it can lead to a skewed reading of the period. For one, Bach's agents were sent not just to Hungary but to all corners of the monarchy. In 1852, Egbert Belcredi wrote of this major state-building campaign, "rule gets more intricate and the rulers become more numerous." The sheer weight of the administration, its new judges and district supervisors, "paralyzes" the creative output of any useful legislation. Belcredi differentiated between the traditional, "organic" rule of autonomous bodies and the nobles with the "synthetic machine" of Bach's administration. The latter "reduced autonomy to dust," and the monarch himself—Emperor Francis Joseph—to "a machine, who himself no longer knows in what form the matter, which he entrusted to the artificial gears of the machine, will see the light of day."[9]

Of course, liberal critics of Francis Joseph's postrevolutionary regime had reason to feel alienated just as much as landed magnates like Belcredi did. Stadion's constitution was suspended, gutted of its provisions covering representation, and finally annulled. Prince Felix Schwarzenberg would die and Francis Joseph would not appoint another prime minister, choosing instead to chair his own cabinet. Finally, Field Marshall Baron Johann Franz Kempen von Fichtenstamm became Austria's chief of police, reporting directly to Francis Joseph.[10] Schwarzenberg's successor as foreign minister, Count Carl Ferdinand Buol-Schauenstein, botched the Crimean War and alienated Austria's sole ally, the Russian Empire, and in the meantime failed to ingratiate the monarchy with Britain or France. The regime's mistakes have made their way into a larger whiggish narrative—and a counterfactual one at that.[11] If only Austria had implemented the Kremsier Constitution, if only it had developed a vibrant public sphere and especially a parliament, it may have been put on a course toward a healthy, modern polity. Instead, the story goes, Francis Joseph turned to a new, rebranded absolutism awash in its own propensity for self-deception.[12]

If the backdrop of neoabsolutism were Francis Joseph's absolutism, the occupation of Hungary, and foreign policy failures, the foreground actually was filled with state reforms, economic development, and foundations for a modern, interventionist state. Under Francis Joseph's government, the Austrian state expanded and took new interest in economic development, building roads, bridges, and canals. In fact, neoabsolutism was the moment when economic liberalism reached its maturity as a leading government principle. Austria abolished its internal tolls, ceased prohibiting imports, and focused on joining international trade.[13] The former head of Austria's Statistical Office, Baron Carl von Czoernig, could write by 1858 of "Austria's re-creation," as he cataloged new canals, roads, and railways that would connect, and thus unite the empire more solidly.[14] Communication networks, such as the telegraph and the post, also tied the vast corners of the monarchy together. Between 1850 and 1856, the monarchy built 828 miles of telegraph lines (71 percent of the total mileage in the monarchy). It duly erected a new state monopoly, the Department of Imperial-Royal State Telegraphs, in 1856. In a period of eight years, between 1848 and 1856, the postal service was handling almost 33 million parcels more per year.[15] Education was reformed from elementary school to the university system under minister of education and religious affairs Leo Count Thun. Professors flocked to the University of Vienna, which now in the German-speaking world rivaled Berlin as a premier research university.

Although the liberal economic thrust of neoabsolutism had many supporters, the administrative and constitutional system needed to undergird it and give it legal and political power. This was a slow process that occurred in stages. With each stage, the system increasingly diverged from Stadion's constitutional and administrative model. Bach built the bureaucratic structures outlined in the constitution, but the representative institutions that were to balance and infuse these new administrative offices never materialized. In fact, Baron Karl Kübeck, the old Josephinist who had served the Austrian state and its emperors for over forty years, would chip away at Stadion's representative provisions. Francis Joseph summoned Kübeck back to Vienna from Frankfurt, where he represented Austria at the German League, and made him president of the Reichsrat. If this "imperial council" was supposed to sow the seeds of parliamentarism in

Austria, those seeds were quickly thrown to the wayside. In a personal audience on November 19, 1850, Francis Joseph told Kübeck that the Reichsrat must "push aside the constitution and in a manner of speaking, replace
it." Two days later Kübeck spoke to Bach about the emperor's wishes. Bach
apparently decided not to throw up any obstacles to the septuagenarian
Kübeck's plans to break apart the provisions for representative government
and to dismantle all vestiges of constitutionalism. Kübeck later noted that
Bach possessed three great qualities: "He is capable of learning from experience, he has the courage to admit recognized mistakes, and he has the
ambition to overcome his vanity."[16] One is left to wonder if Kübeck would
have seen Bach equally as favorably if Bach held on to a commitment to
parliamentarism, representation, and civic rights.

In his diaries, Kübeck contemplated the problem of simply changing the foundations of the monarch again. "[The emperor's] utterances
[on abolishing the constitution] were unclear. But this much is clear: one
wishes and seems to wish to break free of the scaffolding of March 4, but
does not know how."[17] Kübeck did not know how either—not at first.
Over the next several months, Kübeck would steer a course from his seat
on the Reichsrat that would eventually jettison Stadion's constitution. In
the process ministers Schmerling, Bruck, and later Karl Krauß (who replaced Schmerling), resigned. Their struggle with Kübeck was really over
the relationship between this Imperial Council—the Reichsrat—and its relationship to the emperor's cabinet of ministers. Kübeck wanted the Reichsrat to stand as an intermediary between the ministers and the emperor,
downgrading the ministers—in C. A. Macartney words—"to the position
of Departmental heads."[18] But in forcing ministers like Schmerling and
Bruck out of office, Kübeck also removed key figures who could have defended Stadion's constitution and its provisions for representation.

Constitutional rule ended on August 20, 1851, as decreed in three
separate memoranda.[19] The first memorandum annulled the principle of
ministerial responsibility and made the Council of Ministers responsible
only to the emperor. The second memorandum annulled the constitutional
monarchy itself, formally making the Reichsrat only an advisory body to
the crown instead of the parliament Stadion envisioned. The third memorandum gave both the Council of Ministers and the Reichsrat the task
of preparing recommendations for the implementation of the suspended
Stadion's March Constitution. Andrian-Werburg was in Munich when he
heard the news of their publication. He noted in his diaries that with the

uncertainty of the monarch's stance after 1848, "finally the bomb has gone off and despite this circumstances appear much clearer."[20]

A week after Francis Joseph published his intentions to abolish Stadion's constitution, he moved to solidify his personal control over the Austrian bureaucracy. In the Council of Ministers on August 28, 1851, he proposed that all bureaucrats who took an oath to Stadion's March Constitution be given the opportunity to resign. The young emperor saw the need to "ensure the obedience and loyalty of officials" for the state under its new form. Bach followed the emperor's wishes and presented the Council of Ministers with a draft of a new oath for officials on September 7, 1851. Under Bach, the vision of the "ideal bureaucrat" was revised again to reassert a personal relationship between the emperor and his civil servants. Francis Joseph—not the system or the state—commanded their loyalty. The oath required that they loyally execute the orders of the emperor and removed any call to uphold the constitution.[21] The wavering in the systemization of loyalty of the civil servants might have been a step backward for a Weberian conception of the state and the process of rationalization. But a new system was emerging that, with all its centralizing elements, formed an important evolution in the process of building Austria's political arena. The foundations of political participation were built with the stones of centralism and state authority, for the 1850s witnessed precisely the structural changes that underlined all the political radicalism of 1848 and its revolutions. This new state system would rationalize and standardize all of Austria's administrative units and abolish Austria's historic, traditional rights and peculiarities. The explosion of the bomb of the end of constitutionalism in August 1851 would be followed by a second, louder salvo: the Sylvester Patent.

Neoabsolutism was legally established on December 31, 1851—St. Sylvester's Day—when Francis Joseph signed three edicts into being. Although St. Sylvester (280–335) was known for his piety and steadfastness in an age of Christian persecution, his name became synonymous with the heavy hand of rejuvenated imperial authority. These memoranda announced that Stadion's constitution would be jettisoned in favor of one which would preserve monarchical authority in the absolute hands of the young emperor. The first edict (*RGBl* Nr. 2/1852) formally abolished Stadion's constitution. The second edict (*RGBl* Nr. 3/1852) rescinded the Statute of Basic Rights.[22] The third edict was a memo from the emperor to his prime minister, Prince Schwarzenberg, which included a supplement,

"The Foundations for the Organic Construction of the Austrian Imperial State in the Crownlands."[23] This supplement laid down the all-important foundations for the neoabsolutist state as well as the ethos for a strictly centralist-minded administration. The "Foundations"—*Grundsätze*, as they came to be called—in many ways made explicit what Stadion's constitution and Bach's subsequent administrative reforms envisioned: rationalization through the expansion of the administration to all corners of public life. This meant the standardization of the administration à la Stadion, but also the return of Joseph II's idea of state and administration. Neoabsolutism sought to bring about a centralized state that was unified in the hands of an absolutist emperor and administered by a bureaucracy, loyal to the emperor and the central state.[24] Francis Joseph's second name may not have recalled the reformer that the 1848 revolutionaries had hoped he would be, but the name invoked instead the absolutist centralizer that Joseph II had been.

## After 1848: Revolution and Evolution

Revolutions are usually thought of as harbingers of sudden, even drastic change. They topple rulers and kings and, in waves of violence, lop off their heads. They replace the rule of one group with another, shifting the channels of law and commerce to favor some over others. In the theory that underpins European political history we tend to pit the idea of revolution against "evolution"—a slower, gradual, and, if we ask Edmund Burke, a more permanent bringer of change. But can there be gradual revolutions? Can the process of change, the fundamental shifts in the way people think about government, society, economics, and politics be in their own way revolutionary? Austria in the 1850s allows us to consider this question, because so much of Austrian politics and political culture was laid down in the 1850s and would remain until the end of the monarchy.

But such things are not always obvious. The flash and bang of revolutionary violence of 1848 continued to shimmer and echo well after the revolutions finished. But while our eyes are often drawn to the cynosure of revolutionary violence, barricades, and bombardments, what lulls us to sleep is what actually effects fundamental change. The two decades between the revolutions of 1848 and the end of the 1860s were a period of constitutional experimentation. If the 1850s was the decade of bureaucracy, the 1860s would begin the era of representation. That decade culminated in the Great Compromise, or *Ausgleich*, which separated Hungary from the rest of the monarchy, and the promulgation of the December Constitution in 1867, which established a complete representative system in the Austrian half of the monarchy. In other words, these decades of experimentation yielded results. In the midst of all its constitutional change, the slate of Austria's government was never again wiped clean like it was in 1848. Instead, each change was built upon the previous structure. After the revolutions, Austria developed a powerful central administration that saw its reach extend into every town and village from the Vorarlberg to the Carpathians. But this administration was expensive and the added expenses of wars—lost wars—forced compromises between the emperor's absolutism and ideas of representation. In a very real sense, the limits of the imperial state-building project were financial. The state could only hire so many bureaucrats and only regulate so much on its own merit and on its own bankroll. Such challenges would result in innovations of statecraft and a return to Stadion's principles of government. But all this happened in time; for the moment, there was a bureaucracy to build.

The revolution of 1848 broke the ossified system of Francis's personal absolutism. It provided hope to liberals, conservatives, centralists, and federalists alike that the monarchy would change for the better. Out of these hopes came a new political struggle over the organization, and thus the relations of power, in the Habsburg monarchy. The newness of this contest rested in the questions of political participation—now introduced into the debate for the first time in central Europe. At the center of these struggles was the administration, which Stadion had prepared for a leadership role in the face of local and regional politics. He had also prepared the blueprints for a new arena of politics in Austria, which would be built over the course of years—and built upon. The task of completing Austria's political system—one that combined both representation and ministerial statesmen—was left to the erstwhile liberal lawyer, revolutionary, "barricade minister" of justice, and now minister of the interior, Alexander Bach.[25]

Bach was in the middle of a great personal transition as he entered the Prince Felix Schwarzenberg's ministry along with Count Franz Stadion in November 1848; some would say he was shifting from a revolutionary to conservative. Before he entered government, Bach had earned a reputation as a fierce advocate of liberal and democratic reforms. In addition to being a highly prominent Viennese lawyer, Bach cofounded the Vienna Juridical-Political Reading Club, which was the meeting society of Vienna's liberal professionals and intellectuals.[26] But Bach had entered government during the revolutionary year and would lose his flair for barricades, and traded his appetite for revolutionary proclamations for ordinances and decrees on ministerial letterhead. After participating in the early chapters of Vienna's revolution, Bach entered government as the minister of justice in the cabinet of Johann von Wessenberg, which lasted a matter of months. During the October uprising, Bach had to don a disguise and flee an angry mob that was out to lynch him. He made it as far as Salzburg before receiving word that the emperor and his court were regrouping in the Moravian city of Olmütz/Olomouc. To everyone's surprise, the next prime minister wanted Bach to join government again and take over the justice portfolio. Despite his revolutionary credentials, Bach's intelligence and energy had thoroughly appealed to Schwarzenberg. However, Schwarzenberg also knew that Bach would have been a hard sell to his reactionary brother-in-law, the general Alfred von und zu Windisch-Graetz, who doubted that Bach could be relied upon to help Schwarzenberg carry out a return to stability and order. Schwarzenberg wrote of Bach to his brother-in-law: "We need Bach. His constitutionalism, combined with a strict monarchical orientation, his decisive parliamentary talent, as well as his completely pure status as a private citizen marks him as a necessary member of this new ministry."[27] Bach straddled two worlds, the world of the liberal salons and the world of the government bureaus. The revolutionary year and the opportunities it brought caused Alexander Bach to eventually opt for the latter.

Thirty-six years old and the youngest member of the cabinet, Bach brought with him an energetic commitment to his task and serving his superiors—namely Schwarzenberg and the new, young emperor, Francis Joseph. As minister of justice, Bach oversaw the étatization of local justice in central Europe. Where the local nobles once functioned as local administrator, judge, and jailor, the revolutions of 1848 had ended the system of patrimonial authority once and for all. Bach standardized the system and structures of local justice according to new state norms. He replaced patrimonial justice with a system of state courts, starting with district courts and winding up through county courts, provincial courts, to superior and supreme provincial courts. In addition, judges could not be replaced on account of their verdicts, justice was to be separated from administration in the newly created districts, and court cases were to be conducted orally and publically. In establishing the system of courts, Bach made clear that the fundamental rights of all Austrian citizens were to be guaranteed equally before the law, including the protection of property and freedom of the individual. This equality was insured through the exercise of justice in state courts led by an objective judge and judicial system.[28]

Bach's work in the administration of justice prepared him to take over the most important portfolio in cabinet, the Ministry of the Interior. Bach took over the post after Stadion became incapacitated in April 1849. If Stadion was the intellectual architect of Austria's governmental transformation following the revolution, its implementation fell to Bach. But Bach had ideas of his own. Where Stadion saw stability through incorporation of public participation, Bach saw possible obstacles to efficiency and objectivity. For Bach, progress and enlightenment ran through Vienna; in the process of implementing Stadion's constitution, Bach would often choose to strengthen the central government at the expense of the representative institutions that Stadion wanted to mold. Stadion wanted officials who could work with representative institutions; Bach wanted the bureaucracy to serve as society's guardians who could "administer" progress and improve public life. In Bach's view, the bureaucracy could do the work of parliamentary and representative institutions better and more efficiently through its own administrative processes. Bach's system renewed the tensions between local and regional political participation and the paternalism of the central state; this tension would repeat itself throughout the course of Austria's modern history. Thus, rather than implement Stadion's structure where responsibility for administration was to devolve onto autonomous bodies, Bach implemented a system where power was concentrated in Austria's imperial civil service, which was to act alone for the good of the state, and so for the good of all.

Bach quickly made moves to ensure that the imperial civil service would play a major role in Austria's "rejuvenation" and the reconstruction of the Austrian state.[29] To implement his new system and infiltrate the state administration at all levels, he needed to quickly create new administrative offices at the local level, and instill in his bureaucrats the sensibility and purpose of the guardians of Plato's *Republic*. Bach's guardians would not only be "philosophic, spirited, swift, and strong,"[30] they would also devote themselves fully to implementing Bach's system. In a memorandum to the imperial governors on August 18, 1849, Bach expressed that the work of the administration "has become new and better." The task of Austria's officialdom has moved beyond the realm of paperwork; rather, officials "are called . . . directly into the current of life, in touch with political and commercial [bürgerlich] activity." Bach wanted officials who could operate in the provinces and towns, who could speak the local language, and could represent the strength of the central state to the populace after the upheavals and the uncertainty of revolution.[31] At this point in time, Bach wanted officials who could navigate local needs and peculiarities, and he was still willing to have them work with the autonomous institutions that Stadion's constitution and municipalities law envisioned.

But in the momentous year of 1849, the constitutional landscape of Austria was quickly changing. Hungary was subjugated by the late summer of that year, and Stadion's constitution was still suspended; its implementation seeming less likely. As 1849 drew to a close it became increasingly apparent that Bach would not implement Stadion's system, which balanced elected representatives and state administrative institutions, the very administrative reforms on which the constitution depended. The first clues came on October 29, 1849, when Bach suspended Stadion's Provisional Municipalities Law. The law was then annulled in March of the following year. At this time, Austria stood in a position of complete uncertainty. The constitution, which promised a complex system of self-administration, had never gone into effect and the subsequent laws which provided the foundations for autonomy were themselves annulled. Yet, cities like Prague, Trieste, Görz, Brünn/Brno, and Vienna had received their own special charters under the provisions of the very municipalities law that had been suspended.

Victor von Andrian-Werburg, viewing the administration of Austria in 1851, found the system in place to be neither fish nor fowl. He saw Bach's administration as having no inherent sense, having neither complete centralism nor the *Länder*-federalism that he endorsed, but rather "bureaucratic absolutism" and an "administrative labyrinth" that expressed an "untimely experimental politic."[32] But Andrian-Werburg was not critical of only Alexander Bach's administrative domination. He was critical of everything that had emerged from Stadion's March Constitution, which was still on the books, though suspended, when Andrian-Werburg's *Centralisation and Decentralisation in Oesterreich* appeared in 1850.[33] For him, Stadion's constitution was also an administrative reform—and a deeply problematic one at that. In this work, Andrian-Werburg criticized Stadion's constitution and the central state that he envisioned. For Andrian-Werburg, the most important question that the monarchy had to address was that of centralization: "The main questions, on which our political parties differentiate themselves, do not rest on the greater or lesser measure of freedom that should be granted to the *Volk*, but rather to what extent power can and must be granted to the central government and what can and must be left to autonomy of the individual crownlands."[34]

At best, Andrian-Werburg's thought-piece on the power of central government can be seen as untimely. Andrian-Werburg was a critic of the old regime, but the revolutions of 1848 and Stadion's constitution and his municipalities law had wiped nearly everything away, including the formal leadership role of the nobility in the countryside, something that Andrian-Werburg—and his cousin Belcredi—wanted to preserve. The year 1848 removed vestiges of the patrimonial system and even the repackaged ideas of states' rights. And state builders like Stadion capitalized on such sudden changes through constitutional and administrative reforms, which achieved a key goal of the revolution of 1848—the emancipation of the peasantry and the disconnection of the nobility's political power from its social status. Political clout was no longer only a matter of blood; just as important, if not more so, were capital, land, and money in the bank. Moreover, nobles had been forced to join communes as ordinary citizens. The communal property on their estates was now administered by the autonomous *Gemeinde*,[35] a development that rankled many. As autonomy once held in common by the nobility became democratized, Andrian-Werburg saw the noble's loss of autonomy as a harbinger of a new absolutism, one that could not be checked. "As everything in politics, so are the extremes reprehensible; the extreme of centralization rests in a bureaucratic organization, which crushes the autonomy of the crownlands and which as an inevitable consequence also that of the communes ('the foundation of the free state'), and which is able, through the electric telegraph like clockwork, to administer the entire empire according to one mind."[36]

For Andrian-Werburg, resisting absolutism in the name of liberty was about resisting the Josephine central state, the administration, and the economic and political forms of modernity it brought with it. Andrian-Werburg has often been cited as a liberal, because he used liberal terms to argue for freedom, autonomy, and cultural development. But in his defense of liberty, Andrian-Werburg looked to the crownlands to provide the territorial and administrative basis for a "state-free" zone, what would be called civil society today.[37] For Andrian-Werburg, the crownlands provided the history, the tradition, and strongest protection of liberties against the central state.[38] Of course, Andrian-Werburg saw those liberties in terms of estates—freedoms were class-based privileges. His voice, then, was a transitional voice, for the crownlands would remain a seat of resistance against crown authority. But as the political arena in Austria continued to develop, the nature of argument shifted from noble liberty to crownland autonomy, and from noble nations to nationalities.

### Bach's Administrative System

During the early 1850s Alexander Bach, the former liberal jurist and revolutionary hero, may have lamented the end of constitutionalism in Austria, but he found himself unable to raise his voice or any objection to the emperor's wishes.[39] Instead of resigning his cabinet post, he brought his organizational talent to the new regime, even participating in the writing of the Sylvester Patent. Baron Kübeck thought that Bach had sold out his young idealism and relished the idea that he had turned Bach away from a revolutionary course. He noted that "Bach [has become] the most eager destroyer of his own revolutionary works."[40] But it is possible that Kübeck, old and backward-looking, did not see the changes that were afoot. Kübeck was focused on the rabble; he forgot how revolutionary a trained bureaucracy could be.

Following the Sylvester Patent, Bach began a relentless and thoroughgoing reform and restructuring of the monarchy's administration. As early as January 2, 1852, Bach proposed that a ministerial commission be established both to erect the administrative structure and to establish guidelines for the bureaucratic functioning of the empire.[41] Over the course of the next two years, Bach created a strictly rationalized administrative structure of municipality, district, county, and crownland that reflected Stadion's rationalization and standardization of the monarchy's administration.[42] Bach built his system based on Stadion's concepts, but without the representative institutions that Stadion had intended to "balance" administrative authority with political participation. As such, the new modern state was more palatable to the emperor and Kübeck. Moreover, Bach intended that his administration would provide all the impetus for innovation, observe the many needs and particular conditions of its posts, and provide the necessary ideas for the state to administer the general welfare of its citizens. When Stadion's Provisional Municipalities Law of 1849 had been suspended and then annulled in 1850, the local townships were exposed to heavy state influence. Bodies which Stadion had intended to act as local organs of self-government lost their rights to autonomy and now had to carry out the orders of the central state.[43] Even the provisions of the Sylvester Patent, which envisioned advisory bodies of notables from the landed nobility and industrialists at the district and county level, were ignored in Bach's plan and never implemented.

But cities and townships could not be simply wiped off the map, and the new state centralism and Bach had no intention of permanently squashing them. Rather, Bach made municipal governments less political, less dependent on elections, and limited their purview to matters of local budgets and fulfilling the state's objectives. In essence, local institutions now had a freer hand, but they were more dependent on the bureaucrats themselves. Elections to township councils were curtailed in favor of imperial appointments.[44] District and county boards were also no longer elected, and instead Bach sought to staff those with imperial appointments—vetted and suggested by Bach's Ministry of the Interior.[45] This "autonomy" was certainly less representative and could not claim to express the wishes of the "free communities." So, while Stadion thought the work of governance needed the creative input of political participation, Bach preferred that such creativity lie with Joseph II's intellectual heirs—the bureaucracy. In Bach's estimation, it made sense for the good of the state to limit autonomous institutions and prevent their capabilities to obstruct state business. So as Kübeck unloaded the autonomy of the various representative institutions, Bach used the increased authority of the emperor to bring more matters under the purview of Austria's imperial officials. As interior minister, Bach—the commoner—became responsible for nobility matters, as well as for the dismantlement of the patrimonial system and peasant emancipation, conscription, citizenship and passports, press and associations. His Ministry of the Interior gathered all these functions under its base as it rested on a deepened and broadened administrative pyramid—a ladder that Bach had altered from Stadion's blueprint.

Bach's administrative ladder had several platforms, or to follow the metaphor, rungs. At the top stood the emperor and his central ministries. From there the administration stretched into the provinces, which were now given the name crownlands (see Map 3.1). The crownlands existed in the same administrative level of the old *Gubernia*. The larger crownlands were divided into counties. Each county was now divided into several districts. Smaller provinces, like Salzburg or the Bukovina, were not divided into counties at all.

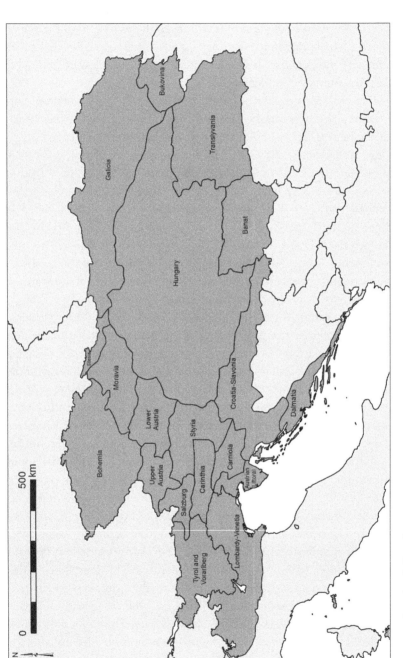

MAP 3.1. Austria, 1848 to 1859

Let us deal first with highest administrative offices, the crownlands. Stadion had actively sought to suppress the crownlands as an administrative unit, because he saw their potential to become the inheritor of provincial and traditional rights—as ministates that could effectively resist the centralizing push of the dynasty. Stadion's administrative structure in the March Constitution sought to limit the crownlands' autonomous functions by decentralizing policy decisions and giving more autonomy to local district councils and regional county councils. Bach, conversely, envisioned the crownlands as an effective administrative unit that could function as the Austrian state in miniature—provided it was completely in the hands of an imperial governor. Bach eliminated the ability of the crownland to serve as a locus for resistance against the crown by strictly centralizing their administration, leaving no form of autonomous representation, no provincial diets, no council of notables. He outfitted the governors with enormous power that went well beyond matters of the Ministry of the Interior. Under Bach's guidelines,[46] the crownland governors were responsible for virtually all state matters in their respective crownlands, including the implementation of directives and laws from the Ministries of Finance, Religious Affairs and Education, Justice, and Trade. As minister of the interior, Bach now had an enormous reach not only into crownland affairs, but also into the ministries of his colleagues.[47] This power of the crownlands and their governors' offices, a key difference between Bach and Stadion, would become even more important over the course of the next fifty years. The crownlands now had the potential to become entities unto themselves. Once representative politics was reintroduced to them in the following decade, it was at this level that national political battles were to become so fierce.

Although the crownlands gathered an increased number of centralized functions just under the minister of the interior, Bach anchored his system in Stadion's concept of the district. Stadion had already created this local unit as the basis of the plan for the "Foundations for the Organization of the Political Administration" of June 26, 1849.[48] In 1849, when the edict was released, one could find the intention to govern according to Stadion's constitution. By 1851, however, this was no longer the case; decentralization proceeded administratively instead. Bach strengthened the districts by making them smaller and more numerous, enabling them to exert a greater state presence in the Austrian countryside. Through these districts, the state could now directly oversee the local communities.

Bach's "Foundations for the Organization of the Political Administrative Authorities," sanctioned by the emperor on June 26, 1849, stipulated that the districts, "which form the lowest political unit, will be led by a district prefect, and stand directly under the authority of the county president."[49] The administrative division of the crownlands into counties and districts occurred almost immediately, in the last months of 1849. By January 1, 1850, the new administrative system was to be fully in place. Upper Austria, which had been part of the Habsburgs' imperial patrimony, was to be divided into four counties and twelve districts.[50] This system was to replace four imperial counties and 111 local administrative units, administered by the nobility and the cities.[51]

Creating new districts on paper in Vienna was one thing; actually putting them into position was another entirely. When we move away from Vienna and into the provinces we see how groundbreaking Bach's system was. It brought the state closer to the people, on the one hand; on the other, the changes and reform the administration brought with it introduced an element of chaos and confrontation. Chaos came from changing the plans as they went along, as well as the struggles implementing the enormous administration that Bach called for. For instance, the regime decided to dismantle Stadion's institutions of local input—elected district and county councils. In their place Bach decided to increase the number of local districts exponentially. Moreover, in the midst of implementing Bach's administrative restructuring, personnel changes abounded. At the beginning, the provincial governments had to hire new people, install them into counties and district offices, and see to it that they were educated and trained. In the process they brought numerous people under the umbrella of state service and refounded the administration—not only in a structural sense but also in terms of a bureaucratic culture. All of this was happening at once, hardly giving Bach or his senior officials the chance to take stock of what they were doing.

In a letter to the new imperial governor of Upper Austria, Dr. Alois Fischer, Alexander Bach admitted that this administrative revolution could not happen overnight and that Fischer would have to exercise a pragmatic attitude to building up a new administration in the crownlands. The new state apparatus was to take effect on January 1, 1850, taking over all local governmental and judicial authority from the patrimonial administration in the new year. But even as the Ministry of the Interior established the new administrative schema and how many bureaucrats were needed in each gov-

ernor's office, county prefecture, and district office, Bach wanted to approve
each new provincial appointment. He wanted a list of applicants by 1 November 1849. He wrote that if "the machinery of state is not to be brought
to a halt or completely ripped out of joint," Fischer would have do his part
in implementing the new system as soon as possible. Bach laid the gravity
of the situation directly onto Fischer's shoulders: "The introduction of new
institutions, the realization of equality before the law, the constitution of
free communes, and the implementation of its institutions and representatives" cannot be implemented without a public service that stands "in direct
contact with the populace" and is committed to the project. And yet, Bach
says: "A less than perfect-looking machine is still worth more than a station-
ary one, the crying needs of the present depend more on the swiftness of the
remedy than at the consolation of an even more satisfying future."[52]

Fischer would have to take on whomever he could. The administrative
plans for Upper Austria foresaw an administration with a new governor's
office, the *Statthalterei*, with a staff of twelve, half of which were upper- and
midlevel officials.[53] But the creation of the districts required that Fischer find
twelve new district prefects, twenty-seven district commissars, twelve district
secretaries, and twelve office attendants or footmen, for a total of sixty-three
new staff members.[54] Fischer and his staff managed to put together a list of
suitable men for the new Upper Austrian administrative staff in early November. For this newly created and important post as district prefect, Fischer
appointed officials who had twenty years or more experience in administration—he essentially sought them out in other state administrative offices.
For instance, Anton Ritter von Schwabenau, the *k.k. Regierungssekretär* and
chief administrator in the *Traunkreis*, had over twenty-six years of experience in the civil service. Fischer commented that "his critical eye and his
familiarity with administration raises him over the other applicants."[55] For
the higher bureaucratic positions directly under the district prefects, Fischer
likewise pilfered from other offices, suggesting people like Eduard von
Pflögl, who served in the governor's office in Linz as a *Ministerial-konzipist*
and had twenty-eight years of service. The irony here was that the new local
branches of the imperial administration were staffed by old men with long
years of service—not new men, but ones taken out of various county and
provincial offices. These men had started service to the state under Emperor
Francis, and yet they were to be the new guard. Even the doormen were
old—between fifty-five and seventy-four years of age—with forty years of
recognized service as footmen to administrators and officials.

## Change Begets Change:
## The Administration Deepens

The sheer size and scope of administrative and judicial expansion in the early to mid-1850s was staggering. For instance, when Bach first took control of the Ministry of the Interior in spring of 1849, he envisioned seventeen district prefectures and nine further local offices (*Exposituren*) for the administration of Lower Austria.[56] But things would change quickly after the promulgation of the Sylvester Patent, which drastically expanded the local level of the administration. For one, Francis Joseph's Sylvester Patent instructed his government to combine administrative offices and judicial offices at the local level. The result: the district prefecture (*Bezirks-hauptmannschaft*) would be replaced by the district office (*Bezirksamt*), which was to be geographically smaller and therefore more numerous.[57] Counties, where they had been dismantled in 1849–50 were reestablished to oversee these much more numerous local district offices, and to review their growing volume of paperwork. By September 1854 Bach had decided to put a district office in every one of the planned local courts (see Figure 3.1). In Lower Austria, the original seventeen planned district offices became seventy offices, one per roughly fourteen thousand residents. The total district offices in the monarchy would reach 1,463, not including separate city districts (an additional eighty districts would be established in the larger cities).[58]

The massive undertaking of building nearly fifteen hundred district courts and administrative offices strained every capacity of the state, and neither the state nor its officials, members of Austria's bureaucratic *Bildungsbürgertum*, were prepared to confront the realities of peasant life in the countryside. An anonymous memoir, published in 1861, by a district official sent to a small town in Hungary tells of the hardships of such officials.[59] Forced to transfer to a new post, the author of the memoir describes his reluctance to take the promotion. First he had to pay an exorbitant sum, five hundred guldens (nearly half his salary), for the Hungarian uniform. The uniform was meant to appease Hungarian sensibilities and evoke legends of Hungarian horsemen, but instead the Hungarian "Attila"—a medium-length coat with golden braids on the front; tight-fitting pants and long, spurred boots; and a feathered felt cap and long saber—inspired ridicule. When he arrived at his new post, the town magistrate gave him, the *k.k. Stuhlrichter* (the district official; Hungarian, *szolgabíró*), quarters

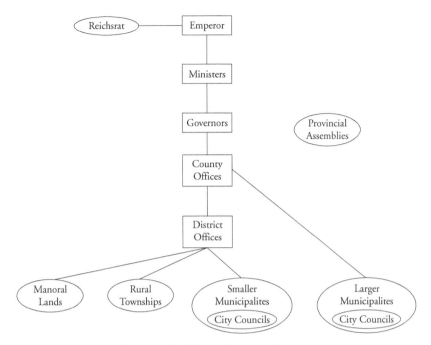

**FIGURE 3.1.** Austrian Administration Under Alexander Bach

in a peasant house, which had no kitchen or proper furniture, and not enough bed space to sleep. The official gave up his bed to his wife, children, and the servant girl, while he slept on the cold floor. His wife cried when she found out that there was no stove even for heating water for coffee. Their servant girl refused to work for him under these conditions and headed back west.[60]

These district officials, whether stationed in Hungary or Upper Austria, were very much pioneers, even though many, including the author of this memoir, were relieved of office and sent back to "the German-Slavic crownlands" (the author's term), when constitutional government returned in the 1860s. Sent to towns that were only loosely entwined in the sinews of power, they had to set up an infrastructure of governance and represent the state authority in the countryside. The district official's job was essentially to create order and good government out of literally nothing. The office of our *Stuhlrichter* had no paper, so he had to track some down through the local merchants and pay it for on credit. The state seemed very far away. Petty cash to pay for printing ordinances took nine months to arrive. Money for the maintenance of the office was two years in coming. After five years, the district official could report that his office had received money for a jail. Before that, the state had put up local criminals at a guesthouse, where they could come and go as they pleased.[61]

Bach's district officials may have suffered mightily on the front lines, but they were the vanguard of a new system and a new era. Larger structural changes were afoot. Under Bach's system, the midlevel of the state administration—the county or *Kreis*—saw its functions reduced as Bach concentrated administrative authority at the two ends of the administrative spectrum: districts and provinces. In terms of the administrative system, this marked another major difference between Bach and his predecessor, Stadion. Stadion had envisioned the counties as being modeled on France's departments and as serving as the keystone on which the weight of Austria's administration would rest, whereas Bach arranged the counties as a subordinate office to crownland governors, the *Landeschefs*.[62] Under the initial neoabsolutist administrative provisions in 1852–53, the county still had a wealth of administrative duties. For instance, the county chairman (*Kreisvorsteher*) approved new buildings for churches and schools and exerted control over the establishment of local businesses and factories by approving the establishment of everything, from new brick factories to coffeehouses.[63] A year later, however, the emperor signed a decree that stripped the county of many of its important functions and gave them over to the governors.[64] Thus, this middle layer of the administration eventually lost all its power and authority, and soon, its reason for being.[65]

Despite impressions from the memoir of our *Stuhlrichter* that the Habsburg state was doing everything on the cheap, state expenditures in fact increased dramatically in the 1850s. Harm-Hinrich Brandt's two-volume study of state finances under neoabsolutism shows that government expenditures on domestic administration (including administrative offices, the police, judicial courts, and public works) roughly doubled between 1847 and 1856, largely due to the creation of these new district offices, courts, and the gendarmerie.[66] In Bohemia alone, the abolition of the patrimonial administration and the creation of district offices saw 1,650 officials employed at the district level in the courts, the administration, and public safety.[67] The surprising finding from Brandt's study is that an increase in tax revenue actually more than covered the enormous expenditure resulting from this incredible increase of bureaucrats and bureaucratic offices. The state's income increased with the increased presence of the administration, judges, and police on the ground, all of whom supported the collection of revenue.

One of the striking qualities of the 1850s and the creation of district offices was how quickly it created an entirely new system of administration, bringing Vienna directly into the provinces with new district offices. Bach created many of them—1,463 to be exact—breaking up the monarchy into manageable units of around ten thousand to twenty thousand people.[68] Diversity still reigned, but it was a diversity that was now limited. In Upper Austria, for instance, the eight districts of Traun County ranged from 7,390 inhabitants in Enns to more than twice as many—17,147—in Kirchdorf.[69] Each district was to consist of a district chief and a support staff similar to those of the larger district prefectures. In addition, in larger provinces like Upper Austria, the county offices were reinstated and the governor had to hire new people while moving experienced officials into leadership positions. Amid the chaotic administrative hustle and bustle of moving people to new positions, the administration became, almost paradoxically, more regimented than before. Despite all the new hires that had to be made, Bach's imperial governors and county chairmen could not put just anyone in the post of district chairman. That position was in the eighth rank—meaning that the office holder had to have completed a university degree, have three years of practical experience as an intern or adjunct, and had passed an additional "political-practical" examination. Upper Austria—forced to find new civil servants to staff all these positions—hired university graduates and made sure that they sat these examinations as soon as they could.

The possibility of climbing into the ranks of salaried, midranking, civil servants meant that the young aspirants were eager to sit the examination as well. Theodor Altwirth, twenty-five years old and provisionally employed in the district office in Schärding, sought admission to sit the political-practical exam in October 1852. He was born in Enzenkirchen, a small township in the Innviertel—not far from Schärding itself. He completed juridical studies at a university—his file does not say which one—and was recruited to work in the Upper Austrian provincial administration in 1850. His superiors noted in his file that he should be given special attention in the future, since he was very talented, knew the laws well, and proved to be more knowledgeable and efficient than those who had been in the office longer than he.[70] The Ministry of the Interior approved his request to sit the examination in October. His exam asked him questions that spoke to the new fiscal responsibilities of the local authorities. "Question 2: Which authorities administer direct taxation? Question 3: What is the relationship between the tax inspector vis-à-vis the district prefecture? Question 4: According to what measure is the land tax calculated? What is cadastral net income and how is it calculated?" Finally, students who took the exam were asked for an essay on the following theme: "Render a decision on the application by the pension administration in Pesenbach for the exemption of the income tax on the brickyard and fish hatchery and [give a] justification for this decision." In addition to the written exam, Altwirth was subjected to twenty oral questions which gave him hypothetical situations which required decisions he had to make and articulate; for example: "Maria Maier, widowed cottager, presents the request on behalf of herself and her two sons, the first an unmarried farmhand and the second a gymnasia-student, for permission to emigrate to America. How is this request to be handled?"[71]

Altwirth passed with good or very good marks, but certainly not everyone did. The civil service was expanding under Bach, but only wanted officials who had the knowledge and will to render important, life-changing decisions for the populace in general. Moreover, tests like these affirmed the role the administration was to have in Austrian society. As the state replaced the local rule of the nobles and abolished the social and economic structures of feudalism, it liberated the peasants to work for themselves, but also left them exposed to the market. Patrimonial administration had been cheap for the state and fostered a paternalistic relationship between peasant and lord. The revolutions of 1848 not only wiped away the legal shackles of the peasants' servitude, it also took away the social and legal obligations of the local lord. The peasants lost easements on their masters' lands and now had to conduct all business in cash, not in kind, often without access to credit.[72] As the district officials stepped in to take over the administrative role of the nobles, they became the new notables of local life. Whether the state would prove up to the task of taking care of the masses of rural citizens still was up in the air in the 1850s.

As befitting the new notables, the prestige and social role of the administration was to be rigorously maintained. Not everyone was taken into the ranks of the civil service, no matter how badly the state needed to fill its positions. Christof Münk, who lived in Linz, sent a letter to the governor's office in 1853 requesting a position as a *Diurnist*—an office factotum. *Diurnisten* had no legal standing as officials (*Beamte*), but served as contract labor: copying forms, filing, or assisting in odd jobs. Münk wrote that he had previously served the state for over twenty-two years as a non-commissioned officer in the military and after his retirement, and served as a *Diurnist* for various state offices in Linz with industriousness and precision. Moreover, his brother worked for the state as a treasury official in Transylvania for over thirty years. Service to the state was his vocation. The problem? He had been found guilty of fraud in 1846 and spent two years in prison. Since then, regulations on state employment barred him from serving the state in any official capacity without a dispensation from the emperor himself. The governor's office in Linz found no reason not to take him in. Since getting out of jail, Münk had served as a temporary worker for the municipality of Linz. He had four children, and according to the police, the municipality, and those who knew him, he seemed rehabilitated. But the government in Vienna, aiming to preserve the extreme correctness of their offices, denied his request, because "in order to safeguard the reputation of the provincial administration it is not considered appropriate to rely on individuals with an obviously dishonorable past."[73] It is unclear what happened to Münk after his request was denied.

How did civil servants find their way to their eventual posting? Officials were hired by the district officials, county chairmen, or the governor himself, but the gateway to the civil service was still the intern post. Interns supplied capable, college-educated grunt labor with little or no pay, and offices often relied on them to handle their burgeoning workload. The provincial government of Salzburg in 1859, for instance, sent out a call for applications for four new posts; they were all for intern positions—two with a stipend of 315 guldens per year and two which were unpaid. Despite the low (or no) pay, the interns were required to have completed their university studies in law and government and to have already passed their state exams in political theory.[74] But the internship meant the possibility of a quick rise through the ranks if a permanent position was ever attained. This pool of college-educated interns would provide ready-made bureaucrats when offices expanded, when new districts were established, or when officials died in office.[75]

For those who were taken into the ranks of the provincial administration, pay under Bach became less appalling. The regime released a pay schema for the lands of the monarchy that raised the pay for the lower ranks of the administration—the masses of servants, clerks, and assistants in the seventh to ninth *Rangsklassen* (official ranks)—and introduced the new upper-level positions of governor, the chief provincial executives (*Statthalter*, or in the smaller provinces, *Landespräsident*), at relatively lower pay than before. This compressed the pay scale—the governor, who earned six thousand guldens, only received as base pay fifteen times more than his doorman, who was paid four hundred guldens per year.[76] Salary compression may have been new, but the ways the central offices and its staff related to the provinces, the counties, and now the districts continued the logic of the Josephine administrative pyramid. Like planets in orbit, the further one traveled from the sun—from Vienna—the colder and darker the world became. The chief executive of a province, the governor, occupied the third or fourth ranks of the pyramid, respectively. County chairmen were in the sixth; district chairmen in the eighth (see Table 3.1). Below these chairmen and their university-educated staff, who occupied the so-called policy-making service—the *Konzeptsdienst*, were the clerks and clerical workers (*Kanzleidienst*), and the wait staff, the *Diener* and *Gehilfen* (see Table 3.2). Again, the further up the administrative pyramid, the larger were the offices and the number of staff needed to populate them, and the higher the pay and rank one could reach. A long-serving clerk could reach the eighth rank as an office manager. That was equivalent to the rank and pay of a university-educated, district chairman. But of course, the majority of the clerks and office staff remained caught in the lower ranks and only a select few, blessed with longevity and great evaluations, rose into the middle ranks of the civil service.

The continuity of organization in the 1850s combined with fundamental change. Bureaucrats were transferred quickly from place to place and they now had new colleagues to train. But this administrative chaos was a managed one—it was never a crisis, but rather, a moment for new opportunities. As such, it did much for refounding the principles and outlook of the administration. We can gain a sense of the newness of bureaucratic penetration into local life from the proliferation of manuals and instructions in the 1850s. These manuals ranged from official productions to books for the public market. The Ministries of the Interior and Justice released an office instruction in 1855 that was meant to standardize administrative practices in the new district offices.[77] The document laid down the foundations of a rational, objective administration in the localities. It described the bureaucratic hierarchy of land, county, and district; stipulated how the districts fit into that hierarchy; and laid down the practices for hiring new officials. Bureaucrats in the new district offices could not be related, they had to meet the necessary qualifications to take up their position, and they had to swear an oath of office. But contrary to Belcredi's complaints cited at the beginning of this chapter, the new regulations did not merely spell the rule of the paragraph sign, §. It bore the imprint of a new optimism in the role of the local official: district personnel were to be the emperor's feet on the ground. Peeking through flat descriptions of the hierarchy and office management were phrases like "of these officials, who stand in direct and daily communication with the populace," which did much to remind the officials of their mission of bringing the state—and thus progress—to the people, without the problems associated with revolution.

Such optimism began with how the officials looked; they were to play their part in the new Austrian story of progress. Bach promulgated new regulations regarding officials' uniforms on August 24, 1849, and made it clear that the bureaucrats, wherever they were to be stationed, would be "recognizable according to his outward appearance."[78] In the course of his duties, on festive occasions and at official ceremonies, officials were to appear in uniform. The daily uniform, from ministers and imperial governors down to the lowly clerk, was to consist of a dark green tunic. Branches and ranks within the service would be differentiated by the collars and uniform's cuffs, which were to be made of velvet. The collars and cuffs of the uniforms mirrored the system of ranks and the new governmental division into ministries. Officials in the offices of the Foreign Ministry wore crimson accents; in the Ministry of the Interior, they wore a darker pompadour; Justice officials wore violet. Such attention to the outward appearance helped to visually reinforce the principles of office hierarchy and rank internally. Externally, uniforms differentiated the bureaucrat from society, making him distinct, identifiable, and observable (see Figure 3.2).[79] The law was timely for Bach, who was in the process of building an administration in the hinterland, sending out men to establish imperial offices where the government had never tread before. These bureaucrats, educated and correct, were to care for the local populace and bring state-funded progress in the form of roads, bridges, and schools. They were to be ideal Austrian citizens, now readily identifiable in their dark green tunics and velvet bars in hues of pompadour, violet, and carnation blue.

The office instructions, along with regulations regarding uniforms, built the local administration into a visible, cohesive unit. Not only did the new legions of bureaucrats dress in the same manner, they ran their office in the same manner as well. The office instructions established a

TABLE 3.1. Rank and Pay Scales in the Higher Civil Service

| Provincial Authorities Konzeptsdienst (higher service) | | | | County Authorities Konzeptsdienst (higher service) | | | | District Authorities Konzeptsdienst (higher service) | | | |
|---|---|---|---|---|---|---|---|---|---|---|---|
| Rank | Title | Salary | Note | Rank | Title | Salary | Note | Rank | Title | Salary | Note |
| III. | *Statthalter* (governor) | 6000–8000 fl. | Free apartment and living expenses allowance | | | | | | | | |
| IV | *Landespräsident* (governor) | 5000 | Free apartment and living expenses allowance | | | | | | | | |
| IV | *Statthalterei* vice president | 5000 | | | | | | | | | |
| V | Ministerial councillor | 4000 | | | | | | | | | |
| VI | *Statthaltereirat* (councillor) | 3000/ 2500/ 2000 | | VI | County chairman | 2500 / 2000 | Living allowance of 500-1000 fl. | | | | |
| VII | Provincial councillor | 2000/ 1800/ 1600 | | | | | | | | | |
| VIII | *Secretäre* | 1400 / 1200 | | VII | 1st commissar | 1400 / 1200 | | VIII | District chairman | 1200 / 1100 / 1000 | Free apartment or rent subvention |
| IX | *Concipisten* (drafting official) | 800 / 700 | | IX | 2nd commissar | 900 | | IX | District adjuncts | 800 / 700 | |
| ... | | | | IX | 3rd commissar | 800 | | | | | |
| ... | | | | IX | County doctor | 600 | | XI | Actuary | 500 / 400 | |
| XII | *Concepts-praktikant* (drafting interns) | 300 | | | | | | | | | |

SOURCE: Law of January 19, 1853; RGBl, 10/1853.

TABLE 3.2. Rank and Pay Scales in the Middle and Lower Civil Service

| Provincial Authorities | | | | County Authorities | | | | District Authorities | | | |
| --- | --- | --- | --- | --- | --- | --- | --- | --- | --- | --- | --- |
| Kanzleidienst (Clerical Service) | | | | Kanzleidienst (Clerical Service) | | | | Kanzleidienst (Clerical Service) | | | |
| Rank | Title | Salary | Note | Rank | Title | Salary | Note | Rank | Title | Salary | Note |
| XIII | Director der Hilfsämter (Office staff manager) | | | | | | | | | | |
| IX | Adjuncten | | | X | County secretary | 700 / 600 | | | | | |
| X | Officials | | | XI | Registrar | 500 | | | | | |
| ... | | | | XII | County clerks | 400 / 350 | | XII | District clerks | 400 /350 | |
| XII | Assessors | | | | | | | | | | |
| | Doormen | 400 | | | Staff | 250 / 200 | Received dress clothes | | Staff | 250 / 200 | Received dress clothes |
| | Kanzleidiener (Office staff) | 300 / 200 | Received dress clothes | | Gehilfen (Aides) | 216 | | | Gehilfen (Aides) | 216 | |
| | Dienersgehilfe (Sub staff) | 216 | | | | | | | | | |
| | Portier | 216 | Received dress clothes | | | | | | | | |

SOURCE: Law of January 19, 1853, RGBl, 10/1853.

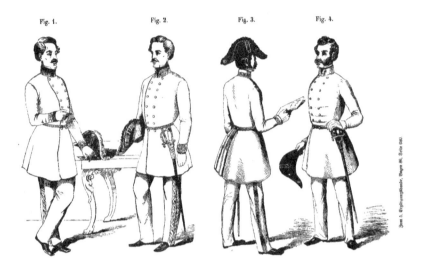

**FIGURE 3.2.** Depictions of the New Uniform Regulations of 1849

SOURCE: *Reichsgesetzblatt für das Kaiserthum Österreich*, Nr. 377/1849.

standard method of management, gave the proper rubrics for entering correspondence and decisions, and taught supervisors how to fill out their assessments in their underlings' *Qualifikation* or *Conduiten* files. These files were to be kept in the strictest secrecy. The instructions reminded officials in leadership positions that these internal evaluation files "were to be filled out with the strictest conscientiousness and with particular attention as to whether the candidate possessed adequate, good, or excellent qualifications."[80] The office also gave a template for these evaluation forms with eight rubrics and a large space for comments. In addition to listing the name, place of birth, age, marital status, social status, rank, and pay, the *Qualificationstabelle* required that officials be evaluated on which languages they spoke and how well they spoke them, their work-related skills and qualifications, and subjective categories such as "morality" and "political behavior." Ignaz Beidtel's complaint about these evaluations in the era of Joseph II and pre-1848 Austria, quoted in Chapter 1, as turning "superiors into despots, subordinates into sycophants," provide a marker of continuity between the first era of state building in the eighteenth century and its refounding under Bach in the 1850s.[81] But here, in the 1850s, these lists were disseminated to the district and county offices and filled out by leagues of conscientious civil servants, sitting at their desks, wearing dark green uniforms. Whether we can say that these evaluations can be elevated to an aspect of national character, as a recent study in historical sociology has intimated, is a matter of debate.[82] What they did do was standardize the qualities of evaluations at the moment when the administration expanded into the countryside and broadened its base. It made a basis for comparing officials, promoting some over others, and especially for transferring qualified officials between offices, provinces, and up the hierarchical ladder.[83]

Further books and pamphlets published by private citizens and officials for the book market only reinforced the expansion of the administration's standardized culture. These works provide glimpses of how important this growing institution was becoming. Professor Moritz von Stubenrauch published the first edition of his *Handbook of Austrian Administrative Law Documents* in 1852.[84] F. J. Johanus, a comptroller official in the Imperial-Royal Treasury records office, published two books in the 1850s to orient the burgeoning civil service with the law. His 1857 *Handbuch der Gesetze, Verordnungen und Vorschriften für k.k. österreichische Staatsbeamte* (Handbook of Laws, Ordinances, and Instructions for Imperial-Royal Austrian State Officials) compiled a compendium of laws and regulations that established the proper conduct and comportment for bureaucrats. The sections were not organized chronologically, but by subject, bringing officials up to the latest demands on their persons. There is also a subtle hierarchy that frames this guide. The first section's title is "The Acceptance of Gifts by Officials Is Strictly Forbidden," while many additional sections further stress correctness, objectivity, and various aspects of the bureaucratic ethos that Joseph II put forward in his pastoral letter of 1783. One such section warned that in hiring new officials, debtors are not to be recommended. Shakespeare's Polonius would have been proud: "Persons, who have not inherited debt, but have themselves have fallen heavily into it, and are notoriously reckless in acquiring debt, are in no way to be recommended for employment in a rank of service." Johanus also provided every section with a reference to the appropriate court decree, giving particularly punctilious officials the chapter and verse of imperial regulations with which to make their point.[85]

As the civil service expanded and penetrated into the countryside, officials were not the only ones who needed some form of orientation. After all, Bach's reforms changed the relationship between the state and its citizens and there was obviously a market for private citizens to understand the new state and its administrative framework as well. Carl Mally wrote a book that provided orientation for members of the general public with their new role as citizens of the state. It was given a title that indicated how new the local system of bureaucracy was and how it indeed had overturned centuries of patrimonial administration, "The New Authorities and Their Jurisdiction; or, A Guide to Whom and to Which Offices We Turn to for Our Matters." The first edition of this book was published in 1851;[86] a second edition was released two years later, completely reworked and twice as long. These books explained in detail the new organization of the Austrian state, from the emperor and his cabinet at the top to the local district offices and courts. The 1851 edition ended with a short guide that directed private citizens to the appropriate governmental offices. In 1851, if private citizens were denied permission to marry, they were to take the matter to the district prefect. If they needed a divorce, they had to go to the district court.[87]

The étatization of local administration and the increase of the number of civil servants generally doubled the expenditures on administration between 1847 and 1855. For instance, the civil administration of Lower Austria in 1847 cost 4.7 million guldens in 1847; by 1855 it was 8.7 million. The lands of the Bohemian crown (Bohemia, Moravia, and Silesia), the alpine lands (Upper Austria, Salzburg, Styria, Carinthia, Carniola, and Tyrol-Vorarlberg, and the Littoral), as well as Galicia, all saw similar increases in expenditure. The administrative costs in Hungary, however, increased by more than twelve-fold in the same period.[88] These increases included, not only personnel and building costs to house all the new local courts and government offices, but also the investment in infrastructure that the administration now oversaw.

In fact, as the government expanded in the 1850s, so did everything with which it came into contact. As the maintenance of law and order fell under the purview of the state police, so did the number of arrests. The statistics regarding citations for disorderly conduct are telling: in 1850 the state security forces made 62,909 citations or arrests, by 1854 that number had increased to over 900,000. But police offices were not the only things this state built. It literally laid the connections between Vienna and the rest of the monarchy in tons of roadstone, in newly dug canals, in railroads, and bridges. Between 1850 and 1853, the state laid 314 million cubic feet of roadstone alone. Carl Czoernig cataloged new imperial streets connecting the Pingau in Salzberg to Tyrol, tunnels between Tyrol and Lombardy, and the raising of road and bridge standards in Transylvania. They converted roads from municipal or local control to imperial control, bringing 173 miles of streets under state control in Transylvania. Between 1850 and

1855, they tore down wooden bridges and replaced them with stone ones, they built ramparts along the monarchy's rivers, from the Adige or Etsch in Tyrol to the Tisza in Hungary, improved the ports of Trieste and Fiume on the Adriatic coast, dredged rivers making them more navigable and invested 8 million guldens on the maintenance of the canals and waterways of Venice alone.[89]

In the 1850s Austria made major investments in its infrastructure, deepening its reach into the provinces and broadening the type of work it did. Over the next decades the administration would build technical offices filled with bridge builders and bridge inspectors, road and building inspectors, veterinarians, sanitation officials, and engineers with the technical expertise the state would now need to draw. If anything, the 1850s saw a new state emerge in central Europe, one which would rely on its administration to build, grow, manage, and nurture the state's new functions. Like much of Europe in the nineteenth century, Austria was becoming an infrastructure state, building wealth and its own legitimacy in the hearts and minds of its peoples.[90] This would be the foundation, the new structures of state building, that would support the edifice as it added new aspects and dimension in the following decades.

### The Age of Bureaucracy and the Long Term

The sheer size of the administration—and its administrators' new role as local model citizens, as bringers of civilization, as creators of order, and as lords of justice—would leave an historic imprint on the culture and ethos of the Austrian administration. In turn, this prominent place in a restructured and rejuvenated Austria would leave a legacy in its politics even once it became a democratic society, precisely because the 1850s saw the administration witness its own capabilities to transform the state and Austrian society. It had now become a power broker in its own right, and would use its authority and expanded place in Austria's political system to protect its own stakes throughout the later periods of constitutional experimentation and constitutional government. The genie, dressed in a Hungarian attila or the green bureaucratic uniform, was out of the bottle.

The transformation of the administration into a political institution itself was a process. The state-political basis for Bach's laws, his ordinances, and his regulations were themselves hardly without precedent. Joseph II, seventy years before Bach's administrative reforms, had charged his civil servants to exhibit "fatherly care" (*väterliche vorsorge*) and to love service to the fatherland and to fellow citizens.[91] Bach's administrative policies, focused on control and interest in the minutiae of public life and welfare, imbued the administration with a rejuvenated Josephinism, just as Bach also hoped his administration would form a central pillar of the rejuvenated Austrian state. Under Bach, the Austrian bureaucracy was to shepherd Austria's public life and economy. It was responsible for policing the press, for approving the assembly of private associations, for proper sanitation, and for enforcing local building codes. It had to approve the establishment of a local café or a new factory.[92] Like the *Stuhlrichter* in Hungary, these men sensed as they entered new towns that had hardly seen the hand of the state, that they were bringing civilization to the countryside.

The idea that the administration acted as society's benevolent and enlightened decision makers—choosing its goals, fostering its economy, and deciding what was best for everyone—would last far beyond Bach's neoabsolutist system. Under Bach, the reach of the central state grew enormously. As the state moved in to fill the shoes of the nobility at the local level, it brought with it a heightened and concentrated control of public life. In the words of the governor (*Statthalter*) of Upper Austria, Eduard Bach—Alexander Bach's brother—the state was now firmly entrenched in local life: "In the essence of the political administration the entire world plays itself out within the framework formed by the district's territory; it accompanies one from the cradle to the grave."[93] Furthermore, the everyday praxis of administrative work intensified the idea that the administration—Austria's political elite—was to act as society's guardians. The newly implemented district offices manifested the rejuvenated power of the central state at the local level. The district officer was responsible for a wide variety of social services, which steadily grew over time.[94] While his administrative duties included the upkeep of roads and canals, care for the poor, and the cultivation of the local economy, the district officer also exercised the power of the central state in a variety of aspects of local public life. His office granted music licenses and permission for theaters to put on plays. He controlled the local press, approved and regulated public auctions, and was responsible for the maintenance of public order in his district, while the governor himself had to approve the establishment of any pharmacy.

Austria's administration under Bach may have been oppressive in the public sphere, but this guardianship of society also came with, and supplemented, both institutional modernization and economic development.[95]

Waltraud Heindl noted in her introduction to the third set of the *Minister-rat* minutes that "free thinking" and liberally inclined bureaucrats were not only appointed to important positions in the administration—despite the reservations of the emperor himself—but these free-thinking bureaucrats were actually instrumental in reconciling the authoritarian and conservative disposition of the government with the pragmatic needs for a centralized and unified Austrian state.[96] The administration of the 1850s did not return to the often paralytic and undynamic role of pre-1848 Austria. Rather, the administration was simultaneously more powerful—because its Josephinist underpinnings were liberated from the enforced stagnation of Metternich, Francis I, and Ferdinand—and more progressive. The "era of bureaucracy" required a balancing act, because it depended on the administration to stoke the fires of economic and social modernization while checking a civil society that had boiled over in 1848. The reinvigorated central administration under Bach would work to enhance the power of the state by co-opting liberal principles of industrial and economic modernization with the modernization of the state itself.

The expansion of the districts and the spreading out of the central administration came at a price. Bach's administration was expensive and Francis Joseph's cabinet was never able to put the lasting debts of military mobilization and war in 1848–49 behind the Austrian state. After the revolutions of 1848, the Austrian government was running yearly deficits between 36 and 49 million guldens. But as Austria responded to the Crimean War of 1853–56 and the international crisis that accompanied it with a partial mobilization, military costs shot holes through the imperial budget. Military expenditure consumed 83.5 percent of total state income in 1855, climbing to 216 million guldens—about 21.6 million British pounds or US$102 million. As the yearly deficit exploded by 160 million guldens, finance minister Baron Andreas von Baumgartner resigned;[97] his course to solve the state's immediate fiscal emergency by selling off state assets, especially the railroads, was a bitter pill. The state had spent over 94 million guldens on the Bohemian and Hungarian rail network; it would lease them for ninety years to the French firm Crédit Mobilier for only 65.5 million guldens in readily convertible gold and silver.[98] The new finance minister, Baron Karl Ludwig von Bruck, set about to raise money through the financial markets, but as the total budget deficit continued to climb, it became apparent that Bach's administration and the enormous state-building efforts would be sacrificed on Mars's altar.

By the late 1850s, foreign-policy disasters, including a war in Italy and the subsequent territorial loss of Lombardy, drove the Austrian state further into financial crisis. Such a crisis created pressures inside and outside the monarchy that necessitated a far-reaching change to cut state expenditures, generate new revenues, or both. As officials and ministers sought ways to save the Austrian Empire from financial ruin, it became clear that military and administrative expenditures far outmatched the state's financial capabilities. Ripples of change reached Count Egbert Belcredi in Moravia in 1859, as well as the district official, the anonymous *Stuhlrichter* in Hungary. Belcredi would help found the conservative daily newspaper *Vaterland*, and left behind the anger and powerlessness he felt on his estates for the new challenges of Moravian and, later, imperial politics. He set out at the end of 1859 for Vienna.[99] The case in Hungary was even more fundamental as Bach's neoabsolutist system would be dismantled and the bureaucrats who had been sent to head all of the district offices were relieved of their duties. The imperial-royal *Stuhlrichter*, after all, was *in Disponibilität*—"available" and therefore unemployed—when he authored the memoir on his eight years of service in Hungary.[100]

Although the face of "neoabsolutism" would be abandoned in 1859, its praxis and its ideas would become deeply ingrained in the Habsburg state's imperial administration and, indeed, would leave lasting imprints on Austrian society. Austria's era of neoabsolutism saw the creation of new networks of state authority that reached deep into the heart of the Austrian countryside. District offices were established in territories with roughly ten thousand to forty thousand residents. Officials traveled through their districts and got to know the local farmers and businessmen, the local notables and the town drunks, sending reports of all kinds back to Vienna. Through these officials, the state struck roots at the local level and acquired a deeper knowledge of its lands and peoples, which could help the state develop comprehensive plans for managing them. Even more importantly, neoabsolutism created internal structures of administration and channels of authority that would persist until the end of the monarchy.

Looking ahead, it was precisely the institutions and innovations of the 1850s which provided the foundations for the representative era, which would emerge in the 1860s. From the local districts to the important crownlands, from district courts to the imperial courts of appeal, the administrative hierarchy of the monarchy was firmly established and this framework, this undergirding of the Habsburg state, would provide the foundations for the arena of Austrian politics for the coming five decades. Less abstractly, political participation was built on the foundation of bureaucratic state building. Crucially, the absolutist bureaucracy, retooled and reinvigorated under Alexander Bach, would form the major partner to representative government. When institutions of representative government and communal and provincial autonomy were reintroduced to the Habsburg lands in the 1860s, they would now exist beside a powerful and interventionist administration.

Together, the age of bureaucracy in the 1850s and the emergence of representation in the 1860s constituted a building process that was based on compromise and would transform both state and society. This process, even more than the flashes of violent change in 1848, transformed the Habsburg polity into a new state that would integrate the two points of tension in Count Franz von Stadion's dream: bureaucratic leadership and political participation. The spark of revolution produced a fire that would burn—and be used to forge the state—until 1914.

# 4

## State Building on a New Track
### Austria in the 1860s

AUSTRIA'S ongoing financial crisis prompted a renewal of constitutional experimentation that would alter once again the administrative structure of the empire. Austria's fiscal situation reached a critical point in the middle of 1859, when a series of defeats in the Second War of Italian Independence culminated in a military disaster at the Battle of Solferino. Francis Joseph would watch Italy unify, despite his best efforts, and take Austria's rich province of Lombardy with it. His great-great grandmother Maria Theresia had faced a similar dilemma in 1740; like her, Francis Joseph would have to find ways to innovate his state and his statecraft. But the transformation of the Austrian state, the innovations to make it financially solvent, depended not only on the creation of officials loyal to the crown and state. These officials already existed and Alexander Bach saw to it that there were a number of them. Rather the means of fighting and winning wars had now departed wildly from the ability to merely raise revenue. States now took on huge debts, floated loans, and had to convince banks and lending firms of their financial solvency. Borrowing monies for war, of course, had been going on in some form for centuries, but by the 1850s, what convinced bankers of future repayment had changed. State innovations now included representative institutions, notions of popular sovereignty, and the people's (whoever they were) control of the purse.

Political representation thus would come to Austria, obliquely, as a cost-saving measure, just as constitutionalism came to Austria to preserve the fantastic drain on Austria's state finances—the army. Even though Bach's large, interventionist state had paid for itself in terms of revenue collection and infrastructure building, the perception of a state weighted down by a bloated, inefficient bureaucracy was enough to scare away investors. Appearance, when it comes to investing, floating loans, and buying bonds, was everything, even in 1860. Reformers could write commentary on the regime, but in the end money would talk. Francis Joseph, plagued by debt and eager to restore his monarchy's position among the great powers, was now willing to listen. Administrative reform, which was previously necessary to reform the state and rejuvenate the monarchy, was now the path of least resistance in the maintenance of the status quo and Habsburg *Hausmacht* in central Europe. Bach was dismissed in 1859. His centralized and far-reaching state—and its civil service—would go next to the chopping block, instead of the real drain on state monies, military expenditure.

State expansion in the form of new government employees and infrastructure in the 1850s would give way to haphazard searches for a way out of a financial mess. The 1860s witnessed a whirlwind of experimentation and change. Nobles would win back control of the provinces—turning the tide against the centralized Josephinist state which they had been fighting and serving since the eighteenth century. This was accompanied by a liberal backlash and the creation of a central parliament. Wars were lost and the Hungarians lobbied for and eventually won their own domestic government and administration. All the while the markets surged, the harvests produced bumper crops, and men got rich. As Austria wobbled, the center of equilibrium began to shift away from the administration as the sole political body, although, tellingly, it would become all the more essential for the functioning of the Austrian state. The Austrian state-building project transformed into one that locked representation and administration together in a revamped and expanded administrative ladder. State building transcended administration in the 1860s.

A series of compromises and constitutional reforms reintroduced representative institutions to Austria's political arena in the 1860s. Many of these institutions were envisioned in Stadion's March Constitution of 1849. This type of constitutional reform, which added political bodies to a system already in place, lent a degree of stability to an era marked otherwise by lost wars, lost territories, and exclusion from the German confederation. It also made Austria's constitutional and legal structure all the more complicated. That complexity would be deepened by the number of political compromises that would have to be made. For despite the magnitude of constitutional change, compromise, and the united criticism of all political spectrums against Bach's bureaucracy, Bach's administrative framework of governors' offices and districts would remain in place. Reforms that introduced representation and autonomy would make that framework stronger than ever. But first, Austria would have to navigate a sea filled with mines and make it to the opposite shore.

## The End of the Age of Bureaucracy: Austria's October Diploma of 1860

On July 15, 1859, Emperor Francis Joseph, having just returned from the lost Battle of Solferino, issued the Laxenburg Manifesto. This document, while praising the valor of the army and explaining the reasons for not continuing the war, also included the all-important passage that the emperor would now turn his attention to "Austria's domestic welfare and international status [Macht] through a purposeful development of its rich intellectual and material strength [Kräfte], as well as through permanently establishing modernizing [zeitgemäße] improvements in legislation and administration."[1] With these words, the liberals of 1848, conservative nobles, and federalists of all stripes joined the debate over the political form the monarchy would soon take and its constitutional future. They fell into two distinct groups—themselves further divided into subgroups: the supporters of a federalist organization and the supporters of centralism.

The crisis may have been precipitated by a lost war, but the real crisis lay in the monarchy's finances. State-building efforts since the Napoleonic Wars had not seemed to escape from under the weight of financial difficulty, and even now military defeat further exacerbated the problem. The defeat at Solferino had shattered minister Karl von Bruck's financial plans for the united monarchy; Austrian government bonds fell by 53.6 percent between April 1858 and May 1859.[2] Austria needed a large loan of more than 500 million gulden, which was nearly twice the government's annual revenue, and cuts would have to be made to make Austria look financially solid to its would-be creditors.[3] For Francis Joseph, however, the military was as sacrosanct as his own person. Not only did he strongly believe that the military had saved the unity of his state in 1848–49 (whether the military in fact saved it is still a matter of debate), but he also thought it necessary to maintain the power of the House of Habsburg in central Europe. In addition to budget cuts, however, the banking community of Europe would not loan the Habsburg state the necessary funds to stay afloat without political guarantees. Both within and outside Austria, Austria's financial crisis was tied to the supposed mismanagement by the neoabsolutist system. For newspapers like the *Neue Augsburger Zeitung*, which heavily influenced public opinion and investors' confidence, neoabsolutism appeared as an anachronism that was not capable of producing the necessary economic growth and tax revenue to be a solid financial investment.[4]

The lost war and the emperor's Laxenburg Manifesto in 1859 signaled that the organization of the monarchy was again up for debate. The emperor's advisory council, the Reichsrat, was expanded—or in the idiom of the day, "reinforced"—to include sixty members. This new forum, which Francis Joseph reluctantly expanded, was to serve as an independent, nongovernmental supervisor of the state's woeful finances.[5] This supervisory role was the idea of the minister of finance, Karl Ludwig Ritter von Bruck, who wanted to secure new loans with administrative reform. Bruck's idea, which was approved after substantial debate in the Ministerial Conference, was to give the Reichsrat a larger and more public function.[6] Austria was, after all, under the watchful eye of Europe's great banking houses. The Imperial Patent of March 5, 1860, thus expanded the Reichsrat to fulfill its new roles as a financial watchdog and a public relations showcase. Under Kübeck, the council had consisted of twelve voting members. Now it was to be reinforced by imperial appointees, including archdukes of the imperial house, high officials of the Church, and men of distinguished military service.[7] In addition to these appointees, thirty-eight representatives were sent as delegates by the crownlands.[8] Although the Reichsrat received the explicit task of monitoring the state budget, it initially did not have the right to approve it—only to advise the emperor. The Reichsrat was also explicitly barred from initiating any legislation and therefore had no parliamentary power. However, if the emperor had intended this body to serve as his rubber stamp for the state budget, it quickly became apparent that this newly reformed institution had the weight to determine its own course. By June, it was fully engaged in the future structure of the Habsburg Empire. By July, it had wrested from the emperor the right to actually approve, or reject, the budget.[9]

As the Reichsrat set out to examine the underlying issues for the monarchy's financial woes, it was clear that it was not divided by financial questions but by political ones. The organizational form of the monarchy had come up for debate and the structures of power and governmental authority had to be reformed and renewed. But what form would the

Austrian state take and how would that state reduce its expenditures and increase its incomes? The crucible years between 1859 and 1867 saw the old divisions between monarchical authority and noble resistance transform into political divisions over the very structures of the monarchy, where autonomy should reside, and the role the administration would play in policy making and governance. In questions of state organization two camps emerged, centralists and federalists, and the political dogmas and attendant ideas of the ideal state that went with them. A coalition of liberals and officials comprised the centralist camp; their political program called for a constitutional parliament and social change. Liberals could agree with centralism on parliamentary and social grounds. For them, a central parliament with budgetary control would protect their core values of economic development and the rights of free individuals. Officials within the administration saw in liberals an ally against their old enemy, the nobility, whose local and regional political networks in the crownlands now took on a federalist character.[10]

The political debates over the structure of the monarchy would take center stage while the elephant in the room—the budget—slept silently in the wings. The conservative nobles on the Reichsrat, who were careful to ignore the most glaring problem facing the Austria state caused by military expenditure, soon found common ground with each other in their stance against Francis Joseph's government. Thus, critics of strict centralism and the rule of bureaucracy, critics like Egbert Belcredi, found themselves in a position to give voice for a federalist reform of the Austrian state. The foundations of their political ideas came from Hungary, in the writings of József Eötvös and the political leadership of Count Antal Szécsen. Like Victor von Andrian-Werburg, Eötvös was a politically engaged aristocrat who was highly critical of Bach's bureaucratic system. For Hungarians like Eötvös, Bach's system was a form of occupation. Eötvös made this Hungarian narrative of events into something more universal, which spoke not only to his compatriots but also to nobles like the Belcredis in Moravia. Writing in exile from Munich in the 1850s, Eötvös made complex arguments that emphasized the need for reconciliation between Austria's various nationalities and the central state through the intermediary bodies of the historical crownlands.[11] Eötvös argued for the reorganization of the monarchy according to the "historical-political" entities.[12] In Antal Szécsen's hands, the historical-political rights were not means to solve the nationality problem, but ends in themselves. In the sessions of the Reinforced Reichsrat,

Szécsen claimed that any future organization for Austria should follow the idea of "historic rights" that each kingdom, each crownland of the monarchy, had inherited before the centralizing interventions of Josephinist statecraft. The strength of Eötvös's ideas lay in their near universal applicability in the monarchy. Soon conservative nobles from Bohemia applied Eötvös's and Szécsen's ideas to their own calls for recognition of the historic rights of the lands of the Bohemian crown.[13]

The political ideas that came out of Hungary turned the centuries-old struggle between the central authority in Vienna and the nobility in the provinces into a political alliance. The nobility banded together in their claims against Vienna, while defenders of Bach's centralism argued for the continuance of the central state, bolstered with political representation. In the closed arena of the sixty-member Reichsrat, Szécsen formed a cohesive group with the Bohemians and other federally minded high nobles—the large landowners, rooted in the countryside, who could trace their lineages for centuries. From this group came the "party of the federal nobility," gathering conservative federalism and its many voices, speaking in different languages, under one roof.[14] In the twenty-one-member budget committee of the Reichsrat, this party quickly drew the construction of the state's administration into a discussion of the monarchy's financial crisis.[15] Meanwhile, the original twelve ordinary members of the Reichsrat combined with the German liberal delegates to oppose any shift in the structure of the monarchy toward federalism. Their representatives on the budget committee endorsed a centralist conception of the monarchy, while Hungarian conservatives and Bohemian and German high nobility proposed the full autonomy of the crownlands. The debates between the two factions in plenary sessions of the Reichsrat spawned two reports—a majority and a minority report—which the Reichsrat presented to the crown on September 27, 1860.[16]

The majority report looked much more like a constitutional draft than a report. It neither advocated for a return to a pre-1848 system nor for a wholly new state system. Rather, its authors, led by Count Heinrich Jaroslav Clam-Martinic and Antal Szécsen, wished to restore Hungary's "historic rights" and apply this "Hungarian" category to other "historic" territories as well, that is, the lands of the Bohemian crown and the Kingdom of Galicia. The majority sought to completely refound the monarchy on a federalist and conservative basis. The main thrust of their argument sought to overturn the centralization of the last eight years of Bach's domestic regime. Essentially, the majority report called into question the survival of the centralized *Gesamtstaat* ("complete-state") that Maria Theresia and Joseph II had created in the eighteenth century—the state that the administration served and actively fostered. By 1860, the stakes of the battle were raised and the entire Josephinian administration sat in the middle of the table. But the very rules of the game had shifted over the preceding twelve years. German liberals would come to the rescue of the central state.

With the stakes so high, the administration transformed quickly from a pillar of the state into a politically active camp of its own. The minority report was authored by the high-ministerial bureaucrats on the Reichsrat, who were the ordinary members carried over from its original form as a twelve-member body, and the German liberals. They heavily criticized the crownland federalism of the majority report, because they believed granting administrative and political autonomy to the crownlands would come at the price of imperial unity and, implicitly, the emperor's imperial authority. The majority report, they maintained, needed language that stated the supremacy of imperial law when provincial laws contradicted it. Moreover, the minority report reminded the emperor that these reforms had to be made toward shoring up the finances of the monarchy and, importantly, appealing to the concerns of Europe's banks and houses of credit. The resurrection of the crownlands as units with administrative and political authority, the report warned, would not provide the optimism needed to secure loans and improve the monarchy's financial situation. It repeated the words of finance minister Ignaz von Plener from a ministry report earlier in the year that "happy political institutions" were necessary to secure the public and the world's general trust. Borrowing those words, the minority report stated that "happy" institutions came from involvement of the public—through local autonomy and an engaged imperial parliament. These institutions could be called happy "when everything . . . regarding the communes and provinces . . . is taken out of the hands of the overburdened cadres of the imperial administration," and "when there exists a legal foundation for the freedom of expression, which allows the needs and wishes of the people in the best and quickest way to be made clear and which alone would save the government from costly supervision and afflictions."[17] The liberals and bureaucrats of the Reinforced Reichsrat saw the devolution of state authority in terms of local autonomy, which would free the communes from state supervision and save the state money; imperial unity would be secured in the central parliament and the central administration.

Shared enemies can make strange bedfellows. While the conservative and federalist alliance of notables and nobles seemed only natural, the ministerial bureaucracy and liberals came together out of necessity. Their connections forged in these days would remain strong, even if, at first glance, the supposed absolutism of the bureaucracy clashed against the supposed liberalism of the middling classes. Bureaucrats and liberals found common ground in the face of the newfound strength of their common enemy—the high aristocracy—and an inimical idea—crownland autonomy. Clam-Martinic and Szécsen's majority report laid the new constitutional foundations of the Austrian state on the bedrock of noble-dominated federalism: that is, crownlands with aristocratically controlled diets. "The invigoration and the future prosperity of the Monarchy demand the recognition of the historic-political particularity of the individual provinces," read their majority report.[18] Their vision of the monarchy turned the provincial diets into nodes of authority and patronage, centered in the provinces and dominated by the local nobility. In effect, constitutionalism was to be centered in the provinces. The diets would make policy, promote economic development, make laws, and preserve the legal and institutional particularities of the realm. This was a program of the aristocracy to be sure, one that was grounded in the resistance to the crown and to the growing bureaucratic apparatus. But in addition to these institutional threats to the bureaucracy, German liberals saw Szécsen and Clam-Martinic's report as a threat to the central state. It was that central state, renewed under Francis Joseph and Alexander Bach, to which the liberals had—almost surprisingly—grown loyal. But more than this, it was the structures of Bach's bureaucratic state, the very structures first conceived by Franz Stadion, that liberals saw as the basis for an economically viable, multinational state.

In such a field of play, liberals and bureaucrats came together to preserve centralism and restore a constitutional government with a central, elected legislative body. In fall 1860, when it was clear that the emperor would at least partially assent to the reorganization of the monarchy on the terms of Szécsen and the federalist nobility, no one in government argued more forcefully for centralism than Ignaz von Plener. His firm grounding in both the Josephinism of the central administration and his connections to Austria's liberally minded financial community brought him to the realization that Austria, to survive financial crises and remain a strong power in the center of Europe, must develop in a constitutional direction with a central government responsible to an elected parliament.[19] Ignaz von Plener was fifty years old when he took charge of the Ministry of Finance in 1860. Born into a family of civil servants, Plener entered the civil service as an intern after he completed his legal studies at the University of Vienna in 1833. Plener's talent earned him the patronage of his superiors and he quickly rose through the ranks of the bureaucracy in the Ministry of Finance.[20] As one of the twelve ordinary members of the Reichsrat and the minister of finance, Plener argued against the federalist reorganization of the monarchy both in the Reichsrat debates and in the Ministerial Conference. He saw granting far-reaching autonomy to Hungary as a slippery slope from which the monarchy could never recover. In a session of the Ministerial Conference which debated the terms of the Reichsrat's minority report, Plener expressed his concern for the future unity of the Austrian state when all of the crownlands were granted the same rights as Hungary: "It is deeply lamentable, if out of consideration of Hungary in all the remaining crownlands a condition of fragmentation is to be synthetically created, a condition which no one demands and for which there isn't the slightest necessity or justification."[21] Plener, along with the liberals, argued that it was better to locate the freedoms associated with autonomy in a central parliament, not in the crownlands. Such an organization, of course, would allow German-speaking liberals like himself to combine voices, coordinate policy, and advocate for larger, empire-wide tax and trade policies.

Despite Plener's forceful defense of the central state, he was outnumbered in both the Reichsrat and in the Ministerial Conference by high nobles who were pushing the emperor toward federalism. Often during debates in the Reichsrat and especially in the Ministerial Conference, the question was not how much "autonomy" should be granted to the crownlands and the local townships, but how much concentration of power in the crownlands would Francis Joseph allow at the expense of the centralization of the monarchy. How many of the duties would he let the autonomous *Länder* institutions take from his *Gesamtstaat* offices, the *Statthaltereien* and the district prefectures? In September and October 1860, Francis Joseph had to decide between two alternatives in the Ministerial Conference, the majority report that emerged from the noble federalists and Plener's call for a constitutionally empowered parliament and continued centralism. In October, Francis Joseph, still firmly opposed to constitutionalism,[22] sided with the aristocratic party and on October 20 promulgated a series of memos and statutes that were to form the "permanent and irrevocable" legal foundation for the empire in the October Diploma.[23]

As news of the October Diploma reached the public in the pages of the *Wiener Zeitung*, the Austrian public learned just how far Francis Joseph acceded to the demands of the aristocratic party and how much he held onto the tenets of neoabsolutism.[24] Although the October Diploma contained federalist elements, more importantly it took the first step toward dualism—giving Hungary a special status vis-à-vis the whole monarchy. Hungary received its former pre-1848 constitution and special legislative powers for its diet, but the October Diploma also allowed Francis Joseph to maintain some facets of absolutism, including his imperial prerogatives regarding the foreign service and the military. Moreover, although Francis Joseph granted the non-Hungarian diets and a new, hundred-member Reichsrat "participation" (*Mitwirkung*) in all legislation (the Hungarians received substantially more rights than just "participation"), he maintained all executive powers in his own hands. In other words, his bureaucrats still had the responsibility to enforce the law.

The biggest achievement of the October Diploma, one that would last until the final days of the monarchy, was the recreation of the crownlands as autonomous polities in the empire. The Diploma called for the revival of the crownland diets, *Landtage*, which would "participate (*mitwirken*) in the exercise of legislative authority." Additionally, Minister of State Agenor Gołuchowski, the new prime minister in Francis Joseph's cabinet, was instructed in the same memorandum to prepare statutes for each crownland.[25] These statutes were to secure the right of the crownlands to decide matters relevant to their welfare and to manage crownland property and monies without interference of the central state.[26] The crownland statutes also provided for the executive crownland board, the *Landesausschuß*, to serve as the administrative presidium of the diets. These institutions formed the basis of crownland autonomy, created as they were in the spirit of the emperor's recognition of the "historic-political" peculiarities of each of the crownlands.

The October Diploma has been characterized as a "constitution of the provincial estates," in the idiom of the nineteenth century.[27] It limited the crown by dividing the right to make laws between the emperor and legislative institutions. Although a central parliament was to be maintained, the most important legislatures would be the individual crownland diets. The crownlands were given a sweeping jurisdiction of legal and policy matters, leaving to the central parliament only legislation that was "common to the rights, duties and interests of all the crownlands," such as legislation on currency, tariffs and trade, the postal and telegraph service, railways and conscription. All other legislative matters were to be determined "according to the constitution" (in the case of Hungary) or by the crownland statutes (in the case of everywhere else) in the respective provincial diets.[28]

Although it was weighted heavily toward the aristocratic parties, the October Diploma pleased no one. For Francis Joseph, the October Diploma was still a compromise, one that chipped away at his imperial authority. As such, the Diploma contained elements of political compromise between centralism and federalism, the nobility and the crown, and absolutism and ideas of constitutional representation. The emperor only consented to the Diploma's revision of the state in the first place because state finances necessitated a reform of some sort that would make the administration more efficient and the monarchy appear more creditworthy to its financial community. In this respect, the Diploma also failed to deliver confidence. The value of the monarchy's paper currency dropped an additional 50 percent in value between October 1860 and January 1861. Europe's financial credit markets backed away from the monarchy's debt as well. The government tried to float a new loan of 30 million gulden in January 1861 and had to pay interest at nearly 9 percent.[29]

What had increasingly become clear to Francis Joseph and everyone was that the Austrian state-building project had become a matter of international attention. Bankers like the Rothschilds wanted to see a central parliament with control over finances and, thus, credit. The constitutional framework of the monarchy was not merely a debate about political ideas. It now became a matter of proving Austria's viability to the outside world. Constitutional organization was now inherently tied to financial questions, not only through how the government would make policy and collect its taxes, but also to how Austria would now finance its army and acquire cheaper debt. Federalization of the monarchy might have responded to the political concerns of the nobles and emerging national political groups, but it did not provide the cover for Austria's need for loans.[30]

Nor did the political solutions that the October Diploma offered gain much traction in the monarchy. Unfortunately for Francis Joseph, the special conditions that the October Diploma granted to Hungary became a source of discontent everywhere. Although the four published crownland statutes were to serve as models for the statutes of non-Hungarian crownlands under the provisions of the October Diploma, it was clear that Francis Joseph had no intention of granting the constitutional privileges he gave to Hungary to the lands on the left bank of the Leitha.[31] For the Bohemian nobility and the nascent Czech national movement, the October Diploma fell far short of their goal for a special recognition of "Bohemian state's rights," which would have united the lands of Bohemia, Moravia, and Silesia into a super-crownland political unit with the same autonomous status as Hungary.[32] In Galicia, the Polish nobility wanted similar political rights as the Hungarian high nobility received in the October Diploma. Moreover, even Hungarians found fault with it. The Pest County Assembly, which was dominated by middle-class liberals, rejected the October Diploma and demanded that the April Constitution of 1848 be reinstated. Ferenc Deák, leader of the Hungarian liberals, made this point the basis for any negotiations with Vienna. In the meantime, Hungarians continued to resort to a low-level civil protest by refusing to pay taxes to the imperial government.[33] The Hungarian situation was bad enough that Plener warned in a session of the Ministerial Conference that Hungary's "half-revolutionary" status had damaged any opportunity for the financial markets to rebound or for Austria to appear any more creditworthy. Among the liberal financial community to which Plener had strong ties, the October Diploma represented a step backward from Bach's neoabsolutism. German liberals like Plener thought the rule of the bureaucracy could be equally ham-fisted and oppressive, but at least it had been infused with the Josephinist ethos that encouraged strong centralism and economic modernization. The bureaucracy itself was also German—at least in its language—which lent it credibility among those who thought the German nation should take a leading role in the monarchy's politics. For Plener and others, centralism put the multinational monarchy in the hands of a German-speaking middle class, who they thought were likely the best stewards of financial solvency, economic development, and the central-state idea.[34] For Plener and his liberal colleagues, financial stability could not be improved without the development of institutions such as a central representative parliament and ministerial responsibility. Finances had become political, but they also had become the constitutional issue of the time. Francis Joseph had, in short order, come around to their line of thinking.[35]

Matters quickly reached critical mass in November 1860. Count Agenor Gołuchowski, who as minister of state was in charge of the implementation of the October Diploma, sought special approval for a vigorous censorship of the press. In his words, "administrative pressure"—censorship and police surveillance—would be the only measure capable of ending "the poisoning influence of the papers on the masses." This position left Gołuchowski increasingly isolated in the Ministerial Conference, as even the minister of police thought better of police pressure on the editors of the press. To Plener, the answer to the problem was relatively simple, because the press merely reflected general anger against the October Diploma and was not leading the resistance to the new order. Instead of "administrative pressure," the Ministerial Conference needed to take steps toward further reform and constitutionalism to restore faith in Austria's stability and thus its credit. Liberal towns and cities in ethnic German areas played into Plener's hands by threatening to overturn the new system by not participating in elections to the diet.[36] Faced with an anemic financial response to a federalist reform and the certain failure of the October Diploma if he stayed on the current course, Francis Joseph dismissed Gołuchowski as minister of state and appointed in his place the former Frankfurt parliamentarian and minister of justice under Schwarzenberg, Anton Ritter von Schmerling. Bureaucrats and centralist liberals like Plener would now have the emperor's ear and an opportunity to set a new course for the Austrian state. But, despite this victory over federalism, this was not a clear victory for Plener. In fact, it was a return to the bureaucratic reformism of 1849 and the ideas of Franz Stadion, tempered by the intervening decade, financial crises, and political failures.

## February Patent, Reichsrat, and Dual-Track Administration

The legacy of Schwarzenberg's three-year ministry between 1848 and 1851 is not only that it wiped out the local administrative vestiges of the old regime. It also produced Austria's leading statesmen through the next decade and a half. Schwarzenberg, Stadion, Bach, and Schmerling were in many ways the founding fathers of the modern Habsburg state. When Schmerling returned to the central cabinet a decade after resigning, he would bring full circle the constitutional reforms of 1849 under Schwarzenberg and Stadion. Following Stadion's 1849 Constitution and Provisional Municipalities Law, Schmerling would introduce representative government, political participation, and local autonomy to work alongside Austria's imperial officials. Bureaucracy and liberalism forged a partnership that would finally end the years of constitutional and political experimentation that had begun among the barricades and fires of March 1848.

Anton Ritter von Schmerling was born into an ennobled family of officials in 1805 which belonged to the Viennese "second society" of officialdom and the upper-class burgher.[37] He followed in the footsteps of his father and maternal grandfather, studying law at the University of Vienna and subsequently entering the ranks of judicial officialdom of the monarchy. Schmerling made the transition from officialdom to politics at a startlingly quick clip, first taking a seat as a member of the Lower Austrian knightage on the assembly of estates in Vienna in 1847. One year later he found himself in Frankfurt as a leading political figure, representing the Lower Austrian district of Tulln in the National Assembly in the revolution of 1848. When the National Assembly turned away from Austria's inclusion in a unified German state, Schmerling packed his bags and returned to Vienna. After Bach took over the Interior Ministry portfolio, Schmerling became minister of justice in Schwarzenberg's cabinet, where he continued the state's takeover of local justice and the building of the network of local courts. Schmerling clashed with the gray eminence of Francis Joseph's early regime, Baron Karl Kübeck, and resigned his post in 1851. This act of passive resistance to the emperor's anticonstitutional course, if nothing else, solidified his standing in Austria's liberal circles.[38] No longer at the center of power, but hardly willing to go into exile, he returned to the ranks of the judicial service, eventually becoming the president of the Superior Court in Vienna. At the beginning of the 1860s, Schmerling's liberal credentials gave him a great deal of credit with Austria's liberal circles, although they would later be disappointed with him.[39]

In the course of his work, Schmerling would become the founder of Austria's parliamentary system through his administrative and constitutional reforms. Even so, he was not a revolutionary democrat. Carrying the torch of progress did not mean using that torch to light a Molotov cocktail, after all. Rather, Schmerling was a transitional figure precisely at the convergence of Austrian political and administrative culture. Schmerling's vision of the state and his vision of liberalism would guide Austria from being a state in which a central bureaucracy administered solely on behalf of the emperor to an Austrian state in which representative bodies had to work with, and coexist with, a specialized and differentiated bureaucratic apparatus that derived its power from a divine-right monarch. With Schmerling, the constitutional reforms of Stadion and particularly his ideas of balance between the state administration and autonomous, representative institutions would rise again to the surface. But such reforms would be met by an uphill climb, since the political landscape of Austria had changed in the intervening twelve years. Schmerling inherited a strong, interventionist bureaucracy from Bach that stretched deep into the localities of the multinational empire, but Bach also shut out the institutions of political participation that Stadion thought were necessary to strengthen the central state and limit the influence of local nobles. Under this system, the state was responsible for almost all aspects of public life, but it also failed to balance its budgets and maintain public trust in the government to repay its debts. Revolution, Crimea, and the lost war of 1859 created an acute financial crisis. The initial results of a search for financial stability, October Diploma, had rearranged the state, but failed to regain the trust of the public and the community of European bankers and capital.[40]

Moreover, despite the need for change and the unpopularity of the October Diploma, the matters upon which Francis Joseph was willing to concede were few. When the emperor approved the October Diploma, he not only informed his Ministerial Conference that the "new institutions [created by the Diploma] are to be maintained as the unmovable basis of the new structure of the Monarchy which is not to be transgressed," but also that the October Diploma is "in no way to be seen as the first step in a series of general concessions."[41] Within this spirit of anticonstitutionalism, Francis Joseph gave Schmerling discrete limits as to how far his new reforms were to go. Schmerling was neither permitted to create anything that abrogated the October Diploma nor to further develop constitutionalism along the lines of what Plener and the liberals wanted. Schmerling's reforms, therefore, had to be constrained within Bach's administrative structure and the October Diploma's system of crownlands. Such limits essentially made Schmerling reach into the chest of Habsburg statecraft, searching for old pieces of value. What he would find were Stadion's old plans for administrative organization, municipal autonomy, and a central parliament.

After becoming the new minister of state (*Staatsminister*) in December 1860, Schmerling went to work on a new administrative framework for the monarchy.[42] The result of his relentless energy was the promulgation of two separate laws which created two new institutions of government, one local and one imperial. The first was the February Patent of February 26, 1861, followed by the Imperial Municipalities Law (*Reichsgemeindegesetz*), which was promulgated on March 5, 1862. The institutions were both representative bodies in the liberal fashion of giving dominance to wealthy and therefore—in the thinking of the time—more interested citizens. In the context of the previous twelve years of constitutional experimentation, what Schmerling created was both old and new. On top of Bach's administrative framework and the October Diploma's system of crownland autonomy, Schmerling transformed the Reichsrat into a central parliament, which would be responsible for legislation and approving the all-important Austrian budget. In addition, like Stadion, he promulgated a municipalities law, which granted autonomy and self-government to rural townships, towns, and cities.

The key feature of the February Patent was its focus on an imperial legislature and the extension of legislative authority. Schmerling, following the ideas of Ignaz von Plener, saw the need for a central legislative authority for the entire *Reich*, with extensive budget-making powers. The February Patent was promulgated by an imperial edict and technically provided the guidelines for the implementation of the October Diploma. In emphasis and spirit, if not in deed, the Patent overturned the Diploma by unequivocally announcing that the crownlands would now "according to the conditions and necessities of the present, be brought into harmony with the entire monarchy [Gesamtmonarchie]." The Patent served to correct the federalist-friendly provisions of the October Diploma by forcing the crownlands to exist as a rung in an administrative and political ladder, rather than the pinnacle of the ladder itself.[43] It did this in two fundamental ways: it focused imperial legislative authority in the Reichsrat and it altered the electoral provisions of the provincial assemblies. Previously, the representatives of the provincial assemblies were determined through indirect elections by city and rural township councils. They were essentially assemblies of the estates, dominated by the nobility. Under the Patent, provincial assemblies would no longer function as an assembly of estates per se, but rather, they would constitute themselves through the election of delegates, elected by a curial system, who would then select the members of the diet. It was still an indirect system meant to give weight to society's propertied classes, but as we shall see, the importance here lay in the weighting. Two addenda accompanied the February Patent that focused on these aspects of legislative authority and suffrage: the first included the statute for the central legislature; the second contained fifteen crownland statutes along with electoral guidelines for the provincial diets.[44]

Above the level of provinces, Schmerling intended to use the February Patent to establish institutions of representation in the center, drawing people to Vienna and making them commit political energy to the central state. The statute for the central legislature (*Grundgesetz über die Reichsvertretung*) created a central bicameral legislature with a House of Lords (*Herrenhaus*) and a House of Representatives (*Abgeordnetenhaus*). The House of Lords would be comprised of those who by birth and position were entitled to a seat (archdukes of the house of Habsburg, heads of the great landowning families), as well as archbishops and prince-bishops in the Catholic Church and those who were given lifetime appointments by the emperor in recognition of their distinguished service to the state or to the Church. The House of Representatives, or lower house, was significantly expanded as well. The February Patent increased the number of its members to 343 from 100 set by the October Diploma. Its members would be sent by the crownland diets, a compromise with the October Diploma's system, and the number of delegates it could send was based on the population and wealth of the crownland.[45] Along with its expanded membership, the Reichsrat received expanded powers at the expense of both imperial authority and the crownlands' newly won autonomy. Additionally, the Reichsrat not only had the right to "participate" in legislation, but also reserved the right to approve all legislation for all-*Reich* matters. It no longer had to wait on the emperor and his ministers to lay bills before it and could now introduce its own legislation. Moreover, the jurisdiction of the Reichsrat was expanded and less delimited in comparison to the crownlands and their legislatures—the diets. In contradistinction to the language of the October Diploma, the jurisdictional division between the Reichsrat and the provincial diets was reversed: article 11 of the *Grundgesetz über die Reichsvertretung* stated that "all matters of legislation, which are not expressly reserved through the crownland statutes" belonged to the jurisdiction of the narrower Reichsrat.[46] In the meantime, the crownland statutes limited the matters that fell under the jurisdiction of the diets to matters of agriculture (*Landeskultur*), public works and buildings erected and maintained out of the crownland treasury.

Although the February Patent laid the groundwork for representative government in the entire monarchy, it and the October Diploma lacked not only a bill of rights, but also the rules and norms of a constitution that limited the government's powers. The Reichsrat, though it gained many parliamentary functions, still did not have the parliamentary rights and norms that were in Stadion's more progressive March Constitution of 1849, for which Plener had so vehemently pleaded in the Ministerial Conference. There was, for instance, no clause in either document that made the ministers responsible to parliament, nor was the concept of parliamentary immunity for the deputies included. The Reichsrat likewise could approve taxes and the budget, but once these were approved they remained valid only until suspended. Finally, the February Patent contained an emergency clause that allowed the Ministerial Council, which replaced the Ministerial Conference, to rule when parliament was not in session.[47]

What the Patent did do, however, was continue the Austrian state-building project and raise it to a new plane, complete with representation, control of the budget, and a shared role for political representatives in policy making. The February Patent was not a constitution, much like the October Diploma before it, but rather an official declaration of a new administrative organization. Together, it and the municipalities law made important and long-lasting changes to the system of governance in Austria by introducing aspects of self-government and autonomy to the administration. The February Patent both recognized the principle of limited representation and safeguarded bureaucratic authority. Meanwhile the municipalities law paved the way for the wholesale expansion of local autonomy, reviving Stadion's ideas for the creation of local self-government, and would have allowed local communities to elect their own officials to run their affairs free from the direct intervention of the central state.[48] But this was not a simple return to 1849. Schmerling had to fit municipal autonomy into the system of crownland autonomy that the October Diploma had created. The Imperial Municipalities Law thus provided the guidelines for municipal autonomy in the monarchy, while also giving room to the diets to draft their own specific regulations for the municipalities and townships. It was a careful balance in which a centralist like Schmerling was not allowed to permanently defeat federalism.

Under the Imperial Municipalities Law, all townships and municipalities shared the same basic structure. Citizens of these *Gemeinde* elected a town council (*Gemeindeausschuss* or *Gemeinderat*). The town council consisted of at least nine members, sometimes more, depending on the number of voters or citizens of the town.[49] Councilmen served between three and six years and were not paid for their work; rather, the position of councilmen was considered an "office of honor" (*Ehrenamt*).[50] Town councils represented the residents of the township, and in addition to their duties as councilmen, they also selected the members of the Township Executive Board (*Gemeindevorstand*) from their own ranks. The executive board consisted of the chairman (*Gemeindevorsteher/Bürgermeister*) and at least two additional members who worked as advisors to the chairman.[51] The chairman served as the head of the autonomous administration. His duties were large and his reach wide, which easily could, and often did, result in some chairmen transforming into "mayor-kings." Essentially, the chairman was in charge of all local projects and administrative business, including management of township assets, and supervising the local police force. Furthermore, he represented the township to other townships and to the state institutions which supervised him. Finally, the township chairman led the local cadre of officials.[52]

The Imperial Municipalities Law and the February Patent comprised a major administrative reform. Together they returned Austria to the principle of the dual-track administrative system first imagined by Count Franz Stadion in his constitution and municipalities law of 1849.[53] A major difference, however, existed between the two systems, because the October Diploma gave the crownlands a large autonomous role. Together, the Imperial Municipal Law of 1862 and the subsequent municipal statutes of the crownlands redefined the role and range of autonomy. The result was that the *Gemeinde*—the local communities, whether cities or rural townships—became the grounding principle of local government. Their work would be supervised under both the autonomous authorities of the crownlands and the imperial officials who manned the districts.

Dual oversight worked to limit the activities of the *Gemeinde*, but these local municipalities and townships could also find room to maneuver between the state and provincial authorities. In matters of some administrative duties, the *Gemeinde* was an instrument of the political administration and stood as a member of the administrative hierarchy. But the higher autonomous corporations, typically the crownlands, also stood administratively over the autonomous townships and had the duty of supervising their legal and financial matters.[54] Additionally, the crownland executive committee acted as an administrative appellate court in cases where citizens brought legal complaints against their municipality. So, autonomous crownland institutions like the provincial assembly and provincial board had oversight of municipal activities in some spheres, while the central state institutions, the districts or the provincial executives (*Statthalter* or *Landespräsident*) supervised in others. In practice, this meant the functions

of the local townships were divided, as they were under Stadion's municipality law, into "independent" (*selbständig*) and "delegated" (*übertragen*)
spheres.[55] The independent sphere of the *Gemeinde* consisted of "everything
that touches upon the interests of the commune and that can be executed
through its own power."[56] Twelve categories belonged to this independent
sphere, including management of township assets; security of persons and
their property; supervision of sanitation, produce and comestibles; building and zoning laws; local fire departments; and care for the sick, poor and
infirm through township institutions. Here was the liberal conception of
autonomy in its truest form. Local institutions could regulate themselves,
their finances, and even erect their own social-service institutions under
their own administration. Although the state stood above the *Gemeinde*,
and reserved the right to intervene in township politics in cases of corruption or mismanagement, it would in principle leave the liberal, socially
active, and well-run *Gemeinde* alone.

The municipalities did have a wide scope of movement, if they
could pay for them out of their own resources. Those resources were further strained by doing the state's work. The "delegated" sphere of activity
(*übertragener Wirkungskreis*) contained activities that were under the control of the central state and which the state subsequently assigned to the
local autonomous administrations for implementation.[57] The philosophy
behind this system reflects the strong legacy of Stadion's ideas: there were
simply some things that the local institutions of government and administration could do better than the central state. These included matters like
registration and residency certification (*Meldewesen* and *Heimatrecht*), the
execution of the decennial census, the management of elections, and the
collection of local taxes.[58] By assigning these types of empire-wide activities
to local institutions, the state could respect local peculiarities and customs,
treating the regions and townships as parts of a multinational empire.

Above the municipalities and townships sat the provinces, or crownlands, which occupied a central position in the administrative ladder. The
Imperial Municipalities Law, the February Patent, and the October Diploma created a system in which the crownlands straddled both sides of
the dual-track administration. In fact, the offices of the crownlands were
split between the autonomous sphere and the imperial sphere. The autonomous institutions of the crownland supervised the independent activities
of the *Gemeinde* and served to administer and regulate the crownland's autonomous activities. The imperial administration, however, continued to

supervise the districts as a bureaucratic organ completely separate from the autonomous sphere. The dual-track administration, revived through these series of laws and administrative reforms, thus divided the crownland into two spheres of policy, while at the same time anchoring much of the monarchy's political questions and debates in each crownland.

The October Diploma resurrected the autonomy of the crownlands and re-created the traditional authorities of the old noble estates. It was, in essence, a compromise with the past and a return to very system that Maria Theresia and Joseph had worked to overcome. Each crownland was given a provincial assembly or diet (*Landtag*), and each assembly selected an executive board (*Landesausschuß*). The emperor appointed a *Landeshauptmann*, or provincial captain, to chair both the diet and the executive committee. While the diet was responsible for all legislation that concerned the crownland, its executive body, the *Landesausschuß*, headed the new autonomous administration of the crownlands as the executive organ of the diet. These committees had between four and eight members, depending on the crownland's size, population, and relative wealth.[59] The executive committee was technically a standing committee of the diet, and met while the diet was not in session. In practice, however, it was much more than a simple legislative committee. Its members were paid out of crownland funds and served six-year terms. Additionally, to fulfill its obligations as an executive body, the *Landesausschuß* could employ its own officials. These crownland officials were not affiliated with the central state; they owed their position and thus their allegiance to the crownland. It is important to note that these autonomous crownland institutions existed *in addition to* the imperial governor's offices that were created after 1848 and built upon by Bach's neoabsolutism. Some crownlands (Galicia, Bohemia, and Styria) also created autonomous district councils that brought self-government to the district level as well.

Schmerling created an administrative system that was more than just a compromise between the ideas of liberalism and self-government and the central authority of the Habsburgs. Schmerling combined a Josephinist concern for justice and social welfare with conservative, pre-Josephine, conceptions of the "historic" rights of the provinces. The February Patent and the Imperial Municipalities Law revived Stadion's conception of dual-track administration. What was added to the mix was the autonomy and administrative significance of the crownlands—that is, the innovations of the October Diploma. Taken as a whole, the period between 1859 and 1862 forged a compromise between the two separate developments of Austrian state building: both Josephinist and the Francist. All the major currents in Austrian constitutional and political thought were now represented: aristocratic, province-centered government in the crownlands; liberalism in the free communes; and last, but not least, the Josephine imperial administration. The result was a complex network of offices, two parallel hierarchical administrative ladders, and the necessity of imperial authorities and elected officials to cooperate at the local, regional, and provincial levels (see Figure 4.1).

Compromise, using tools from the toolbox of Habsburg statecraft, helped Schmerling sail the Austrian ship of state through stormy political waters after the Battle of Solferino and the Peace of Villafranca. What made Schmerling, the bureaucrat who was steeped in Josephinist étatism and centralism, allow such far-reaching autonomy? Josef Redlich has argued that Schmerling's position as a member of the estates diet of Lower Austria and thus his "*ständisch* past," is the answer.[60] I would add that Schmerling not only tolerated an autonomous administration but he actively promoted it, because he expected it to be populated with Germanic liberals and centralists much like himself. The proof of this lies in his "electoral geometry"; Schmerling had constructed an electoral system for returning representatives both to the diets and communes that blatantly favored German

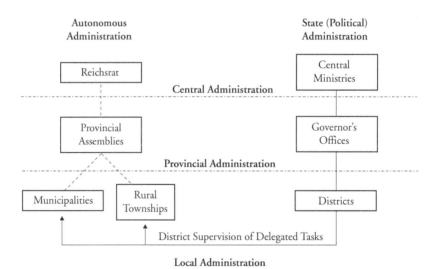

FIGURE 4.1. Dual-Track Administration After 1862

liberals in the cities and towns. Schmerling, like Stadion before him, expected autonomy to supplement the work of the central government, not to compete with it. Schmerling's dual administrative apparatus depended on the electoral victories of those who supported centralism alongside progressive economic development and liberal social values.[61] Local elections in the communes occurred by direct election and according to the three-class, or curial, system (*Dreiklassenwahlrecht*) of landowners, towns and markets, and rural communities or townships.[62] This curial system allowed the basic functioning of direct democracy while giving significantly extra weight to the wealthiest segments of society which paid the highest taxes.[63] Rich landowners and the upper bourgeois dominated electoral politics well beyond their numbers, while the proletariat was generally excluded.[64] In all cases, this allowed liberals to dominate much of the communal councils in much of Cisleithania, which importantly now formed the lowest level of both the central and autonomous administrations.

This curial voting system in crownland elections gave weight to political groups that were safe to the central Austrian state, usually the liberally dominated urban (and therefore German) areas, and thus served to tie Austria's administration firmly to German liberalism. Voters elected representatives by curiae to the diets indirectly in a two-stage process.[65] First they elected delegates who then elected deputies to the diet for six-year terms. The deputies in the diet then selected members from their own ranks to represent the crownland in the House of Representatives in the Reichsrat. The first class of mandates in the *Landtag* belonged to the so-called *Virilisten*, who, due to their rank and position, automatically received seats in the diets. These mandates belonged to members of the "spiritual" class, bishops and university rectors, whose numbers were rather small.[66] The remaining mandates of the diets belonged to members who were elected through three curiae. The first curia belonged to the large landholders (*Großgrundbesitz*) who generally paid direct taxes in excess of one hundred gulden.[67] The second curia belonged to the cities, market towns, and chambers of commerce. The third and final curia consisted of the rural communities and townships.

Schmerling's administrative and constitutional innovations on the one hand and returning to the framework and principles of Stadion on the other added political representation to the larger Austrian state-building project. But the dawn of constitutionalism was more than just a brick in the proverbial wall. Schmerling's electoral geometry gave German-speaking liberals in the towns and cities more than their fair share of the votes. Schmerling, in turn, expected them to be more conciliatory to Austria's powerful bureaucratic apparatus and more favorable to the central state. But more than this, more than a simple narrative of the creation of representation or the staging of political practice, Schmerling's system and the addition of representation would, over the long term, transform the Austrian state-building project. Elected officials, parliamentarians, and mayors all over the monarchy would now participate in and share administrative responsibilities with Bach's bureaucratic apparatus. At the same time, Bach's bureaucratic apparatus would become enmeshed in the monarchy's emerging political world. But first, that bureaucracy would have to be molded and adapted to fit the realities of the dual-track system.

## Dismantling the Bureaucracy, Building Representation?

The years of constitutional experimentation and new constitutional laws like the October Diploma, February Patent, and the Imperial Municipalities Law meant the continuation of fundamental administrative change. Many officials, some newly hired, others not, found their positions taken away from them to make room for crownland governance under the October Diploma and municipal autonomy under the new municipalities law. For instance, the October Diploma outlined many changes for Hungary's administration, restoring to that land a separate justice and administrative hierarchy. In the non-Hungarian lands, the Ministry of the Interior began to disassemble the intricate network of district offices and county offices. The result of such change was personnel chaos and an army of unemployed officials, who were described in the distinctly euphemistic tone of Austrian bureaucratese as "in a state of availability"— *in Disponsibilität*. In other words the 1860s were just as much a period of ruptures and change as the 1850s.

Nowhere was the administrative pain more acute for Austria's officials than in the lands of the Hungarian crown. The arrangements of the October Diploma meant that "Bach's hussars" were pensioned off, dismissed, or like the anonymous *Stuhlrichter* (district official), held *in Disponsibilität*—suspended without pay and awaiting further orders.[68] Our *Stuhlrichter* relates in his memoir his personal anguish when, relieved of his post, he was ordered to remove the imperial eagle from the facade of his office. "The eagle, the symbol of my imperial lord, to whom I swore obedience and loyalty, under whose wing I served honorably and truly for many years; the eagle, to whom I dedicated my youth, my strength, my knowledge, my industry, all of my senses and endeavors, my entire life; now I had to hide this august palladium in a corner!"[69] He could not bear to watch it be removed, so he arranged to have the imperial shield taken down while he was out of the office. When he returned, he found it casually thrown on the floor. Forgetting the decorum of imperial service, the *Stuhlrichter* broke down in tears.

The anguish and humiliation of this official was shared by many. During 1860 and 1861, between two thousand and five thousand midlevel, educated officials were labeled as *disponsibel*.[70] Who were they? They carried names like Johann Psogner, from Hall in Tyrol, who earned 420 gulden a year as a clerk in the Betics-Csanader County Office. Psogner had been a clerk for seven years and fourteen days when he was rendered *diponsibel*. Luckily, his compatriots in Tyrol found a place for him in an administrative office in Bregenz. Psogner was evaluated by his superiors as an impeccable civil servant. Some of his colleagues weren't so lucky, especially the more qualified. Wilhelm Ritter von Pauly, born in Vienna in 1821, had joined the civil service in 1843 as drafting intern in Lower Austria. He completed a university degree in politics and juridical studies and passed the practical civil service exams. He spoke numerous languages—German, Italian, Hungarian, French, and even English. His evaluation noted that his work ethic was "praiseworthy," and that his "moral and political behavior" was impeccable. Pauly was a striver. He left Lower Austria to rise through the ranks faster in the provinces. By 1849 he was in Hungary, seeking better prospects for promotion there. He was promoted repeatedly, moving to Nagyvárad/Grosswardein/Oradea in 1850, and then to Pressburg in 1854. He was in Kassa/Kaschau/Košice and working as a *Statthaltereirat*, second class, making the large sum of 2,625 gulden per year when the hammer fell. After seventeen years, six months, and eight days as a civil servant, Pauly was *disponsibel*; he had no income and was forced to wait on the mercy of another office somewhere to take him on. Initially at least, this ambitious civil servant had no offers.[71]

We have some sense of the scope and gravity of these administrative ruptures in Hungary because the government tried to find positions for many laid-off officials. Charts with names, ages, length of service, and short evaluations and lists of skills were compiled and distributed to various provincial and regional offices throughout the monarchy. The Ministry of the Interior followed up with updates, indicating which civil servants had found positions elsewhere. *Statthaltereirat* Franz Hallina, from Neuhaus / Jindřichův Hradec in Bohemia, was let go from his high-paying (2,100 gulden per year) position in Buda. He eventually found a position in Graz. Emil Sombart was not so lucky. He was also a *Statthalterei*-councillor, a position in the sixth rank, but he was older, forty-seven years old, and single. He was passed over for positions which went to his married colleagues. They had, after all, families to provide for. In practice, the administration continued to evaluate its bureaucrats in ways that went beyond skills and work performance. This allowed for some to be promoted over others for moral standing and political disposition, enabling superiors a personal control over their underlings that went beyond the simple metrics of rationalization and standardization which we associate with modern bureaucracy and state building. But the very potential for social control also had its softer side: the social triage of dismantling Hungary's bureaucracy meant that the state found married men—presumably with families—positions first. Of the four *Statthalterei*-councillors of his rank who were unemployed in 1861, Sombart—who had served the longest—was the only one who was not found a new position. He was the only bachelor.

Additionally, though anecdotally, we see that officials dumped from their positions in Hungary often were taken back by officials close to their origins. *Offizial* Paul Scharf, born in Lower Austria, was rendered *disponsibel* while serving as a county clerk in Sároser, was taken on as a clerk in Klosterneuburg. Anton Schrader was born in Hainburg in Lower Austria in 1819. In 1862, he left his position as a clerk in Eperjes/Prešov and found a position in Vienna. Felix Heinrich was born in Schwaz in Tyrol and, by 1862, he had returned to Schwaz after nearly thirteen years in Hungary.[72] Franz Karl Theodorovich was born in Rann/Brežice in Lower Styria. He found work in Pettau/Ptuj in Styria, ninety kilometers away.[73] Despite these happy stories, many officials, at least two thousand by contemporary reports, came from the "German-Slavic" lands and found themselves laid off in a land that did not want or need them. These officials were looked on with suspicion by the Hungarians and felt orphaned by the central state that sent them there. Many faced derailed careers and financial ruin. As the state would take it upon itself to find work for these civil servants, the process was slow, dragging out into 1864. Thus, dismantling Bach's system had very real effects on the civil servants who were meant to do the work of state making and of policy making. The October Diploma rendered thousands "available," as it sought to turn over so much of the state's work to the crownlands. In 1860, state bureaucracy looked as if it would have to become smaller, too, as diets and councils would hire their own employees to do the work of administration.

At the same time that major ruptures were taking place in Hungary's administration, Bach's bureaucratic apparatus was being evaluated and partially dismantled in the other crownlands too. Following the financial crises in the midst of the Crimean War, the Austrian state began a thorough evaluation of its local and regional offices.[74] Evaluations of these statistical data came to a head after the war with Piedmont and France and the Treaty of Villafranca. The accompanying financial crisis resulted in major administrative cutbacks and a pulling back of state supervision in the provinces. The last law of 1859 was published on December 31. Following the Sylvester Patent by exactly eight years Law Nr. 237, dissolved the four counties of Upper Austria and placed their staff in *Diponsibilität*.[75] Their activity was to cease by April 30, 1860, and their judicial and administrative responsibilities handed partially to the districts on the one hand and to the provincial governors on the other.[76] The Ministry of the Interior abolished the counties in Lower Austria and Styria by the same ministerial decree. The county authorities in Moravia were dissolved by decree in June 1860. Counties remained only in Bohemia and Galicia—but only for a few years longer. The counties in these provinces were eventually eliminated over the course of the 1860s.[77] The county, which was established under Maria Theresia and which first indicated her government's determination to reach into the provinces, had come to an end.

In other words, the major constitutional changes wrought by the fall of "neoabsolutism" and the establishment of constitutional and parliamentary government under the provisions of the October Diploma and February Patent only tell one part of the narrative. Beneath the surface of constitutional change, the tectonic plates of Austria's administrative structures were already quaking. Two aspects are key to understanding the entangled web of administrative and constitutional change. The first has been demonstrated here already: that administrative changes preceded and accompanied constitutional change. Second, the establishment of constitutional government with representative bodies like school boards, town councils, provincial assemblies, and a central parliament, actually was a solution to the monarchy's finances. It made the administration cheaper by sloughing off expenditures onto "autonomous" institutions. For instance, the Imperial Municipalities Law granted autonomy to cities and townships, allowing for the election of local officials who managed local treasuries and funds. But for all the talk of autonomy, there were pragmatic fiscal and financial reasons to give townships their fiscal freedom. On the one hand, the devolution of authority to the townships boosted financial confidence in the fiscal solvency of the monarchy and relieved it of the cost of the day-to-day work of administration. On the other, however, the townships were responsible for the costs of implementing the duties "delegated" by the state, unlike under Bach's system. Although this gave a free hand to richer cities and towns with resources to manage these duties according to their local wishes, it would prove to be financially ruinous for smaller and poorer townships across the monarchy that did not have such resources at their disposal.[78] In the five decades between the promulgation of the Imperial Municipalities Law and the First World War, the state imperial and provincial legislation would add to the various duties of the townships, pushing their finances well over the breaking point. While larger cities and towns could count on innovative direct and indirect taxes, city services and fees, or even service monopolies to cover their expenditures, small rural townships had virtually nothing to draw from.[79] The devolution of the state onto the local communities provided a civic schooling to both well-heeled townsmen and illiterate farming communities, because these communities had to regulate for themselves so many activities. However, this autonomy, which passed a heavy burden of state building onto local communities, also passed financial crises down to the local communities. In the meantime, the central state climbed out of its crushing debt.

In a very real sense, then, constitutional changes of the 1860s were part of a larger process of administrative downsizing and a paring down of state expenditures. By 1864, the Ministry of the Interior had turned its attention to the most local unit of administration—the district office. Officials in the Ministry of the Interior planned for the wholesale retreat from the extreme local presence of the district offices.[80] In fact, planners began to imagine the individual crownlands divided into larger district prefectures, with three to four times as many souls to manage, while simultaneously shrinking staff sizes. For Upper Austria this meant taking the forty-five district offices and combining them to make twelve district prefectures. In fact, the Upper Austrian governor's office projected that the new organization would cost only 68,650 gulden per year—an administrative cost reduction of nearly 120,000, or about two-thirds of current expenditure! In fact, total costs—which included salaries, per diem costs, building rents and maintenance, and monies for day laborers—were projected to be a mere 27 percent of what they had been in 1863. The Upper Austrian government's budget was projected to be reduced from 288,593 gulden in 1863 to a mere 110,246 after the reforms.[81] Even with these staggering numbers, the Ministry of the Interior in Vienna pressed for more cuts and reductions. State minister Friedrich Ferdinand von Beust wrote to Count Eduard Taaffe, then the governor of Upper Austria, in 1867 asking for an appraisal of an even smaller administrative presence in the crownland. Could Taaffe imagine their being only nine district prefectures instead of twelve or thirteen?[82]

The reality of constitutional government was that it made for sharp reductions in administrative personnel and costs. For Upper Austria this meant that the 371 staff members for the forty-five district offices would be reduced to merely 83 public employees stationed across twelve district prefectures. In other words, the local presence of the state—the massive influx of Bach's bureaucrats—would be reduced by 288 (77 percent) in one medium-sized province. The total numbers of state officials in the 1860s are hard to come by—so much so because they were constantly in flux. Karl Megner's economic and sociological study of the Habsburg bureaucracy estimates that there were 52,320 officials, functionaries, and employees in the civil service in 1862. By 1874, the introduction of "reforms" and the displacement of the bureaucracy by autonomous organs, town councils and board, had reduced them by half, to 26,969.[83]

If bureaucratic reductions preceded and accompanied Austria's constitutional reforms and, therefore, if bureaucracy was making way for representatives of the people to step up and take their place in policy making, this did not translate into an immediate representative success. Schmerling may have established a parliamentary system alongside the very real authority of Bach's central bureaucracy, but constitutional parchment did not translate into frictionless practice. Parliamentarism faced an uphill climb and not just from the supposedly absolutist bureaucracy. From the very beginning, jurisdictional questions plagued the Reichsrat. Federalist representatives from Bohemia called into question the competence of the imperial parliament, even going so far as to organize a boycott of its sessions.[84] These noble or even Czech national politicians were merely the most openly hostile to the central parliament. Conservative groups from Galicia to Tyrol denied that the central parliament had the right to legislate on matters affecting the internal affairs of their crownland. Czech national politicians and Bohemian magnates could unite on the idea of Bohemian "state right," while members of the Polish parties from Galicia and clerical conservatives from Tyrol wanted similar arrangements for their provinces.[85] All in all about seventy deputies formed an oppositional union, which was bound, not by an ideological or even nationalist program, but by a constitutional resistance to the central state. For among the federalists, autonomy not only meant that legislative authority rested in the provincial diets, but that executive and supervisory authority stayed with elected officials and their own staffs—not with imperial officials. Whereas federalists used national cultural development and promoted the use of other languages in the state administration as a way of loosening Vienna's grip on the provinces, German liberals defended their mother tongue as the multinational empire's state language.[86] The "language question," and thus "the national question," quickly became the chief weapon in the hands of federalists to wield against the central state.

Opposition to imperial Austria's politics produced its own reaction of solidarity among German liberals. Liberals circled the wagons to defend Schmerling's central parliament and local autonomy, and by doing so, Bach's central state apparatus. However, such politicking would not be enough to save Schmerling's government; it fell in late July 1865 in the face of the intransigence of Slav federalist and Magyar calls for home rule. In fact, the Hungarians' diet had been suspended in 1861 and never recalled—the Magyars never sanctioned the February Patent and were loath to do so. Schmerling would not let them reassemble unless that was their first order of business. Liberals eventually abandoned the government over tariff policies and procedural issues. Francis Joseph responded to the fall of the government by suspending the Basic Law on Imperial Representation entirely. There would be no parliament and no representation for two years. But this period of suspension would mark the last, intense period of constitutional experimentation that first began in 1848.

The state continued to wobble and it was unclear at the time that the wobbling was slowly coming to an end. The failure of Schmerling's constitutional arrangements under the February Patent to satisfy the Hungarian liberal parties, which still demanded the reinstatement of their constitution of 1848, brought Francis Joseph and his advisors back to the constitutional drawing board. In selecting a replacement for Schmerling, Francis Joseph signaled that he was willing to steer a less centralist course. He appointed Count Richard Belcredi, the younger brother of our Moravian magnate Egbert Belcredi, as the head of a new government. Belcredi had made his career, like many of Francis Joseph's prime ministers, as a civil servant in the imperial administration. But Belcredi, unlike Schmerling, was a federalist who hoped to overturn much of his predecessor's work. In fact, Belcredi constituted the first of several scares to the German liberals, who counted on a unified state to preserve the constitutional safeguards for local autonomy. During Belcredi's tenure, Francis Joseph hoped that his personal intervention into Austria's domestic politics would settle the Austrian state question and, at the very least, end once and for all Hungary's active resistance to the *Gesamtstaat*. In June, Francis Joseph had already begun negotiating privately with the Hungarian leadership, Ferenc Deák and Gyula Andrássy; he did not notify Belcredi that he was doing so. In the negotiations, each side had signaled its willingness to compromise with the other. Deák authored the "Easter Article" in the *Pesti Napló*, in which he recognized Hungary's incorporation and subordination to the larger empire;[87] Francis Joseph made an official visit to Budapest in July and by December had reopened the Hungarian diet, which he had previously dissolved in November 1861. However, looming war with Prussia delayed further negotiations between Francis Joseph and the Hungarian liberals. Thus, 1866 was a year of waiting. Then came Königgrätz. Austria's quick defeat by Prussia and its exclusion from Germany removed any reason for further delay. Francis Joseph's new foreign minister, Baron Ferdinand Beust, impressed upon the crown the need to settle immediately the monarchy's organization and constitutional questions. Such a quick settlement of the state problem would allow the monarchy to devote more energy to foreign affairs—and to revising the monarchy's position vis-à-vis Bismarck's Prussia.[88] Francis Joseph returned to the negotiation table with the Hungarians and eventually reached an agreement that would partially solve the riddle of Austria's political organization.

The Great Compromise, or *Ausgleich*, was agreed upon by Francis Joseph, Deák, and Andrássy on February 18, 1867, constructing a new state system that resolved the 125-year constitutional struggle with Hungary. The compromise created two states, each with their own parliament, government, and judicial system. One of these had an official name: the Kingdom of Hungary. The other state did not; it would be known in long hand

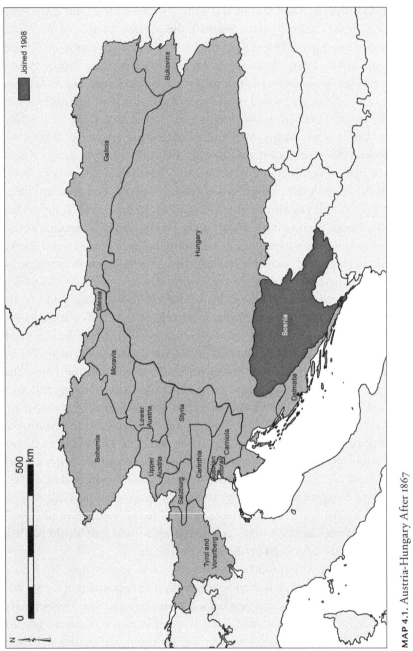

Joined 1908

Bukovina

Galicia

Silesia

Hungary

Moravia

Bohemia

Lower
Austria

Styria

Bosnia

Upper
Austria

Salzburg

Carinthia

Austrian
littoral

Carniola

Dalmatia

Tyrol and
Voralberg

500

km

0

N

MAP 4.1. Austria–Hungary After 1867

for the next fifty years collectively as the "kingdoms and lands represented in the Reichsrat." Subsequently, historians and others have resorted to Latin. "Transleithania" stood for the lands governed after 1867 from Budapest, which included Transylvania, Croatia, and Hungary proper. "Cisleithania" stood for all the lands on the near side of the river Leitha—but in reality it meant "not Hungary." Although these two states were now administratively independent, they were also bound to each other through the monarch (emperor of Austria, king of Hungary), and through common institutions for the military, foreign service, and finances. In addition, the Austro-Hungarian monarchy (as it was now called) comprised a single customs-union and currency zone, which maintained the economic unity of the Habsburg's lands (see Map 4.1). Thus, the Compromise created a unique hybrid state, which Robert A. Kann termed a "political structure *sui generis*."[89] The Great Compromise was in no way a constitution, however. Rather, the document enumerated how common institutions, such as the military and the foreign service, would function, and how public monies would cover their expenses. The compromise resembled a treaty between two states—states that now formed the two halves of Francis Joseph's monarchy.

Now that Francis Joseph had come to an agreement with the Hungarians, it was time to ensure that the Great Compromise was ratified. The Hungarian diet, now the primary legislature in the Hungarian half of the monarchy, ratified the Compromise in March 1867. The Austrian parliament, however, was not even in session. In fact, Francis Joseph had suspended provisions of the February Patent that regulated the convocation of the Reichsrat in September 1865. But now, in the early spring of 1867, Francis Joseph needed parliament to grant its assent to the *Ausgleich*. Unfortunately, Francis Joseph did not enjoy much popularity there and his prime minister, Belcredi, was enormously unpopular with the German liberals, the strongest faction in parliament. Francis Joseph needed their support to have any chance to push through the *Ausgleich*. Moreover, Belcredi was nonplussed that the emperor negotiated with the Hungarians behind his back; the prime minister was thus not likely to energetically deal with parliament on Francis Joseph's behalf. The result of the emperor's foreign-policy disasters and bad faith vis-à-vis the Reichsrat was to turn the page. Francis Joseph pragmatically dismissed Belcredi and replaced him with foreign minister Friedrich Ferdinand Baron von Beust. Beust, as foreign minister, was also given the task to settle the domestic affairs of the non-Hungarian lands.

Beust, a Saxon, was convinced that the *Ausgleich* could only be passed by a parliament dominated by the German liberals, the group least unhappy with the emperor's negotiations and settlement with the Hungarians. The alliance of national and conservative parties lamented that crownland autonomy only applied to the Hungarians. Czech politicians went so far to as show their disapproval by attending an exhibition in Moscow, where they hailed Russia as the "the rising sun of the Slavs."[90] Conversely, some of the liberals seethed at the disintegration of the *Gesamtstaat*. In addition, the liberals distrusted the monarch, who had prorogued parliament and settled with the Hungarians without them. The Reichsrat essentially had been handed the Compromise as a *fait accompli*.[91] It now had the duty of approving the Compromise and also of drafting a new constitution for Cisleithania. This constitution—the December Constitution—was intended to align Austria's parliamentary, state, and governmental institutions with the new dualist system.[92]

In June 1867, the House of Representatives formed a constitutional committee that, over the course of nearly seven months, drafted and debated the five laws which would come to be known as the December Constitution.[93] These laws included a law that altered the Basic Law Concerning Representation,[94] a new Basic Law on the General Rights of Citizens,[95] a law that established the Imperial Law Court (*Reichsgericht*),[96] a Basic Law on Judicial Powers,[97] and finally, a Basic Law on the Exercise of Governmental and Executive Power.[98] These five laws received the emperor's sanction on December 21, 1867.

The December Constitution can generally be read as a new beginning in Austrian politics and social life. The liberals turned their position of weakness into a moment of enormous strength. Since the emperor needed their approval for the dualist system, which he had forged without them, the liberals were determined to use this moment to enact many of the reforms they had been striving to achieve. This included the establishment of the rule of law (*Rechtsstaat*) and the creation of an Austrian citizenship that guaranteed personal freedoms, freedom of worship, freedom of speech, and the right to associate. Thus the December Constitution formed a clear step toward the creation of a *Rechtsstaat*, the sanctification of the rights of individuals, and the recognition of the rights of national groups. Liberals had hoped with this constitution that Austria would enter into "modernity" and the wider western league of democratic, industrial, and forward-looking states.[99] They also demanded a reform of the administration. Although parliament passed some constitutional laws in 1867—beyond the five Basic Laws—that were simply altered versions of government-sponsored bills, the lower house of the Reichsrat also produced laws that showcased their independence from the government and their intention to create a new modern, liberal state. Not all of their laws were new. The Basic Law on the General Rights of Citizens—the Austrian Bill of Rights—repeated much of the constitutional draft produced at Kremsier eighteen years before,[100] including provisions for equality of all citizens before the law, freedom of movement, the inviolability of property, the liberty of persons, the privacy of personal mail, the right of petition, the right of assembly, and provisions for the freedom of speech.

Many of the liberals on the Reichsrat's constitutional committee had served in the Reichstag in 1848 at Kremsier. However, they found the Austrian state and its politicians had changed remarkably in the two intervening decades. National conceptions entered into political programs and thus into the discussion of the organization of the empire. Peter Urbanitsch has noted how these administrative and constitutional questions quickly became the divisive issues for national political parties. Centralism "became wedded more and more to the national-political intentions of the Germans," while "the national principle had begun to transform the concept of 'historic-political individualities.'" This meant nothing less than the supersession of "historical *Staatsrecht*" as the achievement of historical constitutional rights for Austria's many crownlands.[101] After the 1860s, the term *Staatsrecht* meant more than constitutional law; it had become the idea of "states' rights" and the principle through which the various non-German national groups could achieve their national aspirations for cultural development and for virtual, if not actual, independence. The monarchy's representative institutions became fora for opposition to the very structures of the state. But even so, these structures of the state would evolve, strengthen, and eventually, pull in the forces of opposition to the system. Dual-track administration would draw the very forces that opposed it over the next several decades.

## The End of Experimentation

While the December Constitution can be read as a new beginning (and it certainly has been read as the beginning of the end), it was also the last major step in the construction of Austria's political arena. Hungary was excluded, but the rest of the old Habsburg territories would continue together on a course that began under Maria Theresia and Joseph II. The constitution was followed by the final revision of the bureaucratic system in the spring of 1868, when the state finally carried out the elimination of the district offices. The new Law on the Organization of the Political Authorities established larger district prefectures, reduced absolutely the number of local officials, and made room for elected members of town councils to influence the course of local life.[102]

The law created a new administrative unit, the district prefecture (*Bezirkshauptmannschaft*), which would encompass "two or more of the existing districts."[103] This significant addition to Austria's administrative organization on the part of German liberals would persist well beyond the era of the First World War into the successor states. Bach's district offices, numbering 886 in the Cisleithanian lands alone by the 1860s, were consolidated into only 324 district prefectures.[104] Tellingly Carl Giskra, the Burgher Ministry's minister of the interior, justified this bureaucratic retreat from local administration in more than just terms of cost. Now that the constitutional system had come to Austria, Giskra claimed, it was time again to beat back the "bureaucratic spirit" that accompanied Bach's neo-absolutism of the 1850s, by reforming the administration to correspond with the constitutional system and its principles—including ministerial responsibility. But more than this, Giskra claimed that by eliminating the 886 district offices and replacing them with 324 district prefectures, the law made an important step toward the promotion of autonomy and freedom from the state, ending the system in which "each and everything is done by the authorities and nothing is done by oneself; rather we just allow all matters to be taken care of by the authorities under this patronizing system."[105] Giskra hoped that by pulling back the central bureaucracy into offices that were fewer in number and more spread out in the Austrian countryside, he would create room for autonomous towns and cities to grow. He held out the future possibility of a time when "the entire civil administration at the local level could be simply handed over to elected [read: autonomous] organs."[106]

The Burgher Ministry's bill to reorganize the administration was transferred to the "Constitutional Committee" of the House of Representatives, which had representatives from every crownland on the committee. After two weeks, the bill came back to the House, where it passed after some amendments. Despite some parliamentary fine-tuning, especially

concerning the rank and salary scales for the civil service that it introduced, the bill received the support of both the liberals and the federalist
members of parliament. Parliament approved the reform bill on May 14,
1868, and the emperor gave it his sanction five days later on May 19.

But the 1868 law was not only a win for liberalism and local autonomy. Rather it represented a new entanglement of bureaucratic expertise with representative life. The bureaucratic spirit would not be
beaten back; instead it would fuse with representation. Essentially the
1868 law sanctioned and preserved much of Schmerling's (and by proxy,
Bach's) administrative system and ensured that it carried over into the
Cisleithanian half of the Dual Monarchy. Bach's bureaucracy had become the muscles for representative government. The power of the state,
now carrying the participation of the people, had transcended personal
rule into the level of abstraction. Within forty years, that representation
would expand and stretch to reach universal suffrage—that is, democracy. Bach's officials, those many servants who ushered in the "rule of the
legal paragraph," much to the chagrin of magnates like Egbert Belcredi,
would become the executors, not just of the emperor's will, but of a constitutional monarchy.

In retrospect, the reform bill of 1868 concluded a twenty-year period
of administrative reform. In the 1850s, a newly retooled and invigorated
central bureaucracy had been created, while in the 1860s, institutions of
local and regional self-government were created alongside the bureaucracy. Over these twenty years, an administrative system emerged which
was built on crisis and compromise solutions. The result was a mixture of
elected officials and bureaucrats employed by the central state who existed
in distinctly separate, but parallel offices. The dual-track system came to
form the constitutional and administrative framework in which Austria
operated and even flourished. The spirit of compromise that reflected Austria's own complex situation as a multinational empire was carved into the
administrative structure. In its ideal form, this double administration was
to combine the driving principles of the empire and its peoples to create a strong state and at the same time bring progress to central Europe:
the principle of local autonomy and self-rule with a strong central bureaucracy. With town councils, crownland diets, and a newly empowered
imperial diet, the bureaucracy had potentially powerful allies or enemies
with which to deal. It had emerged stronger from the twenty-year period
of constitutional experimentation, imbued with an interventionist ethos

by which it saw itself as the guardian of Austrian society. But those same twenty years had seen the birth of representative politics, political parties, and elected offices, which could challenge the bureaucracy's leadership role in Habsburg central European society. Time, however, would forge its own compromises. This process is the subject of the next chapter.

# 5

## The Years of Procedure, 1868–1900

### The Evolution of *Homo Austriacus Magistratus*

In March 1881, the Ministry of the Interior instructed one of its high-ranking civil servants, *Ministerialrat* Emil Maczak von Ottenburg, to begin to reorganize and recategorize the laws, ordinances, decrees, and norms that concerned the functions of the imperial civil service. Maczak, who as a *Ministerialrat* earned between thirty-six hundred and six thousand kronen per year with a thousand-kronen supplemental living allowance for Vienna, had been in charge of the files in the Ministry of the Interior.[1] For the past decade he had arranged the files chronologically, assembling them in a linear fashion, one file after the other. Additionally, from his own money he had bought empty books and paper to create registration books to aid someone who needed a particular file. Now, per the Ministry of the Interior's instructions, Maczak was to locate the files that created precedents or new administrative norms, give those files a subject heading, and then file them alphabetically, according to their subject. He also had to create new aids for finding them.[2]

Maczak penned a bitter response to the Ministry of the Interior's presidial office. He did not have the necessary staff to help him produce the new reference books that would be needed, nor did he look forward to reorganizing the many years of norms according to new subject entries. In restrained prose, Maczak wrote that he "knew he did not need to remind the high ministry" that his many years of service included paying for materials out of his own pockets. He would not be doing this anymore. Furthermore, he could not understand why there needed to be a new system of cataloging and preservation. The existing aids, which he had produced with his own hands and out of materials bought with his own money, had been rendered useless by these administrative reforms and by these bureaucratic changes. Maczak plucked up some courage in his letter and asked to be allowed to take these obsolete record books, cataloging the last fifteen years of the ministry's activities, home. The ministry rejected his request. Those books, however obsolete, belonged to the state.[3]

. . .

The task that burdened Maczak von Ottenburg was no small one. In a very real sense, Maczak was ordered to create an archive, to do what Jacques Derrida would call the "domiciliation" of power and authority.[4] Derrida called the selection and gathering of laws in an archive a form of violence. The archive gathers and houses the law, and enables the exercise of state authority to seem perfectly consistent, restrained, regulated, and all the more powerful in its exercise and execution. The archive saves what the archon, and thus what the state, sees as important. Other voices, other documents, other possibilities are silenced. There is, of course, a certain irony in this. While Derrida saw the archiving of paper as an exercise of power, the archivist himself felt powerless. But more than this, the Austrian context for Derrida's ideas provides a new wrinkle. For while the archivist's job is to help articulate the abstract and arbitrary authority of the state, the context for Maczak's struggles was nothing less than the expansion of representative government in Austria. The creation of an archive in Austria was not the dispossessing act of power, but the result of an expanding representative government. This expansion brought with it a proliferation of elected officials who, in turn, placed new demands on the state and its administration. Political representation, public participation in governance through town and district councils, provincial assemblies, and parliament itself pushed Maczak to get his papers in order.[5]

As Maczak looked at all the files before him in the ministry's archive, he stood on the threshold of a new era. The world was changing and he wanted it to stay the same. He was an old bureaucrat from a more positivist age. During his tenure in the Ministry of the Interior, the realms of administrative knowledge had changed; they had specialized and fragmented into a spectrum of activities the state had not performed before.[6] Twenty years of parliamentary government and more than a decade under the December Constitution had flooded the administration with new rules, norms, and procedures. Austria's officials needed new ways of understanding their own legal and administrative past. They needed to see their work in terms of subject and themes instead of in chronological narratives. The relationship between the two institutions, the cadres of imperial civil servants and the legions of elected public servants, deepened in these three decades as new ways of doing things emerged—as procedures opened channels of governance and political involvement where they had never been. Determining the complex arrangements among autonomous officials, politicians, and imperial civil servants created precedents or resulted in new norms and laws, which caused the workload of the administration to explode. Thus by 1881, when the Ministry of the Interior instructed Maczak to rebuild and recatalog the archive, the Austrian imperial civil service had become partnered with elected officials—somewhat uneasily— and had to rethink the way it stored its files and thus how it remembered.

## Years of Procedure: Political Participation and Bureaucratic Governance

This chapter will discuss the period roughly from the dawn of constitutional government in 1868 to the middle of the 1890s, which I term the "years of procedure."[7] The procedures and norms of statecraft, the "living constitution" of imperial Austria, were built during this period through relationships, frictions, and compromise.[8] The dual-track administrative system with its separate autonomous and state administrations, which had emerged from two decades of constitutional changes and experimentation, made this inevitable. Of fundamental importance in these two and a half decades, then, was the modus operandi reached between the century-old imperial administration and the newly reborn institutions of autonomous government and political participation: the town councils, district assemblies, provincial diets, and the imperial parliament itself. During this period, these newly reconstituted forms of autonomous government had to find ways to work with the administration, which had been retooled and strengthened under the systems of Count Franz Stadion and Alexander Bach after the revolutions of 1848. Part of this search for procedures and how to work together was defining jurisdictional boundaries. The new institutions of political participation had to find the scope of their autonomy and thus define themselves in terms of the written constitution and the bureaucratic structures of the state. The relationship and the procedures and norms that governed the cooperation between political institutions and the administration would become the living constitution of the Austrian monarchy, a system in which participatory politics and technocratic administration found ways to work together to create policy and run the state.

The reverse side of this coin meant that Cisleithanian Austria became a state in which the administration would not only continue to play a role in policy making, but also in imperial politics. This dynamic would form the basis for much of the criticism toward the Habsburg monarchy's political system, its "bureaucratic absolutism," and specter of an overly powerful administration that worked behind closed doors, or up in Kafka's proverbial castle, beyond the gates which closed out the populace. Certainly this was the way that the long-time London *Times* correspondent in Vienna, Henry Wickham-Steed, wrote about the Austrian administration in the years preceding the First World War.[9] By 1913 Steed would refer to the bureaucratic exercise of power as "anonymous tyranny exercised through a dozen Departments and a hundred divisions of State by thousands of hierarchical potentates."[10] For Steed, the bureaucracy—over the course of the constitutional period, the "years of procedure"—gradually abandoned the principles laid down for it in the eighteenth century, during the pinnacle of enlightened absolutism under Joseph II. The onset of political participation and the new frictions from working alongside elected officials had forced the Austrian imperial civil service to jettison its ethos and its concern for the general welfare for political self-preservation.[11] For Steed, the constitutional period had the effect of making the administration an end in itself.

History writing on the Habsburg Empire in the late imperial period has, for a long time, tacitly followed Steed's lead. Moreover, scholars only have to look down the academic hallway to political science to find its theoretical underpinnings for this interpretation. Conventional wisdom in the realm of politics tells us that bureaucracies are a threat to democratic institutions since they have a capacity to be "instruments of coercion." Political science theories in particular have seen administration as an inherent problem for democracy, because of the independence of the bureaucracy vis-à-vis democratic institutions and elected officials.[12] But recent work in the social science of public administration tends to see administration in more positive terms, arguing, for instance, that democratic societies need the expertise in policy making that bureaucracies offer in order to bolster their own governmental legitimacy.[13] Social science now increasingly emphasizes a "governance perspective," which sees both elected officials and representative bodies in play with bureaucracy: either can "facilitate democracy" or impede it.[14]

The structures of Austria's December Constitution provided for and demanded engagement between politicians and the officials of the state. But lest we think that Austria suffocated under the weight of an oppressive administration while tied up in a constitutional "straight jacket," the political world hardly remained static.[15] To begin to see the dynamism inherent in the Austrian state project, we need to begin to question the assumptions that have underlined Steed's analysis of the Austrian bureaucracy from a century ago. The years of procedure remind us that the emergence of a constitutional system and elected officials in no way reduced the activities of the imperial administration. If anything, those things we tend to label as "bureaucracy" increased exponentially. Constitutionalism gave the imperial administration more to do and a more complicated political environment in which to work. But these developments did not mark a fundamental rupture. Rather, as I have argued in the first four chapters of this book, the constitutional government—as complex as it was—emerged out of the gradual building process in which the administration played an integral part. What would be added to this complexity was the way politicians and bureaucrats conducted the business of state and the rules of the political game. After all, Austria's political arena, built over four generations, now housed political competition within institutions of the state.

### The Political Procedures of the 1870s: Liberalism and the Autonomy of the Bureaucracy

The emergence of a constitutional system in the 1860s was not the result of a revolution. Between 1849 and 1867 heads did not roll, the emperor was not deposed, the landed nobles were not dispossessed. There was no revolutionary army marching on Vienna, nor was there a Lenin, a Garibaldi, or even a Napoleon III who promised a new way of doing business. Rather, Austrian constitutionalism was the product of almost twenty years of continual revision. At the dawn of constitutionalism neither politicians nor bureaucrats knew where the lines of demarcation and jurisdiction would be drawn. They would have to draw those lines themselves. While the December Constitution was written, signed by the emperor, and registered in the law books, the "living constitution" of procedures, precedents, and simply the ways in which the business of government was done, had yet to be written.

The "living constitution" was written by Austrians of all nationalities on many different levels. Bureaucrats and politicians found means of co-operation and obstruction, ways of working with each other, or not, in the twenty-five years following the signing of the December Constitution. But these years of procedure were hardly a flat surface on which to work. The years of procedure circumscribe a period of great growth, modernization, and change. In the current idiom of contemporary Austria, the period between the promulgation of the December Constitution in 1867 and the turn of the century is called the *Gründerzeit*, or the years of the founders. The "foundations" of the Austrian state and its economy ran deep into the bedrock of the administrative past. The rail lines that were built in neoabsolutist 1850s became conduits for economic investment, urbaniza-tion, and communication. The economy grew, the rural population moved to cities and towns. By the turn of the century, Vienna had become the fourth largest city in Europe with a population of nearly 2 million. Major manufacturing centers emerged in Bohemia, Moravia, and Styria.[16] As the economy grew, so too grew the electorate. Political participation began a step-wise progression toward universal suffrage with the dawn of the con-stitutional era, through suffrage reforms in 1873, 1882, and again in 1893 and 1907. The world of politics was growing and changing—and politics increasingly mattered in Cisleithanian Austria.

Politicians mattered too, and at first the liberals seemingly mattered most of all. Once the laws that comprised the December Constitution were approved by imperial sanction, the work of the liberals in building the liberal state was just beginning. State building *begins*—it does not end—with the promulgation of a constitution.[17] At the beginning of this constitutional era, the liberals appeared ascendant as they emerged from the previous twenty years of constitutional experimentation. In the writing of the December Constitution, parliament had acquired new powers and strength to assert itself in matters of state. Moreover, in passing the actual laws of the constitution the Reichsrat set up a judiciary independent from the domestic administration, which would aid parliament in establishing its own status as pillar of the state.[18] However, whether these liberals, from the German-speaking towns in the Alpine valleys and especially from Bo-hemia, would be able to mold the "living constitution" as they had the written one was unclear.

With the sanction of the constitution, the liberals in parliament formally turned their attention away from the constitution to the administrative structures of the state. Moreover, the liberals had often spoken of the need to reform the administration "in the spirit of modern civilization [Cultur] and freedom."[19] When Count Friedrich Ferdinand von Beust resigned as prime minister in December 1867, many questions remained open. What would reform look like and how would it be brought about? Beust still remained foreign minister, but his resignation as prime minister made way for the liberal centralists to take over the government. This "burgher" ministry, so named because it was the only government which ruled on the basis of its parliamentary majority, remained in office for two years.[20]

Despite their threats or intentions to put much of local and regional administration in the hands of elected officials, the German liberals, who dominated the lower House of Representatives, kept much of Schmerling's system as they hammered out the constitution in 1867–68. They ended the twenty-year process in which, through compromise and experimentation, Austria had built the foundations of political participation and an arena for political engagement. Notably, however, parliament changed its relationship to Austria's governmental system, to the emperor and to the administration as well. Parliament carved out a greater role for itself in Austria's political life, by making itself responsible for the Cisleithanian budget, and by setting itself up as a law giver alongside the emperor. Parliamentary control, the ability of parliament to write laws and make policy was a direct challenge to the bureaucracy's role and self-perception as the sole representative of the Austrian state.[21] This challenge, in turn, had profound implications for the political role of Austria's administration.

The work of parliament in 1867–68 transformed Austria into a state based on the rule of law in which the laws would be written by the representatives of the people.[22] Moreover, liberal politicians like Carl Giskra, who took over the post of minister of the interior in the first postconstitution government, adamantly fought for the right of parliament to intervene both in how the imperial administration was structured and in how it would be used to do the work of government. Giskra claimed in 1868 that the old "means of ruling by decree has been curtailed by the reestablishment of constitutional rule and changes in the constitution have generally solidified the constitutional jurisdiction" for parliament to participate in the organization of the imperial administration.[23] Giskra stood for many of his colleagues who thought the sovereignty of the people meant that parliament should control the administration, which had served the emperor in a semi-independent status since the death of Joseph II in 1790.

Liberals like Giskra, who wanted parliament to control the administration and extend parliament's authority over the imperial civil service, faced opposition from many sides—including their fellow liberals and Germans. Giskra's optimism in the transformative power of legislative authority clashed with other voices in parliament, which echoed different ideas about where the center of legislative authority should lie. Parliamentarians from small towns and from Czech-, Slovene-, and Polish-speaking areas spoke up for the other parts of the empire—the crownlands and the cities, muddling parliament's voice. Under contention was the question of where important legislative powers—and thus modernization—would lie: in the central institutions of government (the Reichsrat, the ministries, the emperor, and the administration), in the crownlands and their autonomous diets, or in the municipalities and their town councils.

These new political divisions tended to mirror the old eighteenth-century divisions between the central state of Maria Theresia and Joseph II on the one side and the regional and provincial power of the landed nobility on the other. However, the struggle between central and regional authorities had changed by the last half of the nineteenth century from a struggle between aristocracy and the crown to one between political parties and national movements. The Polish delegation in parliament (the Czech national politicians had boycotted the session of parliament entirely) used constitutional negotiations in 1867 to revise their dominance in Galicia and wrest power away from the central government. Florian Ziemiałkowski from Lemberg, claimed for instance, that "if independence cannot at this time be granted to the kingdoms and lands [of the monarchy], then they should be given self-rule, which—without endangering the unity of the monarchy in the least—enables their natural development."[24]

Such wishes for crownland autonomy appeared again and again during the initial sessions of the Reichsrat; any attempt to definitively answer the riddle of the *Reich*'s organization drew a stalemate.[25] Moreover, the questions of municipal autonomy, self-rule for the crownlands, and state centralization continually emerged in the debates, but these jurisdictional questions and issues were left up in the air in order to secure crucial support for the passage of the basic laws.[26] Politicians could create the legal basis for public participation in policy making and legislation, but they could not agree on the proper hierarchy of participatory institutions themselves. Was the central state more powerful than the provinces? Should the local towns be the center point of public life? Among all the town councils, the district and provincial assemblies, or the imperial parliament that they had helped create, politicians could not create hierarchy, order, or harmony.

By the middle of the 1870s the imperial parliament was set for a clash on the path forward for a new state. Francis Joseph had briefly turned toward federalism in 1870 with the appointment of Count Karl von Hohenwart as prime minister.[27] His government's plan to grant the Czech national politicians their wish for a constitutionally autonomous "royal Bohemia" within the confines of the empire would have federalized the monarchy and rendered moot the centralist program of German liberals since Anton Ritter von Schmerling. German-speakers were outraged and even the Hungarians protested against the constitutional change that these "Fundamental Articles" would cause.[28] The emperor was forced to drop the issue in the fall of 1871, to the great disappointment of Czech advocates for Bohemian state rights.

The clash over the state and its organization would continue—but it continued not on the stage of big structures, but on procedures. The organization of the empire was still up in the air. Federalism—at least for a trialist system with Hungary, Bohemia, and the German- and Polish-dominated "leftovers"—had failed. The system of administrative and political structures of Cisleithanian Austria (a central parliament and central ministries; provincial assemblies and imperial governor offices; district prefectures and cities and towns) was only four years old by the time the federalist experiment of 1871 had failed. Having reached a stalemate, Austria's politicians and officials would have to make do and move on. They would have to navigate the administrative system they had within the confines of the state structures of Stadion, Bach, Schmerling, and the December Constitution.

### August Göllerich, Small-Town Liberalism, and the New Politics of Reform

In 1873, a new suffrage reform brought new people into the imperial parliament. Under the reform, the provincial assemblies no longer selected the representatives to populate the Reichsrat; instead, the people directly elected the representatives. These elections were weighted, organized through four curiae, giving the richer members of Austrian society more of a voice.[29] But they were direct elections nonetheless and brought new blood into the Reichsrat. One member of the freshman parliamentary cohort of 1873 was August Göllerich, a German liberal from Upper Austria, who had a long career in the Austrian civil service behind him.[30]

Göllerich was fifty-four years old in 1873, when the suffrage reform allowed direct election of representatives. Born in 1819 in Moravia, he was the son of an army officer, who had been stationed in many places of the monarchy while August was growing up. After graduating from a gymnasium in Udine, August Göllerich studied government at the University of Vienna and successfully passed the exam for entry into the civil service. In 1848, the twenty-nine-year-old Göllerich was—despite his employment in the state service—an active participant in the revolution. He belonged to the Vienna Citizens' Brigade (*Wiener Bürgergarde*) and was selected by his peers for a leadership position on the organization's security board. With the failure of the revolution, Göllerich retreated from public life and took up farming on an estate in Styria. But Göllerich was drawn to public life and public service. In 1860, he applied for the position of municipal secretary of the Upper Austrian city of Wels, the town in which his mother grew up. Wels was looking for someone with an official's background, someone who had gone through the juridical and governmental training at university to help reorganize the city and establish its municipal administration. Göllerich was the man for the job. At the very moment that Bach's neo-absolutism was making way for constitutional government and the return of municipal autonomy, Göllerich was informed that he received the position. At the end of 1860, Göllerich moved his family to Wels.[31]

Göllerich brought many perspectives to his job as municipal secretary and imperial parliamentarian and occupied many positions within the various autonomous bureaucracies. He was a municipal official and a member of the provincial assembly; he sat on the executive board of Upper Austria and therefore oversaw the provincial administration there; finally, after 1873, he served as a member of the imperial Austrian parliament, the Reichsrat. In Upper Austria, Göllerich was active in the *liberal-politische Verein*, of which he served as chairman between 1874 and 1878 in addition to active duty as a member of both the Upper Austrian provincial assembly and its executive board.[32]

An active political life mattered for a town like Wels. 1861 saw the expansion of the municipal council (*Gemeindeausschuss*), doubling its size to twenty-four members. Moreover, new regulations for the municipality under Schmerling's constitutional government meant that these officials were now elected and no longer appointed by the minister of the interior. The 1861 elections turned out to be a sea-change for municipal administration. Only two former members of the municipal council were returned to office by the voters. The remaining twenty-two council members were new politicians, men like the new mayor, Dr. Franz Gross, a lawyer and state prosecutor, who was active in local liberal circles.[33] In this era of great changes, both the local politicians and the local administrators could carve out new jurisdictions for themselves. Their job descriptions changed as Bach's neoabsolutist state began to withdraw its hands from all the inner workings of local life. Dr. Gross as mayor took on a lot of authority for himself. He was a man with a flair for showy gestures and grandiosity. He founded Wels's *Volkesfest*, still the biggest country fair in Austria, and would tear down the town's walls and gates to build Wels's own Ring boulevard on the model of the imperial capital, Vienna.

But just as a man like Gross would write his own job description as mayor, August Göllerich created his own portfolio as head of Wels's municipal administration.[34] What Göllerich discovered in Wels—as many other small and midsized municipalities in Cisleithania were finding out—was that the much sought-after municipal autonomy had a double edge. Liberal burghers all over Cisleithania may have greeted Schmerling's Imperial Municipalities Law as creating a state-free zone where freedom and economic progress would reinforce each other, but the law was also government on the cheap, and largely left the empire's towns to fend for themselves financially. The state had simply passed many of its administrative duties that were handled locally, such as issuing passports, administrating issues of right of residence (*Heimatrecht*) and justice, onto the cities and townships in the form of "the delegated sphere of activity" (*übertragener Wirkungskreis*).[35]

Göllerich's vision, coupled with his recognition and acquaintance with the law, led him to be naturally cautious even in this era of heady optimism. He quashed Wels's application for charter city status, arguing that more independence would mean an even greater tax burden on Wels's six thousand residents. The scope of municipal autonomy—free of direct state interference—was limited only by the imagination of city officials. Göllerich saw danger and opportunity as he watched the imagination of cities grow. Slowly and surely, Göllerich watched other cities expand from maintaining streets and sanitation into managing municipal monopolies for new services like transportation and electricity. He saw other cities take out loans for gas works and electric works. They built slaughterhouses to supply their rapidly expanding populations with meat. They managed markets in their districts, and public baths and swimming pools, and they used the profits from their enterprises to build orphanages and hospices for the aged poor.[36]

The Imperial Municipalities Law of 1861 essentially had given cities and towns free reign to venture into any form of public service that did not conflict with the prerogatives of the imperial government. The years of procedure saw Austria's cities grow, industrialize, attract large swaths of Austria-Hungary's rural population, and create a professional, permanent staff of technically and juridically trained officials to manage its affairs. Vienna had been completely reborn as a major, modern city.[37] Vienna had municipalized public transportation, created gas works, connected the city to an Alpine water supply, and was steadily expanding, not only in population but also geographically.[38] Smaller and poorer cities—cities like Göllerich's Wels—would be left behind, because nineteenth-century liberal ideals put autonomy ahead of all else. Wealth made the possibilities of freedom larger, and shared public responsibilities less onerous.

The drastic and sudden political changes of the 1860s occurred against the backdrop of long-term economic sea-changes. The social achievements of 1848, the abolition of feudal privileges and duties, allowed citizens to move to Wels to seek new opportunities for work. However, the social achievements of 1848 also deprived this old town of many traditional sources of income: the milling rights, the tolls and taxes, the rent on property and on land it collected, the services in cash and in kind from its peasants. The new social and economic basis for Austrian society had changed quickly and utterly. Wels lost its income and now had to provide the social safety net that had fallen away: the endowment of its poorhouse depended on supplements from feudal income as well.[39]

As Göllerich managed the town's administration, he was faced with questions on how an old town like Wels could find its way in the modern, increasingly capitalist world. Autonomy meant freedom to make policies and to make investments and choices that local notables and businessmen wanted. But autonomy, the "state-free" zone created under the Imperial Municipalities Laws of Stadion and Schmerling, also meant that cities and towns lived and died by their own economic resources. Wels was big enough to have a small proletarian class; to have urban poverty, and to need social welfare institutions, but whether the town could generate the income to pay for these institutions was questionable.

Towns like Wels, drowning in autonomy, still needed and still wanted an interventionist state and state administration. So when Göllerich received leave from the city of Wels to take up a mandate in Cisleithania's parliament in 1873, he joined up with the liberal party, but stayed very much his own man. His liberalism reflected the growing financial insecurity of all the small cities and towns, for which autonomy meant a dangerous balance. When Göllerich joined parliament, it was still engaged in battles over the framework of the Austrian state. The expansion of administrative services at all levels of society (local, provincial, and imperial) meant not only that bureaucracies grew—though that certainly was the case. It also meant that administrative jurisdictions, which administration provided what services, became political questions and a source of rigorous political debate. The dual-track administrative system, which featured the imperial administration sharing executive power and jurisdictions with politically controlled autonomous bureaucracies of the cities and provinces, made for a constant political struggle and thus, a forum for compromise and policy discussions. Political struggles in parliament focused on deciding what was imperial and what was provincial; what was Caesar's and what the lord mayor's. Such questions became more complicated as the role of the state in social and public welfare increased. But what was the "state" in the eyes of the average Austrian citizen? Was it the imperial government, centered in Vienna? Was it the provincial governments or would it be the cities and townships? Göllerich was a small-town statesman, but a statesman nonetheless. He, perhaps unknowingly, helped to lay down the tracks of political procedure.

.    .    .

When Göllerich looked up the administrative ladder from his city of Wels through the tangled vine of Austria's administrative system, in which government and policy making was shared between autonomous units and the imperial administration, he saw uncertainty and blurred boundaries. Barely a year into his first term as a representative, August Göllerich presented a motion in the Reichsrat that called for the government to commit itself to a "detailed investigation of the present condition of the political administration in Austria."[40] Göllerich's motion made mention of the problems he saw as a municipal administrator: the unclear boundaries between the activities of the central state and the autonomous institutions of the crownlands and the cities and towns, and the lack of norms for each branch of the "dual tracks" of state and autonomous governments.

Göllerich's motion attempted to balance the German liberals' divided loyalties—local autonomy and the central state. In a speech before parliament ten days after submitting his motion, Göllerich defended his bill. He cited "unavoidable clashes" between autonomous governments and the political administration, and he pleaded for a healthier autonomy for Austria's rural townships and municipalities. His motion states that "it appears desirable to outfit the autonomous administrative organs—namely the municipal boards and crownland executive boards with a sufficient executive authority."[41] Since Göllerich defined liberty as more than simply "freedom from the state," he was in fact pleading for more than just an increased level of autonomy or for less state interference. Rather, Göllerich believed—despite his favorable opinion of autonomy—in a large and important role for the central state and its officials. In Göllerich's view, an educated, elite bureaucracy would promote the state's capacity for modernization and economic development, and bring an enlightened civic patriotism to the Austrian peoples. Göllerich's perspective—emerging from the small developing city of Wels—had given a new twist to the enlightened absolutism of Joseph II. The state, through its administration, was still the guiding hand and the motor for progress, but now the state had the duty to intervene "exactly where a lack of education or a lack of understanding of decisions of the autonomous authorities falls short." For Göllerich and his brand of small-city liberalism, the eighteenth-century Josephinist mission of the Austrian state administration still had a powerful role to play in the economic and civic development of the modern Austrian state.

In fact, Göllerich spoke directly to this "mission" as he presented his motion before the House of Representatives on November 17, 1874. Göllerich hoped to disentangle the central state's work from that of the autonomous municipalities, so that each could more efficaciously do its own work. This would relieve a town like Wels of the ever-growing administrative and financial burden of "delegated" duties and allow the state to "fulfill its mission of instruction and enlightenment—which although it cannot be found in their office manuals, lies in the heart of every constitutionally loyal bureaucrat and friend of the people."[42]

Göllerich did not want to attack the state or chip away at the jurisdictions of the state's imperial bureaucracy. Rather, his problem with Austria's administration was twofold: the jurisdictional boundaries between the local autonomous administrations and the imperial administration were not clearly defined; and furthermore these unclarities led to an unwieldy financial burden for the autonomous townships and an unwieldy amount of work for the district prefectures. The lack of coherent norms for the cooperation of local autonomous authorities and the central state bankrupted the former and pushed the latter away from close contact with the populace. Göllerich's motion demanded that the government draft and present legislation in parliament that would "overcome the present deficiencies and in consideration of the real needs, restore the necessary order in the political administration."[43]

As Göllerich defended his motion in the provisional House of Representatives in the Währingerstrasse, he looked out over a politically divided parliament, but he felt fairly confident that his fellow liberals would see his motion through. Of the House of Representatives' 353 members, the parties supporting the government totaled between 218 and 272 votes.[44] His motion received the co-signatures of forty-five of his colleagues, mostly from the block of "constitutionally loyal magnates" (*Verfassungstreuer Grossgrundbesitz*).[45] Göllerich counted on all the government-supporting parties to finally untangle the vine of the dual-track administrative system and bring order to the relationship between autonomy and the bureaucracy. He and his fellow parliamentarians wished—as they had in 1871 during the Hohenwart government when they attempted to federalize the monarchy—to settle the relationship between the empire and its constituent parts, between the central state, the crownlands, and townships. The Viennese liberal daily, the *Neue Freie Presse*, which would comment as Göllerich's motion came to a general debate almost two years later, remarked that finding a majority to back any constitutional and administrative reform would be difficult, because "so many voices call out for a reform of the political administration, but suggest their own particular plan."[46]

Göllerich's motion to reform the administration was really a motion to reform the political architecture of the empire, and soon many voices crowded out his own. At first, though, the political ball rested in Göllerich's hands. Parliament established a twenty-four-member committee to draft an administrative-reform legislative program. The committee was stacked with men with ministerial experience like Karl Giskra and Count Karl Hohenwart, and with representatives of the various corners of the vast monarchy, from Galicia to Dalmatia and from Silesia to Görz/

Gorizia/Goriška.[47] Göllerich and Giskra were able to control the thrust of the committee's work, directing it toward strengthening small-town autonomy and also the public role of the state administration. To address his concern for the financial stability of the small city, Göllerich had to use a flanking maneuver, namely reorganizing and restructuring the local organization of the state administration. After three months of repeatedly meeting between December 1874 and February 1875, the committee produced a report and a motion for the government to embark on a reform of the administration.[48] More specifically, the committee proposed a reform of the law of May 19, 1868, which established the structure and function of the imperial administration at the local level.[49]

According to the committee's report, the problem with the 1868 Law on the Establishment of Political Administrative Offices was the amount of work and supervision for which the district prefectures were responsible. This law not only separated the political administration from Austria's legal system, but also eliminated the district offices (*Amtsbezirke*) that Alexander Bach had created and expanded. In their place, this law created district prefectures (*Bezirkshauptmannschaften*) by combining several of the former districts. As a result, the state administration took a step back from contact with the populace, leaving many of its former tasks to the municipalities and, to be sure, many of the costs as well. Moreover, by creating larger and more populous districts by combining many smaller ones, this law had, according to the committee, actually increased the amount of work for district administrators. This additional workload, coupled with the expanding role of the state in matters of education and social welfare, overburdened the small number of personnel responsible for the district's administration.

The committee's idea of administrative reform in the era of a liberal parliament, spurred on by a motion to preserve the autonomy of cities and towns, paradoxically was to create more bureaucratic offices and bureaucrats, not less. The committee proposed new branches of the central government in every local court circuit (*Gerichtsbezirk*). This solution signified a complete about-face among Giskra and the liberals from their position in 1868. Their change of heart had much to do with their newfound positions of power in parliament and in the ministries of the state. Instead of pushing the state away from the cities and local townships, Göllerich and his colleagues now wanted to draw the state back in. Although not in explicit terms, the report proposed creating over five hundred new local district suboffices, each complete with a district commissar and a modest staff of secretaries and servants.[50] Essentially, this proposal would reinstate, at least in terms of administrative divisions, the district office system of Alexander Bach and the neoabsolutist 1850s, while at the same time maintaining the district prefectures that were instituted only in 1868. And like the administration of neoabsolutism, the committee's report proposed an enormous increase of expenditure on state administration for these new offices, as well as the increased presence of the state—in the form of imperial officials—in the monarchy's towns and villages.

In November 1876, after some delay, parliament took up the committee's report on administrative reform. The debate stretched over four days, with nineteen members of parliament delivering long and detailed speeches for and against the committee's proposals. On paper it appeared that the committee's report had the necessary votes—246 members of parliament sat in the government's loose coalition in 1876—but making liberals from Bohemian towns, democrats from Vienna, Poles from Galicia, and landowners from Styria and Carniola agree to back this specific administrative reform program was nigh impossible. The committee's proposal failed by a clear majority—so much so that the vote was not even counted. The evening edition of the *Neue Freie Presse* reported that "unrest and agitation" fell upon the house after the vote. Eduard Herbst, in the meantime, was dealing with the defection of his party members from his "Club of the Left" party.[51] What should have been a clear victory for Göllerich had not slipped through his fingers—it never had a chance. What had happened?

The proposal laid out by this parliamentary committee in 1875 and its subsequent defeat point to a larger system of politics that emerged in the first seven years of the constitutional state. As Austrian citizens were elected to parliament, town councils, and provincial assemblies, they—like August Göllerich—found themselves as political advocates for their corner of the empire. And just as they brought their own political interests into the representative organs of the Austrian state, the very structures of the Austrian state shaped their imagination, channeled their ideas, and framed their political possibilities. Once given the keys to parliament, politicians took on the political battles formerly fought by Maria Theresia and Joseph II with the aristocratic estates. The old centralist/federalist divide became much more complicated and was now fought by representatives of the people. What had happened in the seven years between the proclamation of the December Constitution and this debate on administrative reform was that each parliamentary faction had latched onto its own platform of the dual-track administrative system. The strange hybrid administrative system of Stadion, Bach, and Schmerling, now found individual backers in parliament. As a result of these political conditions, the parliamentary debate quickly changed from focusing simply on the merits of Göllerich's proposals to the constitutional organization of all of Cisleithania. The debate also jump-started a discussion on the constitutional entanglements of administrative reform that would continue well into the era of the successor states.

In practical terms this meant that politicians of Austria's various factions became advocates for parts of Austria's dual administrative structure. Structures of the state had become political patrimony, patrimony that Austria's politicians would be loath to concede. While August Göllerich, the municipal official from the small city of Wels, found the local district prefects as powerful allies to municipal autonomy, Ferdinand Kronawetter, a Viennese democrat, defended the rights of the autonomous chartered cities. Kronawetter was a gifted speaker and vigorously defended municipal autonomy from the growing specter of bureaucratic interference. Kronawetter—like August Göllerich—had once been a municipal official.[52] But the criticism that he levied at the committee's proposals demonstrated—in distinction to Göllerich—Kronawetter's complete distrust of the imperial administration. He saw the bureaucracy as an army of drones who follow orders and not the law: "So long as a bureaucrat, who is dependent on the government, is called to execute the laws, [the laws] will be forever and always administered according to administrative instructions instead of according to the laws themselves."[53] For Kronawetter, the institutions of self-government were the sole line of defense against a government that would operate in its own interests outside the law. In this perspective, municipal autonomy became the guarantee of constitutional government in which the people's representatives make laws "which are implemented by their own institutions, that is, through the citizens themselves and not through bureaucratic institutions."[54] Kronawetter thus saw municipal autonomy as the bedrock for building a state based on the rule of law because the laws would be enforced by the citizens themselves. He rejected the committee's proposals on the grounds that it would give this authority to enforce laws back to the administration.

Part of the distinction between August Göllerich and Ferdinand Kronawetter, both municipal officials and parliamentarians, lay ultimately in their common municipal background. Kronawetter's Vienna had over seven hundred thousand inhabitants in 1876 and was municipally more than capable of taking on all the roles of state with which its status as a charter city and imperial residence of the Habsburgs had endowed it.[55] Meanwhile, Göllerich's small city of Wels could claim little more than seven thousand residents and would have had a much harder time finding the necessary officials with the proper training to conduct the business of state, or, for that matter, the necessary funds to pay them. Whether municipal autonomy was feasible and affordable for one's own city divided liberals not only along ideological lines but also along geographical ones. Kronawetter certainly did not wish his beloved city of Vienna to lose any of its authority to the central state; while Göllerich wanted to save Wels by giving it much less to do. For *Wiener* like Kronawetter, preserving Vienna's independence from the state was a path to wealth and prosperity. No proposals called for a flexible system that would have catered to the expanded abilities of large cities like Vienna and still come to the aid of a town like Wels that could only afford a much humbler administrative role.

There was little time for a radical like Kronawetter to reach any agreement with Göllerich and the liberals on these matters of municipal size and capability. Almost immediately as the debate began, conservative representatives launched themselves into it. And they were not the only ones. Kronawetter's position against the expansion of the state administration found allies among the Polish Club from Galicia, clerical conservatives, and even from liberals who wanted a more rigid, less local centralism.

The Göllerich proposals were assailed first by a fellow liberal, Baron Ludwig von Zschock, a member of the Progressive Party from Styria. Zschock, whose politics placed him in the center-left of the political spectrum, would have seemed a natural ally for the proposals of Göllerich and his fellow liberals. But Zschock complained that autonomy was a wrecked system, dominated by "village tyrants," who stepped into local positions of power once Bach's hussars had been forced to pack up and leave town. Zschock, despite his liberal credentials, believed that matters of state should be left in the hands of a "qualified, appointed, paid, and responsible official, who would be responsible to the district" for legislative matters and "to the government for the strict execution of the laws."[56] Such independent and qualified bureaucrats would be free from local pressures and the political agendas of local politicians who contaminate the work of self-government. Zschock wanted expertise and objectivity at the local level, not elected officials who could wield the state's authority as their own.

With liberals divided, the conservatives attacked the proposal on the grounds of protecting the autonomy of the crownlands. Michael Hermann, a delegate from Styria, began the conservatives' criticism, by calling Göllerich's proposal nothing more than an increase in the number of bureaucrats.[57] After this, the conservatives began a more programmatic attack. The Clerical Party, the Polish Club, and agrarian magnates emerged as staunch defenders of the autonomous crownlands in the administrative system.

The main force of the conservative front was led by Count Karl Siegmund von Hohenwart, the former prime minister and governor of several crownlands. Hohenwart defended the traditional prerogatives of the autonomous crownlands in the face of the committee's proposals, which he said would only mean more bureaucrats, more paperwork, more mistakes, more useless supervision, interoffice conflict, and wastage of public resources.[58] Hohenwart castigated the liberals for throwing themselves behind the power of the central state while throwing overboard their tradition of protecting "autonomy" and political freedom. Hohenwart asked how it could happen that the German liberals, who pressed so hard for municipal autonomy and who "campaigned so sharply against the propensity [of the state] to overrule [Vielregiererei], against the constant paternalism of the state toward the free municipality, and so decisively fought for the liberation of the people from their chains," could now, in parliament, deny their heritage and find the answer to all society's problems in "a bureaucratic organism that will take over everything and strangle the autonomous activity of the populace?"[59] Hohenwart then argued that the division of jurisdictions between the imperial parliament and the crownland diets meant that parliament could not enact the committee's proposals. He reasoned that any legislation that affected the autonomous administrations, be it of the crownlands or the townships, fell under the legislative jurisdiction of the individual diets.[60] In other words, he claimed that Göllerich's proposal and the Reichsrat's discussion of it was unconstitutional.

Hohenwart found support among the Poles who backed Hohenwart's style of crownland autonomy, because they were particularly keen to maintain the rights of the crownlands as a matter of principle.[61] The leader of the Polish Club, Kazimierz Grocholski, admitted that reforms of the system were needed, but they should be discussed within the individual crownlands themselves.[62] Moreover, Grocholski made an argument that echoed a century worth of tension between the Habsburg crown and the provinces: the problem of uniformity. The problem with any major administrative reform would be its application in the seventeen different and varied crownlands. Thus, in addition to the jurisdiction issue, in which Hohenwart and the Polish representatives called into question the legality of any empire-wide legislation on administrative reform, Grocholski also questioned the efficacy of such legislation.[63] Grocholski's compatriot and fellow member of the Polish Club, Julian Ritter von Dunajewski, echoed this sentiment when he, in making the closing arguments for the opponents of the committee's proposals, stated that parliament should "not disregard the needs of the individual crownlands," nor should it force the crownlands to give up their individuality in order to adapt to a system of uniformity.[64] Here, Hohenwart and the Poles could come together, not only on the legal side of the argument (i.e., the idea that any intervention of the Reichsrat into municipal autonomy was unconstitutional), but also in defense of the heterogeneity of the *Reich*, or more specifically, the heterogeneity of the crownlands.[65]

The result of the proposals and the surrounding debate was a stalemate. Parliament rejected the bill on November 24, 1876. As the *Neue Freie Presse* commented on the five sessions, spanning two weeks, which had been taken up with the reform bill, "The debate had not even a minimal result—it had no result at all."[66] The bill was seemingly an afterthought. In the debate, the reform bill was forgotten and left by the wayside: parliamentary discussion had entered the plane of constitutional politics and the nature of parliamentary authority.

During this debate it became clear that the dual-track administrative system, which provided the very structures of the Cisleithanian state, had become politicized. Clericals and conservatives had allied with the Polish parties to champion the autonomy of the crownlands. German liberals had fragmented: they were split between small and large city autonomy, the authority of the central state and the imperial parliament. When the Czech national parties returned from their boycott of parliament in the 1880s, crownland autonomy would find new parliamentary allies.

Administrative reform had become anchored in a matrix of larger constitutional issues that quickly overshadowed the importance of reform. The largest issue was the question of the empire's organization: the age-old question of how to properly organize such a vast and disparate empire. "Administrative reform" in November 1876 quickly became a channel to the larger questions of centralism and federalism. As we know, the liberals' newfound allegiance to the central state did not find success in this reform bill, but an equally large issue here was the independence of the administration. Attempts by parliament to reform the administration were caught up in the political debates on the larger structures of the Austrian state. If liberals tried to make the state their own by taking control of the administration and molding it to fit their ideas of parliamentary and municipal autonomy, conservatives of all stripes would block them in defense of crownland autonomy. The fact that the arena of politics had been built over twenty years of compromise and debate meant that all factions in Austria had something to lose when the structures or system changed. As a result, the imperial administration, which was a key component in the middle of these debates, surprisingly would achieve a wide freedom for movement and so have the most opportunities for expansion and growth. This part of Austria's living constitution was established in parliament, in these days of stalemate over administrative reform, in mid-November 1876.

The heterogeneity of the state and the fact that political parties identified with aspects of the dual-track administrative hierarchy created a stalemate that empowered the persistence of an independent, politically active, and technocratic bureaucracy. Stalemate meant that if the parties could not agree how to restructure the administration and adapt it to a constitutional system, they tacitly agreed to keep the bureaucracy as they inherited it from the absolutist past. But, as we will see in the next section, the fact that this administration was inherited did not mean that it would be unchanging. As the divided parliament laid down a system of political culture that split over administrative questions but could not find solutions to them, it essentially created a fertile ground for the administration to grow and flourish.

### Procedures and Growth: Administrative Resurgence After 1867

The Austrian parliament, dominated in the 1870s by liberals from German-speaking regions and cities, failed to impose a new administrative structure on the state because of its own national political divisions. The larger point at stake in the debates surrounding Göllerich's proposals for administrative reform was the relationship of the imperial bureaucracy to the parliament. Here too the parliament failed to impose a political dependence on the imperial administration by forcing it into a subservient relationship to parliamentary power. Although the debate came to nothing, the Austrian state continued to evolve. The path the state took after 1876 allowed the imperial administration to become a political entity in its own right.

The imperial administration had been an independent force since Bach's reforms. Political life since the 1860s had made it into a political entity in its own right. Yet, despite its independence and its ability to pursue its own political interests, the role for it that Stadion conceived and which was implemented over the next thirty years made it unquestionably interdependent with the new, emerging representative institutions. The first decade of Cisleithanian Austria had established the rules of Austrian politics and erected the arenas where political battles would be fought. This process began in the 1870s under the liberal parliament and would continue in the 1880s, after the liberals were pushed into opposition. In many ways, this settling of the "rules" of politics meant that the emperor, who in 1879 was nearly fifty years old and had been on the throne for over thirty years, became less involved in politics. But as Francis Joseph gave the wheel to his confidantes in domestic politics, the liberal coalition ran aground and collided with the emperor's foreign policy. In that same year, 1879, the liberal firebrand Eduard Herbst led a group of 112 liberals in a vote against the treaty that certified Austria-Hungary's occupation of Bosnia. They walked out on the governmental coalition as well. While Emperor Francis Joseph could allow the liberals the leeway to bicker about domestic matters, he would not tolerate this criticism of his foreign policy. Determined not to allow the liberals back into government, Francis Joseph appointed his childhood friend and confidante, Count Eduard Taaffe, prime minister and put him in charge of building a new government after new elections. Thus the 1870s ended with the German liberals back in opposition.

Taaffe formed a conservative coalition, built with members of the Polish Club, Hohenwart's clerical conservatives, and the Old Czechs, whom Taaffe had persuaded to end their long boycott of the imperial parliament. This loose coalition, known as the "Iron Ring," would control Austria's parliament and government for the next fourteen years.[67] Both Taaffe and the emperor saw the role of prime minister, and the role of cabinet minister, as that of an impartial imperial official.[68] Taaffe formed a government with other civil servants, as well as with politicians with past administrative careers like Karl von Stremayr. Czech and Polish national politicians received minister positions without portfolio. Under Taaffe, the precedent for Austria's ministries to be hybrid ministries with bureaucrats taking the post of prime minister and, often, the specialist portfolios like minister of the interior or minister of finance, became a firmer aspect of Austria's living constitution.

Taaffe and his parliamentary coalition sailed the ship of state on a more or less straight course, refusing to reengage in debates over the constitutional and administrative structures of the state other than by slowly expanding the suffrage. However, even though Taaffe did not take up any sort of administrative reform, the bureaucracy continued to evolve under him. How could it not? The period of Taaffe's government, which stayed in power from 1879 to 1893, witnessed major changes within Austria's political landscape and, even more than this, changes in the role and size of the Austrian state.[69] Procedures and precedents—the political culture of the way things get done—had their own way of shaping the nature of the game played in the arena of politics. In the 1880s the political ground quieted enough to let procedure take over. The state could quietly and slowly build, develop, and therefore—when viewed over the span of years—fundamentally change, as the imperial administration constructed its own norms, as well as its infrastructure, in order to participate in Austrian politics on its own, nonnational terms.

After the direct political struggles over the administration ended in the 1880s, tensions and compromises switched from debates over the relationship of the state and the public to the bureaucracy to the ways in which policy was made and work was done: the procedures of governing, now shared by representatives of the people and imperial administration. Just as Taaffe's government was a hybrid of technocrats and politicians, the administration took on a hybrid role itself, characterized by expert policy makers and political interventions. We will discuss the politics further in the next chapter, but for now, we will concentrate on the foundations of the administration for playing these two roles.

The 1880s would see the administration grow and its relationship to the state and its representative bodies transform into an independent political body of its own. How this happened was a process that paralleled the growth and expansion of the Austrian state itself. Democratic development has a paradoxical habit of making the role of the administration larger, not smaller. As the role of the state expanded, the state built new bureaus, expanded its facilities, and increased the number of bureaucrats to do its work.

We can follow several larger trends in this period that built the procedures—the living constitution—of the Austrian half of the empire. The first trend was growth of the bureaucratic role in Austrian society coupled with the expansion of the administration itself. To a large extent this growth paralleled the emergence of constitutional government and political participation. Municipal councils, school boards, provincial assemblies, district assemblies, the imperial parliament, and the imperial and administrative courts established a network of public places that would attend to policy making and governance alongside the bureaucratic apparatus. As we shall see, the interactions between the administrative apparatus and political institutions increased the size and the scope of the administration, just as they increased the interactions between it and the representatives of the people. As legislatures passed new laws, regulations, and spending programs to improve the working and living conditions of Austria's citizens, to build Austria's economic infrastructure, or to promote economic growth, the Austrian administration was given more to regulate, to research, and to do. This brings us to the second trend: the growing apprehension of the expanding state within the administration itself. As the role of the Austrian state exploded in the 1880s, the high-ranking policy makers in Austria's government worried that the tasks of administration outpaced the ability of the state to hire, train, and pay for officials to do the work. Political participation demanded a bigger state, a different type of state, and pushed the limits of a rational administration.

### Administrative Optimism: Growth and State Building in Cisleithania

The 1880s were a time of expansion. The years of the Taaffe ministry witnessed a broadening of services at the provincial and local levels. The central and crownland authorities built libraries, hired archivists, and collected their procedures to standardize and regiment the increasing amount of work that needed to be done. Moreover the records from the various provincial governors' offices to the minister of the interior show us the burdens of an expanding administration. The governors sent missives requesting permission to hire new people and to rent more space in the cities and towns for their own offices or for the district captaincies under them.

The records of provincial expansion—those that still exist—are not especially numerous, but they do indicate that much attention was paid to the expansion of the administration's infrastructure in the 1870s and 1880s.[70] The correspondence between the minister of the interior and the

Bohemian governor's office, for instance, indicates that many of the local district offices, the accompanying district courts, the tax offices, and the tax adjustors had grown, and therefore outgrown the spaces that the provincial governments had rented for them since district offices had been set up under Stadion and Bach in the 1840s and 1850s. The growth of the state, its presence in the countryside in municipalities whose names were (in the official German of the central ministries) Smichov, Kolin, Leitomischl, Pilgram, Strakanitz, or Deutsch Brod, required new spaces for their growing offices, officials, papers, compilations of ordinances and decrees. In 1881, for instance, the governor sought final financial approval from the minister of the interior, the Ministry of Justice, and the Ministry of Finance for the district prefecture to move its offices in Smichov to larger quarters. The district prefecture had been renting its building from the town of Smichov since 1875, but after 1881 had been experiencing an "acute lack of space."[71] The district prefect, by negotiating with the tax offices and the local landlords had managed to find a bigger space that would cost the Ministry of the Interior the same outlay in rent; but this was unusual. Governors often wrote in to the Ministry of the Interior asking for approval for new quarters which ultimately would require additional state expenditures. In Trieste, for instance, the governor had proposed public buildings that would combine tax offices, courts, police, the local Finance Ministry offices, as well a building by the Ministry of Trade which would house all the local offices of the imperial-royal marine authorities, including the harbor authority, post and telegraph authority, and finally an education building. The original sum for these three buildings was calculated at 1,479,367 gulden in 1873—a cost that was revised upward in the 1880s.[72]

State building in the years of procedure was not metaphorical. In the beginning of the 1880s the state undertook the construction of a new building in Kolin to house the local offices of the "princely authorities," a common term for the state administration. Kolin had no suitable space to house both the district prefecture and the local tax offices, so the finance minister was forced to assent to build a new building for them.[73] The city of Pardubitz/Pardubice in Bohemia likewise offered to build a new building in the center of town to house all the state local administrative offices. The district officials had been setting up shop in rented quarters in the local Baron's castle. While the district official noted that they had enough light and space, the hike up to the castle's second floor, two kilometers from the train station and sixty-six steps in the castle itself, made the state's officials remote.[74] The writer Franz Kafka, in his novel *The Castle*, might have presented the bureaucracy as supernaturally kept from the public's view in the keep on the hill, but these officials wanted to be in the center of town, among the populace and not housed in the old lord's quarters—such an image reminded everyone of the old days of patrimonial administration. New buildings in central locations were a sign of the times. The state was setting up permanent residence on high street.

The question of space and place, summed up in the Austrian bureaucratic idiom *Lokalität*, or locality, filled the files of Taaffe's Ministry of the Interior in the 1880s. *Lokalität* not only concerned where to house the civil servants but, increasingly, their files. The governor's office in Prague reported in 1885 that it was having difficulty procuring a suitable *Lokalität* for the purposes of maintaining their archive. Not only was the archive not housed in a place convenient to the province's officials and clerks, but it was becoming a more necessary part of everyday work. The Bohemian archivist reported that the number of initiated researches had increased from 258 to 683 in one year. By 1886, the archive was initiating research in 2,929 volumes or cartons of documents.[75] The archive and library of the Ministry of the Interior was likewise keeping track of a steady increase in the number of its consultations. The archivist, Emil Maczak von Ottenburg, sent a report to the Ministry of the Interior which detailed the volumes from the library that were being consulted by ministry officials. The top three categories were "legislation," "legal and political sciences," and "parliamentaria."[76] The library was growing too. The librarian reported that their collections had reached 50,529 volumes by the end of 1883. They were buying periodicals on political economy, Germany's administration, Hungarian law, Prussian constitutional law, statistics, as well as the official governmental publications on Cisleithania. They kept Mayrhofer's indispensable *Handbook for the Political Administrative Services*,[77] a compendium of administrative and constitutional law. Next to this, they collected the party newspapers of Austria's various political parties. Bureaucrats were mustering expert knowledge to continue on as Austria's policy makers, even after elected officials took their places in the governmental system. The administration was recasting itself in the age of politics. It was becoming a political institution in its own right and retooling itself to play in Austria's arena of participatory politics. For this knowledge of politics, books on "parliamentaria" were essential reading and reference material.

### Growth, Independence, and Nationality Politics

Austria's civil servants had not been displaced by Austria's new co-horts of elected majors, city councilmen, and crownland board members. Rather, public service in Austria had added new dimensions to Austria's living constitution as elected officials stood by imperial bureaucrats in public ceremonies, church services, Corpus Christi processions, and in the council halls and political board rooms. In fact, ministerial officials and imperial governors put particular emphasis on the bureaucracy's public role in making their appointments and promotions. Imperial officials had to exude competence, virility, and objectivity—even as they were partisans for a public good that was defined differently than by their political colleagues and political opponents.

The official's carefully cultivated image of strength would persist well after the end of the monarchy. In the iconic novel *Radetzky March*, Joseph Roth captured the wide-ranging political importance of the local district prefect with his depiction of Franz von Trotta, the father of the novel's main character, a young military cadet. This district prefect, stationed in Austrian Silesia, "represented no one less than His Majesty the emperor." In one particular scene, the military band begins to play a Sunday afternoon concert in the main square, where the prefect's apartments are located. The official and his son step out on to the balcony and the son, Carl Joseph, takes in the concert and "felt almost related to the Habsburgs, whose power his father represented and defended, and for whom he would one day go out himself, to fight and to die." Roth's district prefect not only legally and administratively represents the crown in the Austrian countryside, but in this case he also serves as a corporeal metaphor. Roth describes District Prefect von Trotta as speaking "nasal Austrian of upper officialdom," in which "his nose and mouth seemed more like wind instruments than facial features." He even wore the black sideburns in emulation of the venerable Emperor Francis Joseph—these too were part of his official uniform, an "emblem of his service to Franz Joseph I and a proof of his belief in a dynastic monarchy." Roth depicts District Prefect von Trotta as a living metonymy, standing in for the emperor himself. In this new era of expanding political presentation, the prefect had to play a public role as the face of the state. In the case of von Trotta—and many real servants—the state wore the emperor's sideburns.[78]

The role of the local imperial official as the embodiment of the greater state should not be underestimated. Moreover, this embodiment was not the unintended consequence of his ceremonial role. Less literary were politician and scholar Josef Redlich's reminiscences of his childhood and upbringing in Göding/Hodonín, Moravia, on the border with Slovakian Hungary. Redlich devotes more than a page and a half of a memoir to the old district prefect, Karl Kandler, who lived in his town and who "with calm and dignity attended to his truly paternal post as district prefect." Redlich describes the prefect as a distinguished man, "early sixties, short, but with a well-cultivated figure." He enjoyed the esteem of everyone, from the local peasants to the townsmen, for whom he represented the "dutiful and just guardian of the police and state authority in old Austria." Redlich remembers seeing the prefect receive the emperor and empress at Göding train station. What struck him about the occasion was not the pageantry of the imperial house arriving in the small border town, but the "simple dignity, which the old man showed in his natural comportment." Redlich writes, almost fifty years after the original event, that this image of the simple, dignified district official remained in his mind when he reflected on "our excellent official of the domestic administration."[79] The local official represented the emperor in Roth's *Radetzky March* and, for Redlich, who looked back on his homeland in the late 1920s as it descended into political turmoil, the district official embodied the Austrian state and the age of security that now seemed lost forever.

The image of the security and paternalism of the Austrian state, embodied by the local official, was carefully cultivated. It is therefore no wonder that Roth and Redlich reveal more than just a twinge of nostalgia in their literary and memoiristic work. The administration often was thrown into local and tangled political conflict. Its survival depended on the cultivation of its image, especially one of benevolent competence. This was yet another aspect of the years of procedure. Bureaucratic appointments became questions of both political acceptability and administrative acumen. Whether local officials were up to the task of serving in politically and nationally divided places proved to be a great concern to the governors stationed in the provinces and the minister of the interior in Vienna. The governors and ministerial bureaucrats took care to emphasize these qualities when they made appointments to local posts and district prefectures.

Moreover, the administration and administrative appointments had become political. In the early days of the Taaffe ministry, government enacted the Stremayr Language Ordinances, which elevated the Czech language to official status alongside German in Bohemia and Moravia.[80] This was a decree that was aimed first and foremost at the language spoken by the bureaucracy. What now mattered was the language in which a citizen initiated any administrative or legal proceedings.[81] Regarding the administration's language of communication with local government, the state administration had to communicate with the individual cities and towns in whichever language they conducted business. Therefore, the central government would now communicate with and supervise Czech-speaking villages and towns in the Czech language. Finally, all official notices had to be disseminated in both Czech and German. In short, the work of the central authorities in Bohemia and Moravia, at least regarding all contact with the populace and autonomous government, would be bilingual.

The Stremayr Language Ordinances produced a major political battle between German and Czech national politicians. Czech nationalists bristled that their mother tongue clearly held a subordinate position to German in the crownlands' administrations, despite the fact that Czech was spoken by a majority of the population in Bohemia and Moravia. German liberals emphasized the cultural superiority of the German language over the Czech language, and maintained that official communication with the populace, as well as internal communication within governmental offices, should be in German.[82] But these nationalist politics, while certainly important, had limited influence on the way the administration staffed its district offices. The Stremayr Language Ordinances did not interfere with the promotion of bureaucrats as district prefects—at least in mixed or Czech-speaking where areas they would have to know both languages. Given our picture of the language question in Bohemia and the prevalence political histories have given to nationality problems, the limited influence of the ordinances should be even more surprising.[83] But, at least in the 1880s, the governor's office in Bohemia found no shortage of bilingual bureaucrats to serve as district prefects. For all the German-liberal handwringing, the Stremayr ordinances did not witness a quick change in the upper ranks of the administration, even though high-ranking civil servants needed to establish their ability to speak Czech. This is because a large number of imperial civil servants in the Bohemian lands spoke Czech as a matter of course.

Rather, when appointing politically important officials, like the district prefects, nationality politics played an insignificant role in comparison to the qualities necessary to represent the empire: the display of calm authority, competence, and the command of public respect. A window into the dynamic of upper-level appointments after Stremayr comes from 1883.[84] In the beginning of that year, the Bohemian governor had to manage the sudden and unexpected death of two high provincial officials. *Titular Statthaltereirat* Julius Czerwenka, who held the important post as the supervisory district prefect in Pilsen/Plzeň, died on March 1. His colleague, *Statthaltereirat* Albans Spengler, who was stationed in the governor's office in Prague as the head of the military-affairs department, died on February 20. As the governor in Bohemia, Alfred Freiherr von Kraus, selected replacements for these two high-ranking officials, he unleashed a veritable domino effect of appointments that would stretch over the course of three months and encompass seven high-ranking positions and the personnel files of nearly thirty civil servants. In the process, the surviving reports and requests for approval that Kraus sent to the Ministry of the Interior give us a rather clear perspective into the higher rungs of the provincial bureaucratic ladder after 1880, when new questions arose over the infiltration of national politics into Austria's growing public administration.

The years of procedure did establish the norm and ideal, however, that bureaucrats had to be on display, participating in the staging of Austrian administration. District prefects were political actors in every sense of the word. Successful applicants for district prefectures, like Emil Janda, whom Kraus appointed as supervisory prefect in the large industrial city of Pilsen/Plzeň, displayed "proven discretion," and "tact"; he had also demonstrated a record of hard work and success in his previous post. In his work, Janda serves "with especial loyalty and resilience, he possesses good qualities, a capacious knowledge of law and management, his political standing is in every way correct, his manner serious . . . and approachable." Finally, Kraus remarked that Janda "enjoys the reputation" of a strictly "proper, unpartisan official" whom the people in the important but contentiously political city of Pilsen/Plzeň will trust.[85] Taaffe would in turn repeat such language to the emperor.[86] As these reports signify, it was important for the district prefect to cut a good figure in public and represent the energy, impartiality, and calm decisiveness of the state. There is no mention of Janda's language capabilities, largely because it is a matter of course that he—like every bureaucrat who has been selected for the prominent positions—can speak Czech. Bilingualism was not limited to the best and the brightest among Austria's imperial administration—it was not a given, but it certainly was not the determining factor either. Far more importantly, the governor was searching for people to "represent" the state in the provinces—much as

Count Wilhelm Haugwitz and Maria Theresia had created local offices 125 years before to represent the crown.

The years of procedure were filled with many such strings of appointments. The pyramidal structure of Austria's imperial administration, whether in the provinces or in the ministries of Vienna, meant that the vacating of positions at the top of the pyramid entailed months of personnel shuffling, promotions, and parallel transfers. The Bohemian case, of course, tells us more than the relative undramatic effects of the Stremayr Language Ordinances in the imperial civil service—especially in the political administration. It is, however, worthwhile to reiterate this aspect, because the Stremayr ordinances did provide a new arrow in the governor's quiver to promote his chosen candidates over others. While the command that officials stationed in Bohemian and Moravian mixed districts had to speak both German *and* Czech unleashed a political backlash in the provincial diets and in the Austrian parliament, such provisions were often superfluous in the administration itself. Moreover, these newly promoted officials did not replace an older, more experienced, "German" bureaucracy; rather they were senior themselves, and often multilingual, due to family background and the lure of promotion. This was, after all, traditionally a multilingual monarchy. Given the normal course of promotion for provincial officials, these men would have been the emperor's age—born in the 1830s and entering their early fifties or even sixties. Within this string of appointments, Kraus had promoted Guido Törply to a *Statthaltereirat* position in his office in Prague. Törply was over sixty and had begun his career in the civil service in 1843! The youngest of Kraus's string of appointments was Paul Appeltauer, who was forty-five years old and began his career in the civil service in 1859. He was fluent in Czech and German, "in word and script," as the phrase went in Austrian bureaucratese. The other civil servants whom Kraus appointed in the early months of 1883, were born in the 1820s and 1830s, and were likewise fluent. Rare were those civil servants available for promotion who "were not completely fluent." The governor would put such men in jobs in the smaller, German-speaking districts.[87] Bilingualism had been the practical order of the day in the provincial civil service since the days of Metternich. And while it was not rare, it was now explicitly necessary for the best and most prominent positions.

The Stremayr ordinances not only provided an extra arrow in the governor's quiver in making appointments, but could also be wielded by the local populace to oust unpopular district prefects. In October 1893, for instance, representatives of Czech parties questioned the government with an official interpellation about the district prefect in Mies/Stříbro. The interpellation claimed that the district prefect in this mixed-language district near Pilsen/Plzeň showed favoritism to German speakers, was not fluent in Czech, and therefore could not associate directly with Czech speakers in the district.[88] When the Bohemian governor's office looked into the matter, however, it discovered that this was an attempt to oust an official on political grounds, an action based on "nationalist fiction rather than in the legal rights of the Bohemian population."[89] The district prefect was, in fact, a Czech speaker, but nationalist agitation in the area had inflamed the population against the government. They took it out on the prefect, with the legal tools at their disposal.

Bilingualism, therefore was a political issue for national politics; it was not an issue for a bureaucracy that depended on its officials to be linguists as a matter of course. It therefore represented part of the larger public comportment and status of the local prefect, who had to display an admirable work ethic, knowledge of the law, and experience leading departments or smaller districts. Such qualities helped them to cut the best possible figure in their prefectures. The district prefectures themselves had an unofficial hierarchy. Smaller and more rural districts, which lacked factories or industry and thus socialist agitation, provided good training grounds for promising civil servants. The lucky officials whom governor Kraus selected for promotion showed a variety of qualities that differentiated them from the college-educated civil servants who would remain forever in the middle ranks as commissars and lower officials in the district offices. Successful climbers displayed energy and virility—more than once Kraus wrote that more senior bureaucrats should be passed over for their "sickliness" or for being too old and tired to lead in important posts.

Moreover, the official emphasis on the qualities of energy and virility could have negative effects for bureaucrats who (for whatever reason) could not display them. In August 1883 Kraus forced District Prefect Anton Wenzel in Rumburg/Rumburk into retirement because of his "advanced age" (he was sixty), and the fact that he was "not at all possessing the intellectual gifts and the energy" that was needed in greater and greater quantities for the civil service. Wenzel, even in such an "unexposed post," the relatively quiet district prefecture of Rumburg in northwest Bohemia, was no longer "up to the task."[90] Kraus, 120 years after Joseph II sent his *Rêveries* to Maria Theresia, followed in Joseph's footsteps by dismissing officials who were no longer able to contribute. At least in the nineteenth century Wenzel would be able to count on a significant pension.

The years of procedure therefore saw an intensification of the administration's old representative function, but now with the onset of participatory politics. As the conservative government under Taaffe sought to bring other political groups into government, it had to open up the administration to Austrians who did not come from the core German-speaking towns and cities. The Taaffe government aimed at long-term changes in the character of the administration. It granted Czech speakers the access to higher education and eventually, to the upper ranks of the state administration. With the foundation of a new Czech language university in Prague in 1882, there was an influx of Czech-speaking technical officials into the Austrian civil service, and an increase in the percentage of Czech speakers in public service in general (including the autonomous administration) between 1880 and 1900.[91] Friedrich F. G. Kleinwaechter could reminisce in his 1947 memoir, *Der fröhliche Präsidialist* (The Happy Cabinet Official), of serving alongside Czechs in the bureaus of the Ministry of Finance before the First World War. One in particular, Dr. Richard Stretti—despite having an Italian name—was a convinced Czech nationalist. The German Kleinwaechter, however, only had good things to say about him. Stretti, always "helped me in the most amicable way. . . . The national antagonism, which in the Austria of those days was bitter, did not bother our relations in the slightest."[92] On the eve of the First World War, Czechs like Stretti could advance as high as the central ministries, and they too were judged on their competence, manliness, and energy. Such political casting helped the administration to navigate the changing and nationalizing political landscape of the late imperial monarchy.

For Redlich, for Roth, and for the governors who promoted them, the local official was increasingly important in his representative function. Not only were they to speak the local language, they were there to embody the qualities of the central state and to deal evenhandedly with local politics by using a "strong and stern hand" with tact, cautiousness, and "a solid character," which would be visible beacon of the state in the localities that stretched across the empire. And so, while the traditional qualities of "representing the crown" still remained since the days of Haugwitz, some major facets of this representation had evolved. Roth's district prefect may have worn Francis Joseph's sideburns, but his superiors expected him to embody more than just the emperor and to push the local paperwork. Rather, the district prefect also had to represent the more abstract qualities of the Austrian state: its multinationalism, objectivity, and a "political correctness" that was clearly visible and would earn the trust of the larger populace.[93] Such skills were necessary in a new world with extensive local political participation, socialist agitation, and the "crisis management" situations that would arise in a world of expanding political activity. But increasingly, the ministries and provincial governors feared that even the best bureaucrats would not be up to the task of keeping pace with the growing state.

### Growing Apprehension

The two and a half decades following the promulgation of the December Constitution in 1867 saw the expansion of the Austrian state in ways that the state administration never envisioned. Instead of sloughing responsibility for economic and infrastructure development onto autonomous bodies and elected councils, it was these elected institutions that called the state back into their lands, their towns, their districts. Elected representatives who sat on town councils, crownland executive boards, and in the parliament hoped to preserve their own autonomy and make their basis of power stronger and more vibrant, but they could only do so with the help of the central state, the imperial apparatus. They needed state funds to help them cover their building and infrastructure expenses.[94] The administration responded with its time and resources as the government responded with special budget items and subventions.

Growth in all forms of public life grounded the years of procedure. Growth itself became a force and ideology, which gathered momentum—and drew the state apparatus into its current. Cities built new institutions and services; provincial assemblies created new social insurance; local district councils built new hospitals and hospice homes. Rail service expanded, the state and the provinces combined forces and resources to jointly finance public works. More bridges, roads, and hospitals meant more oversight, supervision, and paperwork. This additional workload put pressure on the administration, which tried to hold the line on government expenditures. Nonetheless, we can see traces of new hirings as the state needed new bridge inspectors, engineers, doctors, veterinarians, and sanitation inspectors. We also find a renewed vision of the state's penetration into the provinces. State sciences had graduated from the fiscalism of cameralism to a more careful promotion of local culture, of business contacts, and of economic and communication infrastructure. The state invested in the monarchy's future, through educational institutions and new administrative offices.[95] In many places it invested heavily. It established new district offices in central towns and moved out of the castle on a hill outside of town into a new building on high street. We cannot know exactly how many people served in the imperial Austrian civil service, from its central ministries to its district prefectures, because the bureaucracy did not wish to be counted. The higher-ups in the ministries knew that the expense brought by the size of the administration would be a sensitive issue in Austria's parliament, so not only did they suppress any information on their numbers, but they refused to be counted in the first place. The first actual "census" of the administration would wait until 1910.[96]

Growth of the public sphere, of Austria's political life, brought more than economic development and political expansion. Within the high ceilings of Austria's imperial buildings, it brought fear and apprehension. Austria's ministers, its *Sektionschefs*, and especially the governors feared that the state had grown so much and had become so complicated, that it had expanded beyond the administration's ability to run it. One of the true ironies of the monarchy's political development was that representative government came out of the financial crises of the 1850s: the central state intended autonomous municipalities, crownlands, and the parliament to create institutions and manage funds that shared the financial burden of administering the state. This should have made government cheaper and balanced the perennially strained finances of the monarchy, but the social welfare and infrastructure building projects that came out of public involvement in government since the 1860s had put renewed pressure on the budget. Between 1870 and 1889 the Ministry of the Interior's budget increased from 13,728,078 gulden to 19,361,281 gulden. The increase in the Ministry of the Interior's budget—47 percent in twenty years[97]—was still lower in percentage than the budget as a whole, which increased by roughly 66 percent over the same period. In these twenty years the ministry's budget increased in part due to a major pay raise for imperial civil servants in 1873, but this was only a fraction of the increased costs.[98]

The differences between the 1870 and 1889 budgets were not even the building and infrastructure allocations to the various crownland authorities. Those allocations had held the line rather firmly in the preceding twenty years. Rather it was special line-item budget earmarks for projects in each of the lands that caused the increase in the Ministry of the Interior's budget. The 1889 budget earmarked funds for bridges and roads, river regulation, canals, and new public buildings that pushed beyond the Finance Ministry's attempts to keep budget items for each of the crownlands constant. By injecting roads and building projects into the provinces during the years of procedure, the imperial Austrian government kept on good terms with the autonomous crownlands and municipalities. These funded projects created good relationships with politicians who were seen as bringing development to their constituencies, but they also required massive state involvement. This level of involvement worried the administrative elites in the provinces, who saw the needs of supervision expanding beyond the personnel that was available.

By the end of the 1880s, governors wrote to the Ministry of the Interior requesting the creation of new districts and the hiring of more personnel. Moreover, the governors did not want copyists and clerks; they needed new university-educated policy officials. The governor in Prague complained that his staff had been working in a "permanently" pathological situation. The overwork, the growing case backlogs, had been created by an ever "increasing workload calamity." The future looked grim. Governor Kraus predicted that these conditions would eventually endanger the mission of the state if more civil servants were not quickly hired.[99] Kraus was not alone. Less-developed crownlands suffered from similar personnel shortages and unsustainable working conditions as did Bohemia. In Dalmatia, not only did the amount of work increase since the district prefectures were instituted in 1868, but the governor was having a hard time keeping his district prefects healthy. Malaria combined with exhaustion and overwork decimated the governor's staff and threatened to cripple the administration's work there.[100] In May 1888, the governor of Tyrol wrote to the Ministry of the Interior to request a budget increase of 13,400 gulden. He needed to hire fourteen new civil servants to serve as district commissars, Lord-Lieutenancy officials, and drafting interns. All of these were midlevel positions requiring university education.[101]

The governors were not only apprehensive of their future ability to meet their increasing workloads, as they wrote to the Ministry of the Interior of a civil service already in despair at their powerlessness in the face of their tasks. They witnessed an ever-increasing jurisdiction: the administration had become responsible for more and more technical matters than it had ever foreseen. The era of constitutionalism and representative politics had produced a new corpus of legislation, passed by representatives of the people. The problem with this, according to the governor in Tyrol, was that the implementation of the people's legislation was left to the imperial civil service.[102] Work had trebled while the numbers of staff had stayed the same. General military service required the participation of district officials to manage recruitment, tax laws needed to be implemented and supervised, elections for all sorts of councils, public offices, and public associations needed to be managed.

By the end of the 1880s, the governors requested more university-educated personnel because they needed more policy-making officials to make sense of all the new laws and regulations that had come out of Austria's elected political institutions. From riparian rights to the supervision of industry and political and voluntary associations, the imperial administration found itself managing a massive influx of new types of work that required time, research, and energy. There seemed to be no end in sight. Public life in Austria came into being through administrative compromise, but it was flourishing to such an extent that the administration could no longer effectively manage it. A "stark incongruity" between the work and the number of officials had come into being. The state had become so complex and yet so successful in integrating public participation, that it needed more and more bureaucrats to make it work. The question became, then, whether such growth in the administration was sustainable.

## Conclusion: Tools of Knowledge Give Way to Ways of Doing Things

In the quarter-century between the promulgation of the December Constitution and the fall of Eduard Taaffe's government in 1893, the living constitution of a representative government took shape. The politics of liberals, as they sought to take over the various institutions of the state, largely failed to tame and control the imperial administration. But these failures in the 1870s helped pave the way for the independence of the administration, its growth, and its expansion in the 1880s and 1890s. The years of procedure helped to build the unique qualities in which the Habsburg imperial bureaucratic apparatus related to representative government and representative institutions. It remained independent of parliament, the provincial assemblies, and town councils, yet it found itself pulled into politics through the multitude of ways in which these representative bodies worked to expand the state.

The years of procedure drew to an end by the 1890s not because the procedures fell apart, but because they had been firmly established. Such administrative expansion brought its own challenges and needed a new type of official and a new way of getting things done. Derrida's talk of violence makes a worthwhile point: creating and maintaining an archive entails a process of selection, a collection of information that will be used to influence and control. It consolidates and anchors power, however arbitrarily, in a legal system that demands compliance and conformity. What makes this especially interesting is the very context of this archival form of "violence": it occurred in the early years of constitutionalism, of an expanding representative government, during a period of political evolution toward a more democratic society in central Europe.

The expanding political world in central Europe expanded the universe of the bureaucracy and this would bring its own challenges. The Austrian state, with its many levels of intertwined administration, was exceptionally good at record keeping. Possibly it was too good. By the end of these two and a half decades, the procedures and growth had created a mountain of paperwork. After two years as the governor of Lower Austria, Erich von Kielmansegg had decided to follow through on his plans to systematically destroy the mountains of files that were crowding out his offices.[103] The very traces of archival violence were systematically erased— not to cover up the violence, but to make room for more people, more files, more laws, more decisions.

When one examines the Lower Austrian Provincial Archives, now housed in the new governmental quarter in Sankt Pölten, one finds large gaps in the very collection of information for which the imperial civil service was known. Tax records, property surveys, all sorts of information gathering conducted by the district prefects, had been removed. In fact, the special Austrian language of administration—influenced by the Enlightenment-era administrative teachings of Joseph von Sonnenfels—has a special word for the systematic destruction of archival documents: *Skartieren*.[104] Not everything was *skartiert*. They found *Lehenbücher* which cataloged the lands and fiefs of Emperor Maximilian I (1459–1519) and thought better of pulping those. Although many of the records of the state-building process were erased, procedures were set in place to make sure that important historical documents were preserved.[105]

The knowledge of the administration had become action; it had become embedded in procedures and norms. The years of making procedures had drawn to a close. Kielmansegg's pulping campaign indicates that by the 1890s, the state building and archive making of Maczak von Ottenburg had given way to the new realities of the administrative, activist state. The years of procedure had paved the way for the rapid expansion of governmental budgets and bureaucratic expansion. But it would also pave the way to administrative crises. The bureaucratic universe had expanded more under the constitutional state than ever before. And, much like our own universe, the administrations of the monarchy began to expand at an increasing rate. For some, like Kielmansegg, the danger was that the expansion would extend beyond control. In the 1890s, Kielmansegg could pulp his way out of the flood of papers, which his predecessors had amassed pell mell. But what would he do about the expanding number of bureaucrats, the growth of city administrations—like that of the city of Vienna, which was becoming one of Europe's largest metropolises right in his very province? What would he do with the expanding budget, which was to pay for the increased services by city, province, and state governments—services that parliament, provincial assembly, and town council had approved on behalf of their constituents? Kielmansegg would face new challenges in the years ahead, as the next chapter will discuss.

# 6

## Bureaucracy and Democracy in the Final Decades of the Monarchy, 1890–1914

IN HIS MEMOIRS, long after the Habsburg Empire collapsed, the one-time civil servant Robert Ehrhart recalled a moment of which he was particularly proud. Of all his colleagues in the civil service, Ehrhart was the only one who could boast of drafting an interpellation for a radical Czech nationalist political party. Ehrhart was not a Czech nationalist, and was hardly a radical. How had he come to drafting a fire-and-brimstone condemnation of the government, specifically for a shortage of coal in 1906? The answer is simple: he was following orders.[1]

Ehrhart was a ministerial secretary appointed to the Cisleithanian cabinet under prime minister Baron Paul von Gautsch. He stayed on through the next two ministries, eventually serving under prime minister Baron Wladimir von Beck. Beck had been tasked by Francis Joseph to push a universal suffrage bill through parliament, but the parliamentary situation in Austria after 1905 had reverted once again to obstruction. Smaller parties, which did not have the votes necessary to block legislation, had begun to use the rules of parliamentary procedure to delay the discussion of bills and the passing of budgets. A particular tactic that they used was the "emergency motion." Politicians could gather a number of signatures from their colleagues and submit an emergency motion, which then automatically forced a debate on whether the motion was an "emergency" or not. In one sitting of parliament, the opposition parties could muster several emergency motions that could whittle away an entire day's proceedings, so that by the time the matter was closed a good deal of time had slipped away.

Despite these tactics of delay and obstruction, the Beck government in 1906 was determined to keep parliament functioning. After all, the latter was in the process of implementing a major suffrage reform that would grant the vote to all men over the age of twenty-four. The success of the ministry depended on the successful implementation of the reform and then the establishment (and functioning) of a parliament elected through universal manhood suffrage. Therefore, when a small group of Czech radicals decided to throw their efforts into obstruction, the government asked them what would persuade them to stand down. The party responded that it would be bringing an interpellation against the government on the shortage of coal. Other parties were planning the same action, but if the government response could be worded in such a way as to give prominence to the interpellation of their own Czech radical party, the party would withdraw its emergency motions. In other words, the party wanted publicity; it wanted to score points in the press and with its voters by denouncing the government. If the government could help them do so, all the better.

Shortly after these closed-door meetings between the Czech radicals and government officials, Ehrhart began drafting the government's official response to this still-hypothetical interpellation on the coal shortage. When, as part of the negotiations, the government showed the Czech radical party its response to their not-yet-written interpellation, the representatives of the party responded, "The text is nice, really nice. Would you please have the same official draft our interpellation too?"

Ehrhart recalled this episode because it stood out in his mind as anomalous: officials in the prime minister's office normally did not pen interpellations for radical parties. And yet, after 1890, the bureaucracy was increasingly enmeshed in parliamentary politics, often negotiating with political parties, nationalist groups, and power brokers to keep government functioning while parliament itself was not.[2] And far from being a simple absolutist institution, the imperial administration was forced to deal with political parties and to become a political player in a complex parliamentary world.[3] On the one hand, the bureaucracy faced the challenge of limiting the effects that mass politics and occupational interests could have on its ranks, while on the other hand, it would have to seek continually to engage representative institutions in the work of governance. This delicate balance depended on the bureaucracy to continue, in a way, the sense of self-sacrifice that Joseph II had hoped to instill in it over one hundred years before. However, that sacrifice depended on being completely immersed in Austrian politics and yet not part of it.

Ehrhart's story provides further insight into how Joseph's bureaucracy adapted to a world that now included political participation. As the role of participation grew, the bureaucracy became increasingly important for maintaining a sense of equilibrium, and yet this careful balance became more difficult to maintain as parties continued to latch onto the various levels of the administration (cities, crownlands, or the central government) as sinecures of their power. Thus the paradox of the Austrian state was not so much that with the expansion of representative government, with sporadic expansion of the suffrage between the 1880s and 1906, the power and size of the bureaucracy grew. Rather, democracy and its accompanying institutions increasingly relied on the bureaucracy—this supposedly undemocratic and absolutist institution—for their survival.

Throughout the 1890s and the first decade of the twentieth century the bureaucracy found itself at the center of a number of political and governmental crises. As the bureaucracy learned to respond to these crises, it became clear to a number of high officials that a reform of the entire system created during the two decades after 1848 would be necessary for political stability as well as rationalized, efficient, and fiscally responsible government. But politicians would not be able to do this alone. Instead, the bureaucracy began to pursue grand state reforms, increasingly with the help of politicians, to solve the monarchy's myriad difficulties. These grand state reforms, however, were conceived of as administrative reforms. The doctor was continuing, as under Stadion and Bach, to be both surgeon and patient. This chapter will follow the course of crises and the proposed solutions, leading up to the assassination of Franz Ferdinand and the end of civilian government in "old Austria."

## State Building in Crisis:
## A Quest for Equilibrium, 1895–1900
### Mass Politics and Kielmansegg's "Officials' Edict"

The expansion of political life in the Habsburg monarchy offered opportunities for the Austrian administration to grow, but also established some of its greatest challenges. The growth of not just its workload but the bureaucracy itself kept pace with the expansion of suffrage in the Habsburg monarchy. The administration built new offices and created new posts to accommodate the growing demands of the public. But with growth came fears that the traditional norms and standards of the imperial civil service had become diluted and lost. Moreover, although Austrian officialdom had typically recruited new members into its upper ranks from established "bureaucratic dynasties"—the children and grandchildren of officials who grew up and were educated in the "state philosophy of Enlightened Absolutism," this was no longer possible in the age of mass politics.[4] Recruitment of new blood into the bureaucracy—especially from national groups like the Czechs, who had only recently been given a university curriculum in their language—raised internal questions as to how to maintain an unpartisan, state-loyal corps of officials. And elections brought moments of uncertainty; bureaucrats had to vote for government parties, but, increasingly after the 1890s, ministerial officials wondered how to continue to foster imperial politics without becoming immersed in them. If the administration was to engage in dirty work, if it was to work with parties and politicians, how could it ensure that its members were clean?

Nationalist party activity did little to allay ministerial anxieties. Nationalist parties in the Reichsrat increasingly registered their influence by an ability to place their co-nationalists in the bureaucracy.[5] Nationality politics in the Reichsrat also led representatives in this body to sell their support for government initiatives through bureaucratic appointments. The appointment of national representatives (*Landsmannminister*) in various cabinets was a major concession to this form of political patronage and deal brokering. These ministers without portfolio represented the interests of their national group in the ministerial cabinet by influencing bureaucratic appointments.[6] The Poles were able to use their national representative in the cabinet so well that Josef Redlich could comment that the *Landsmannminister* "had placed officials of Polish nationality in the higher positions of the civil service in all the departmental Ministries, so that within their staffs they formed a sort of Polish enclave, which, under his invisible direction, watched over the interests of Polish citizens in Galicia and throughout the Empire."[7]

Increasingly, nationality and radical politics mattered, all the more so because they threatened the appearance of the bureaucracy as a nationally neutral institution. Although Alexander Spitzmüller—who was at one time the minister of finance—could praise the objectivity and the Austrian loyalty of his fellow public servants in his memoirs, he also recounts one particular story of how he had to deal with a subordinate in the civil service who became caught up in nationality politics. In Spitzmüller's circles, these national agitators were not Czechs or Poles, but German nationalists. At the time of this story, Spitzmüller was head of the Lower Austrian finance office (*Finanzlandesdirektion*), and was asked to take into his department a civil servant by the name of Schmidt, who was being transferred as part of a disciplinary decision.[8] Spitzmüller recounts a conversation that he had with the finance minister regarding Schmidt's case: "the Minister stressed that this was a question of an excellent *employé* who had gotten into the wrong ways through political agitation and was to be set right again."[9] When Schmidt reported for duty, Spitzmüller informed him that he was to "avoid political activity as much as possible in the future for his own sake." By doing so, Schmidt could "mend his reputation as a government official."[10] The upper echelons of the imperial bureaucracy were careful to be corrective, not demonstrative, with punishments, in particular not to draw public attention to any deficiency in the imperial administration's objective character.

While the upper strata of Vienna's bureaucracy increasingly feared political infiltration in the form of nationalist agitation and bigotry, such as in the case of Schmidt above, "politicization" could also take the form of active political agitation by the occupational interest groups of an increasing assortment of officials.[11] This too worried the higher-ups, because it exposed the bureaucracy's deficiencies in the press and at political meetings and demonstrations. These interest-group politics emerged slowly. Bureaucratic organizations started as reading societies and public information groups soon after basic civil freedoms were established in the 1860s under the February Patent and the December Constitution.[12] Gradually, these associations waged public campaigns on behalf of bureaucrats' occupational interests, promoting pay raises and greater benefits, but early occupational interest group organizations rarely challenged the government.[13] By the 1890s, however, bureaucratic organizations had joined in a movement willing to wage political battles based on their occupational interests. They had become a political force that challenged their superiors (and by proxy the emperor himself).[14] The conventions of the *Verein für Staatsbeamten Österreichs* (Association for State Officials of Austria), for instance, were loud and boisterous and its members spoke and wrote direct and sharp criticisms of the government. Moreover, the *Verein* no longer abided by the norm of submitting its petitions *internally* to the higher-ups in the imperial bureaucracy; rather, it made direct and public appeals to parliament.[15]

Through their interest groups, officials found new allies outside the bureaus of the state. Political parties attacked the government and demanded better salaries and pensions for their new constituents. The nature of how civil servants viewed their service to the state had changed, even if slowly. The self-sacrifice of service had transformed in the constitutional era into interest-group politics. It took twenty-five years of "social frustration and political education" before officials learned to combine their interests as an occupational group and "deal more aggressively with the Imperial government as employer."[16] What is more, such interest-group organization naturally turned to the public, political sphere as the proper arena for the defense of occupational interests. Officials were in the process of transforming from a caste to a class, and quickly became part of a larger political process of developing middle-class political radicalism in Vienna and elsewhere in the monarchy. While occupational interest groups transformed "group interest into political power," parties also took notice of these new centers of activity and began to compete with one another for their votes.[17] The larger movement, therefore, engaged in interest-group politics, when Austria's bureaucrats attempted to maintain their "self-idealization as a privileged cultural stratum with corporate claims to honor."[18]

Emperor Francis Joseph found politicization of the imperial civil service deeply troubling, and he was not the only one. In the minds of senior officials like the governor of Lower Austria, Count Erich von Kielmansegg, national political agitation and interest-group politics threatened to erode the self-image of bureaucrats as Joseph II's heirs. Bureaucrats were to be servants of a neutral, objective, enlightened state. They should not hold political signs or make inflammatory speeches in makeshift-tent meetings. What is more, political agitation threatened not only the self-image of the bureaucracy but its image to the outside world. The bureaucracy depended on the veil of neutrality for its legitimacy, and as the civil service sought to maintain its institutional role in Austria's larger political world, it needed to maintain the image of objectivity and political impartiality at all costs.

Interest-group agitation stirred the emperor and his senior officials to action. In 1895, the emperor summoned Count Erich von Kielmansegg from the Lower Austrian governor's office to head a caretaker government. The emperor chaired the caretaker government's first cabinet meeting on June 20, 1895, and specifically addressed the lack of discipline among civil servants.[19] Kielmansegg wrote in his memoirs that the emperor read reports in newspapers of officials participating in political demonstrations, in which they denounced their superiors. But speaking out was not all that they were doing: the emperor was particularly incensed by inflammatory newspaper articles, which could have been written only with the help of officials who leaked confidential information to the press. Francis Joseph insisted that a crackdown was necessary. In that first meeting of the Council of Ministers, he charged Kielmansegg's caretaker government with finding a way to bring the imperial bureaucracy back under control.[20]

Over the next six weeks Kielmansegg's ministry discussed ways in which to rein in the politics of the civil service.[21] The result of these meetings was the *Beamtenerlass*, or Officials' Edict, which Kielmansegg's ministry released on August 10, 1895.[22] Kielmansegg's edict highlights two important facets in the growing discussion in Austria about the role of the imperial bureaucracy in the body politic. First, there was the question of administrators and civil servants as citizens. To what degree could the civil servants be integrated into the larger sphere of political parties, interest groups, or national politics? Second, and less directly, how much could and should the bureaucracy as an institution become engaged in Austria's political life?

In the Officials' Edict, Kielmansegg sought to find the seam between civil servants' rights as citizens and the traditional ideals of bureaucratic self-sacrifice and service to the state. While much of the edict confirmed civic rights (the right to publically express opinions, the right to assemble, the right to petition the government), it also asserted that civil servants should refrain from exercising those rights. The imperial bureaucracy was attempting to stay relevant in the new age of political participation by hanging on to its Josephinist traditions. In fact, the language of the edict compares the obligations of the official to the other pillars of the regime that held special importance for Emperor Joseph II—priests and army officers. From this comparison, the edict contraposes the exercise of civil and political rights with the concept that the "nature of public service" demands restraint and the strict observance of service regulations (*Dienstvorschriften*). Thus, while civil servants obviously enjoyed rights as citizens, the edict expressed the opinion that "it is just as undoubtable that state officials are given special obligations through their office and their oath." Failure to exercise self-restraint would result in punishment, which could include transfer without remuneration or negative evaluations in the offender's file.

In a practical sense, Kielmansegg's edict was a signal to the monarchy's civil servants to tone down their strident political protests and their visibility in any public criticism of the government. The second point was a key concern: it was the visibility of officials in public protests, a reality that tarred the Josephinist ideals of neutrality and objectivity in government. Kielmansegg posited that bureaucrats must maintain much self-denial, harkening back to Joseph II's "pastoral letter" of 1783: "Self-interest . . . is the spoiler of all activity and is the most unpardonable vice of the state servant."[23] As political life expanded and officials exercised their rights of citizens in public protest, ministerial officials like Kielmansegg thought that the exercise of rights also threatened the authority of the administration. Kielmansegg's edict is careful throughout, to remind government officials that mixing in political activism goes against their oath as well as harms the public "standing and dignity" of the bureaucracy. Just as important, however, was that the edict did not condemn the civil service's occupational associations but expected them to play a leadership role in the enforcement and maintenance of the public comportment of its membership. Again, the public face of the bureaucracy had to appear unified and solid. Kielmansegg expected the civil service occupational associations to "limit themselves to their own occupational concerns and in so doing provide the bureaucracy with a worthy and appropriate organ for expression." In return, the edict stated that the government would promise to review resolutions vetted through the associations more favorably. This use of the carrot to entice proper comportment—as well as the stick for future violations against the dignity of office—reinforced the general idea that governmental and administrative matters must be kept *in-house*, out of the public sphere. The government and its ministers were not to be tried in the court of public opinion and the bureaucrats themselves were to stay out of activist politics.

Kielmansegg's solution for the exercise of civil rights foreshadowed the emerging answer to the second question facing the bureaucracy: what was its general political involvement? Although Kielmansegg may not have thought so, the next generation of bureaucrat-politicians would attempt to preserve the traditional ideals of the bureaucracy, because it was precisely those ideals of objectivity and neutrality that were useful in the world of Austrian politics. The bureaucracy would have to keep its members clean and clear of political stain because as an institution, it would be diving into Austria's political world. This realization would become even more important once parliamentary political life shifted outside the shuttered doors of parliament itself.

## Administration and Parliamentary Problems:
## Prime Minister Badeni's Language Ordinances

Count Casimir Badeni's main priority when he became prime minister in 1895 was to bring to fruition programs that had broken apart Count Taaffe's conservative political coalition, the Iron Ring, some three years earlier. His first priority was to propose and implement yet another electoral reform, which would expand the suffrage and further weaken the exaggerated representation of the centralist German liberals. Once this was done, his second priority was to bring about a compromise between German and Czech national politics in the provinces of Bohemia and Moravia by addressing the hierarchy of languages in those provinces. This second priority was not only a question of language; it was an administrative question that would burst the seams of parliament and of politics in general.

Badeni began his term with an impressive array of accomplishments, in which he had skillfully managed the Austrian parliament to pass his sponsored legislation. He was able to sail the 1897 budget through while also implementing suffrage reform rather quickly—by June 1896.[24] It is one of those true ironies of history, however, that his second priority—working out a political compromise between the Czech and German parties in Bohemia—would fail in part because of the success of the first. The electoral reform expanded the suffrage considerably but had, as a result, altered the constellation of the parties which composed parliament. Hoping to upset the balance between German liberals and nationalists and the rest of the parties—both conservative and those representing individual Slavic national groups, Badeni's electoral reform had tilted the balance to more socially radical parties on both sides. It would be these new elements which would eventually lead parliament's more moderate elements against him in 1897.[25]

Badeni released his language ordinances, one each for Bohemia and Moravia, in April 1897.[26] Like the Stremayr ordinances of 1880, these language ordinances dealt with the use of language of the imperial administration, but Badeni's ordinances expanded the use of Czech in the administration in Bohemia and Moravia beyond what the Stremayr ordinances already decreed.[27] While the Stremayr ordinances allowed Czech to be the language in which ordinary citizens communicated with the imperial authorities (i.e., the "outer" administrative language), Badeni's ordinances decreed that now cases would be adjudicated in either Czech or German—depending on how they were submitted. This meant that if a

224 Bureaucracy and Democracy

Czech speaker initiated a case with the imperial bureaucracy, even in an area inhabited by a majority of German-speakers, officials would have to review the case *internally* in Czech (the "inner" administrative language).[28] A corollary of this was that every member of the state administration of Bohemia and Moravia would have to be fluent in both languages. If the administrations in Bohemia and Moravia had to be bilingual collectively under the Stremayr ordinances, Badeni decreed that each individual civil servant in Bohemia and Moravia now had to know both languages.[29] State officials in Bohemia and Moravia had four years—until July 1901—to prove themselves fluent in both Czech and German. This, of course, favored Czech speakers in Bohemia and Moravia over their German-speaking neighbors: educated Czech speakers learned German through school and the military service, while German speakers rarely deigned to learn Czech.[30]

Although Badeni hoped to create a lasting political and national compromise in Bohemia and Moravia between Czech and German national parties, his efforts to reach a compromise brought about the most serious political crisis that Austria had known in the constitutional era. The result of such hubris landed Badeni in a wholly unworkable position vis-à-vis Germans in parliament.[31] The Germans in parliament reacted initially with shock; shock soon gave way to violent opposition, bolstered by waves of local protests and violent demonstrations in German towns throughout the monarchy. The Badeni ordinances had once again put the bureaucracy on the center stage of Austria's political world. But here the "language and *Beamten*-problem" had become a matter of national prestige and thus a matter of politics.[32] For the Czech nationalists, access to positions in the imperial administration was a crucial step toward recognizing the cultural progress of the Czech nation. For Germans, the ordinances presented a serious threat to their self-perception as the cultural anchor of the monarchy; they also threatened many German speakers in the provincial administration with an eventual transfer or dismissal from service—if they failed to learn Czech within four years.

In retrospect, the tumult in parliament that resulted from the Badeni ordinances has been seen as the beginning of the end of the monarchy. German representatives began to obstruct the work of the Reichsrat through endless procedural delays and filibusters. When the ordinances were eventually repealed, the Czech national politicians followed suit and ensured that parliamentary activity, having ground to a halt, did not start back up again.[33] The Badeni fiasco not only deepened growing rifts in the monarchy's political arena, it also opened up new ones. While the events in parliament further strained relations between Czech and German politicians, the stature and authority of parliamentary democracy also suffered. Obstruction brought a new public face to Austria's parliament: elected representatives who behaved very badly. The German left used all the means of parliamentary procedure to obstruct the business of parliament, including the renewal of the *Ausgleich* with Hungary.[34] While delegates hurled inkwells and insults at one another, they undermined the authority of the body as a whole. The governmental coalition eventually responded with unconstitutional measures to end the obstruction: they passed new standing orders for parliament (the *Lex Falkenhayn*), while summoning the police to arrest deputies who still engaged in obstruction. The sanctity of the legislators had been thrown out the window with the respect for order and dignity among the legislators. Moreover, Badeni and his successors could rule without parliament if they were forced into such a position by employing the constitution's emergency paragraph, article 14.[35]

The denigration of parliament in Austria has long been a topic of historical debate. Adam Wandruszka pointed out in an article from 1976 that despite the many positive achievements of Austria's parliament in the last twenty years of the monarchy, "parliament remained a place, described in a crude and clichéd manner, as a public crisis, where concerts were improvised with desk boards and children's trumpets, where inkwells and ashtrays were thrown about, and where otherwise thoroughly honorable men, who in their private lives would never have let themselves descend to such excesses, cursed each other in unflattering tones and even threatened each other with their fists."[36] And so the story goes, Austria's parliament, nearly forty years old in 1897, was committed to the mad house. The larger moral of the story of the Badeni ordinances has long been that Austria was an immature polity in the late nineteenth century, and therefore it was too weak to provide a halt to the First World War and too lame to provide any model for future democratic exercise in the 1920s and 1930s when fascism easily broke down democracy in the monarchy's successor states.

However, the elegance of this version of Austria's decline and fall, the ruptures in Austrian parliamentary politics and the hodge-podge of hastily assembled cabinets in the next three years, did not mean that politics or negotiation stopped.[37] Moreover, the Badeni Language Ordinances, while producing a major crisis, also launched an intense collective soul searching, both in the public press as well as among the bureaucratic elite.[38] The "best minds" from all backgrounds and from all different positions "began to wrangle intensively with the nationality-problem and with the Austria *Reich-* and state-problem that was closely bound to it."[39]

When parliament shut its doors in 1897, new doors of dialogue and ideas opened. Moreover, these discussions did not just focus on parliament and nationality politics, but also on the relationship of the administration to the public sphere and how political participation should work in a multinational, constitutional, and representative state. The Badeni crisis opened up a new period of reform and compromise, one that harkened back to the era of reforms after 1848. The bureaucracy became involved in a larger Austrian discourse on the Austrian state, one that was held in the press, in lecture halls, and behind the closed doors of Austria's ministries. While the Badeni crisis had created a constitutional vacuum, it had also opened up new channels for the bureaucracy to reclaim its reformist spirit and possibly even laid an open road to restructure the monarchy.

The bureaucracy emerged from these discussions aiming to place its officials collectively in the center of Austrian politics, as referees of the political process, the adjudicators of interest-group conflict, and as priests of citizenship. The administration in these years did not become absolutists, as the story is often told. They attempted to transform themselves into technocrats of democracy. This transformation would be cut short by the complete overturning of the long state-building process by the First World War. But it is essential, if we are to understand the final years of the monarchy, not to see the last decades of the monarchy as leading to collapse in the war. For one, we have been so conditioned by the decline-and-fall narrative of the monarchy that we miss elements of contingency and roads not taken. If we see this time period as bound up in the events that came later, we miss the very discussions and debates that sought to refine the state and the practices of citizenship. We miss the vibrancy of a multinational polity in its attempts to retool itself once again for a new era: in this case, democracy, mass politics, and social welfare. It was not only these discussions that were cut short by a state of emergency and war, but the very possibilities for multinational democracy in the twentieth century.

### Autonomous Difficulties

If we return to the Upper Austrian town of Wels, we see that by the early twentieth century, there wasn't much reason for drama. In 1908 Emperor Francis Joseph, celebrating his diamond jubilee, visited the city for a few hours, but that was the most excitement the city had seen.[40] Local life in Wels was supposed to be boring; the great administrative upheavals had happened fifty years before. The years of procedure had created a state whose administration sat in the countryside and had become part of that countryside. This was what made the Habsburg state predictable, secure, and seemingly permanent as the public buildings seemed as they reflected the sunlight in their yellow hue. In other ways, too, Wels was a quiet town. The district prefect keeps an eye on socialist agitation, looks over a few reports from gendarmes patrolling the countryside, and supervises a few cases of complaints sent to the local school board, but nothing remotely serious comes across his desk. The preparations for the emperor's visit are mostly in order. He helps orchestrate and choreograph the imperial visit. Who gets to stand where? The prefect is the one who knows. He also is the first person to greet the emperor and the last person to see him off. He promotes a few charity events in the district, though the one for the Red Cross is the most important. That one is being run by the governor's wife, Baroness Elisabeth Handel.

But the good life in Wels and other localities spread across the monarchy was hard to maintain. It was expensive. We see that Wels grew in the years of procedure precisely in the ways that city director August Göllerich had feared. In less than twenty years, the municipal bureaucracy of Wels saw the number of cases increase more than fourfold. Much of the caseload came from the increase of "delegated" tasks, regulations passed by the central state but enforced—and paid for by local and regional governments.[41] Wels added new governmental offices for building inspections and city planning, municipal police, lighting, poor care, schools, vocation education. By 1902 it had built a gasworks, a theater, and a savings bank. Austria's deep and complex political world owed much of its vibrancy as well as its difficulties to the cumbersome dual administrative system. The years of procedure had seen the autonomous governments of the crownlands, cities, and townships grow as well. Their growth came through new social welfare programs and the general momentum of a growing public sector. In a very real sense, Austria took part in the larger trends of the nineteenth-century European state, as its government took on new roles in the realm of social welfare and public education.[42] What made Cisleithania exceptional was that such increased expenditures were borne in no small part by crownland and municipal budgets. These new tasks, from the building of local railroads to army barracks, to lighting the city, to building sewers, and to electrification, were meant to improve the quality of life of Wels's citizenry, but Wels had to borrow heavily to pay for all this new infrastructure. By the middle of the first decade of the twentieth century, nearly 40 percent of its material expenditures (what it did not pay to municipal officials) went toward interest on loans, which had reached 7 million kronen.[43]

The financial situation of many of the provinces was even worse. The crownland of Moravia took out four major loans to cover its own building and infrastructure projects between 1890 and 1899, totaling more than 10.4 million gulden (5.2 million kronen). Increasingly, maintaining its buildings and personnel led to permanent budget shortfalls. By 1899, Moravia's expenditures eclipsed its incomes by nearly 1.5 million gulden. It had to take out loans just to cover its operating expenses.[44] Moravia, like many other crownlands of the empire, given the vague and expansive nature of its responsibilities as self-governing bodies, simply had stepped up both to pay for and to administer Austria's entire social welfare system, as well as to build institutions and infrastructure for economic development. But its administrative imagination had outgrown the realities of the Austrian tax system. The crownlands set up special funds to pay for all kinds of new programs and institutions for the public good: sanatoriums, orphanages, care of the poor, public buildings and roads, public health and inoculation programs, promotion and improvement of crownland agriculture, and— drawing the largest share of any crownland's budget—public education.[45] The fundamental role of the crownlands as the provider of social welfare and the expensive nature of this role was not lost on the political economists of the time. Nevertheless, the crownlands steadily increased their services and, of course, the monies they spent on them. As Baron Josef von Friedenfels, in an article presenting the state of crownland budgets in 1893, remarked: "Almost every administrative period increases the number of responsibilities, which in exact circuitous fashion bind the public funds of the crownland—without limiting the areas which remain free—since progressive times bring with them new necessities and new goals for the promotion of the social welfare of the land."[46] Altogether, the fact that the crownlands administered so many different programs on behalf of public welfare was not so unusual. But problems, both political and national, rose as expenditures outpaced the income that the crownlands could bring in.

For one, Cisleithania's tax policies compounded the lack of spending restraint. An article on the state of Galicia's finances in 1901, in the official statistical journal *Statistische Monatschrift*, sets the blame for Galicia's financial troubles on the lack of sufficient tax resources coupled with the fiduciary responsibilities of the crownlands: "It [a reform of crownland finances] has in no way anything to do with overcoming abuses, with a fundamental reform of hitherto existing public finances, but simply with the opening of new sources of income for our crownland budgets, since the sources of income presently at our disposal are no longer capable of covering all the unavoidable necessities of autonomous finances."[47] For the centralist administrative scholars and political economists of the early twentieth century, the problem of crownland finances arose from the fact that the constitutional experiments of the 1860s gave much of the responsibility for social welfare to the crownlands, but they did not also turn over, in any measurable way, the absolute control the central state had on taxes. The ability of the crownland to collect taxes to support its budget was firmly bound to the tax collection of the central state. Crownlands could collect income through agricultural and banking institutions, or through fees collected by crownland hospitals; however, most of their income came through taxation. The problem was that the crownlands did not have a tax system that was independent of the central state. Crownlands could appropriate surcharges on direct taxes (and some indirect taxes, like beer and wine consumption taxes) that the central state collected.[48] In other words, the only way for crownlands to raise money for their increasing responsibilities was to levy surcharges on imperial taxes already being collected. They could not invent taxes of their own in the form of toll roads, spa or hotel taxes, or taxes on luxury items.

By 1905, provincial surcharges reached legal and financial ceilings: the average surcharge that the crownlands levied equaled 55 percent of the Cisleithanian direct tax. The Bukovina, for instance, levied a 95 percent surcharge on its citizens, while Galicia's surcharge equaled no less that 81.5 percent.[49] The finances of Moravia were propped up by a tax surcharge on top of imperial income and inheritance taxes of 54 and 60 percent, respectively. But these tax surcharges only brought in 7,215,778 gulden, which barely covered 70 percent of the expenditures (10,239,634 gulden) in 1899. The rest of the budget was covered by contributions by the imperial government for pensions, policing, sanitation, and poor relief. Institutions like hospitals brought in some monies (covering only 1 percent of the state's expenditure), while townships and cities contributed monies via local school funds and pension contributions for teachers. But, all in all, it took creative ways and much cooperation in the province to keep Moravia financially afloat.[50]

While the central state monopolized the best sources of income for itself, it left both the crownlands and the municipalities to bear much of the costs of social welfare. This inequity was not lost on Ferdinand Schmid, who—while arguing for a stronger presence of the central state—recognized the impossibility of the crownland's situation: "The state has already requisitioned all the important means of income for itself and so the crownlands and the autonomous municipalities mainly depend on the irrational surcharge-system, whose effects become more and more ruinous—especially for the rural taxpayer."[51] The nearly bankrupt state of the 1860s would have financial consequences for Austria as it entered the twentieth century. The financial egg of the nearly bankrupt state of the 1860s had hatched into a fiscal dragon at the turn of the century.

At the start of the twentieth century, when the crownlands found their surcharges on direct taxes had reached the limits of feasibility, crownland finances would become an even bigger concern when coupled with runaway expenditures, especially in the nationally mixed crownlands. Ernst Mischler notes in an important contemporary analysis of Austria's financial situation from 1909 that the expenditures of the crownlands increased twenty times between 1862 and 1905.[52] Moreover, the crownlands increasingly sought to cover expenditures by borrowing money.[53] Unclear statistics hid the depths of the problem, but a governmental effort to investigate crownland finances in 1908 discovered that the crownland administrations had loans totaling more than 300 million kronen—with over 225 million kronen of the debt shared by the multinational crownlands Galicia (108 million kronen), Bohemia (77 million kronen), and Moravia (41 million kronen).[54] Among professors of political economy and *Verwaltungslehre* in the Habsburg monarchy, there seemed to be a consensus that education and the promotion of agriculture (*Landeskultur*) in the crownlands were driving the expenditures skyward. Moreover, other "cultural" programming was appropriated by nationalist groups. Crownlands with multiple national groups, such as Galicia, the Bukovina, Bohemia, and Moravia, would thus have to equitably fund cultural programming for each of its national populations. The percentage that the crownlands spent on the maintenance of their own administrative apparatus fell from 28 percent of the total expenditure in 1862 (and this included the salaries for an ever-increasing number of bureaucrats) to only 4 percent by 1904. In the same year, however, the crownlands spent over 41 percent of their income on public education and the promotion of crownland "Kultur."[55]

Nationally mixed crownlands had the most trouble covering their expenditures. By 1910, the Bukovina's expenditures exceeded its budget by 46 percent, Moravia's by almost 35 percent, and Bohemia and Galicia each spent 23 percent in excess of their revenues.[56] Again, Austria's own academics blamed national politics for the financial woes of the nationally mixed crownlands. Ernst Mischler was certainly not alone when he laconically described how national politics and even national compromises pushed crownland expenditures beyond revenues: "Each party seeks in the period of its national hegemony to satisfy its national needs as much as possible and it is not seldom (e.g., in several districts in Moravia) that these 'needs' are nationally parallel or doubly satisfied, which very often leads to exorbitant expenditure."[57]

During the wide discourse of administrative reform at the start of the twentieth century, national politics were blamed for more than inflating crownland expenditures. In 1905 Ferdinand Schmid criticized national politics for infecting the entire administration of the crownland and crippling the executive boards and the diets in the exercise of their duties. "In the last decades an objectionably high measure of national and political bickering [Hader] has crept openly into the administration of the crownlands." Moreover, the executive boards, Schmid complained, "are already—thanks to their peculiar standing—hardly able to function as objective authorities or to develop any beneficial activity in the area of their autonomous jurisdictions."[58]

The larger struggle between the central and autonomous bureaucracies, and their financial competition, filtered down from policy making into not so petty battles over public standing. As the autonomous institutions of the crownlands and the townships increased their reach, they asked silent questions about what their role was alongside the imperial authorities. Such silent questioning would regularly boil to the surface in ceremonies, such as the Corpus Christi procession, which was (and still is) held sixty days after Easter. The Corpus Christi procession, as an expression of the fusion between public authority and religious piety, necessitated the participation of elected officeholders, governors, and other imperial officials in the ceremony.[59] The questions that inevitably arose were: in what order should these officials walk in the procession and where should they sit during the mass? District officials often complained to their superiors about local city officials asserting a higher place in line—often ahead of the imperial bureaucrats in the town. Or conversely, town officials would formally lodge a complaint against the local imperial officials. These complaints often reached the desk of the minister of the interior himself.[60] The unclarity of administrative hierarchy; the boundaries of public participation; and the authority of the emperor thus expressed itself in various towns and cities of the empire in the simple order and seating of personages. Naturally egos of local officials and administrators played a role, but just as important was the need for these local centers of governance, as well as the regional officials of the imperial administration, *to know where they stood*—both literally and figuratively. These questions were becoming increasingly difficult to answer. As the bureaucracies of both the autonomous and imperial trees grew, they became more entangled.

## Bureaucracy as Political Salvation
### Ernest von Koerber's Government, 1900–1904

When Ernest von Koerber came to power on January 18, 1900, the emperor entrusted him, not only with the helm of the Austrian half of the Austro-Hungarian monarchy, but also with the task of extracting Austria from the political mire of the nationalities conflict. If he could crack the administrative fiscal nut, all the better. Koerber was, like Taaffe or Kielmansegg before him, first and foremost a civil servant. Koerber was born in 1850 in Trent, Tyrol, to a family that achieved its status, and indeed its noble title, through generations of service to the Habsburgs and the state.[61] Koerber followed the typical, and privileged, course of Austria's "second society," who were the lesser, service nobility and bureaucratic elites.[62] He attended the Theresianum gymnasium, which had been responsible for the education of Austria's elite administrators since 1745;[63] he then received a doctorate in law from the University of Vienna. By the time he was twenty-four, Dr. Koerber gained a post in the Ministry of Trade; by the time he was thirty-seven, he had become chief of the presidial office of that ministry. He had distinguished himself by his enormous energy, intelligence and devotion and, in 1895, became the *Sektionschef* in the Ministry of the Interior under Prime Minister Badeni. In Austria, at such heights in the bureaucracy, the air not only became thinner but it was also infused with high politics. Koerber served twice as a cabinet minister between 1895 and 1899; first as the minister of trade in Baron Paul Gautsch's first ministry (December 1897–March 1898); then as the minister of the interior in the provisional government of Count Manfred Clary-Aldringen in late 1899.

The emperor and many in Austria's civil service viewed Koerber as a savior-like figure at the dawn of 1900: he was the man who finally and ultimately would solve the language question; the prime minister who would set the deadlocked parliament in motion again.[64] How Koerber would attempt to do these things is of utmost importance to this study, for Koerber hoped to change the constellation of power in Austria, and to place most of the important weight of governance and legislation, not in the hands of parliament, but in those of the bureaucracy.[65]

The Koerber government was neither the first nor the last *Beamten*-government that Austria saw, but in many ways this government encapsulated that term. For the German liberal *Neue Freie Presse* the unique qualities of a government of civil servants were crucial to bring the Czechs and Germans to an agreement and to lead Austria out of its political morass.[66] In fact, the *Presse* saw nothing other than a *Beamten*-government as viable given Austria's unworkable parliamentary situation. Key to this hope was the idea that a cabinet of public officials would not favor one party or one national group over the other—in other words, this cabinet would exhibit the "neutrality" or "objectivity" for which Austria's officials were known. Thus, with the relative lack of esteem for parliament, the prestige of the bureaucracy had grown. Moreover, the German liberal press had optimistically looked to the bureaucracy as both a nationally neutral and objective guide for the ship of state after nationalist conflict had derailed parliamentary government.

Koerber's cabinet consisted of several fellow officials, men of talent and energy who, like Koerber himself, rose through the various departments of government and policy making. Koerber took the most politically sensitive ministry for himself, the Ministry of the Interior. Dr. Eugen von Böhm-Bawerk, senate president in the administrative supreme court, was named as minister of finance. Baron Alois Spens-Boden, who had been governor of Moravia and *Sektionschef* in the Ministry of Justice, became the minister for justice. The minister of trade, Baron Call, was a diplomat in Austria-Hungary's foreign service. In addition, Koerber named Dr. Baron Karl Giovanelli, who served on the administrative supreme court, as minister for agriculture and a professor of Roman law, Dr. Leonhard Piętak, as minister without portfolio.[67] As we will see, Koerber's *Beamtenkabinett* not only stood "above the parties" but wielded considerable power and could withstand political pressure. Koerber would use the skills and knowledge of a *Beamter* to lead Austria's politics to a solution and, if forced, to break the backs of the parties which threatened his work.

Of course, the various German and Czech political parties viewed this Koerber government—faced with the task of taming them and bringing them to a table of compromise—with high suspicion. The *Neue Freie Presse* worried that the Koerber government could never be seen as objective and neutral by the German parties, since Koerber had planned to have two Slavic ministers without portfolio, one Czech and one Polish, while not appointing a *Landesmannsminister* for the Germans. *Narodní Listy*, on the Czech side, completely refused to entertain the idea of Koerber's objectivity: "The Koerber Ministry is a German ministry, whose national unity will be broken by a Pole and a Czech as a fifth wheel on the wagon. The Koerber Ministry will be centralist and German, therefore it is nonsense to refer to it as neutral. Each one of us knows this, and this is the reigning opinion among the Czechs."[68] However biting this indictment of Koerber's government may seem, this Young Czech paper was correct. Koerber indeed harbored strong Josephinist and centralizing plans for the government. What the Young Czechs, as well as other national political parties, did not see was the energy and strength that Koerber would bring to bear against them and, for that matter, against autonomist government in Austria generally.

But all of this remained unseen on January 18, 1900, as Koerber first took the helm of state. Contemporary observers predicted that Koerber's government would be made or broken by its ability to bring parliament back into peaceful action. Koerber indeed planned to make parliament work again, but his methods called for an unprecedented reorganization of the Austrian state-system, which would take away parliament's ability to cripple government. His plan would require the repositioning of the constellation of the major pillars of the Habsburg state: bureaucracy, government, and parliament. In this new constellation the bureaucracy would initiate innovation while parliament would serve as a rubber stamp.

The quest to restore parliament, however, was only a part of the larger crisis and public discussion on governance. The larger quest was one of equilibrium: as ministers, officials, politicians, and academics considered Austria's parliamentary crisis, they asked questions that concerned how to rule, manage, or self-govern a diverse, multinational empire. These questions pointed to parliament's position within the larger framework of the Austrian state, its size, and its roles in public life. These discussions were gradually lumped under the same heading, as the word *reform* became the word pursed on the mouth of the public. From speeches held in parliament, to published discussions of the Viennese Associations of Jurists, academic studies, internal bureaucratic reports, angry anti-government pamphlets, and several official imperial inquiries, the quest for the proper balance between executive authority and public input, between bureaucracy and representation, pointed to revisiting the structures of the imperial state. These structures had been cast, forged, and refined in the twenty years of constitutional experimentation between the revolutions of 1848 and the promulgation of the fundamental laws that made up the "December Constitution" in 1867.

By the twentieth century politicians and administrative reformers began to reconsider the 1850s and 1860s and Austria's own peculiar state-building process. The decisions of Stadion, Bach, and Schmerling were still relevant and their contributions to functioning and nonfunctioning governance slid further under the public's microscope. Such debates were significant, the more so because they force historians to thoroughly revise the lingering depiction of the final years of the Habsburg monarchy as marked by imperial decline, parliamentary crisis, and bureaucratic absolutism.[69] The period of "parliamentary crisis" between 1897 and 1914 unleashed an equally vibrant period of political discussion, participation in important debates, and, most of all, considerations of imperial reform. If anything, the final seventeen years of peace in the monarchy would have constituted another period of constitutional experimentation and renewal had they not been cut short by the First World War.

Under Koerber, imperial reform took on a certain shape and it was to keep that shape until the end of the monarchy. Koerber sought to reform the Austrian state by reforming its structures—the bureaucracy. He used administrative reform in place of constitutional or political reform.[70] Under Koerber, administrative reform took on special qualitative aspects and was often shorthand for major constitutional changes. In a very real sense, then, Koerber followed in the footsteps of Stadion, Bach, and Schmerling: the minds behind the era of constitutional experimentation between 1848 and 1867.

Austria's problem at the beginning of the twentieth century, as Koerber saw it, boiled down to a lack of stable, responsible politics. In Koerber's view, the Austrian state in July 1900 needed a new parliament, a parliament that would work with the state, enacting beneficial legislation for Austria's citizens. Since Badeni's ordinances in 1897, nationalist rabble-rousers and

delegates more interested in disrupting the work of government had dominated Austria's parliament. Koerber wanted to replace these nationalists and
extremists in parliament with delegates whose sense of duty to the populace
and to the state resembled that of his willing and able civil servants. In
order to make parliament fulfill a legislative function and more consistently
serve the state, Koerber suggested that the emperor, in a striking coup d'état,
completely alter suffrage law and create a new three-curia parliament, which
would leave little room for the national rabble-rousers from the *bürgerlich*
parties.[71] Instead, his new parliament would consist of two curiae of notables, based on Austria's wealthiest taxpayers and its leading minds.[72] These
two curiae would bring to Vienna a new generation of venerable, eloquent
statesmen, who supported the *Gesamtstaat* Austrian idea. Not wanting to
appear anachronistic or out of step with the prevailing zeitgeist of 1900,
Koerber allowed for 60 percent of the parliament to be generally elected.
Koerber hoped that social democrats would dominate this third, generally-
elected curia, because he could count on them to support state-sponsored
progress and social-welfare programs. Moreover, the social democrats' anti-
nationalism, with their tempered but still existent belief in German cultural
superiority, would have lent support in parliament to Koerber's belief in the
viability of the Austrian central state.

Koerber's political habitus was marked by the belief that parliament,
and representative bodies in general, function as a pillar of the state. He
intended to endow the legislature with the mantle of state service. Koerber
even went so far as to propose that all delegates upon their admission into
parliament would swear an oath, which he based on various "service oaths"
(*Diensteid*) that had to be sworn before any civil servant could perform the
functions of his office: "To the emperor I will be loyal and obedient, I will
give unwavering observance of the Basic State Law, I will promote on all
sides the work of this House, especially concerning the counsel and execution of all the drafts of laws and bills brought forward by the government
and the conscientious fulfillment of all its duties."[73] Sharing their oath
with civil servants, the parliamentarians were not to use their position as a
defense of interests or an assertion of rights against another faction or the
government; instead they were, like enlightened officials, to make policy
for the good of the whole.

This memorandum never left the offices of the emperor's cabinet,
but it showed that Koerber was willing to revisit Austria's constitutional
framework, which had been established in the 1860s to limit the potential

disruptiveness of parliamentarism. Over the course of his five-year term, Koerber continually revisited piecemeal approaches to force parliamentary bodies, whether the central parliament in Vienna or the diets in the provinces, to pass budgets, approve governmental legislation, or help his government show a unified front in budget and army recruitment negotiations with Hungary. His economic infrastructure programs did not bring the nationally warring parties of parliament to the negotiation table, but their promises of railways, roads, and waterways did serve to temporarily end the Young Czech Party's parliamentary obstruction and allow the Young Czechs to come together with their German-speaking antagonists to support government projects.[74] Parliament actually passed a budget for 1902, but long-term stability eluded Koerber in subsequent years.[75] Koerber's attempts to negotiate with Czech and German parties in the autumn of 1902 once again stirred up national conflict and obstructionist tactics; his government would implement budgets and the recruitment contingent for the military over the next two years using the emergency paragraph—article 14—but this hardly offered Koerber much sleep.[76] Attempts to open parliament and get it working again failed repeatedly in 1903 and 1904, culminating with Koerber's appearance before the House of Representatives in the Reichsrat on March 8, 1904. Koerber lambasted the members of parliament for their obstruction, chiding them for all the budget and tax bills, the sixty imperial decrees which they failed to debate, the bills for industrial development or trade that they failed to discuss, and the failure to pass humanitarian aid for the city of Laibach/Ljubljana—which suffered an earthquake in 1895. Near the end of his speech, Koerber worked himself into a rhetorical frenzy, saying that the delegates "truly present the picture of a parliamentary ghost town."[77] Koerber woke the ire of the parliamentarians who shouted him down, as the president repeatedly clanged the bell, calling for order. But order was increasingly elusive and Koerber, who invited all parties to the negotiating table, would eventually try to steer the ship of state clear of the Reichsrat.

### Koerber's Study for Administrative Reform

The culmination of Koerber's search for a workable solution to restoring politics in the multinational monarchy culminated in *Prime Minister Koerber's Study for a Reform of the Domestic Administration*.[78] Released to parliament and subsequently to the press in late 1904, Koerber's study became a public bombshell. In incredibly blunt language, the study bared the inefficiencies and problems inherent in Austria's dual-track administrative system. Jurisdictional conflicts and unclear lines of authority came under fire for creating an inefficient governmental system that was out of step with the larger development of the modern welfare state. Austria's administration was complex, confusing, and too susceptible to political influence. In the words of the study, Austria's administration had "fallen utterly short."[79]

Koerber's study planned, in the words of a contemporary, "a grand state-reform,"[80] which entailed a massive overhaul of the Austrian administrative system. In effect, the *Studien* endorsed decentralizing the administration by shifting administrative power and responsibility from the *Land* and the central offices in Vienna to the district and superdistrict offices of the county. At the same time Koerber wanted to centralize the administration by taking away duties, responsibilities, and power from autonomous offices and instead give them to their counterparts in the central administration. The end product of such a reform was to foster a local and regional democracy that was cleansed of national and mass political parties and which would focus itself toward policy.

To effect such groundbreaking changes in the political and administrative culture of the monarchy, Koerber had to alter the political culture of the monarchy. Once again, this played out as Koerber reached into the Habsburg administrative toolbox to find a familiar instrument. The tool was once again, following Stadion almost six decades before, putting Austria's officials in the center of the storm as mediators and fixers. Koerber sought to restore the imperial bureaucracy to a leading policy-making role in the monarchy, one that would step into the vacuum left behind by a stalemated and diminished parliament. To restore the bureaucracy's policy-making role, however, the administration would have to restore politics to some kind of working order. It is telling that Koerber and other domestic officials in his ministry did not share the "cultural despair" of many of the elites in the foreign ministry. Instead of seeing the parliamentary crisis as a sign of impending dissolution, Koerber saw parliamentary unrest as a means and as a moment to correct the many political and administrative idiosyncrasies of Austria's constitutional government.[81]

While Koerber's study sought to restore politics to a constructive component of government, he believed that political life had to be managed. His *Studien* relegated politics to increased bureaucratic supervision at local and regional levels. Koerber's reforms called for the bureaucracy to fulfill the work that Austria's constitutional system had given to political representatives. In his mind, politicians had lost their mandate and were no longer serving the good of the people or the state. The stability of the central state was of utmost importance to Koerber, not only because as an idea it shared the "neutrality" or "objectivity" of the bureaucracy which served it; but also because, in the mind of a progressive Josephinist like Koerber, the state was best equipped to manage the increasing tasks of public welfare. As such, the Koerber reform plan proposed administrative changes that would have brought bureaucrats much closer to the populace at large—to a position to see firsthand the needs of citizens. It also called for new forms of training and new structures, which would have enabled the bureaucracy to take on new roles of social welfare; with its new skills and power, the bureaucracy could wrest other forms of public works and expenditures away from the autonomous administrations. These goals were hidden in more pedestrian administrative language that veiled a very Josephinist antipolitical stance, or at the very least, a faith that the bureaucracy could fulfill the needs of the populace better than politicians.

The thrust of Koerber's *Studien* was to manipulate the structures of administration to rechannel political life into one that was not based on the assertion of rights and the promotion of interests; rather political life should serve the state and, so serve the good of all. To change the administrative structure, however, was to alter the foundations of the state that arose in the 1860s. Koerber aimed his piercing criticism at the root of the inefficiency of the Austrian *Verwaltung*: its bad organization. As such, Koerber subtly attacked the unclear and muddled constitutional foundations of the Austrian state, which were born out of compromises to Austrian liberals and Hungarian nationalists after the military failures of the 1850s and 1860s. He lays much of the blame on the structure of the administration, which placed too much emphasis on the autonomous units which did not have the financial means to fulfill the growing duties of a modern administration, nor the independence or objectivity to institute good policies.[82] Hence, Koerber shifted the discussion of administrative reform of intra-office measures to a reform of the monarchy's structure—and the state itself. Administrative reforms once again, as they had since Maria Theresia, became a heuristic device for understanding and correcting the larger conflicts in public law and parliamentary life.

Koerber's *Studien*, underneath its stern analysis of governmental problems and Koerber's public assurances for the continued maintenance of autonomy, proposed—in its details—an administrative coup. There were a few aspects central to Koerber's sprawling plan for administrative reform. The first was decentralization. Koerber proposed redrawing district prefectures, making their boundaries contiguous with district court precincts. This would have increased the number of district prefects in Cisleithania from 342 to 749, more than doubling their number. Public power would be further "decentralized" by grouping four or five districts under a county, which Koerber wanted to reintroduce to Austria's administrative framework. Koerber argued that this would help unburden the provincial governments, which were all too often called upon to make decisions in local matters and also too far removed from the populace to make those decisions well. By expanding the districts and re-creating the *county* as their supervisory unit, Koerber's *Studien* essentially removed crownland politics from any power to make decisions on local matters.

In addition to taming politics, the proposal sought to hollow out all the administrative and political work done at the provincial level. Districts and counties would be outfitted by representative assemblies of elected delegates. These elected officials were to become the vessel for political activity and would help create, in the words of the study, "an organic connection between the state and autonomous authorities."[83] They would take over many of the autonomous features of government, leaving the crownlands left to manage funds, but little else. The matter of politics, the pursuit of interests, would be pushed down the administrative ladder to counties and districts, which would be smaller, more nationally homogenous, and less likely to devolve into national conflict.

Rather than seeing Koerber's study as an exercise in blatant bureaucratic absolutism, the *Studien* envisioned limited local and regional democratic representation. But the democracy that Koerber wanted was local and absent of party political machinery. As such, Koerber's strategy was not to rid the administration of the dual-track system, even though his *Studien* identified it as the root of the problems in Austria's bureaucracy. Instead, he wanted to maintain the "mix" of autonomous and centralist units in the administration, but he also wanted to alter the power constellation in it. Koerber wanted to subsume the autonomous elements into centralist institutions by placing the autonomous offices under the leadership of a state official who would take orders from Vienna.

Koerber's *Studien* likewise envisioned a new type of civil servant, who would be able to demonstrate the local face of the state. As minister of the interior, Koerber had continuously reminded his local officials that they were the public face of the state and that their comportment was of utmost importance for maintaining the good will of the populace.[84] Koerber wanted an administration composed of officials willing and able to tackle problems and make appropriate decisions. Part and parcel of this transformation of the ethos of the bureaucracy was the idea that civil servants must no longer be able to defer difficult decisions to their superiors and hide within the hierarchy of command; instead, they must learn to handle decisions in their own offices. Koerber needed to retool and retrain officials to act independently and confidently. In service of these goals, bureaucrats staffing the districts and counties would also need to acquire deep technical knowledge of business and industry, because such bureaucrats would have to make decisions regarding these important matters by the time they reached the offices of the county. Koerber's *Studien* proposed reforms for the education of future officials at the universities, and in their on-the-job training once they took up a position in the civil service. University-trained civil servants, who entered the bureaucracy as *Konzeptsbeamte* in the ninth class, overwhelmingly had graduated with a degree in law. Koerber proposed that civil service exams which emphasized practical education and experience would be administered after the third and tenth years of service. In addition, these civil service exams offered a standardized gateway for advancement into the higher ranks of the ministerial bureaucracy, barring anyone who did not pass the second exam from proceeding past the sixth class. This would keep unexceptional civil servants from entering into any important bureaucratic posts at the level of the crownlands or the ministries, effectively banishing them forever to the Austrian countryside as underlings in a district or county office. These structural changes would have caused a major shift, not only in the administrative framework of the state, but also in the way Austrian citizens related to the state. Koerber's proposal would decentralize state authority, but it did not necessarily take authority away from state officials. Instead, it called for decentralization into the hands of state officials who were stationed locally. At the same time, however, Koerber's proposed reforms directly attacked the autonomous crownland authorities. Koerber's reforms had a representative element that sought to fly the work of government under the stormy clouds of nationality conflict.

In the long term, Koerber's plan returned to many ideas that Stadion first outlined for the dual-track system in 1849. This was representative government, carefully defined and kept in a glass aquarium. It would be the state's pet, not its master. Koerber's study sharply collided with vested political interests. Polish aristocrats wanted to preserve their influence in the governor's office in Galicia; Czech national politicians and German conservatives hoped to expand the scope of provincial autonomy from Bohemia to Styria; the Christian Socials in Vienna looked to preserve their power base in Vienna and thus jealously guarded the special political concessions to charter cities. Liberals worked to maintain local self-government in the smaller towns. Everywhere, then, the structures of Austrian politics worked against Koerber's reform plans. Thus, it was hardly a surprise that the publication of the study unleashed a maelstrom of criticism and discontent in Austria's political parties. *Narodní Listy*, the Czech liberal daily, accused Koerber's study of exaggerating the scope of Austria's problems, especially his criticism of autonomous government. That the Young Czech Party's political power base rested in the sinecures within Bohemia and Moravia's autonomous administration was left unmentioned. *Słowo Polskie*, in Lemberg/Lwów, more brazenly stated that Poles, for reasons of national interest, should resist Koerber's plan to unify the administration and reduce the administrative purview of the autonomous authorities.[85] Koerber's plan rankled German speakers in cities and towns, too. The Christian Socials in Vienna recognized Koerber's study for what it was—an attack on their authority as the political elite in the imperial capital. They tacitly withdrew their support from Koerber's regime.[86]

Koerber handed in his resignation to the emperor on December 28, 1904; the emperor released him from office on December 31, after almost five years in office.[87] Officially, Koerber stepped down due to his failing health: he was plagued with stomach problems, increasing nervousness, and, reportedly, fits of rage in the later stages of his minister-presidency. One can indeed see, both in the press and in various memoirs of Koerber's contemporaries, evidence of Koerber's failing mental and physical health, as well as an exhaustion that stemmed from almost five years of wrestling with the political complexities of the time. However, as Kolmer and others rightly note, Koerber was still planning sweeping changes and ambitious projects in the last months of his government. His many legislative drafts, a pending trade agreement with the German Empire, as well as his *Studien* on administrative reform, offer no evidence that he was planning an escape from the minister's bench. And though Koerber's increasing physical and mental weakness may indeed have been real, his growing political isolation may very well have been the fundamental cause for his departure. But, like

Joseph II over a hundred years earlier, it was Koerber's energy and ideas that would have lasting currency. Koerber's *Studien* unleashed a discussion which would last for the next decade or more, only interrupted by Europe's great catastrophe, the First World War.

## Universal Suffrage and State Reform

Koerber's study demonstrated not only the room for improvement, but the awesome potential for the bureaucracy in the Austrian state-system. It would leave a lasting legacy for the first half of the twentieth century in Austria. Koerber's crafty release of the study to the press brought these grand state-reform ideas and the bureaucracy's role in civil society into public discussions and into publications on politics, political economy, and parliamentary government. "Reform," in all its permutations and guises, became the order of the day. The next several years saw a number of private works on administrative reform, from Social Democratic ideologues like Otto Bauer to political economists like Ferdinand Schmid.[88] Far from being a moribund monarchy without friends, instead socialists and liberals, bureaucrats and radicals thought through ways to reestablish the monarchy for a new century.

The monarchy by 1904 had become a state built on the basis of prosperity, reform, and progress. Joseph II's goal of "the general best," which encompassed the "greatest number of citizens" and made "all the provinces of the monarchy into a whole," had been rearticulated many times during the long nineteenth century.[89] Through the constitutional experiments of the 1850s and 1860s, to the establishment of Austria's dual-track administrative system, and finally to the promulgation of universal male suffrage in 1906, the "public" in Austria was based on a combination of old and new. This tradition of compromise continued into the twentieth century, as Austria's supreme administrative and constitutional courts contemplated new forms of group rights for national communities and as regional politicians brokered "compromises" that split provincial electorates into national cadasters.[90] In the last decade before the outbreak of the war, between the promulgation of Koerber's study and the assassination of Franz Ferdinand, Austria's politicians and ministerial elites experimented with new political institutions and implemented new public laws.

The administration, including the imperial bureaucracy and the framework of the imperial state, remained at the center of public reform discussions. But the very nature of "reform" in the final years of the monarchy meant that the bureaucracy had become an essential component of constitutional law, parliamentary politics, and democratic governance. The Austrian state had reached a level of complexity and intricacy that it needed *public input* and *bureaucratic authority*. The outbreak of war in 1914 would shut off this vital channel of communication, but not before there were movements to rethink the relationship between bureaucracy and democratic society in the twentieth century. The decade between 1904 and 1914, then, was one of possibilities. Questions, of course, remain: How much reform was possible? What would the Austrian state have been capable of doing with national politics in parliament and an old conservative emperor on the throne? Lest we judge the capacity of the Austrian state too harshly in this moment, we have to keep in mind that thinkers of the day thought reform possible. Francis Joseph had entered his eighth decade and was bound to pass away soon. The heir presumptive, Franz Ferdinand, had established a military chancellery in the Belvedere Palace which did much more than supervise maneuvers or organize military inspections. In reality, Franz Ferdinand's military chancellery prepared for the day when Franz Ferdinand would become the emperor. In the meantime, the old emperor's advisors wanted to change as little as possible.[91]

What resulted from a restless heir presumptive—who wanted to change everything but could not—and an old emperor on the throne was a period in which political thinkers could dream. And dreaming was the order of the day. Everyone expected that Franz Ferdinand would change the monarchy; the point was to come up with the best plan for him to do so.[92] In the world before the First World War, the Austrian state had a chance to reform again, like it did sixty years before. We can look therefore at the vibrancy of the debate as a clue into the wide-ranging avenues for change. The possibilities were there. That they were cut off by the violence and tragedy of the war does not mean that they had no chance to succeed.

Ernest von Koerber's *Studien* emerged too late in his tenure and was far too uncompromising, but it certainly caught the attention of the press and politicians. It began a decade of debate about reform and the future of the empire. Moreover, Koerber's *Studien* imbued new energy into a public debate on imperial reform that centered on the administration. The Viennese Juridical Society held a series of lectures in January and February of 1905; these lectures were given by experts from Austria's academic and legal professions, as well as by members of the civil service (including a district prefect and *Statthaltereirat*) and members of the Supreme Administrative Court (*Vewaltungsgerichtshof*).[93] Academic debate ensued with a flourishing of articles,[94] but increasingly the debate on administrative reform reached a wider public audience.[95] This public engagement included political analyses that were meant for a larger, educated audience and which called for various sweeping administrative reforms. In many ways, these more popular political tracts reproduced and repackaged older, well-established ideas for Austrian state reform.[96] Although the entries into the public debate represented diverse ideas—from advocacies of centralism, national councils, or even a return to a federal system and a shrinking of the central authority—what united them was a viewpoint that saw administrative reform as the access point to a larger constitutional reform.[97] As Count Ludwig Crenneville noted in the conclusion to his tract, in which he advocated an administrative reform that would shrink the central authorities of the civil service and therefore turn over regional administration to the autonomous authorities of the crownlands, "The administration is not the object of our interest, but rather the question, whether it [the administration] should be primarily autonomous [i.e., belong to the crownlands and cities] or of the central state."[98]

Moreover, the introduction of universal male suffrage in 1907 pushed the idea of administrative reform further into the public eye. Reformers, bureaucrats, and politicians believed that the administration would have to be retooled to adapt to a modern, democratic system. Reform of the administration returned to the tables of parliament again—much like it had in 1876. As I have argued in Chapters 4 and 5, the imperial civil service found that parliamentary government was a new institution with which it would have to work after the promulgation of the February Patent in 1861. Since that time, the suffrage in Cisleithanian Austria had undergone an expansion in progressive stages. Suffrage laws in April 1873, October 1882, and June 1896 were sanctioned by the emperor; by 1897, every male citizen over twenty-four years of age with six months of residence in his current domicile could vote in the parliamentary elections. However, all votes were not equal, since they were divided among five different curiae. The 1907 suffrage reform, which received the emperor's sanction on January 26, changed all of this. It destroyed the curial system of suffrage; now 510 representatives would be elected to the lower house of parliament by equal, universal male suffrage.[99]

Elections were held in May 1907 for the first democratically elected parliament; this new parliament, which only returned 216 members (300 of the 516 were newly elected), convened in June.[100] The suffrage reform of 1907 swept out a great many experienced politicians and brought in new ones. Experienced statesmen who were forced out by the elimination of the privileged curiae of landowners and the chambers of commerce and industry included well-known figures such as Josef Maria Baernreither and future prime minister Count Karl Stürgkh. Thus the suffrage reform created new divisions and gave strength to the mass parties, especially the Social Democrats and the Christian Socials. It also meant that the representatives of the people were now constituted differently and would express different interests. On another level, the suffrage reform and the new crop of parliamentarians it inevitably introduced to *Reich*-level politics meant that the imperial Austrian bureaucracy would have to work alongside a new, democratically elected parliament. The bureaucracy not only faced a newly constituted interlocutor in the state system, but it also lost powerful allies in parliament—the representatives of the state-supporting Loyal Constitutionalists of great landowners and the various liberals who were elected through the separate curiae for chambers of commerce.

Emperor Francis Joseph followed these debates closely. In his speech opening the eighteenth session of parliament on June 19, 1907, Francis Joseph remarked that "it would be a rich benefit for the state, if an accomplishment of equal worth in the field of the administration could be implemented beside the constitutional reform [i.e., the establishment of equal, universal male suffrage]—which in the previous session of the Reichsrat was so successfully implemented." The emperor furthermore believed that such an administrative reform was necessitated by the new, democratically elected parliament. What was needed, according to Francis Joseph, was a "better administrative foundation," "a quickened decision-making process," and shorter links in the chain of command between district prefects and imperial governors. All this would be to the purpose of "adapting the state administrative apparatus to the increasing demands" that now would be made on it.[101]

Following Francis Joseph's speech, members of this parliament began calling for a reform of the administration: one which would be able to accommodate and accompany democracy into the twentieth century. In the fourth sitting of the new parliamentary session, a newly elected representative from Moravia, Josef Redlich, brought the need for a thoroughgoing administrative reform to the forefront of parliamentary discussion. The fourth sitting began with a debate of an emergency motion by Dr. Albert

Gessmann, the parliamentary leader of the Christian Socials, on the need for a thorough reform of the financial situation of the crownlands.

Redlich claimed any solution to the crises of crownland finances must begin with an administrative reform of the central bureaucracy. Moreover, like Francis Joseph, he made the link between the institution of universal male suffrage and an administrative reform: "Consider that every improvement in the public policy [staatliches Leben]—take, for example, the institution of a general, equal suffrage law—in all civilized states [Kulturstaaten] is accompanied by a significant reform of the administration."[102] But more than this, Redlich claimed that the entire administrative system—the dual administration for which Redlich blamed Anton Schmerling—was outmoded and devoid of an "inner logic" or "cohesion."[103] Moreover, Redlich was willing to go into details, criticizing the "colossal growth of personnel," and thus cost, in the central authorities, while the autonomous administrations of the crownlands and municipalities bore the brunt of providing new social services. "Our bureaucracy," Redlich claimed, "is a costly apparatus, which operates half-empty, which doesn't accomplish much more than follow routine, or which even throws obstacles in the way of the promotion of economic interests."[104]

Redlich's opinions in many ways expressed, although with a different tenor, the criticisms of the administrative system that Ernest von Koerber had published in his *Studien* two-and-one-half years before. Redlich thought that the domestic administration of the Austrian state cost too much for what it provided and, in the end, that it was "far removed from the actual duties of a modern *Verwaltung*."[105] In the middle of his speech to parliament, Redlich reiterated the need for the administration of the state to harmonize with the various provincial and autonomous administrations. Unlike Koerber, Redlich was much more ready to lay the blame on the expensive central administration than on the irresponsible autonomous authorities. To bring harmony to the administration, Redlich exclaimed that an appeal must be made to government, so that it would "undertake a truly serious reform of the administration; a reform that will also offer the public a financial benefit; a reform that is now made necessary with the institution of a universal, direct, and equal suffrage law."[106]

Two years after his plea to the government, Redlich followed up with his own motion to form an extraordinary imperial commission on June 15, 1909.[107] Redlich's bill called for the government to "immediately take steps to assemble an extraordinary imperial commission which would be given the task to submit suggestions, based on its own investigations and studies, for the reform of the entire domestic administration of state finances and railways." Redlich reiterated that the expense and relative inefficiency of the administration necessitated such a large and important project. But his bill went further than this; in fact, it stated that a grand reform that solves the problems of the central administration "cannot be accomplished by the administration which is itself to be reformed." Rather, Redlich's bill instructed that a commission be established, which would consist of representatives of the administration, but also members of the autonomous administrations of the crownlands and large cities, as well as university academics who specialized in constitutional and administrative law. Additionally, Redlich wanted to include representatives of Austria's various business communities: agriculture, industry, chambers of commerce, and trade unions.

Redlich, although a rather new parliamentarian, was no stranger to the complexities of administrative organization. After studying law and political economy at various universities in the Habsburg monarchy and in Germany, Redlich had joined the Cisleithanian civil service as an unpaid intern in the imperial governor's office in his native Moravia.[108] As a student, he had taken a strong interest in the study of public administration, especially that of England. His family's independent wealth allowed him the financial freedom to make research trips to England throughout the 1890s. He put these efforts and resources to good work, producing a thorough survey of the English administration, *Englische Lokalverwaltung: Darstellung der inneren Verwaltung Englands in ihrer geschichtlichen Entwicklung und in ihrer gegenwärtigen Gestalt* (1901). This work not only won Redlich significant acclaim outside Austria—the volume was translated into English at the urging of Sir Courtenay Hirst[109]—it certified Redlich's academic reputation as an expert in administrative law.[110]

By the time Redlich took a seat in the Austrian House of Representatives in 1907, he had published a second study on England, this time on the House of Commons;[111] he had taken up a post as Professor Extraordinarius at the Technical University of Vienna in administrative law; and he had been elected to the Moravian diet from his home town of Göding/Hodonín. Additionally, he had taken up a study of local government in Austria in conjunction with his status as a representative for Austria in the editorial commission for the *Verein für Sozialpolitik* (Association for Social Policy).[112] It was precisely in terms of administrative questions that Redlich attempted to put his academic expertise to practical effect. What is more, Redlich's bill in parliament found traction within the government. On November 27, 1909, almost five months after his original motion for the establishment of an imperial commission, the minister of the interior, Baron Guido von Haerdtl, summoned Josef Redlich to a meeting.[113] According to Redlich's diary, Haerdtl informed Redlich that if he were to remain minister of the interior, he would put Redlich's idea for a special commission on administrative reform into action. In this regard, he hoped Redlich would offer his assistance and support to get the effort set into motion.[114]

Of course, Haerdtl was likewise no stranger to questions of administrative reform. Not only was he a high-ranking civil servant in the Ministry of the Interior during the tenure of Ernest von Koerber, but he also worked very closely with Koerber on his *Studien*. By the end of Koerber's term in office, Koerber had promoted Haerdtl to the highly coveted rank of department head (*Sektionschef*) of the ministry's legislative section. By 1908, Haerdtl had become interior minister in Count Richard Bienerth's cabinet. In his appointment letter, Bienerth recognized Haerdtl's "work as *Sektionschef* in one of the most important sections of the Ministry of the Interior," and Haerdtl's "rare full perspective of the entirety of tasks and goals of the central administration," as well as Haerdtl's "mature statesmanlike conception toward the more important questions" that faced the ministry.[115] As minister of the interior, Haerdtl intended to use his thorough understanding of administrative matters to take up the torch of administrative reform. He leapt at the chance that Redlich's parliamentary bill had offered him. These efforts nevertheless took over a year to bear fruit: on May 22, 1911, Emperor Francis Joseph gave his official permission to establish an imperial "Commission for the Promotion of Administrative Reform" (*Kommission zur Förderung der Verwaltungsreform*).[116]

### Commission for the Promotion of Administrative Reform

Koerber's practice as prime minister and interior minister and his groundbreaking study on administrative reform encapsulated the inner tensions between the expansion of the state and ideas of far-reaching reform. As the prime minister, Koerber sought to build roads, canals, and bring more people into contact with the largess of the modern state. The expansion of political participation, with the step-by-step expansion of suffrage, only fueled these trends. The increased need for inspectors and regulatory officials pressured bureaucratic bosses to hire new types of officials with technical training. Moreover, they had to staff their central offices with more general policy-making officials, who would be able to understand increasingly technical reports, queries, and make decisions forwarded up the chain of command. Koerber's state needed a bigger civil service.[117] Governors in the provinces especially pressured the Ministry of the Interior in Vienna for more personnel. For them, the increased tasks of the state and the lack of a corresponding increase in personnel had created a crisis. The governor in Trieste, for instance, complained that the Littoral, with its ever-increasingly important position in the monarchy as a military and shipping center, as well as its linguistic complexity (four official languages: German, Italian, Slovene, and Serbo-Croatian), experienced a "colossal increase in the amount of work." The changes that the state bureaucracy underwent since 1900, he argued, due to an "intensification of state activity in all areas of public administration," had not only expanded its responsibilities, but—combined with little changes on the ground, either in organization or number of personnel in the Austrian Littoral—had caused an acute administrative crisis. The governor did not mince his words either: chiding the government for handling his province and its administrative needs in "stepmother-like fashion," he wrote that "the general overabundance of work forces the bureaucracy into cursoriness, causes large and harmful delays, dulls any interest in the work to be done and suppresses many insightful initiatives."[118] For the governor in Trieste, more men meant better work and a better administration.

However, Koerber's study emphasized the importance of efficiency and offered ways to completely rethink the state apparatus. Out of such grand ideals for a newly outfitted multinational state came the projects of the Commission for the Promotion of Administrative Reform. Over three years, between May 1911 and June 1914, the commission, consisting of politicians, academics, and former ministerial officials, examined all facets of administration in Cisleithania. Their studies produced reports and, more importantly, suggestions for reform of everything from legal education at universities and periodic training for active civil servants to the structure of the bureaucracy itself.[119] The chairman of the commission, Erwin von Schwarzenau, was one of Koerber's protégés, and like Koerber, he had a most capacious idea of what administrative reform meant.[120] In the inaugural meeting of the commission on June 28, 1911, Schwarzenau highlighted that the work of the commission would be to rebuild the state for a new century. "Out of the chaos of conflicting opinions and strivings," Schwarzenau philosophically intoned, "the gradually recognizable form of a welfare state emerges."[121] It fell to the commission to sort out the form that this welfare state would take. For Schwarzenau and for his fellow colleagues, the keystone in rebuilding the future state was not parliamentary life alone, but the administration in all its parts, autonomous and state, central and local. Schwarzenau emphasized that the administration stood in the center of the chaos, as it tried to meet and make sense of the competing claims of Austria's citizens. Only the bureaucracy could grasp the needs of the whole, fragmented society; only it could find the right path to fulfillment of the common good. Reforming the administration, therefore, was the key to reforming all of Austrian society for the twentieth century.

But, of course, the administration had become fragmented, presenting the commission with a daunting task. The commission's members spent the first two years collecting information and writing reports. Josef Redlich and Guido von Haerdtl even staged an *Enquête*—an imperial commission of inquiry—bringing eighty industrialists, businessmen, lawyers, academics, local notables, and officials to Vienna for sessions of the *Enquête*, which stretched over fourteen days of meetings in late October and early November 1912. As Redlich stated in his letter of invitation to the participants, the purpose of the *Enquête* would be to "assemble the observations and experiences of practical men in regards to the effectiveness of the state and autonomous administrations."[122] Topics of conversation ranged from the structure of the administration, the amount of time it took for the administration to reach a decision, the division of labor of state and autonomous authorities, as well as legal obligations on behalf of the state for unconstitutional or illegal actions on the part of the bureaucracy. The stenographic minutes of these group interviews were quickly published, consisting of over five hundred folio pages.[123]

For historians today, the sheer size and contents of the inquiry indicate two general trends of imperial reform by 1912. First, Austria's administration had become so complicated that it took a sizeable membership of reform commissioners a significant amount of time and research to "find out" fundamental aspects of its structure, functioning, and even its size and expenditure. Second, contrary to what Josef Redlich would write about the commission after the fall of the monarchy, the work of reform included both insiders and outsiders: ministry officials and representatives of Austria's national groups, political parties, and the public at large.[124]

The *Enquête* provided a basis for much of the second year of the commission, which consisted of the various commission members researching various aspects of the administration and writing reports. As the committee members dug deeper into the depths of administrative practice, they found a system that again had become encrusted by years of muddling through, bad practices, and a pattern of supervision that turned a blind eye to inefficiency. Guido von Haerdtl's report on the rising costs of the administration, found that while the state had become responsible for so much more of public life since 1890, its structures had not changed. Rather, more and more civil servants had been hired, without an eye directed toward efficiency. Haerdtl's report not only found that the costs of the domestic administration had skyrocketed since 1890 (from almost 4 million kronen in 1890 to over 18 million in 1911), but it also laid out in clear statistical tables the numbers of officials and how few cases they actually produced over a given year. Ministry officials found Haerdtl's report so troubling that they sought to suppress its contents.

In the midst of more detailed calculations, Haerdtl determined that much of the costs could be spared by a better organization. In his research he found numerous departments that were so overspecialized that they had hardly any work. Citing numerous examples, including a department that was created in October 1911 to oversee the "organizational and juridical-administrative matters of state building," he ridiculed such useless overspecialization: "Gentlemen, I beg your forgiveness, but I spent days trying to find out what 'the organizational and juridical-administrative matters of state building' means. . . . And, gentlemen, since October 1911 this department has handled forty-two files." Haerdtl's report, in general, found that technical specialization of the bureaucracy had created so many minidepartments, many of which were staffed with juridically trained—and thus more expensive—midlevel officials. This type of specialization caused the number of officials in the central ministries in Vienna to more than triple between 1890 and 1911. Moreover, in this same period, the number of officials in the provincial offices barely doubled. Despite the greater growth in Vienna, the governments in the provinces took on a much greater case load than the departments in the central ministries. Haerdtl discovered that the average official in the central offices handled less than two cases per day; one third of officials in the central ministries averaged less than one case per day.[125]

Haerdtl offered the commission several ideas for a reform, all of which touched on fundamental issues of both the administration's organization and the way it employed its officials. Haerdtl based his ideas on the dual action of reducing the costs of the administration and improving its organization and efficiency to meet the growing challenges of modern social welfare. However, his suggestions cut at the heart of some of the developments in the bureaucracy in the constitutional era. First of all, Haerdtl hoped to reduce the number of tenured, university-trained officials. Much of the work of the offices should be met by increasing the relative size of clerical support staff, *Kanzleibeamte*, to the number of policy-making, university-trained officials. Such a reorganization of the bureaucracy writ large would be enhanced by streamlining the organization of the bureaucracy itself. Haerdtl wanted to reduce jurisdictional conflicts and overlapping offices between the various ministries.[126] In the end, he hoped to use this rationalization of the entire domestic administrative organization to increase the pay of the civil service and attract better and smarter officials for work in the administration, while retaining those who were tempted to find better pay in the private sector.[127]

His report and suggestions certainly touched a nerve. Count Erich Kielmansegg ironically spoke at length on how part of the growth in personnel and the lack of efficiency was due to *Vielschreiberei*—administrative graphomania—that manifested itself in the tendency to write down everything. Moreover, Kielmansegg had noticed in his almost forty years of service at every level of the administration, that this tendency to write too much had become a veritable part of the entire administrative system—a system that in fact depended on a hydrocephalic administration in which so much of the ministerial staff consisted of university-trained officials instead of clerical staff.[128]

The combined subcommittees decided to continue the discussion the next day so that they could agree on principles for reform. At Haerdtl's insistence, the suggestions for reform were expressly described as "provisional" (*vorläufig*) and thus, dependent on other reform proposals that the commission expected to produce at a later date. Haerdtl's report was groundbreaking for the work of the commission. His findings underscored the political independence of the commission and his conclusions and suggestions for reform made claims for the commission's involvement in all areas where the administration reached. As some members rightly claimed after reading his report, Haerdtl's findings that the central bureaucracy had ballooned in the preceding two decades gave statistical voice to the problem of political infiltration and patronage in the bureaucracy. Cutting costs and improving efficiency became tied to the sticky issue of how the bureaucracy would free itself of largely unnecessary appointments going to the cronies of national interest groups and political parties. Moreover, could parliament be expected to aid in an administrative reform that loosed these problematic connections between politicians and the bureaucracy? Such questions were put off until the commission could finish more of its work, but they would shape the way the commission continued and widened its scope. It would consider all facets of the Austrian state and its role in a modern, democratic society.

Members of the commission filed other reports with the commission over the next two years. They slaughtered sacred cows, at least on paper. Josef Redlich's report on Austria's financial administration identified its tax-collection policies as a system whose many jurisdictional conflicts allowed politicians and district prefects to meddle in tax collection and revenue projects.[129] The result was haphazard management, political interventions by members of parliament, and crass inefficiency.[130] For instance, Redlich found that the Ministry of Finance spent more than 4 million kronen collecting 2 million kronen worth of taxes in Dalmatia.[131] Redlich proposed removing the work of revenue collection from the state administrative organs of districts and the provincial governments and giving them to an independent revenue-collection authority. Redlich hoped to mold the Ministry of Finance into a more distant supervisory body. As it stood, it intervened too readily in local matters of collection and expenditure while not keeping a watchful eye on the state budget as a whole.[132]

Redlich's proposals sought to push decision making in revenue collection closer to the local level. Vienna had too much say and often meddled—to the detriment of efficiency and transparency. But such proposals needed to be integrated into a larger system of reforms, ones that reinforced the *freies Ermessen*, "the freedom of discretion," on the part of local state officials. Other reform proposals put forth by the commission sought to create the necessary conditions to support independent professionalism at the local level. The subcommittee on the education and training of civil servants was particularly productive. Count Franz Merveldt, a career civil servant and former imperial governor, and Dr. Heinrich Rauchberg, a professor at the German university in Prague, had produced a study on the reform of university curriculum in political economics and legal studies.[133] This curriculum reform targeted degree programs that prepared university graduates for work in the civil service. It suggested that reforms be implemented that aimed at improving the practical knowledge and experience of civil servants. Merveldt and Rauchberg had also produced drafts of two separate administrative ordinances that would have revised the qualifications and process of hiring university-trained civil servants as well as revised early on-the-job training for these civil servants once they were hired. This report was followed by a study of the education and training of civil servants who were "technical specialists" (in engineering, agriculture, forestry, veterinary and regular medicine) by former *Sektionschef* and cabinet minister Dr. Heinrich von Wittek.[134]

As the commission moved to examine the larger role of the bureaucracy in public life, Dr. Erwin von Schwarzenau issued a report suggesting "new rules of procedure" for district prefectures and the "declaration of principles for actions by the central state [*politische*] authorities."[135] In the main, Schwarzenau hoped to push through a fundamental retooling of the bureaucracy, weighing its decision-making abilities toward the point of direct contact of the state bureaucracy with the general populace: the district prefect. Schwarzenau presented his proposals during the ninth plenary meeting of the commission on July 1–2, 1913. Although the minutes of this meeting have not survived in the archives of the Administrative Reform Commission in the Allgemeines Verwaltungsarchiv, it was the scene of an important debate.[136] The ninth plenary session stayed up well into the night debating the legality of Schwarzenau's plans. The sticking point of Schwarzenau's reform was that Schwarzenau hoped to promulgate all aspects of the reform by administrative ordinance—not by going through parliament or the various crownland diets.[137] Haerdtl and the legal scholar Edmund Bernatzik disapproved of Schwarzenau's proposals on constitutional grounds: Bernatzik held that ordinances can only be decreed on the basis of the law, according to article 11 of the Fundamental Law on the Governmental and Executive Authority (one of the laws comprising the December Constitution). In Bernatzik's estimation, the ordinances that Schwarzenau was proposing encompassed far more than setting norms within the bureaucracy. Rather they set up new legal norms "binding subjects vis-à-vis the administration."[138] This, of course, was the point: since Koerber, administrative elites like Schwarzenau thought of administration reform in terms of ersatz constitutional reform.

Schwarzenau's new rules of procedure for district prefectures sought to make the district prefect a greater presence in Austria's local communities by releasing him from many of his paper-pushing responsibilities and by giving him better training to enable him to make more administrative decisions on his own.[139] Through these new procedures, Schwarzenau sought to fulfill Koerber's concept that the district should be the "middle-point of all matters of the inner administration."[140] Schwarzenau declared that the purpose of these new rules of procedure was to correct Alexander Bach's administrative instruction of March 17, 1855, which had made the district administrators responsible for every file that their office processed.[141] Schwarzenau explained that "this instruction initiated a sudden rift in the progressive development of the political administration," which had important consequences for the relationship of the bureaucracy to the people they were to oversee.[142] In other words, Bach's instruction had made district officials and other juridically trained civil servants into paper-pushers unable to achieve any sort of close contact with the local populace. In freeing the district prefect from his primary role of paper-pusher, Schwarzenau hoped to speak both to Haerdtl's suggestions on the reduction of administrative costs (by making the districts carry a greater administrative load and by shifting the weight of office work onto clerical staff), and to Koerber's plan to bring the central administration directly into contact with the populace:

Full commitment and faithfulness for the supreme service, careful observation of the common good—of which the most possible accord with local public interest as with the official pursuit of defending the interests of individuals; the promotion of all endeavors that are legally allowed and in the public interest; friendliness and helpful assiduity toward the populace, a comportment which grounds a trust of the authorities in mutual understanding and a regard for its directives . . . represent in essence the general obligations of the district prefectures.[143]

Schwarzenau's proposals betrayed a high degree of paternalism, but they also reflected the larger concerns of Koerber to push politics closer to the local level, as well as Redlich and Haerdtl, who wanted decentralization of state authority to be standardized, more carefully delineated, and more cost-efficient.

Even if Redlich subsequently wrote in his analyses of late-imperial Austria that the commission was a general failure, in 1913 Schwarzenau's proposals had a chance of success. The commission, after long debate, eventually accepted his proposals. Tellingly, even Bernatzik's strong objections of unconstitutionality could not deter the commission's liberals or autonomists, like Adalbert Schönborn, from approving this report. Even parliamentarians like Redlich, who called Schwarzenau's plan "Liberal progress," could envision administrative reform plans such as Schwarzenau's capable of being implemented over and beyond the limits of constitutional law.[144] The Ministry of the Interior welcomed Schwarzenau's proposals and intended to implement his plan on a trial basis.[145] The exigencies of war put these plans on hold, but in and of themselves, Schwarzenau's proposals indicated a possible future of central Europe—a future vision shared by administrative intellectuals and the ministerial bureaucracy in the waning days of the Habsburg Empire. This future would soon be lost.

But the commission fought hard to give the Austrian state constructive reform ideas. The commission spent much of the spring of 1914 debating Guido von Haerdtl's *Foundations of a Reform of the Organization of the Domestic Administration*, which thoroughly revisited the constitutional and administrative organization of the Cisleithanian state.[146] In many ways Haerdtl's proposals revisited the entire framework of imperial Austria, the very framework that emerged in many compromises and debates between the revolution of 1848 and the promulgation of the December Constitution in 1867. Haerdtl's proposals sought to—in his words—"decentralize the administration," making room for district prefects and other local officials to have the freedom of judgment to render decisions locally, unburdening the governors' offices and central offices from their propensity to solve sticky issues, or worse, meddle in affairs that wasted time and resources. Haerdtl proposed to make districts more uniform throughout the monarchy and capping their population below eighty thousand people. He proposed methods to limit the ability of cases to be kicked up the chain of command. He envisioned the need for a new type of official, "the *Amtsmann*," to consult and conduct state business delegated to small towns and rural townships. Finally, like Koerber's study ten years earlier, he proposed the reintroduction of the county as an administrative district.[147] All of this, Haerdtl hoped, would create clearer lines of authority, rationalize decision making, and—most importantly—depoliticize, especially in terms of nationality politics, the work of the state. Haerdtl, again much like Koerber with his proposals, hoped to set a course below the stormy clouds of national politics. Smaller districts could separate national groups; counties would likewise keep them separate; crownlands with reduced responsibilities would give national politicians fewer opportunities to clash. Haerdtl repeated in many ways during these sessions that the reform program's purpose was to "liberate the administration from the damage of national hatred."

Haerdtl could not single-handedly revise the foundations of the Austrian state, which had been built over 150 years of compromise and experimentation. The state had grown too organically and provided too many pockets of fertile ground for vested interests of all kinds to grow amid the various levels of the administration. Haerdtl repeatedly had to defend his proposals during the spring of 1914. His proposal for the reintroduction of the county was voted down in the subcommittee on March 6, 1914, by a vote of five to four. Nonetheless, it was presented to the entire commission in its tenth plenary session at the end of March, where it was likewise voted down by eleven votes to seven.[148]

These failures sent Haerdtl back to the drawing board, but he found it difficult to press on. Haerdtl conceived his proposals as an organic whole and he found trouble fulfilling his larger goals without their central component. He complained with bitterness during the next meeting of the subcommittee that the underlying deficiencies of the administration remain untouched by these emasculated reform proposals: "There is nothing one can do, after the high commission chooses to shoot down all the proposals we present to it."[149] Yet, the subcommittee pressed on, meeting without a quorum on June 27, 1914, to salvage and possibly rebuild Haerdtl's proposals for the reform of the administrative organization of the monarchy.[150] Redlich emphasized that they should, in Koerberesque fashion, publish Haerdtl's original proposals·and allow a public debate to unfold, but the rest of the subcommittee ignored him so they could discuss Haerdtl's reworked proposal, *Reform of the Organization of the Domestic Administration*.[151] Haerdtl once again brought up limiting the size of districts, expanding the number of technical experts, and limiting the number of administrative levels a case could pass through without a decision. The topics of his proposals ranged from the state authorities to the autonomous governments of the crownlands, cities, and townships, but any unifying spirit of the reform proposal was notable for its absence. The subcommittee's discussion likewise centered on residual disagreements between competing centralizing, federalist, and local ideas of governance, specifically problems over which level of the administration can make appointments, which levels should be in charge of approving the plans for new public buildings, and—most telling—which administrative bodies should be in charge for the sanitation of public toilets on trains and in train stations. They were drowning in the details, unable to unite on a vision of the whole any longer.

## Descent into War

The joint subcommittee meeting ended with plans to reconvene in the fall, but by the fall the world had completely changed. The very next day in Sarajevo, June 28, 1914, Gavrilo Princip fired two shots into Archduke Franz Ferdinand's car, killing the archduke and his wife, Sophie, duchess of Hohenberg. Within a month, the monarchy would be at war with Serbia and the Allied powers.

The onset of the war cut short many other visions of the future. The twelfth and last meeting of the Commission for the Promotion of Administrative Reform occurred on December 15, 1914. At this meeting the commission's members (those who were able to attend) hammered out the language of the third and final yearly report. They had already decided that the remaining reports and resolution of the commission would be published in this report as addenda.[152] The hope was that the war would be short and that the commission, or some forum of experts, would soon be able to pick up where the commission was forced to leave off. The meeting contained a mix of resignation and optimism. For Haerdtl, the war shattered whatever hopes he had of reforming the entire governmental system and brought him to the brink of despair.[153] Josef Redlich showed optimism that the war would force a change in Austria's governmental system and break through the political stalemate. By tearing down the state, they could look to building up a new and better one in the future. Schwarzenau saw the emergency measures of the war as "superseding" the work of the commission.[154] For him, the war would allow a greater range of reform—a future free of the stalemate that had occupied administrative reformers since the Badeni crisis.

In a real sense, Schwarzenau saw the work of the commission as laying down a future path for reform—one that the war would make more viable, not less. On January 25, 1915, the emperor officially recognized the end of the activity of the commission.[155] Nevertheless Schwarzenau was persistent in his belief that the onset of the war had changed the nature and the relevance of the commission's work, though it was still unclear to him what exactly would change. Still, Schwarzenau was optimistic that the war would offer an opportunity for a large-scale transformation—one that could be pushed over the constitutional entanglements of the preceding half-century and that would benefit from the commission's work. At the end of the plenary session, Schwarzenau addressed the committee members, saying that the war would be the true successor to the Commission for the Promotion of Administrative Reform: "The greatest and most powerful administrative reformer will be the war." He thought that the war would give new goals to the state and that it would bring forth a "new generation," which would be up to the challenge of solving the state's pressing questions.[156]

It is only in hindsight that we can see Schwarzenau's optimism was deeply misplaced. The war would launch a coup d'état in which the military took supreme command of civilian policy. Austria would go down a different path from the one in which it had followed since the days of Joseph II; it was a path from which it could never return. State building and reform would be jettisoned in favor of arrests, prosecution, and persecution. The state no longer would bring civilization and progress to the countryside; it would bring troop recruiters, gendarmes, food commissars, and then, after years of war, death, hunger, and suffering.

The end of the state-building project and the state of emergency under military government should not color how we see the last decade of the monarchy. In the world of participatory politics and universal suffrage, Austria's ministerial elites had forged their own political identity. They had shaken off the attempts of parliamentarians to curtail their independence in the 1860s and 1870s to become a political institution in their own right. The bureaucracy's attempts to reform itself and the constitutional framework of the state was less a mark of bureaucratic absolutism than a search for solutions to a multinational and increasingly democratic polity. When the war broke out, this longer state-building process failed along with the possibilities for multinationalism in twentieth-century Europe.

# Epilogue
## The State of Exception:
## Austria's Descent into the Twentieth Century

IN MAY 1911 Field Marshall Oskar Potiorek became the imperial and royal army inspector in Bosnia-Herzegovina as well as its governor. As an Austro-Hungarian province, Bosnia-Herzegovina belonged to neither constitutional entity, but had an extraterritorial status and was placed, as an internal colony, under the direction of the common finance minister. It had received a provincial assembly in 1910, but sent no delegates to the Reichsrat or the Hungarian parliament. As an internal colony, Bosnia-Herzegovina was essentially under Potiorek's leadership, for he combined the muscle of the military with the political authority of the governor. Within the military establishment, Potiorek was a high-flyer. He had been several times on the short list for chief of the general staff: in 1906 when he had been the assistant to the then chief of staff, and again in 1911 when the post went to a rival general, Blasius Schemua. As compensation for these career disappointments, Potiorek had essentially been given Bosnia as his own kingdom. Bosnia was a fief to rule as he saw fit, far away from the politics of the general staff, where someone of his stature could prove to be a distracting influence.

Potiorek's work as military inspector led him to travel throughout the province, where he inspected fortresses and garrisons. But as the territory's governor, he also paid particular attention to the quality of roads and rail, the loyalty and industriousness of civilian authorities, and he held numerous discussions with religious and political elites. This is a key point, because for the three years that this high-ranking military general worked as the chief civilian official in Bosnia, he was taken by the optimism of administrative politics, the idea that deepening the role of the state can bring progress, just as it brought roads, bridges, rails, and schools to new localities, connecting them to the wider world. This same reforming spirit had affected administrative reformers and politicians for the previous decade and a half: reformers like Ernest von Koerber and Erwin von Schwarzenau, Josef Redlich and Guido von Haerdtl. For three years, Potiorek seemed to believe in the state-sponsored "cultural" and infrastructure investments, for a *Wohlstands- und Wohlfahrtstaat*. Potiorek worked hard during these years to keep Bosnia's politicians working and negotiating in the provincial diet. He wanted them to build schools, improve education, and to approve funds for rail improvements and better roads. The latter would bring investments and open up the colony to the monarchy. Moreover—Potiorek was ever the military man—infrastructure improved the mobility of the armed forces in case of war.

Of course, Potiorek had to prepare for the possibility of war. It came first in October 1912, in the form of the First Balkan War, when Serbia, Montenegro, Bulgaria, and Greece declared war on the Ottoman Empire. A month later, pro-Serbians in southern Hungary, in Dalmatia, and Bosnia-Herzegovina staged demonstrations to celebrate the early victories of Serbia and Montenegro—in the name of their southern Slav brethren. As Austria-Hungary's leading ministers and military elites considered mobilization and took efforts to suppress any perceived separatist radicalism, Potiorek hoped to hold his ship together and keep the political world open. He wrote to the common finance minister, his immediate superior in civil affairs, that he wished, "if it is somehow possible," to avoid the state of exception before a possible mobilization, so that "the work of the provincial assembly can continue as much as possible without interruption."[1] He explained: "As soon as the state of emergency is declared or a general mobilization is ordered—as painful as it be for us—the work of the provincial assembly will come to an end."[2] Potiorek himself thought that mobilization would ruin the work to which he had committed himself during his sixteen-month tenure as governor. This took no small act of bravery on his part: his colleagues in the military pushed repeatedly for implementation of emergency measures and the order for mobilization. They hoped to shut down Austria's political institutions, and thus debate, treasonous speech, and obstruction. Potiorek, as military governor, had traded in his sabre for the pen—at least for the moment.

But Field Marshall Potiorek would become tragically disillusioned with politics, for when the heir to the Habsburg throne, Franz Ferdinand, visited Sarajevo on June 28, 1914, the heir would die visiting Potiorek's army and his fiefdom. Potiorek sat in Franz Ferdinand's automobile as it came to a halt near the Latin Bridge along the Miljacka River. The car had followed the first two automobiles in the heir's motorcade as they mistakenly turned onto Franz Joseph Street. Potiorek stopped the driver, who slowly backed out onto the Appel Quay. At that moment on that fateful day, Potiorek watched in horror as a Bosnian Serb, Gavrilo Princip, gunned down Archduke Franz Ferdinand and his wife, the duchess of Hohenberg, Sophie Chotek, with merely two bullets. They died quickly, each with a severed artery. The act famously set off a chain of events which led to the First World War.[3]

But this major conflagration was still far off when Potiorek reexamined his three-year tenure in Bosnia. Potiorek had seen bloodshed. He was, after all, a career soldier. But the assassination of the heir to the throne struck him down on the road to Damascus. Potiorek fundamentally changed his mind about politics; he exchanged his optimism to engage the people in their own governance for a severe pessimism. Above all he wanted to punish those responsible and seek his own redemption. Two days after he witnessed the murder of the heir apparent, he sent the emperor's military chancellery his final political report. The report contained his activities in the week leading up to Franz Ferdinand's visit and death. The tone was melancholic. In the report, Potiorek let it be known that all his political activities, all his aspirations for the land of Bosnia-Herzegovina had been pointless. It was all moot to Potiorek now. He blamed himself for Franz Ferdinand's death, for having "deceived himself that the deterioration of the situation already has gone much further and become more serious" than he had previously thought. The "atrocity" of June 28 had showed him that Austria needed to take decisive action against its enemies, both internal and external. The time for talking, for negotiations, for patience with politics, was over. Not even Potiorek's civilian chief, the old, cautious Pole, Common Finance Minister Biliński, could convince Potiorek otherwise. Biliński, on June 30, asked Potiorek to keep the provincial assembly open and preserve the good political situation there, which Potiorek had worked so hard to build over the previous three years. "I am convinced," Biliński added, "that the speedy resumption of the Diet's work will not only save the situation but will have a quieting effect on the general political tenor of the territory."[4] Potiorek could not comprehend such optimism. He ignored Biliński's suggestions and, the day after the assassination, declared martial law in the province. The diet closed. Within five weeks, Potiorek would command three armies which would invade Serbia, seeking revenge and redemption. With Potiorek, the entire empire would enter a state of exception. Politics and state building would become a forgotten era of the past.

. . .

The drafters of the imperial Austrian constitution—the December Constitution of 1867—had unintentionally constructed laws that would pave the way for the end of the constitutional era: the law of May 5, 1869, on the Suspension of Fundamental Rights and the Declaration of a State of Emergency.[5] This law went into effect on July 26, 1914, giving the emperor emergency powers to lead the state through a time of crisis. But this constitutional trust of one man's benevolence and his good intentions did not take into account age and the ability to hold together all of the reins of state. In July 1914 Emperor Francis Joseph was nearly eighty-four years old—too old to lead the military in a time of war. Forced to delegate his authority, the emperor named Archduke Friedrich, the grandson of the famous Archduke Karl von Österreich-Teschen, as the supreme commander of the army. Friedrich resembled Shakespeare's Falstaff more than his grandfather, whose statue stands on Vienna's Hero's Square. The emperor's delegation of authority is of consequence. The willing spirit of the kaiser to lead met the realities of his weak body. The military would step into the breach. In reality, Archduke Friedrich was a figurehead leader who gave the chief of the General Staff, Conrad von Hötzendorf, free rein.

Between July 26 and 28, 1914, the Habsburg monarchy changed forever. The declaration of war on Serbia on July 28, 1914, would be accompanied by a new series of laws which represented a significant shift in the way the Habsburg state—especially the imperial Austrian state—operated.[6] But beyond the words on paper, the legal transformation of the Austrian state was just as much a change in praxis, as the imperial administration now found itself in a bewildering struggle for the soul of the state with the Austrian military.

The First World War brought to end a long-term state-building project in the Habsburg Empire. If Charles Tilly's oft-quoted maxim, "War makes the State and the State makes war," is true for the world of early modern Europe and enlightened absolutism, the First World War adds a new wrinkle. War unmade the Habsburg state. The Habsburg Empire was not ultimately defeated on the field of battle. In 1918 there were no areas of the Habsburg Empire under enemy occupation. Rather, the state itself unraveled during the war. In many ways, however, this process of unmaking had much to do with the new ways in which the Habsburg state functioned. It also had much to do with who was now in charge of much of its policy making.

The initial flurry of emergency laws would be supplemented over the next three years by 154 further emergency laws and 510 additional ordinances which were promulgated by the cabinet ministers themselves.[7] Emergency measures erected a War Surveillance Office overnight in Vienna in late July—without any law or announcement calling attention to it.[8] Additional emergency legislation addressed everything from industrial production to veterinary medicine, as Austria-Hungary's resources were now controlled for maximum efficiency in the war effort. Together a new system emerged, which completely reversed the trends of state administration from material concerns, the development of economic infrastructures, and the channeling and accommodation of political participation, to a focus on military provisioning, control, censorship, and retributive justice which would mark Austria-Hungary as one of the most repressive states on the European continent. A major transformation of the Austrian state had taken place, a reversal of policy, a veritable U-turn from the order of things before the war. The administration became responsible for the management of the homefront and the domestic economy. What this meant in practical terms was a centralization of bureaucratic measures. The local officials who had become the lynchpin of Habsburg administration in the decades before the war were no longer in charge of local policies; these local officials were now forced to implement measures that would alienate them from the peoples whose friendships and loyalty they previously had been instructed to cultivate.

With a simple letter of July 26, 1914—two days before the declaration of war on Serbia—to all the *Statthalter* and land-presidents—minister-president Count Karl von Stürgkh hinted strongly at the coming of war and reminded the *Landesschefs* of their duty to serve the state. "The martial events which stand before us make it completely irrefutable that all organs of the state administration must unite with their full effort and collective strength around one goal: the mobilization and application of the military forces in the service of the fatherland."[9] And while Stürgkh would remind the *Landeschefs* to cultivate and encourage the patriotic cooperation of all the monarchy's peoples without regard to class, nation, or confession, it was also clear that the political administration was to set aside all matters of internal politics and to "orient all the collective energies of the state to the assured, quick, and complete achievement of our war aims." The political administration was now to find itself the handmaid and executive of the military, and, as some of the files from the early months of the war indicate, the army high command (*Armeeoberkommando* or AOK) was frequently to remind the bureaucracy of its secondary status.[10]

Much has been written about the Habsburg military's mobilization. But beyond military histories of moving troops from the Serbian front to the Russian front, mobilization itself did much to change the fabric of the home front. For instance, mobilization was accompanied by the systematic arrest and detention of politically active Slovene politicians and priests in Styria and Carinthia in the early days of the war. In Styria, the military and the Gendarmerie—which was under military supervision—arrested countless teachers, priests, and politicians in response to the fear of anti-Habsburg activity or even military sabotage. In the South Styrian village of Maria-Rast, arrests of numerous Slovene speakers marked what Martin Moll called a scenario of "blind rage on the part of the domestic security organs and military justice."[11] In the mixed-language villages and towns of Carinthia, civilian authorities targeted the Slovene Catholic clergy, often in response to denunciations on the part of German speakers.[12] But while Governor Fries-Skene encouraged and justified the arrest campaign against the Slovene intelligentsia in Carinthia, Count Manfred Clary-Aldringen, the governor in Styria, complained to his fellow Styrian, Minister-President Stürgkh, as well as the Ministry of the Interior that the military was overstepping its authority and arresting many loyal elements. In fact, Clary-Aldringen asked his underlings for reports on the arrest of Slovenes, which he forwarded on the Ministry of the Interior. They had cataloged ninety-five arrests of Styrian Slovenes by September 19, 1914.[13] Clary-Aldringen complained about the "over-eagerness" of military garrisons and gendarmes leading to "unfounded internments."[14] In fact, the governor found himself employing an extensive campaign of damage control, suppressing the German-language press which had focused on the arrests and disloyalty of Styria's Slovenes. For Clary-Aldringen the "mistakes and mishandling" of the gendarmeries and the military during mobilization had presented him with major difficulties regarding the morale and attitude of the Slovene population which had been unfairly targeted and largely innocent.[15]

The campaign of arrests was such that Francis Joseph responded in September. Suggesting that the military's campaign of arrests and detentions often involved loyal, innocent subjects, he ordered the military to only arrest suspicious persons when they have good grounds to do so.[16] While the Austrian Ministry of Home Defense (*k.k. Ministerium für Landesverteidigung*) responded that it would instruct the k.k. Landwehr and gendarmes to not arrest politically suspect people, but turn them over to civilian courts, the Ministry of War responded to the kaiser's decree defending the arrests of "serbophile elements." Rather, the Ministry of War promised that now that they have arrested all the people they knew about before the war, but could not, the number of arrests will slow down and won't seem like there are so many.[17] The military was slipping out from under the kaiser's control—much to the consternation of the civilian officials in the Austrian provinces, like Clary-Aldringen, who were scrambling to repair the damage done to the belief in the Rechtsstaat and the Habsburg state.

Moreover, once the war started, the military caught civilian authorities completely off guard by their instrumentalization of justice. Law became a tool of the military state, an anvil upon which military authority could hammer the population into obedience. Baron Johann von Eichhoff, in an unpublished memoir, "Von Miramar bis St. Germain," described a chasm that existed between the military and civilian officials like himself.[18] Eichhoff had served as a liaison between the Ministry of the Interior and Franz Ferdinand's cabinet before the war. After the assassination of Franz Ferdinand, Eichhoff went through a deep depression; leaving Austria for Italy to collect his thoughts, he realized his impatience with the "Austrian" way of doing things: the legal correctness, the spirit of compromise. As July neared August and war preparations were being made, Eichhoff reported to Vienna and personally asked the minister of the interior for some type of military position.

Eichhoff—like imperial reformers and bureaucrats—initially looked to the leadership of the military in war as something that could energize the state and break through political stalemate. Eichhoff describes how he—along with many others—had given up on the old, legal, strenuous way of doing things. He wanted to go down a new path and let a master battle or war sort things out. This impatience with the administrative way, the procedurally delimited way of making government work, however, was nothing in comparison with the approach of military men. In praxis, the Rechtsstaat and particularly the procedural Rechtsstaat—the idea that the state and justice must rigidly follow protocols and procedures to limit the arbitrary use of authority—were thrown to the side. But, Eich-hoff, like many others in government who saw the military emergency as means of starting over, did not fully understand the mindset—and the extremism—of their new dancing partner.

Eichhoff received his desired appointment to work with the military. He was to represent the Ministry of the Interior to the army high com-mand. Almost immediately, the scales fell from Eichhoff's eyes. He writes: "Right in the initial days of my new position I recognized that—according to the military mindset—the civilian working with the military command will always be treated with a measure of mistrust and a style of polite dis-dain, even given the personal amiability of the individual officers."[19] Eich-hoff found that all his legislative and administrative work in the military headquarters—meant to aid the military regime as it made decisions that affected civilian governance in occupied areas and internal regions that fell under the jurisdiction of the military—needed the approval of a General Staff officer. Such oversight by nonexperts, which could be arbitrary, cer-tainly got under Eichhoff's skin: "I had to put up with hardheaded and uncomprehending interventions, depending on the chief of the [respec-tive] General Staff Department and in the interest of working together, I had to silently look on as tasks, which I naturally understood better than the most capable officer, were badly done and botched."[20]

Eichhoff recounts such a story in his memoirs:

A military jurist reported to the Corps Commandant, who appeared very merciful: "Servus Jurist! I know people like you and I have no intention of causing you diffi-culty; you have your instructions as we have ours. You have nothing to fear from me!" A few days later, the commandant summoned the jurist: "As I've told you, I have no intention of making things difficult for you. Here is a list of persons guilty of high trea-son. Tell me, which ones you will take over in order to convict. Number one, well he's been spending his summer vacation in the Crimea. I wonder, what the rascal has been doing there, eh? What? You're not going to prosecute him? Fine, let it go! Number two: suspicious correspondence with Russians."—"I'll look into that, your excellency," says the jurist.—"Good man. Number three is married to a Russian woman. Nothing to do with that one? Fine." And so on. The jurist could begin an investigation in two [of the ten] cases. There wasn't a trace of guilt in the others. The Corps Commandant then called for his aide-de-camp: "Here is a list of ten persons guilty of treason. $X$ and $Y$ are to be taken over by Herr Lieutenant-Colonel [the jurist]. The others are to be shot immediately without trial. This is my decision. [Turning to the military jurist:] As you can see, I'm not making any problems for you lawyers."[21]

As Eichhoff learned very quickly, Austria's entry into the war put the bureaucratic method of governing, through contact and negotiation with local notables and party representatives, to an end. It ended the trends of state growth and the more efficient use of personnel, but also the relationship between the state and citizen that depended on following strict protocols of procedure. The war would place the bureaucracy in an unenviable position as the military became its new interlocutor in matters of politics, policy making, and administration. How would the administration respond to its new wartime roles? How would it deal with a new administrative partner—the army—and the limitation of movement that this new partner would create for the imperial bureaucracy? The bureaucracy's legitimacy, and the legitimacy of the Cisleithanian state itself, had rested for a long time on the bureaucracy's ability to flexibly deal with the complexities of multinational, popular participation in policy making. With the onset of war, with the shuttering of the Reichsrat and all of the provincial diets, the bureaucracy was left without its erstwhile dancing partner. But more than this, it was left scrambling to run a state whose legal framework was rearranged to produce arrests and to suppress disloyalty rather than one that was based on correctness and procedure.

## September 1914: The Collapse of Order

At the same time that the state of emergency altered the careful frameworks and legal structures of the monarchy, mobilization and war threatened to tear the bureaucracy apart. Amid the confusion and destruction of war, the local benevolence of the Habsburg administration was crippled by invasions and left in shambles by the new regime under mobilization. The Lower Austrian district prefect in Bruck an der Leitha wrote *Statthalter* Biernerth as early as July 26 that he expected to lose four officials (two drafting officials and two interns) when the Second Corps mobilized.[22] Such a loss of personnel could stop a small office from functioning properly. More dramatic was the situation at the beginning of August in Waidhofen an der Thaya, a district in the Waldviertel of Lower Austria. The district prefect, Alexander Bosizio Ritter von Thurnberg und Jungenegg, reported to Biernerth on August 5 that by the end of the month, he would no longer have any political drafting officials in the prefecture. Moreover, he himself expected to be called up at any moment.[23] Bosizio's letter expresses a dramatic but rather common experience of the district prefectures as they stood on the brink of a great unknown. All the while, new directives were flooding into the local officials of the administration, the administration was simultaneously being stripped of the independently minded, juridically trained personnel. These *Konzeptsbeamten* were the very men that the prefect needed to carry out the new orders in a way which promised efficiency as well as the flexibility to deal with the populace on the ground. In a letter to a fellow district prefect, Bosizio comments that he did not request any replacements for the officials his office has lost, even though he desperately needs them, because he fears that the *Statthalterei* has a "dreadful amount to do." "The young workforce will all be off soon," he added. "In these times one must endeavor to get by as one can."[24]

By August 1914, the administration in the provinces, which in mid-July was desperate for more personnel (and was caught in the process of a general restructuring of manpower and work-related bureaucratic norms) was becoming responsible for much of the requisition work, local industrial production, and the distribution of food. Moreover, the administration was being depleted at exactly where the rubber met the proverbial road. As we learned from Bosizio's letter, mobilization called up the very class of officials, *Konzeptsbeamten*, which the *Statthalter* felt were in short supply. In addition to the strong personal qualities of leadership which allowed the district prefect to act as the emperor's representative in the countryside, Bosizio reflected the general idea that the motor of the Austrian administration was fueled by the work of the educated officials who populated the middling ranks of Austrian officialdom. But, these drafting officials were likewise the very class of officials which men like Erwin von Schwarzenau had proposed to eliminate in his draft for an administrative reform of the district offices. In essence, the complex of administrative questions which had dominated the inner core of Austrian policy making since the dawn of representative government in the 1860s had centered on Vienna's presence in the hinterland. These questions asked essentially how the Austrian state would evolve as it sought to incorporate but also manage and channel increasing popular participation in politics and policy making. Such a long-term discussion reached its climax in the days leading up to the war. This discussion came to a crashing end with the declaration of war. The exigencies of war not only meant that the Austrian state shifted its focus from state building to military necessity; it also meant that the very trends of building a more efficient and a more penetrative bureaucratic apparatus were undercut by the vigor of mobilization and its demands of personnel.

While the Lower Austrian offices in the hinterland were in danger of losing all their junior staff to the war effort, the provinces of Galicia and the Bukovina—bordering on Russia—were shattered by invasion. At the beginning of the war, the military establishment expected to make speedy inroads into Russian Poland. The AOK had sent missives to the Ministry of the Interior in August 1914, asking for the names and résumés of all Polish-speaking civil servants, as they would be needed to administer the military zones of occupation.[25] Such pride came before a terrible fall. By late August 1914, these eastern provinces of the empire—those which had been economically underdeveloped and had received so much state investment over the years—had been overrun. The bureaucracy—the institution which had linked these far-flung provinces, a day's journey by fast train from Vienna, to the center of the empire—had crumbled under the pounding knout of Russia's army. The administration of Galicia and Bukovina scattered, winding up in refugee camps as far away as Upper Austria or Bohemia. They offered their services to the state, begged for the resumption for their salaries, and waited for a hopeful counterstrike by the k.u.k. army.[26]

.    .    .

We can read signs of decline in the long sweep of history in Habsburg monarchy, no doubt. From Joseph II renouncing his more radical reforms, to the stagnation in the years preceding 1848, military defeats in the 1850s and 1860s, to the parliamentary crisis of 1897, historians have judged that this was a monarchy on the wane and that the First World War was just the final stage of a long fatal illness. But if we view the long sweep of history from another perspective, from the center, without privileging ideas of decline or a particular nation's rise, a different narrative emerges. The national divisions of the present, the near century-long focus on nationally centered history often obscure a shared, common past. One can see the story in the buildings, in the roads, and sometimes even in central European political culture.[27] If one travels the rails of central Europe from the spires of Prague to the now border town of České Velenice, one finds the remnants of this infrastructure state in the stations and the rails themselves. From art nouveau in Prague's booking hall to the *Schönbrunner* yellow in the small Bohemian town, the empire, the provinces, the cities, and towns built public buildings to last. Moreover, if we look at these buildings as part of a much larger and longer project, one of investment, of building and forging a political polity of benefit to a large and diverse citizenry, we can see that the buildings are merely an architectural remnant of a vibrant, dynamic polity, which could and did justify its existence to its members.

And yet, this state fell quickly despite the long process of state building that has been the focus of this volume. What I have argued in this book is that Frederick the Great's invasion of Silesia sparked a transformation in the assortment of kingdoms and lands of Maria Theresia. She and her successors, raising the funds to fight Prussia and protect the lands from new technologies and larger armies, created an infrastructure of state and a central bureaucracy, along with the further development of state-science— a technology of governing taught in universities. Joseph II had taken this bureaucracy and infused it with an attitude of the state's supremacy. Service to that state and the self-sacrifice and efficiency that service entailed was sacralized. The bureaucracy developed an ethos that would persist and develop despite the nearly sixty years of political stagnation after 1790.

After Joseph II, the Austrian state-building project became a good in itself, rather than merely a technique for building a larger army. The Austrian military maintained its importance in the state system, with firm and unbreakable links to the dynasty and the men of the House of Habsburg. Yet, over the course of the nineteenth century, and especially after 1848, the imperial bureaucracy reforged the Austrian state into something much more than a dynasty with an army. Bureaucratic reformers drew up plans for a state that accommodated and channeled public participation—still believing in Joseph II's ideals as the state as a good in itself. In the view of great reformers like Count Franz von Stadion, participatory politics was the next step in the development of the state, bringing in the opinions and expertise of the population. These ideas took time to develop into a constitutionally established regime, but it did happen by 1867 with the promulgation of the December Constitution for the non-Hungarian half of the monarchy. In the following half a century political participation expanded and the state grew with it. What followed were massive building campaigns, public works, roads, cultural institutions, and educational funding—all of which could generate political friction and heat. Moreover, the administration became a weak point of the state, held in suspicion in some quarters to the dark influence of party and national politics. White-gloved military officers sniped derisively at the bureaucrats sullied in politics, but what they failed to see was that the state *worked* well enough that many from all over the monarchy scrambled to reform its government in the years preceding the war.

Prior to 1914, the Austrian state had devoted much more of its resources to building infrastructure and keeping its denizens content with public-sponsored progress in the form of cultural intuitions, schools, commercial infrastructure, and the like instead of weapons, soldiers, and fortresses.[28] The Habsburg state, and Cisleithanian Austria in particular (though the same could be said for the Kingdom of Hungary) was out of step with the rest of Europe, which was preparing precipitously for war. Ironically, it would be the Habsburg Empire that would take Europe over the cliff and plunge it into the greatest conflagration that it had ever known.

When war came in 1914 and the civilian government declared the state of emergency, military rule took over. War, mobilization, and the state of emergency began to fray the web that connected the state of Joseph II in Vienna to the surrounding provinces. The military assumption of police and justice alienated the monarchy's peoples from the state and squandered what good will the bureaucracy had worked to forge. Further east, an onslaught of over a million Russian troops, parceled in forty-five infantry divisions and eighteen cavalry divisions, completely destroyed the network, sending the bureaucracy into exile and scattering Austrian officials to the seven winds.[29] Over the next four years, however, Austria-Hungary resiliently withstood the brutality of total war. Its army would be completely destroyed only to be raised again. This was hardly a weak, decrepit state. Rather, the state that Joseph II and Maria Theresia built was able to withstand a three-front war for four years, raise over 8 million troops to its flags, while suffering staggering losses, hunger, and shortages. The limits of loyalty—which itself was multilayered and diverse—were tested, but nevertheless it took a conflagration that the world had never known before to tear the old monarchy apart.

Nevertheless the Habsburg multinational experiment fell. On October 16, 1918, the thirty-one year-old Emperor Charles declared that Cisleithanian Austria would be transformed into a league of nation-states, but that failed to bring about an immediate peace with the allies, or keep the peoples of the empire together. National committees took over various parts of the empire and already—in a resurgence of provincial politics—had begun the virtual liquidation of the Habsburg monarchy. By the end of October 1918, a Czecho-Slovak republic had been proclaimed in Prague, the Poles had begun to solidify a Polish nation-state, Croatians in Zagreb proclaimed a new state, and the province of Carniola had severed ties with the empire. The provinces had transformed into national states—they were

the largest institutions that the prosecution of the war and the management of the homefront had not discredited completely.

The fall of the monarchy would not bring peace, either. The Ruthenians of eastern Galicia proclaimed independence as well, only to be attacked by the Poles. The Kingdom of Hungary likewise was in the process
of dissolution. While Romanians in Hungary moved toward self-determina-
tion, the Romanian state invaded, sparking a war with Hungary that would
last nearly a year. Italy occupied Fiume/Rijeka and parts of Dalmatia, following on its claims on Habsburg territory in the Treaty of London. The
state died in late October and the self-appointed heirs began to fight over
its property. The prosecution of the war had torn it apart, alienated all its
peoples, and pushed them away from each other. An experiment lasting
over a century and a half had come to an end in little more than four years.
Czechoslovakia and Austria had become republics, Hungary was in the
throes of communist revolution, the Poles had formed a republic with their
co-nationals from Prussia and Russia, and Romanians and Southern Slavs
had conjoined themselves to the monarchy's enemies. By the time Charles
I formally renounced his sovereign powers on November 11 (without formally abdicating), the state that Joseph II and Maria Theresia had built was
already in shambles. Nobody cared anymore what Charles had to say; they
had turned their back on him, on Austria, and on the multinational state
that had squandered their lives and sent them into the great tragedy of the
First World War.[30]

The larger moral of this story is that states are fragile things. The
Austrian state collapsed despite its modern welfare state features, despite
its expanding political participation, and despite the resources it mobilized
to making the state work. In the end, we can see that the war ended a long-
running process, one that would bring millions of people into political
participation, formal education, cultural literacy, and economic promise.
War does not make states, but it gives them reason and purpose to deepen
their power, their infrastructure, and their focus. As this process took hold
in the multinational empire, the purpose of the state shifted from making
war to building a multinational community of educated, happy citizens.
In such a polity, war did not continue the process of state making, but
ended it. This is a lesson worth keeping in mind, both in how it helps us
understand the past and how we make choices in our democratic, liberal
polities, to shape the future.

# Reference Matter

# Notes

## Abbreviations

### Archives
AVA    Allgemeines Verwaltungsarchiv
HHStA  Haus-, Hof-, und Staatsarchiv
KA     Kriegsarchiv
NÖLA   Niederösterreichisches Landesarchiv
OÖLA   Oberösterreichisches Landesarchiv
ÖPA    Österreichisches Parlamentsarchiv
ÖstA   Österreichisches Staatsarchiv
VwGh   Archiv des Österreichischen Verwaltungsgerichtshof

### Other Abbreviations
A      Akten
AOK    Armeeoberkommando
EOK    Etappenoberkommando
*HM* 2   *Die Habsburgermonarchie, 1848–1918*, vol. 2
HR     Hauptreihe
K      Karton
k.k.   kaiserlich-königlich (imperial-royal)
k.u.k. kaiserlich und königlich (imperial and royal)
MI/MdI Ministerium des Innern
MK     Ministerkonferenz
MKSM   Militärkanzlei Seiner Majestät
MR     Ministerrat
MRZ    Ministerratszahl
*NFP*    *Neue Freie Presse*

| NL | Nachlass |
|---|---|
| ÖMR | Österreichischer Ministerrat |
| ÖMRP | Österreichisches Ministerratsprotokoll |
| *ÖZV* | *Österreichische Zentralverwaltung* |
| Pr. | Protokoll |
| Praes. | Praesidium |
| *RGBl* | *Reichsgesetzblatt* |
| Sch. | Schachtel |
| *SPAR* | *Stenographische Protokolle des Abgeordnetenhauses des Reichsrates* |
| SR | Sonderreihe |
| StM | Staatsministerium |
| StP | Staatshalterei-Präsidium |
| VÖAW | Verlag der Österreichischen Akademie der Wissenschaften |
| VRK | Verwaltungsreformkommission |
| *WZ* | *Wiener Zeitung* |
| Z | Zahl |

## Introduction

1. Waltraud Heindl, *Josephinische Mandarine: Bürokratie und Beamte in Österreich, 1848–1914* (Vienna: Böhlau, 2013), 92.

2. For the role of education in the eighteenth and nineteenth centuries in Europe, see both James Van Horn Melton, *Absolutism and the Eighteenth-Century Origins of Compulsory Schooling in Prussia and Austria* (Cambridge: Cambridge University Press, 1988); and Eugen Weber, *Peasants into Frenchmen: The Modernization of Rural France, 1870–1914*, 1st ed. (Stanford, Calif.: Stanford University Press, 1976).

3. For instance, see Jo Guldi's new book on infrastructure building in Great Britain, Jo Guldi, *Roads to Power: Britain Invents the Infrastructure State* (Cambridge, Mass.: Harvard University Press, 2012).

4. Mack Walker, *German Home Towns: Community, State, and General Estate, 1648–1871* (Ithaca, N.Y.: Cornell University Press, 1998).

5. Josef Redlich, *Das österreichische Staats- und Reichsproblem: Geschichtliche Darstellung der inneren Politik der Habsburgischen Monarchie von 1848 bis zum Untergang des Reiches*, 2 vols. (Leipzig: P. Reinhold, 1920); Viktor Bibl, *Der Zerfall Österreichs* (Vienna: Rikola Verlag, 1922); A. J. P. Taylor, *The Habsburg Monarchy, 1809–1918: A History of the Austrian Empire and Austria-Hungary* (London: H. Hamilton, 1948); A. J. May, *The Hapsburg Monarchy, 1867–1914* (Cambridge, Mass.: Harvard University Press, 1951); Robert A. Kann, *A History of the Habsburg Empire, 1526–1918* (Berkeley: University of California Press, 1974); H. Seton-Watson, *The "Sick Heart" of Modern Europe: The Problem of the Danubian Lands* (Seattle: University of Washington Press, 1975); Carl E. Schorske, *Fin-de-Siècle Vienna: Politics and Culture* (New York: Vintage Books, 1981); Erich Zöllner, *Geschichte Österreichs* (Munich: R. Oldenbourg, 1961). For a summary and criticism of this body of work, see Gary B. Cohen, "Neither Absolutism nor Anarchy: New Narratives on Society and Government in Late Imperial Austria," *Austrian History Yearbook* 29, no. 1 (1998): 37–61.

6. For a recent, and excellent, treatment on the Habsburg Empire's First World War, see Alexander Watson, *Ring of Steel: Germany and Austria-Hungary at War, 1914–1918* (London: Allen Lane, 2014). Yet, it is fascinating to examine that these failure narratives of the Habsburg state themselves emerge out of British propaganda in the First World War. See R. Seton-Watson, *German, Slav, and Magyar: A Study in the Origins of the Great War* (London: Williams and Norgate, 1916); R Seton-Watson, *The Southern Slav Question and the Habsburg Monarchy* (New York: H. Fertig, 1969); Arthur J. May, "R. W. Seton-Watson and British Anti-Hapsburg Sentiment," *American Slavic and East European Review* 20, no. 1 (February 1, 1961): 40–54; Mark Cornwall, *The Undermining of Austria-Hungary: The Battle for Hearts and Minds* (Basingstoke: Macmillan, 2000).

7. G. W. F. Hegel, *The Philosophy of History*, trans. J. Sibree (New York: Dover Publications, 1956), 453; Georg Wilhelm Friedrich Hegel, *Sämtliche Werke*, 20 vols., ed. Hermann Glockner, Jubiläumsausgabe (Stuttgart: Fromanns Verlag, 1949), 11, 564.

8. David Fromkin, *Europe's Last Summer: Who Started the Great War in 1914?* (New York: Knopf, 2005), 24.

9. Our readings of German history in the nineteenth century rest on this important moment in the early nineteenth century, when the eventual victor in Germany (Prussia) committed itself to reforms and the eventual loser (Austria) did not. See, for instance, the masterwork of Thomas Nipperdey, in which he states that Austria's lack of reform in the period between 1806 and 1812 was "of great significance for the way German history progressed." Thomas Nipperdey, *Deutsche Geschichte, 1800–1866: Bürgerwelt und starker Staat* (Munich: C. H. Beck, 1983; repr., 1998), 80.

10. Charles Tilly, "Reflections on the History of European State-Making," in *The Formation of National States in Western Europe*, ed. Charles Tilly and Gabriel Ardant, Studies in Political Development 8 (Princeton, N.J.: Princeton University Press, 1975), 28.

11. Rogers Brubaker's sociological studies of nationalism have been instrumental in shaping the way historians of central Europe have reimagined the national political disputes in the region. See Rogers Brubaker, *Nationalism Reframed: Nationhood and the National Question in the New Europe* (Cambridge: Cambridge University Press, 1996); and the essays in Rogers Brubaker, *Ethnicity Without Groups* (Cambridge, Mass.: Harvard University Press, 2006).

12. Some of the most influential works in this regard since the 1990s have been Larry Wolff, *Inventing Eastern Europe: The Map of Civilization on the Mind of the Enlightenment* (Stanford, Calif.: Stanford University Press, 1994); Gary B. Cohen, *The Politics of Ethnic Survival: Germans in Prague, 1861–1914*, 2nd ed., Central European Studies (West Lafayette, Ind.: Purdue University Press, 2006); Tara Zahra, *Kidnapped Souls: National Indifference and the Battle for Children in the Bohemian Lands, 1900–1948* (Ithaca, N.Y.: Cornell University Press, 2008); Jeremy King, *Budweisers into Czechs and Germans: A Local History of Bohemian Politics, 1848–1948* (Princeton, N.J.: Princeton University Press, 2002).

13. Tony Judt, *A Grand Illusion? An Essay on Europe* (repr., New York: New York University, 2011), 115.

14. Charles Tilly, *Big Structures, Large Processes, Huge Comparisons* (New York: Russell Sage Foundation, 1984).

15. This often takes the form of "roads not taken" and "missed turns." For the most articulate expressions of this literature, see Redlich, *Staats- und Reichsproblem*; Robert A. Kann, *The Multinational Empire: Nationalism and National Reform in the Habsburg Monarchy, 1848–1918*, 2 vols., expanded ed. (New York: Octagon Books, 1964); Ian Reifowitz, "Francis Joseph's Fatal Mistake: The Consequences of Rejecting Kremsier/Kroměříž," *Nationalities Papers* 37, no. 2 (2009): 133–57.

16. For a nuanced discussion of these characteristics that does not doom the monarchy to failure, see Michael Mann, *The Sources of Social Power*, vol. 2, *The Rise of Classes and Nation-States, 1760–1914* (New York: Cambridge University Press, 1986), 330–32.

17. Kenneth J. Meier and Laurence J. O'Toole, *Bureaucracy in a Democratic State: A Governance Perspective* (Baltimore: Johns Hopkins University Press, 2006), 1; Ezra N. Suleiman, *Dismantling Democratic States* (Princeton, N.J.: Princeton University Press, 2003), 2–3.

18. For a recent meditation on paperwork and state power that looks at the "materiality" of paperwork, more than the content, see Ben Kafka, *The Demon of Writing: Powers and Failures of Paperwork* (New York: Zone Books, 2012), chap. 1.

19. Robert Musil, *Der Mann ohne Eigenschaften* (Reinbek bei Hamburg: Rowohlt, 2011), 94.

20. Heindl, *Josephinische Mandarine*, 24.

21. C. A. Bayly, *Empire and Information: Intelligence Gathering and Social Communication in India, 1780–1870* (Cambridge: Cambridge University Press, 1996); Bernard S. Cohn, *Colonialism and Its Forms of Knowledge* (Princeton N.J.: Princeton University Press, 1996).

22. On the Pragmatic Sanction, see Friedrich Walter, *Österreichische Verfassungs- und Verwaltungsgeschichte von 1500–1955*, ed. Adam Wandruszka, Veröffentlichungen der Kommission für Neuere Geschichte Österreichs 59 (Vienna: Böhlau, 1972), 81–83; Charles W Ingrao, *The Habsburg Monarchy, 1618–1815*, 2nd ed., New Approaches to European History 21 (Cambridge: Cambridge University Press, 2000), 129; Jean Bérenger, *A History of the Habsburg Empire*, 2 vols. (London: Longman, 1994), 2: 35–37.

23. Reed Browning, *The War of the Austrian Succession* (New York: St. Martin's Press, 1993), 39–89.

24. "Maria Theresa's Political Testament," in *The Habsburg and Hohenzollern Dynasties in the Seventeenth and Eighteenth Centuries*, ed. C. A. Macartney, Documentary History of Western Civilization (New York: Walker, 1970), 94–132; quote on 97.

25. Ingrao, *Habsburg Monarchy*, 160.

26. P. G. M. Dickson, *Finance and Government Under Maria Theresia, 1740–1780*, 2 vols. (Oxford: Oxford University Press, 1987), 1: 212–26.

27. Ibid., 1: 222–23.

28. Samuel E. Finer, "State- and Nation-Building in Europe: The Role of the Military," in *Formation of National States in Western Europe*, ed. Charles Tilly and and Gabriel Ardant, 84–163; Arthur A. Stein, *The Nation at War* (Baltimore: Johns Hopkins University Pres, 1980); for a recent comparative perspective, see Miguel Angel Centeno and Agustín Ferraro, eds., *State and Nation Making in Latin America and Spain: Republics of the Possible* (Cambridge: Cambridge University Press, 2013).

29. For a thorough discussion of Haugwitz's reforms and the resistance to them in 1748

see above all, Friedrich Walter, *Die Theresianische Staatsreform von 1749*, Österreich Archiv (Vienna: Verlag für Geschichte und Politik, 1958), 44–56.

30. See Dickson, *Finance*, 1: 224–25; Franz A. J. Szabo, *Kaunitz and Enlightened Absolutism, 1753–1780* (New York: Cambridge University Press, 1994), 77–78; Walter, *Der Theresianische Staatsreform*, 56–57.

31. The county as an administrative unit already existed in the lands of the Bohemian crown—dating back to the days of King Ottokar in the thirteenth century. Under Haugwitz, however, these offices took new importance as the local agents of the crown and were extended to the other provinces in the hereditary lands as well. Again, Hungary, and Transylvania remained distinct from the system and were allowed to maintain their "traditional rights." For more on the *Kreisämter* see, Arnold Luschin von Ebengreuth, *Grundriss der österreichischen Reichsgeschichte: Eine Bearbeitung seines Lehrbuchs der "österreichischen Reichsgeschichte"* Edition Classic (1899; repr., Saarbrücken: VDM Verlag Dr. Müller, 2008), 317–18.

32. For a discussion of Kaunitz's *grundregeln*, see Friedrich Walter, *Die Geschichte der österreichischen Zentralverwaltung in der Zeit Maria Theresias*, vol. 1, bk. 1 of *Die Österreichische Zentralverwaltung. II. Abteilung. Von der Vereinigung der österreichischen und böhmischen Hofkanzlei bis zur Einrichtung der Ministerialverfassung (1749–1848)* [hereafter *ÖZV* II/1/1], Veröffentlichungen der Kommission für neuere Geschichte Österreichs 32 (Vienna: Adolf Holzhausens Nachfolger, 1938), 282–86; Szabo, *Kaunitz*, 83–84.

33. An edited form of Kaunitz's *grundregeln* is available in Harm Klueting, ed., *Der Josephinismus: Ausgewählte Quellen zur Geschichte der theresianisch-josephinischen Reformen* (Darmstadt: Wissenschaftliche Buchgesellschaft, 1995), 62–75; quote on 67.

34. *ÖZV*, II/1/1: 282.

35. See the work of Helmut Reinalter, who made the examination of Joseph II and enlightened absolutism in Austria the focus of his academic work. The body of his scholarship is excellently summed up in his book, Helmut Reinalter, *Joseph II: Reformer auf dem Kaiserthron*, Beck'sche Reihe 2735 (Munich: C. H. Beck, 2011), esp. 20–25.

36. See Ingrao, *Habsburg Monarchy*, 203–4.

37. Gerald Stourzh invokes the idea of *isonomia*—a society based on the equality under the law—as a fundamental category to understanding the transformation of society to one based on equality. This is, in his words, the "Tocquevellian Moment." See especially his essay "Equal Rights: Equalizing the Individual's Status and the Breakthrough of the Modern Liberal State," in Gerald Stourzh, *From Vienna to Chicago and Back: Essays on Intellectual History and Political Thought in Europe and America* (Chicago: University of Chicago Press, 2007), 275–303.

38. For our purposes here, cameralism combined new and specific practical knowledge of administration. It offered Maria Theresia and Joseph II a body of knowledge and practitioners on which to call for their reforms. Cameralism has been notoriously difficult to define since historians have split on whether it was a form of academic theory or a vocation, applied to the facets of knowledge necessary for state service. Andre Wakefield has made the case for a holistic viewpoint, combining cameralists of the book and of the bureau. See Andre Wakefield, "Books, Bureaus, and the Historiography of Cameralism,"

*European Journal of Law and Economics* 19, no. 3 (2005): 311–20; and his more recent book, *The Disordered Police State: German Cameralism as Science and Practice* (Chicago: University of Chicago Press, 2009). See also David F. Lindenfeld, *The Practical Imagination the German Sciences of State in the Nineteenth Century* (Chicago: University of Chicago Press, 1997), 14–20.

## Chapter 1: The Dynamics of Austrian Governance

1. Joseph to Leopold, January 21, 1790, in Derek Beales, *Joseph II: Against the World, 1780–1790* (Cambridge: Cambridge University Press, 2009), 628; the letter is printed in the original French in *Joseph II. und Leopold von Toscana: Ihr Briefwechsel von 1781 bis 1790*, ed. Alfred Ritter von Arneth, 2 vols. (Vienna: W. Braumüller, 1872), 2: 312.

2. For the best expression of this narrative, see the now classic work C. A. Macartney, *The Habsburg Empire, 1790–1918* (New York: Macmillan, 1969), esp. 1–2.

3. See, for example, the treatment by Thomas Nipperdey, *Deutsche Geschichte, 1800–1866: Bürgerwelt und starker Staat* (1983; repr., Munich: C. H. Beck, 1998), esp. 31–82.

4. Historians have traditionally become entangled in debates that define Josephinism according to its relationship to reform Catholicism or the state's subjugation of the Church. Although I think this debate informs and enriches our conception of Josephinism and its ideas of the primacy of the state in society, I also think this debate focuses too narrowly on Church matters and thus misses the very important and wider statist resonances of many Josephinist policies. In this book, Josephinism, broadly defined, represents the peculiar form of enlightened absolutism that existed in Austria, and which put the state up as the greatest good and looked to state institutions to be the progressive force in society. This peculiar form, of course, includes matters regarding the relationship of church and state. The literature on "Josephinism" is immense. The term has become an entry point for discussing the legacy of enlightened absolutism in the nineteenth century. For recent work on the term, see Helmut Reinalter, "Einleitung: Der Josephinismus als Variante des Aufgeklärten Absolutismus und seine Reformkomplexe," in *Josephinismus als Aufgeklärter Absolutismus*, ed. Helmut Reinalter (Vienna: Böhlau, 2008), 9–16; Irmgard Plattner, "Die josephinische Bürokratie und ihr Fortwirken im 19. Jahrhundert," in *Was Blieb vom Josephinismus?* Edited Book Series (Innsbruck: Innsbruck University Press, 2010), 57–74; Derek Beales, "Joseph II and Josephism," in *Enlightenment and Reform in Eighteenth-Century Europe* (London: I. B. Tauris, 2005), 287–308. For the older literature and debates on Josephinism, which are still relevant, see Ferdinand Maaß, *Der Josephinismus: Quellen zu seiner Geschichte in Österreich, 1760–1850* (Vienna: Herold, 1951); Fritz Valjavec, *Der Josephinismus: Zur geistigen Entwicklung Österreichs im achzehnten und neunzehnten Jahrhundert* (Munich: R. Oldenbourg, 1945); Eduard Winter, *Der Josefinismus und seine Geschichte: Beiträge zur Geistesgeschichte Österreichs, 1740–1848* (Brünn: R. M. Rohrer, 1943); Eduard Winter, *Der Josefinismus: Die Geschichte des österreichischen Reformkatholizismus, 1740–1848*, Beiträge zur Geschichte des religiösen und wissenschaftlichen Denkens 1 (Berlin: Rütten & Loening, 1962).

5. James J. Sheehan, *German History, 1770–1866*, ed. Alan Bullock and F. W. D. Deakin, Oxford History of Modern Europe (Oxford: Clarendon Press, 1989), 276–81; Paul P. Bernard, *Jesuits and Jacobins: Enlightenment and Enlightened Despotism in Austria* (Urbana:

University of Illinois Press, 1971); Paul P. Bernard, *From the Enlightenment to the Police State: The Public Life of Johann Anton Pergen* (Urbana: University of Illinois Press, 1991).

6. For Joseph's tenure as co-regent, see above all Derek Beales, *Joseph II: In the Shadow of Maria Theresa* (Cambridge: Cambridge University Press, 1987).

7. Peter Becker, "'Kaiser Josephs Schreibmaschine': Ansätze zur Rationalisierung der Verwaltung im aufgeklärten Absolutismus," *Jahrbuch für europäische Verwaltungsgeschichte* 12 (2000): 223–54. Waltraud Heindl, "Bürokratie und Aufklärungskultur," in *Europa im Zeitalter Mozarts*, ed. Moritz Csáky and Walter Pass, Schriftenreihe der Österreichischen Gesellschaft zur Erforschung des 18. Jahrhunderts 5 (Vienna: Böhlau, 1995), 247–51.

8. Helmut Reinalter, *Joseph II: Reformer auf dem Kaiserthron*, Beck'sche Reihe 2735 (Munich: C. H. Beck, 2011), 20.

9. Waltraud Heindl, "Beamte, Staatsdienst und Universitätsreform: Zur Ausbildung der höheren Bürokratie in Österreich, 1780–1848," *Das achtzehnte Jahrhundert und Österreich: Jahrbuch der österreichischen Gesellschaft zur Erforschung des 18. Jahrhunderts* 4 (1987): 35–53; Heindl, "Bürokratie und Aufklärungskultur."

10. *Beamter* is the German word meaning "official," "civil servant," "appointee," "magistrate," or "bureaucrat"; I translate it in various ways throughout this book, depending on the context.

11. Such decrees are available in the multiple-volume work, edited by Joseph Kropatschek and now available online in the digital library of the Österreichische Nationalbibliothek: Joseph Kropatschek, ed., *Sammlung aller k.k. Verordnungen und Gesetze von 1740–1780*, 5 vols. (Vienna: Joh. Georg Mößle, 1786); Joseph Kropatschek, *Handbuch aller unter der Regierung des Kaisers Joseph des II. für die k.k. Erbländer ergangenen Verordnungen und Gesetze in einer Sistematischen Verbindung*, 18 vols. (Vienna: Joh. Georg Mößle, 1785).

12. Waltraud Heindl, *Gehorsame Rebellen: Bürokratie und Beamte in Österreich 1780 bis 1848*, ed. Christian Brünner, Wolfgang Mantl, and Manfried Welan, Studien zu Politik und Verwaltung 36 (Vienna: Böhlau, 1991), 21–47; Karl Megner, *Beamtenmetropole Wien, 1500–1938: Bausteine zu einer Sozialgeschichte vorwiegend im neuzeitlichen Wien* (Vienna: Verlag Österreich, 2010), 178–88; Heindl, "Beamte, Staatsdienst und Universitätsreform," 36–37.

13. There is a recent and burgeoning literature on cameralism as a both the science of statecraft and good governance. See Andre Wakefield, *The Disordered Police State: German Cameralism as Science and Practice* (Chicago: University of Chicago Press, 2009); David F. Lindenfeld, *The Practical Imagination: The German Sciences of State in the Nineteenth Century* (Chicago: University of Chicago Press, 1997); Keith Tribe, "Cameralism and the Science of Government," *Journal of Modern History* 56, no. 2 (June 1984): 263–84; Keith Tribe, *Strategies of Economic Order: German Economic Discourse, 1750–1950* (Cambridge: Cambridge University Press, 1995).

14. Gernot Stimmer, "Zur Herkunft der höchsten österreichischen Beamtenschaft: Die Bedeutung des Theresianums und der Konsularakademie," in *Student und Hochschule im 19. Jahrhundert: Studien und Materialien*, ed. Christian Helfer and Mohammed Rassem, Studien zum Wandel von Gesellschaft und Bildung im Neuzehnten Jahrhundert 12 (Göttingen: Vandenhoeck & Ruprecht, 1975), 303–45; Gernot Stimmer, *Eliten in Österreich, 1848–1970*, 2 vols. Studien zu Politik und Verwaltung 57 (Vienna: Böhlau, 1997), 1: 96–98;

Eugen Guglia, Rudolf J. Taschner, and Heinz Kröll, *Das Theresianum in Wien: Vergangenheit und Gegenwart* (Vienna: Böhlau, 1996).

15. *Polizei* in this eighteenth-century sense means regulation and policy making. See Marc Raeff, "The Well-Ordered Police State and the Development of Modernity in Seventeenth- and Eighteenth-Century Europe: An Attempt at a Comparative Approach," *American Historical Review* 80, no. 5 (December 1975): 1221–43.

16. Simon Karstens, *Lehrer, Schriftsteller, Staatsreformer: Die Karriere des Joseph von Sonnenfels (1733–1817)*, Veröffentlichungen der Kommission für Neuere Geschichte Österreichs 106 (Vienna: Böhlau, 2011); Karl-Heinz Osterloh, *Joseph von Sonnenfels und die österreichische Reformbewegung im Zeitalter des aufgeklärten Absolutismus: Eine Studie zum Zusammenhang von Kameralwissenschaft und Verwaltungspraxis* (Lübeck: Matthiesen Verlag, 1970).

17. Keith Tribe, *Governing Economy: The Reformation of German Economic Discourse, 1750–1840* (Cambridge: Cambridge University Press, 1988), chap. 4.

18. Heindl, *Gehorsame Rebellen*, 99–103.

19. Heindl, "Beamte, Staatsdienst und Universitätsreform," 36.

20. Ibid., 36–39.

21. Heindl, *Gehorsame Rebellen*, 103–6. Heindl's analysis rests on the list of lectures and courses at the University of Vienna after 1784.

22. Ibid., 116–17.

23. For Sonnenfels's important work in the fiscal and administrative reforms of the monarchy in the era of Maria Theresia and Joseph II, see Karstens, *Lehrer, Schriftsteller, Staatsreformer*; Robert A. Kann, *A Study in Austrian Intellectual History: From Late Baroque to Romanticism* (New York: Praeger, 1960); Osterloh, *Josef von Sonnenfels*.

24. Joseph von Sonnenfels, *Über den Geschäftstyl: Die ersten Grundlinien für angehende österreichische Kanzleybeamten, zum Gebrauche der öffentlichen Vorlesung, nebst einem Anhange von Registraturen*, 4th rev. ed. (Vienna: J. G. Heubner, 1820). For analysis of the text, see Heindl, *Gehorsame Rebellen*, 106–9; Leslie Bodi, "Sprachregelung als Kulturgeschchte: Sonnenfels; Über den Geschäftsstil (1784) und die Ausbildung der österreichischen Mentalität," in *Pluralität: Eine interdisziplinäre Annäherung: Festschrift für Moritz Csáky* ed. Moritz Csáky et al. (Vienna: Böhlau, 1996), 122–48.

25. See the insightful analysis on Sonnenfels, written communication, and bureaucratic knowledge in the essay by Becker, "Kaiser Josephs Schreibmaschine," esp. 231–42.

26. Waltraud Heindl, "Bürokratie, Staat und Reform: Überlegungen zum Verhältnis von Bürokratie und Staat im aufgeklärten Absolutismus in Österreich," in *Etatisation et bureaucratie: Staatswerdung und Bürokratie; Symposion der Österreichischen Gesellschaft zur Erforschung des 18. Jahrhunderts*, ed. Moritz Csáky and Andrea Lanzer, Beihefte zum Jahrbuch der Österreichischen Gesellschaft zur Erforschung des 18. Jahrhunderts 2 (Vienna: Verband der wissenschaftlichen Gesellschaften Österreichs, 1990), 39–48. See also Heindl, "Bürokratie und Aufklärungskultur."

27. Max Weber, *Wirtschaft und Gesellschaft: Grundriß der Verstehenden Soziologie*, rev. 5th ed. (Tübingen: Mohr Siebeck, 2002), 553; italics in the original. English translation taken from Max Weber, *Economy and Society: An Outline of Interpretive Sociology*, ed. Gerhard Roth and C. Wittich 2 vols. (Berkeley: University of California Press, 1978), 2: 959.

28. Although nationalist and National Socialist scholars of the early twentieth century saw Joseph's elevation of German as sign that he was their forerunner, such assessments entirely miss the character of Joseph's outlook and the purpose of his reforms. See, for instance, Viktor Bibl, *Kaiser Josef II: Ein Vorkämpfer der grossdeutschen Idee* (Vienna: J. Günther, 1943).

29. See Karstens, *Lehrer, Schriftsteller, Staatsreformer*, 228–29, on how Sonnenfels's stylistics corresponded to Joseph's drive for centralization.

30. For Joseph's stance to the German language with regard to the Austrian administration and the idea of a unified monarchy, see R. J. W. Evans, "Language and State Building: The Case of the Habsburg Monarchy," *Austrian History Yearbook* 35 (2004): 6–13. For an older, but more detailed treatment, see Alfred Fischel, *Das österreichische Sprachenrecht*, 2nd ed. (Brünn: Friedrich Irrgang, 1910), xxviii–lvi.

31. For the process of Germanization that Joseph carried out in the civil service see the highly illuminating memoir by Ignaz Beidtel, *Geschichte der österreichischen Staatsverwaltung, 1740–1848*, ed. Alfons Huber 2 vols. (Innsbruck: Verlag der Wagner'schen Universitäts-Buchhandlung, 1896–98), 1: 200–204.

32. Derek Beales, *Joseph II: In the Shadow of Maria Theresa* (Cambridge: Cambridge University Press, 1987), chaps. 4 and 6, for the evolving role of Joseph in policy-making affairs.

33. For analysis of Joseph's first memorandum, see ibid., 95–97; the original memorandum is reproduced in Alfred Ritter von Arneth, ed., *Maria Theresia und Joseph II: Ihre Correspondenz, sammt Briefen Josephs an seinen Bruder Leopold*, 3 vols. (Vienna: Karl Gebold's Sohn, 1867), 1: 1–12. See Derek Beales's analysis as well as a full copy of the text, Joseph's *rêveries*, in Derek Beales, "Joseph II's Rêveries," in *Enlightenment*, 157–81; quote on 169.

34. Beales, "Rêveries," 171.

35. Ibid.

36. Original text is reprinted in French in Arneth, ed., *Correspondenz*, 3: 335–61; quote on 339. A German translation of the text is available in Harm Klueting, ed., *Der Josephinismus: Ausgewählte Quellen zur Geschichte der theresianisch-josephinischen Reformen* (Darmstadt: Wissenschaftliche Buchgesellschaft, 1995), 88–107; quote on 91. For a thorough discussion of the document in English, see Beales, *Joseph II*, 1: 164–76.

37. Arneth, *Correspondenz*, 3: 358.

38. The administrative reforms of Joseph II once were a rich topic of historical exploration. See the classical exposition published in the "Austrian Central Administration" series Friedrich Walter, *Die Zeit Josephs II. und Leopold II*, vol. 1, bk. 2, pt. 1 in *Die Österreichische Zentralverwaltung. II. Abteilung. Von der Vereinigung der österreichischen und böhmischen Hofkanzlei bis zur Einrichtung der Ministerialverfassung (1749–1848)* [hereafter ÖZV, II/1/2/1], Veröffentlichungen der Kommission für neuere Geschichte Österreichs 35 (Vienna: Adolf Holzhausens Nachfolger, 1950), esp. 1–69. For recent correctives to the classical approach, see Hamish Marshall Scott, "The Problem of Government in Habsburg Enlightened Absolutism," in *Europa im Zeitalter Mozarts*, ed. Csáky and Pass, 252–55.

39. This dynamic is the story of the second volume of Derek Beales's biography of Joseph, fittingly titled, *Joseph Against the World*. Beales, *Joseph II: Against the World*, esp. chaps. 10 and 14.

40. Joseph's "pastoral letter" (*Hirtenbrief*) is reprinted in Klueting, *Der Josephinismus*,

334–40; Friedrich Walter, ed., *Die Zeit Josephs II. und Leopolds II. (1780–1792). Aktenstücke*, vol. 4 of *Die Österreichische Zentralverwaltung. II. Abteilung. Von der Vereinigung der österreichischen und böhmischen Hofkanzlei bis zur Einrichtung der Ministerialverfassung (1749–1848)* [hereafter *ÖZV*, II/4], Veröffentlichungen der Kommission für neuere Geschichte Österreichs 36 (Vienna: Adolf Holzhausens Nachfolger, 1950), 123–32. Kleuting has edited his version, for this reason I will refer to Walter's. For differing summaries and commentaries on the text itself see Beales, Joseph II: Against the World, 2: 343–62; Walter *ÖZV*, II/1/2/1: 52–53.

41. *ÖZV*, II/4: 126.

42. Ibid.

43. For Beales's gloss on Joseph's "pastoral letter," see Beales, *Joseph II: Against the World*, 343–52; quote on 352. Friedrich Walter likewise finds that the pastoral letter displays another example of Joseph's misanthropy and his mistrust of people in general and of his officials and ministers specifically. For Walter's own gloss of the "pastoral letter," see *ÖZV*, II/1/2/1: 52–53.

44. Wolfgang Reinhard, *Geschichte der Staatsgewalt: Eine vergleichende Verfassungsgeschichte Europas von den Anfängen bis zur Gegenwart*, 3rd ed. (Munich: C. H. Beck, 2002), 141–83.

45. *ÖZV*, II/4: 127.

46. For a fuller and more explicit explication of Max Weber's theory of modern bureaucracy and its creation in the Austrian Enlightenment, compare Weber, *Wirtschaft und Gesellschaft*, 124–26; Heindl, "Beamte, Staatsdienst und Universitätsreform," 35 n. 1.

47. Harm-Hinrich Brandt, "Der österreichische 'Staatsbankrott' von 1811," in *Staatsfinanzen—Staatsverschuldung—Staatsbankrotte in der europäischen Staaten- und Rechtsgeschicht*, ed. Gerhard Lingelbach (Cologne: Böhlau, 2000), 55–66.

48. Ibid., 56–57.

49. José Luis Cardoso and Pedro Lains, "Paying for the Liberal State," introduction to *Paying for the Liberal State: The Rise of Public Finance in Nineteenth-Century Europe* (Cambridge: Cambridge University Press, 2010), 1–26.

50. Iryna Vushko, "Enlightened Absolutism, Imperial Bureaucracy and Provincial Society: The Austrian Project to Transform Galicia, 1772–1815" (Ph.D. diss., Yale University, 2008).

51. For a contemporary overview of public law in the Austrian *Vormärz*, roughly 1815 to 1848, see Johann Springer, *Statistik des österreichischen Kaiserstaates*, 2 vols. (Vienna: F. Beck, 1840), especially 1:245–83.

52. *Ah. Handschreiben an den Kronprinzen Erzherzog Ferdinand vom 28. Februar 1835*, printed in Friedrich Walter, ed., *Die Zeit Franz' II. (I.) und Ferdinands I. (1792-1848). Aktenstücke*, vol. 5 of *Die Österreichische Zentralverwaltung. II. Abteilung. Von der Vereinigung der österreichischen und böhmischen Hofkanzlei bis zur Einrichtung der Ministerialverfassung (1749–1848)* [hereafter *ÖZV*, II/5], Veröffentlichungen der Kommission für neuere Geschichte Österreichs 43 (Vienna: Adolf Holzhausens Nachfolger, 1956), 266.

53. Sheehan, *German History*, 277–81.

54. Helmut Rumpler, *Österreichische Geschichte, 1804–1914: Eine Chance für Mittel-*

*europa; Bürgerliche Emanzipation und Staatsverfall in der Habsburgermonarchie,* Österreichische Geschichte (Vienna: Ueberreuter, 1997), 38–42; Ernst Wangermann, *From
Joseph II to the Jacobin Trials: Government Policy and Public Opinion in the Habsburg Dominions in the Period of the French Revolution,* 2nd ed. (London, Oxford University Press, 1969);
for a skeptical treatment of the Jacobin plot see, above all, Bernard, *From the Enlightenment,*
chaps. 8 and 9.

55. For an example for the changing meanings of Austria, see Grete Klingenstein, "The
Meanings of 'Austria' and 'Austrian' in the Eighteenth Century," in *Royal and Republican
Sovereignty in Early Modern Europe: Essays in Memory of Ragnhild Hatton,* ed. Robert Oresko,
G. C. Gibbs, and Hamish Marshall Scott (Cambridge: Cambridge University Press, 1997),
423–78.

56. Heindl, *Gehorsame Rebellen,* 110–12; Heindl, "Beamte, Staatsdienst und Universitätsreform," 47.

57. Heindl, "Beamte, Staatsdienst und Universitätsreform," 44–47.

58. Vorschrift über die allgemeinenen Pflichten und besonderen Obliegenheiten der
Stellen und Beamten, und über die wechselseitigen Befugnisse und Verbindlichkeiten
der Oberen und Untergebenen. Ah. Cabinets-Befehl, December 30, 1806, in HHStA,
Kabinetsarchiv Kaiser Franz Akten, K 69. Historians have labeled this decree as Francis's
"pastoral letter"—in contrast to Joseph II's from 1883. For corroborating commentary
on this executive order see Heindl, *Gehorsame Rebellen,* 44; Plattner, "Die josephinische
Bürokratie," 61–62.

59. Karl Friedrich Kübeck von Kübau would enjoy a long and illustrious career in the
Austrian administration. Karl Friedrich Kübeck von Kübau, *Tagebücher des Carl Friedrich
freiherrn Kübeck von Kübau,* ed. Max Kübeck von Kübau, 2 vols. (Vienna: Gerold, 1909),
I/I: 206–7. Brief and instructive on this topic is Hellmuth Grausam, "Der österreichische
Staatsbeamte im Spiegel der Memoirenliteratur. Vom josephinischen Jahrzehnt bis zum
Beginn des Konstitutionalismus" (Ph.D. diss., University of Vienna, 1965), 72–76.

60. Heindl, *Gehorsame Rebellen,* 44–45.

61. Franz Leander Fillafer, "Eine Gespenstergeschichte für Erwachsene: Überlegungen
zu einer Geschichte des josephinischen Erbes in der Habsburgermonarchie," in *Was Blieb
vom Josephinismus?* ed. Christian Ehalt and Jean Mondot, Edited Book Series (Innsbruck:
Innsbruck University Press, 2010), 39–44; See also, Matthias Rettenwander, "Nachwirkungen des Josephinismus," in *Josephinismus als Aufgeklärter Absolutismus,* ed. Reinalter, 317–
425, which makes the argument that Josephinism is precisely the bureaucratic ethos that
arises after Joseph, and serves as a center of resistance in the Metternich-Franciscan era.

62. Heindl, *Gehorsame Rebellen,* 116–26; Waltraud Heindl, "Beamtentum, Elitenbildung
und Wissenschaftspolitik im Vormärz," in *Vormärz: Wendepunkt und Herausforderung,* ed.
Hanna Schnedl-Bubenicek, Veröffentlichungen des Ludwig-Boltzmann-Institutes für Geschichte der Gesellschaftswissenschaften 10 (Vienna: Geyer-Edition, 1983), 47–64.

63. Beidtel, *Staatsverwaltung,* 2: 110–14.

64. Rettenwander, "Nachwirkungen des Josephinismus," 357–65.

65. Irmgard Plattner, "Josephinismus und Bürokratie," in *Josephinismus als Aufgeklärter
Absolutismus,* ed. Reinalter, 53–96.

66. In the meantime, see Gerd Holler, *Gerechtigkeit für Ferdinand: Österreichs gütiger Kaiser* (Vienna: Amalthea, 1986).

67. Alan Sked, *Metternich and Austria: An Evaluation* (Basingstoke: Palgrave Macmillan, 2008), 117–18, 238; A. J. P. Taylor, *The Habsburg Monarchy, 1809–1918: A History of the Austrian Empire and Austria-Hungary* (London: H. Hamilton, 1948), 47.

68. See Hans Bankl, *Die kranken Habsburger: Befunde und Befindlichkeiten einer Herrscherdynastie* (Vienna: Kremayr & Scheriau, 1998), 85–89, for a description of Ferdinand's afflictions. For a partial rehabilitation of Ferdinand, see Lorenz Mikoletzky, "Kaiser Ferdinand I. von Österreich und 'Seine' Wiener," *Jahrbuch des Vereins für Geschichte der Stadt Wien* 52 (1996): 277–88.

69. For descriptions of Ferdinand during the Bohemian coronation, see Hugh LeCaine Agnew, "Ambiguities of Ritual: Dynastic Loyalty, Territorial Patriotism, and Nationalism in the Last Three Royal Coronations in Bohemia, 1791–1836," *Bohemia* 41, no. 1 (2000): 14. Interestingly, the latest interpretation of Ferdinand's coronation emphasizes it as a boon to the Czech national movement, not as a way for the landed estates to assert their authority. This speaks to the now longstanding and unfortunate tendency in central Europe to subsequently nationalize constitutional and administrative history: Milada Sekyrková, *7. 9. 1836, Ferdinand V.: poslední prazská korunovace*, Edice Dny, které tvořily české dějiny 10 (Prague: Havran, 2004), esp. 51–55.

70. Christiane Thomas, "Ornat und Insignien zur Lombardo-Venezianischen Krönung 1838: Entwurf und Ausführung," *Mitteilungen des Österreichischen Staatsarchivs* 32 (1979): 165.

71. Waltraud Heindl, *Josephinische Mandarine: Bürokratie und Beamte in Österreich; 1848–1914* (Vienna: Böhlau, 2013), 26–34.

72. Heindl, *Gehorsame Rebellen*, 140–42. Heindl uses the official *Tafeln zur Statistik der oesterreichischen Monarchie* (Vienna, 1828–78), for these figures.

73. For the relation to Joseph's own renunciation of his most unpopular policies in Hungary, see Beales, *Joseph II*, 2: 628–30.

74. Becker, "Kaiser Josephs Schreibmaschine," 231–42.

75. See Friedrich Walter, *Österreichische Verfassungs- und Verwaltungsgeschichte von 1500–1955*, ed. Adam Wandruszka, Veröffentlichungen der Kommission für Neuere Geschichte Österreichs 59 (Vienna: Böhlau, 1972),120.

76. Quoted in Friedrich Walter, *Die Zeit Franz' II. (I.) und Ferdinands I. (1792–1848)*, vol. 1, bk. 2, pt. 2 of *Die Österreichische Zentralverwaltung. II. Abteilung. Von der Vereinigung der österreichischen und böhmischen Hofkanzlei bis zur Einrichtung der Ministerialverfassung (1749–1848)*[hereafter *ÖZV*, II/1/2/2], Veröffentlichungen der Kommission für neuere Geschichte Österreichs 42 (Vienna: Adolf Holzhausens Nachfolger, 1956), 163.

77. The feud between Metternich and Kolowrat is legendary. The best orientation to this feud, which often expressed itself in battles in and through the offices of Austria's administration, is Heinrich Ritter von Srbik, *Metternich: Der Staatsmann und der Mensch*, 3 vols. (Munich: F. Bruckmann, 1925), esp. 1: 540–56; for Metternich's attempts to isolate Kolowrat in the State–Conference, see 2: 2–28.

78. See *ÖZV*, II/1/2/2, chap. 5, for more detailed information on the Staatskonferenz.

Also see Srbik, *Metternich*, 2: 6–9 for a detailed account of Metternich's relations with members of the Imperial family.

79. Walter, *Österreichische Verfassungs- und Verwaltungsgeschichte*, 123.

80. Ernst Carl Hellbling, *Österreichische Verfassungs- und Verwaltungsgeschichte: Ein Lehrbuch für Studierende*, Rechts- und Staatswissenschaften 13 (Vienna: Springer, 1956), 329–30.

81. For useful summaries of the powers and roles of the *Council of State*, see Hellbling, *Verfassungs- und Verwaltungsgeschichte*, 328–29; Rudolf Hoke, "Österreich," in *Deutsche Verwaltungsgeschichte*, ed. Kurt G. A. Jeserich, Hans Pohl, and Georg-Christoph von Unruh, vol. 2 (Stuttgart: Deutsche Verlags-Anstalt, 1983), 155.

82. Springer, *Statistik*, 1: 220. See also Wilhelm Brauneder, "Die Verfassungsentwicklung in Österreich 1848 bis 1918," in *Die Habsburgermonarchie, 1848–1918*, ed. Helmut Rumpler and Peter Urbanitsch, vol. 7/1, Verfassung und Parlamentarismus (Vienna: Österreichische Akademie der Wissenschaften, 2000), 74.

83. For a more exhaustive list of the *Vereinigte k. k. Hofkanzlei*'s duties and responsibilities, see Springer, *Statistik*, 2: 19–20. See also Hoke, "Österreich," 358.

84. Springer, *Statistik*, 2: 19–20.

85. Franz de Paula Hartig, *Genesis der Revolution in Oesterreich im Jahre 1848*, 3rd ed. (Leipzig: F. Fleischer, 1851), 28–29. See also Hoke, "Österreich," 357.

86. Hartig, *Genesis*, 28–29.

87. The twelve provincial government offices encompassed the following lands and were located in the following cities (1) Lower Austria–Vienna; (2) Austria over the Enns–Linz; (3) Styria–Graz; (4) Tyrol and Vorarlberg–Innsbruck; (5) Illyria (Carniola and Carinthia)–Ljubljana; (6) Coastal Provinces [*Küstenland*], which encompassed Görz, Gradiska, and the Istrian Peninsula–Triest; (7) Bohemia–Prague; (8) Moravia and Silesia–Brno/Brünn; (9) Galicia and Bukovina–Lemberg/Lwów/L'viv; (10) Venetia–Venice; (11) Lombardy–Milan; (12) Dalmatia, Ragusa and Cattaro–Zara. See Springer, *Statistik*, 2: 20–21.

88. For a discussion of Kaunitz's work to establish the Gubernial system, see Franz A. J. Szabo, *Kaunitz and Enlightened Absolutism, 1753–1780* (New York: Cambridge University Press, 1994), 83–95.

89. The governor was known by different names in different provinces. In Bohemia, the governor was known as "Supreme Burgrave" (*Oberstburggraf*); in other places he was known as "President" (*Präsident*) or "Governor" (*Gouerneur*). See Hoke, "Österreich," 369. Of course, titular variation is yet another indication of the general status of the provinces themselves as substates or state-fragments. Austria, in other words, was not fully unified as central state, nor did it have uniform titles for analogous positions across its provincial administrations.

90. Springer writes that the "responsibility of this office [the Gubernia] encompasses the entire political administration of its province, but also additional areas which according to their nature or in part are financial or military matters; on the actual business of civil justice are strictly excluded from its departmental purview." Springer, *Statistik*, 2: 22. See Springer for a detailed account of the staffs of the individual Gubernia: ibid., 21–28.

91. Hoke, "Österreich," 369.

92. For a description of Hungary and Transylvania's administration in the early nineteenth century, see Springer, *Statistik*, 2: 34–42.

93. See Becker, "Kaiser Josephs Schreibmaschine," 242–51.

94. Hoke, "Österreich," 370.

95. The translators of Otto Brunner's *Land und Herrschaft: Grundfragen der territorialen Verfassungsgeschichte Österreichs im Mittelalter* have rendered the term *Grundherrschaft*, alternately as "lordship over land," or simply "land lordship," and "seigneury." Brunner himself explains that *Grundherrschaft* "lumps together a broad assortment of rights that were in no way restricted to lordship over land, even though this must have been present in every seigneury." Otto Brunner, *Land and Lordship: Structures of Governance in Medieval Austria*, trans. Howard Kaminsky and James van Horn Melton, Middle Ages series (Philadelphia: University of Pennsylvania Press, 1992), 200–01. See also the translators' introduction in Brunner, *Land and Lordship*, xxvii–xxxiii. I have decided to keep the German in the original.

96. See Gerhard Putschögl, "Zur Geschichte der autonomen Landesverwaltung in den zisleithanischen Ländern der Habsburgermonarchie," *Mitteilungen des Oberösterreichischen Landesarchivs* 13 (1981): 290–94; Gerald Stourzh, "Länderautonomie und Gesamtstaat in Österreich," *Bericht über den neunzehten österreichischen Historikertag in Graz* 19 (1993): 39–40.

97. Leopold II attempted to ensure that his mother's state-building reforms remained intact by distancing himself from his brother's more radical program. In this vein, Leopold, to calm down the various protests of the landed nobility in the wake of Joseph II's far-reaching and penetrating reforms, reinstated the provincial diets his elder brother had disbanded and even assented to be crowned King of Hungary in Pressburg. Adam Wandruszka, *Leopold II: Erzherzog von Österreich, Grossherzog von Toskana, König von Ungarn und Böhmen, Römischer Kaiser*, 2 vols. (Vienna: Herold, 1963), 2: 249–90.

98. Heinrich Börnstein, *Fünfundsiebzig Jahre in der alten und neuen Welt: Memoiren eines Unbedeutenden*, ed. Patricia Herminghouse, Crosscurrents, Writings of German Political Emigrés in Nineteenth-Century America (New York: Peter Lang, 1986), 220–21. See also Hans Sturmberger, *Der Weg zum Verfassungsstaat: Die politische Entwicklung in Oberösterreich von 1792–1861* (Munich: R. Oldenbourg, 1962), 44–5.

99. Sturmberger, *Weg*, 44.

100. The following discussion builds on the work of Ralph Melville on the Bohemian nobility and Otto Brunner in general. See Ralph Melville, *Adel und Revolution in Böhmen: Strukturwandel von Herrschaft und Gesellschaft in Österreich um die Mitte des 19. Jahrhunderts*, Veröffentlichungen des Instituts für Europäische Geschichte Mainz. Abteilung Universalgeschichte 95 (Mainz: Philipp von Zabern, 1998), 15–60; Ralph Melville, "Von der Patrimonialverwaltung zur Gemeindeselbstverwaltung in Böhmen und Österreich um 1848," in *Mezi liberalismem a totalitou: Komunální politika ve středoevropských zemích, 1848–1948*, ed. Jiří Pešek and Václav Ledvinka, Documenta Pragensia 14 (Prague: Scriptorium, 1997), 54–59; Otto Brunner, *Adeliges Landleben und europäischer Geist: Leben und Werk Wolf Helmhards von Hohberg, 1612–1688* (Salzburg: O. Müller, 1949), chap. 5.

101. Brunner, *Adeliges Landleben*, 324–25.

102. In areas that had belonged to French satellite states during the Napoleonic Wars, however, the central state actually had taken over the local administration. When these areas

reverted back to the Habsburgs (Tyrol, Vorarlberg, Carinola, the Villach county in Carinthia and the Coastal Lands) or were given to the Habsburgs as part of the post-war settlements, (Salzburg, the Innviertel), Austria did not put local administration under the yoke of the Grundherren, but maintained the local state institutions. See Andreas Gottsmann, *Venetien, 1859–1866: Österreichische Verwaltung und nationale Opposition*, Zentraleuropa-Studien 8 (Vienna: VÖAW, 2005); Brigitte Mazohl, *Österreichischer Verwaltungsstaat und administrative Eliten im Königreich Lombardo-Venetien, 1815–1859*, Veröffentlichungen des Instituts für Europäische Geschichte Mainz; Abteilung Universalgeschichte 146 (Mainz: Philipp Von Zabern, 1993); Brigitte Mazohl-Wallnig, "Überlegungen zu einer Verwaltungsgeschichte Lombardo-Venetiens im Neoabsolutismus," in *Gesellschaft, Politik und Verwaltung in der Habsburgermonarchie, 1830–1918*, ed. Ferenc Glatz and Ralph Melville, Veröffentlichungen des Instituts für Europäische Geschichte Mainz, Abteilung Universalgeschichte 15 (Stuttgart: Franz Steiner, 1987), 87–104.

103. Melville, *Adel und Revolution*, 16.

104. Ibid., 17.

105. Melville, *Adel und Revolution*, 19.

106. Melville, "Von der Patrimonialverwaltung," 55.

107. Melville, *Adel und Revolution*, 33–44.

108. Melville, "Von der Patrimonialverwaltung," 56.

109. Helmuth Feigl, "Der Adel in Niederösterreich 1780–1861," in *Der Adel an der Schwelle des bürgerlichen Zeitalters, 1780–1860*, ed. Armgard von Reden-Dohna and Ralph Melville, Veröffentlichungen des Instituts für Europäische Geschichte Mainz, Abteilung Universalgeschichte 10 (Stuttgart: Franz Steiner, 1988), 202. Also, for a general discussion of the nobility in pre-March Lower Austria, see Viktor Bibl, *Die niederösterreichischen Stände im Vormärz: Ein Beitrag zur Vorgeschichte der Revolution des Jahres 1848* (Vienna: Gerlach & Wiedling, 1911).

110. According to Springer, the counties were called "quarters" (*Vierteln*) in Austria under the Enns, and "provinces" in Lombardy and Venetia. Moreover, the county offices in Lombardy and Venetia were known as "delegations" (*Delegationen*). Springer, *Statistik*, 2: 27–29.

111. Ibid., 27–28.

112. Hoke, "Österreich," 370.

113. Springer, *Statistik*, 2: 28.

114. Brunner, *Adeliges Landleben*, 320.

115. Ibid., 317.

116. Matthias Rettenwander, in a recent article, calls attention to the neglected interpretation that Josephinism was an attitude that developed *after* Joseph. Rettenwander, "Nachwirkungen des Josephinismus"; see also the original pioneering work of Valjavec, *Der Josephinismus*.

117. For more information on von Andrian-Werburg's life and career, see Franz Adlgasser, "Viktor Franz Freiherr von Andrian-Werburg (1813–1858)—Eine Lebensskizze," in Victor-Franz von Andrian-Werburg, *"Österreich wird meine Stimme erkennen lerner wie die Stimme Gottes in der Wüste": Tagebücher 1839–1858*, 3 vols., ed. Franz Adlgasser, (Vienna:

Böhlau, 2011), 1: 11–35. Fritz Fellner, "Die Tagebücher des Viktor Franz von Andrian-Werburg," *Mitteilungen des Österreichischen Staatsarchivs* 26 (1973): 328–41; Madeleine Rietra, *Wirkungsgeschichte als Kulturgeschichte: Viktor von Andrian-Werburgs Rezeption im Vormärz; Eine Dokumentation mit Einleitung, Kommentar und einer Neuausgabe von "Österreich und dessen Zukunft" (1843)*, ed. Cola Minis and Arend Quak, Amsterdamer Publikationen zur Sprache und Literatur 143 (Amsterdam: Rodopi, 2001).

118. Andrian had applied as an intern for the position as *Kreiskommissär* in 1837 and was turned down because of his relatively young age. He attempted to enter the diplomatic corps and was refused entrance. Then, he was appointed as unpaid *Kreiskommissär* in 1839 in Pisino, Istria—nearly six years after joining the civil service—against his own will. Fellner, "Die Tagebücher von Andrian-Werburg," 331; Rietra, *Wirkungsgeschichte als Kulturgeschichte*, 12.

119. Victor Franz von Andrian-Werburg, "*Österreich wird meine Stimme erkennen lernen*," 1: 67 (entry on December 15, 1839). See also Rietra, *Wirkungsgeschichte als Kulturgeschichte*, 13.

120. Victor Franz von Andrian-Werburg, *Oesterreich und dessen Zukunft*, vol. 2 (Hamburg: L. Giese, 1847); quoted in Rietra, *Wirkungsgeschichte als Kulturgeschichte*, 13–14.

121. See the two thoughtful essays on the legacies of Josephinism in the nineteenth century: Rettenwander, "Nachwirkungen des Josephinismus"; Fillafer, "Eine Gespenstergeschichte."

122. Melville, *Adel und Revolution*, 61–66.

123. Carl E. Schorske writes that Andrian-Werburg was a member of the "liberal aristocracy" while Georg Franz quotes Paul Molisch, calling his work "the program of the liberal landed estate." Georg Franz, *Liberalismus: Die deutschliberale Bewegung in der habsburgischen Monarchie* (Munich: Georg D. W. Callwey, 1955), 32; Carl E. Schorske, *Fin-de-Siècle Vienna: Politics and Culture* (New York: Vintage Books, 1981), 304.

124. Fellner, "Die Tagebücher von Andrian-Werburg," 330. For a recent presentation of Andrian-Werburg's reception in central Europe, complete with reprinted letters to the author and newspaper articles, see Rietra, *Wirkungsgeschichte als Kulturgeschichte*.

125. Melville, *Adel und Revolution*, 61–64.

126. Beidtel, *Staatsverwaltung*, 2: 234–36.

127. Heindl found that while the high nobility indeed increased in percentage among the bureaucracy, their increase came at the expense at the lower nobles—nobles like von Andrian and not burgher like Beidtel. See Heindl, *Gehorsame Rebellen*, 142–59.

128. See for instance, Beidtel, *Staatsverwaltung*, 1: 20–22.

129. Beidtel, *Staatsverwaltung*, 2: 352–54.

130. See, for instance, Kübeck von Kübau, *Tagebücher Kübeck*, 1/2, 282; Josef Karl Mayr, *Wien im Zeitalter Napoleons: Staatsfinanzen, Lebensverhältnisse, Beamte und Militär*, vol. 6, Abhandlungen zur Geschichte und Quellenkunde der Stadt Wien 6 (Vienna: Gottlieb Gistel, 1940), 176. Mayr also tells us that many officials died in poverty, leaving nothing to their children. See, Josef Karl Mayr, *Geschichte der österreichischen Staatskanzlei im Zeitalter des Fürsten Metternich* (Vienna: Selbstverlag des Haus-, Hof- und Staatsarchivs, 1935), 126–27; Heindl, *Gehorsame Rebellen*, 170.

131. Mayr, *Geschichte*, 126.

132. Heindl, *Gehorsame Rebellen*, 149. To be sure, the burgher and their recently enno-

bled cousins still dominated the central offices of the civil service in *Vormärz* (678 persons to 209 high nobles in 1841).

133. Ferdinand Leopold, Count Schirndinger von Schirnding, published a four-volume examination of imperial Austria's government and society in 1840, which considers the bureaucracy as divided into these two classes, *Konzepts- und Kanzleipersonal*. To this, he also includes a third subtier—consisting of "doormen, office servants, prison guards, porters and house servants." Ferdinand Leopold Schirnding, *Oesterreich im Jahre 1840: Staat und Staatsverwaltung, Verfassung und Cultur, von einem österreichischen Staatsmanne*, 4 vols. (Leipzig: O. Wigand, 1840), 1: 83–84.

134. Weber, *Economy and Society*, 2: 959. Civil service also brought special privileges, such as paid vacations and the right to wear medals of distinction.

135. Johann Georg Megerle von Mühlfeld, *Handbuch für alle kaiserlich-königlichen, ständischen und städtischen Beamten, deren Witwen und Waisen, oder Darstellung aller ihnen durch die neuesten allerhöchsten Gesetze vom Jahre 1806 bis 1822 zustehenden Rechte und obliegenden Verbindlichkeiten*, expanded ed. 3 vols. (Vienna: J. G. Ritter von Mösle, 1824), 1: 353–99.

136. Sociological and categorical evaluations of the Austrian civil service are numerous. My own pragmatically descriptive approach follows that of Otto Hintze. See Otto Hintze, "Der Beamtenstand," in *Otto Hintze: Gesammelte Abhandlungen*, 3 vols. ed. Gerhard Oestreich (Göttingen: Vandenhoeck & Ruprecht, 1964), 2: 67–68.

137. Beidtel, *Staatsverwaltung*, 1: 20.

138. See Table 1.2 for examples. A drafting-intern (*Konzepts-pratikant*) in Vienna was assigned to the eleventh class, while his colleague in a provincial governor's office (*Gubernium*) or county office was assigned to the twelfth class.

139. For the career of Eder, see Stefan Sienell, "Die Beamtenlaufbahn des Johann Nepomuk Eder (1794–1873): Ein Beitrag zur Verwaltungsgeschichte im 19. Jahrhundert," *Zeitschrift des Historischen Vereins für Steiermark* 85 (1994): 313–34; For the corresponding ranks of Eder's positions, compare with the lists and descriptions in Megerle von Mühlfeld, *Handbuch*, 1: 353–99.

140. Herman Bahr, *Die Hexe Drut*, 5th ed. (Berlin: Sieben Stäbe-Verlags- und Druckereigesellschaft, 1929). See also Donald G. Daviau, *Hermann Bahr*, Twayne's World Authors Series, German Literature (Boston: Twayne Publishers, 1985), 95–98.

141. For a further discussion on the service nobility as the second society see Adam Wandruszka, "Die 'Zweite Gesellschaft' der Donaumonarchie," in *Adel in Österreich*, ed. Heinz Siegert (Vienna: Kremayr & Scheriau, 1971), 56–67. The quote is located on page 57.

142. The Austrian dramatist Franz Grillparzer, who worked by day as an archivist in the Imperial-Royal Court Treasury, is a prime example. Adalbert Stifter, though, also was engaged in public service as a public school inspector. On this topic, see the excellent essay by Heindl, "Beamtentum, Elitenbildung und Wissenschaftpolitik," 56–60.

143. There is no biography of any kind on this prime example of a learned official. See his entry in the *Österreichisches Bibliographisches Lexikon*: s.v. "Hock, Carl Frh. von," *Österreichisches Biographisches Lexikon und biographische Dokumentation* (2003), www.biographien.ac.at/ (accessed June 11, 2012); and Heindl, "Beamtentum, Elitenbildung und Wissenschaftpolitik," 55–56.

144. Heindl, *Gehorsame Rebellen*, 102. Beidtel describes local officials taking a year vacation to enter the universities to study law, lest they lose their post. Beidtel, *Staatsverwaltung*, 2: 149–50.

145. Heindl, *Gehorsame Rebellen*, 102; See Heindl, "Beamte, Staatsdienst und Universitätsreform," for how the will to reform the civil service and its training were "lamed" during the reign of Francis.

146. For a detailed description of the civil-servant uniform, see Georg Kugler, "Der Hofstaat des Kaisers Franz," in *Kaisertum Österreich, 1804–1848: Ausstellung Schallaburg, 27. April bis 27. Oktober 1996*, ed. Gottfried Mraz, Henrike Mraz, and Gottfried Stangler, vol. 387, n.s., Katalog des Niederösterreichischen Landesmuseums (Bad Vöslau: Niederösterreichisches Landesmuseum, 1996), 87–88.

147. Beidtel, *Staatsverwaltung*, 2: 258.

148. Ibid., 1: 352–54.

149. In the statistics that Waltraud Heindl put together for her analysis of the bureaucracy between 1828 and 1846, the number of officials increased from 26,231 to 29,995, or roughly by 14 percent. At the same time the number of interns almost doubled (98 percent) in the same time span—increasing from 3,212 to 6,363 persons. See table 2, in Heindl, *Gehorsame Rebellen*, 141.

150. Julius Bunzel, *Der Lebenslauf eines vormärzlichen Verwaltungsbeamten*, Studien zur Sozial, Wirtschafts- und Verwaltungsgeschichte 5 (Vienna: C. Konegen [E. Stülpnagel], 1911), 42–43.

151. Attrition clearly worked to clear the ranks of interns. Bunzel reports that in the same treasury office, only two of twenty-five interns who worked in the treasury office from 1817 to 1837, were promoted into officialdom. Bunzel, *Lebenslauf*, 41.

152. Heindl, *Gehorsame Rebellen*, 148–58.

153. The best description of the generally tough financial conditions of the interns is still Grausam, "Der österreichische Staatsbeamte," 43–47. See also Megner, *Beamtenmetropole Wien*, 240–47.

154. Kübeck von Kübau, *Tagebücher Kübeck*, 1/1: x–xiii, and the diary entry from October 16, 1801, 1/1: 74–75. See also Schirnding, *Oesterreich im Jahre 1840*, 4: 74–75.

155. For information regarding Kübeck's life in the civil service, see his published diaries Kübeck von Kübau, *Tagebücher Kübeck*. See also, Friedrich Walter, "Carl Friedrich Freiherr Kübeck von Kübau," *Neue Österreichische Biographie ab 1815* 16 (n.d.): 16. The best interpretive essay on Kübeck is a short piece on how Kübeck exemplified tensions in the bureaucracy between the heritage of Josephinism and nineteenth-century absolutism, Jean-Paul Bled, "Le Baron Kübeck, un modèle de haut fonctionnaire," *Études Danubiennes* 12, no. 2 (1996): 209–14.

156. Alfons Huber, "Ignaz Beidtels Leben und Wirken nach seinen Memoiren," in *Geschichte der Österreichichen Staatsverwaltung 1740–1848*, ed. Alfons Huber, 2 vols. (Innsbruck: Verlag der Wagner'schen Universitäts-Buchhandlung, 1896), 1: xiv.

157. Bunzel, *Lebenslauf*, 41. This study was based wholly on files in various Styrian archives and offices.

158. Bunzel reports that in 1805 there were 2,041 case files and 493 "Videat" files, which

were for review only. By 1807, the number of case files climbed to 2,819 plus 943 "Videat" files. The year 1808 saw 3,025 files. After 1815, the files began increasing yet again. He counts 2,344 files in 1815; 3,569 in 1820; 4,400 in 1822; 5,258 in 1825. By 1829, the number of files topped 7,000! All the while the office staff was insufficient to keep up with the increasing work. Despite the fact that the number of files increased by almost 1,750 files between 1825 and 1829, the office staff actually shrank. In 1824, it consisted of the *Prokurator* (Varena), two deputy officials (*Adjunkten*) and five unpaid interns (*Praktikanten*); in 1830, the same number of deputy officials was supplemented by only four interns. Bunzel, *Lebenslauf*, 8, 10, 14, 17, 19, 33.

159. Ibid., 37.

160. The *Conduiteliste* formed a major complaint of civil servants from the time of Joseph II until nearly the end of the monarchy; occupational interest groups, advocating on the part of officials in the last decades of the monarchy hoped to abolish the secrecy of these performance evaluations. The literature on them, therefore, is extensive. See Beidtel's own explanation of the reports, their status as confidential, and his assessments of the problems associated with them in Beidtel, *Staatsverwaltung*, 1: 197–200.

161. Ibid., 2: 112.

162. Ibid., 42–44. See also Heindl, *Gehorsame Rebellen*, 27–28.

163. Weber, *Wirtschaft und Gesellschaft*, 553.

164. Beidtel, *Staatsverwaltung*, 2: 43–44.

165. Schirnding, *Oesterreich im Jahre 1840*, 1: 84–85.

166. This very tension between the courtly servility and rationalism has been elevated to an aspect of Austrian national character in Helmut Kuzmics and Roland Axtmann, *Autorität, Staat und Nationalcharakter: Der Zivilisationsprozeß in Österreich und England, 1700–1900*, Schriften zur Zivilisations- und Prozesstheorie 2 (Opladen: Leske & Budrich, 2000), chap. 6 and 8; see esp. 281–88. This work has recently been translated into English: Helmut Kuzmics and Roland Axtmann, *Authority, State, and National Character: The Civilizing Process in Austria and England, 1700–1900*, Studies in European Cultural Transition 36 (Aldershot: Ashgate, 2007).

## Chapter 2: The Madness of Count Stadion

1. Rudolph Hirsch, *Franz Graf Stadion* (Vienna: Eduard Hügel, 1861), 102.

2. No extensive biography exists on Count Franz Stadion—a situation which historians have lamented for at least a century. Stadion died young and left no private papers, though some of his letters have survived in others' *Nachlässe*. A good start on Stadion, his background and his term as minister of the interior is Rudolf Till, "Innenminister Franz Graf Stadion," in *Gestalter der Geschicke Österreichs*, ed. Hugo Hantsch, Studien der Wiener Katholischen Akademie 2 (Innsbruck: Tyrolia-Verlag, 1962), 379–87; Joseph Alexander Helfert, *Geschichte Oesterreichs vom Ausgange des Wiener October-Aufstandes, 1848*, 4 vols. (Prague: F. Tempsky, 1869–86), 3: 16–44. See also the recent works by Ralph Melville, especially Ralph Melville, "Der böhmische Adel und der Konstitutionalismus: Franz Stadions Konzept einer postfeudalen Neuordnung Österreichs," in *Die Chance der Verständigung: Absichten und Ansätze zu übernationaler Zusammenarbeit in den böhmischen Ländern, 1848–1918*, ed. Ferdinand Seibt (Munich: R. Oldenbourg, 1987), 135–45.

3. Helfert, *Geschichte Oesterreichs*, 3: 19.

4. Ibid., 23. See also the contemporary portrait of Stadion in *Reichstags-Gallerie: Geschriebene Portraits der hervorragendsten Deputirten des ersten österreichischen Reichstages* (Vienna: Jasper, Hügel & Manz, 1849), 53–56. Finally, Andreas Gottsmann, *Der Reichstag von Kremsier und die Regierung Schwarzenberg: Die Verfassungsdiskussion des Jahres 1848 im Spannungsfeld zwischen Reaktion und nationaler Frage*, Österreich Archiv (Vienna: Verlag für Geschichte und Politik, 1995), 37, gives a short and insightful analysis of Stadion, not as a liberal, but as a progressive Josephinist.

5. Officials made up one of the leading social groups in the Constitutional Assembly, claiming 87 mandates out of 383. See table 3 in Andreas Gottsmann, "Der Reichstag 1848/49 und der Reichsrat 1861 bis 1865," in *Die Habsburgermonarchie 1848–1918*, vol. 7/1, *Verfassung und Parlamentarismus*, ed. Helmut Rumpler and Peter Urbanitsch (Vienna: Österreichische Akademie der Wissenschaften, 2000), 587.

6. *Reichstags-Gallerie*, 55–56.

7. Heinrich Friedjung, "Reformen unter dem Grafen Stadion," *Österreichische Rundschau* 18 (1909): 23.

8. Hannes Stekl and Marija Wakounig, *Windisch-Graetz: Ein Fürstenhaus im 19. und 20. Jahrhundert* (Vienna: Böhlau, 1992); Paul Müller, *Feldmarschall Fürst Windischgrätz: Revolution und Gegenrevolution in Österreich* (Vienna: W. Braumüller, 1934).

9. Otto Urban, *Die tschechische Gesellschaft, 1848 bis 1918*, trans. Henning Schlegel, 2 vols. (Vienna: Böhlau, 1994), 74–87; Stanley Z. Pech, *The Czech Revolution of 1848* (Chapel Hill: University of North Carolina Press, 1969).

10. Schwarzenberg wanted the minister of justice, the "Barricade Minister" Alexander Bach, to take the post of minister of the interior in order to buy credibility with the revolutionaries. Windisch-Graetz posed Stadion as a compromise. For events surrounding the appointment of the Schwarzenberg cabinet, see Stefan Lippert, *Felix Fürst zu Schwarzenberg: Eine politische Biographie*, Historische Mitteilungen 21 (Stuttgart: F. Steiner, 1998), 158–65.

11. R. John Rath, *The Viennese Revolution of 1848* (repr., New York: Greenwood, 1969), 34–35.

12. Rath writes that the Hungarian journalist Ferencz Pulszky translated the speech and began circulating it in Vienna: ibid., 36. Pulszky reproduces a German text of Kossuth's speech in his memoirs. See Ferencz Aurelius Pulszky, *Meine Zeit, mein Leben*, 4 vols. (Pressburg: Carl Stampfel, 1880), 2: 36–50.

13. Pulszky, *Meine Zeit*, 2: 39.

14. Friedrich Walter, *Die Geschichte der Ministerien Kolowrat, Ficquelmont, Pillersdorf, Wessenberg-Doblhoff und Schwarzenberg*, vol. 1 of *Die Österreichische Zentralverwaltung. III. Abteilung. Von der Märzrevolution 1848 bis zur Dezemberverfassung 1867* [hereafter *ÖZV*, III/1], Kommission für neuere Geschichte Österreichs 49 (Vienna: Adolf Holzhausens Nachfolger, 1964), 3–4. Wilhelm Brauneder, "Die Verfassungsentwicklung in Österreich 1848 bis 1918," in *Die Habsburgermonarchie 1848–1918*, ed. Rumpler and Urbanitsch, vol. 7/1, 84.

15. Thomas Kletečka, ed., *Die Protokolle des Österreichischen Ministerrates, 1848–1867, Abteilung I: Die Ministerien des Revolutionsjahres 1848. 20 März 1848–21 November 1848*. Die

Ministerratsprotokolle Österreichs und der Österreichisch-Ungarischen Monarchie 1848–1918. 1. Serie [hereafter ÖMR I] (Vienna: öbt & hpt, 1996); Brauneder, "Verfassungsentwicklung," 85–86.

16. Thomas Kletečka, "Einleitung," in ÖMR I, ix–xiii. See also the minutes of the Cabinet of Ministers in the same volume, Nr. 1–3.

17. For a detailed study of the drafting of Pillersdorf's "April Constitution" as well as the work of the Central Committee, see the two articles by Karl Hugelmann: "Die Entwicklung der Aprilverfassung von 1848," *Jahrbuch für Landeskunde von Niederösterreich* 17–18, n.s. (1918): 235–78; "Der ständische Zentralausschuß in Österreich im April 1848," *Jahrbuch für Landeskunde von Niederösterreich* 12, n.s. (1913): 170–260.

18. For a full discussion of the Pillersdorf Constitution, see Brauneder, "Verfassungsentwicklung," 84–106.

19. The Pillersdorf Constitution is reprinted in Edmund Bernatzik, *Die österreichischen Verfassungsgesetze*, Studienaufgabe österreichische Gesetze 3 (Vienna: Manzsche k.u.k. Hof-, Verlags- und Universitätsbuchhandlung, 1911), chap. 4.

20. Rudolf Hoke, "Österreich," in *Deutsche Verwaltungsgeschichte*, ed. Kurt G. A. Jeserich, Hans Pohl, and Georg-Christoph von Unruh (Stuttgart: Deutsche Verlags-Anstalt, 1983), 2: 375.

21. Ibid.

22. Thomas Kletečka, "Einleitung," in ÖMR I, ix–xiii. For a narrative of these events, see the classic study Heinrich Friedjung, *Österreich von 1848 bis 1860*, 2 vols., 2nd ed. (Stuttgart: J. G. Cotta, 1912), 1: 26–27.

23. Joseph Alexander Helfert, *Geschichte der österreichischen Revolution im Zusammenhange mit der mitteleuropäischen Bewegung der Jahre 1848–1849*, 2 vols. (Freiburg im Breisgau: Herdersche Verlagshandlung, 1907), 1: 213–22, for an account of the storm petition and the concessions wrung from the Council of Ministers and the kaiser. For a description of the complicated electoral process and the resulting membership of the Constituent Assembly that met in July, see Rath, *Revolution*, 275–77.

24. Brauneder, "Verfassungsentwicklung," 107.

25. Gottsmann, "Reichstag und Reichsrat," 586–92.

26. Friedjung, *Österreich*, 81–85.

27. For an account of the initial debates of the court and officials following the emperor's retreat to Olmütz, see Thomas Kletečka, "Einleitung," in *Die Protokolle des Österreichischen Ministerrates, 1848–1867. II. Abteilung: Das Ministerium Schwarzenberg*, 5 vols. ed. Thomas Kletečka, 1: 5. Dezember 1848–7. Jänner 1850, Die Ministerratsprotokolle Österreichs und der Österreichisch-Ungarischen Monarchie, 1848–1918. 1. Serie [hereafter ÖMR II/1] (Vienna: öbt & hpt, 2002), ix–xi; Lippert, *Felix Fürst zu Schwarzenberg*, 158–63.

28. Wolfgang Häusler, *Von der Massenarmut zur Arbeiterbewegung: Demokratie und soziale Frage in der Wiener Revolution von 1848* (Vienna: Jugend & Volk, 1979), 382–97.

29. ÖZV, III/1: 231–32.

30. The literature on Schwarzenberg is extensive. The most-recent study is Lippert, *Felix Fürst zu Schwarzenberg*. A classic biographical sketch of Schwarzenberg is Rudolf

Kiszling, "Fürst Felix zu Schwarzenberg," in *Gestalter*, ed. Hantsch, 359–70. One could also consult the same author's full biography of Schwarzenberg, Rudolf Kiszling, *Fürst Felix zu Schwarzenberg: Der politische Lehrmeister Kaiser Franz Josephs* (Graz: Hermann Böhlaus Nachfolger, 1952) a classic only recently supplanted by Lippert's volume. Additionally, one should consult the sketch in Helfert's history of the later days of the revolution: *Geschichte Oesterreichs*, 3: 1–15.

31.  See Lippert, *Felix Fürst zu Schwarzenberg*, chap. 3, for an examination of Schwarzenberg's years of service in the diplomatic corps.

32.  The conditions surrounding the appointment of these two ministers is well documented. Schwarzenberg wanted Bach to be his all-important minister of the interior, but his brother-in-law, the imposing military commander Prince Alfred Windischgrätz, distrusted Bach and forced Schwarzenberg to accept Franz Stadion, whom he thought would be more likely to uphold the rights of the dynasty. See Friedjung, *Österreich*, 1: 92–102.

33.  For a detailed description of this event, as well as an analysis of the speech's reception, see Helfert, *Geschichte Österreichs*, 3: 302–12. In addition, see *ÖZV*, III/1: 143–48; as well as the relevant sections of Lippert's biography, Lippert, *Felix Fürst zu Schwarzenberg*, 181–86. Unfortunately, though this speech has garnered much attention by historians, it remains unprinted in any widely available collection of documents. It is, however, in Andreas Gottsmann's 1988 doctoral dissertation, Andreas Gottsmann, "Die Regierung Schwarzenberg und der Reichstag von Kremsier" (Ph.D. diss., University of Vienna, 1988), appendix F.

34.  Helfert, *Geschichte Oesterreichs*, 3: 302–6.

35.  Gottsmann, "Regierung Schwarzenberg," appendix F.

36.  Quoted in ibid. Lippert also reminds us that autonomy and strong central power reflected the ideas of Schwarzenberg's minister of interior, Stadion. Lippert, *Felix Fürst zu Schwarzenberg*, 182–83. For further details of Stadion's reform plans, see below.

37.  Victor Franz von Andrian-Werburg, *"Österreich wird meine Stimme erkennen lernen wie die Stimme Gottes in der Wüste": Tagebücher 1839–1858*, 3 vols. ed. Franz Adlgasser, Veröffentlichungen der Kommission für neuere Geschichte Österreichs 98 (Vienna: Böhlau, 2011), 2: 191, 193 (entries from December 6 and 8, 1848).

38.  The decree is reprinted in Friedrich Walter, ed., *Die Geschichte der Ministerien Kolowrat, Ficqelmont, Pillersdorf, Wessenberg-Doblhoff und Schwarzenberg*, vol. 2 of *Die Österreichische Zentralverwaltung. III. Abteilung. Von der Märzrevolution 1848 bis zur Dezemberverfassung 1867* [herafter *ÖZV*, III/2], Veröffentlichen der Kommission für neuere Geschichte Österreichs 50 (Vienna: Adolf Holzhausens Nachfolger, 1964), 32–34. Walter also discusses the same decree in *ÖZV*, III/1: 276–77.

39.  This decree likewise can be found in *ÖZV* III/2, Nr. 12, 34–36. Walter also discusses the same decree in *ÖZV* III/1: 276–77.

40.  *ÖZV* III/2: Nr. 12, 34–36.

41.  See R. J. W. Evans's excellent revisionist assessment of the innovativeness of post 1848 absolutism in Austria in R. J. W. Evans, "From Confederation to Compromise: The Austrian Experiment, 1849–1867," in *Austria, Hungary, and the Habsburgs: Essays on Central Europe, C. 1683–1867* (Oxford: Oxford University Press, 2006), esp. 268–70.

42.  Gottsmann, "Reichstag und Reichsrat," 599; The minutes of the two subcommittees

are available in published form in Anton Springer, ed., *Protokolle des Verfassungs-ausschusses im oesterreichischen Reichstage, 1848–1849* (Leipzig: S. Hirzel, 1885).

43. Gottsmann, "Regierung," Ph.D. diss., appendix F.

44. Gottsmann, *Der Reichstag*, 103; Kletečka, "Einleitung (ÖMR II/1)," xviii–xix.

45. Kletečka, ed., ÖMR II/1: 69, Nr. 11 (January 2, 1849).

46. *WZ*, Abend-Beilage, January 5, 1849, 19.

47. Gottsmann, "Reichstag und Reichsrat," 600.

48. See, for instance, the proposal by trade minister Karl Ludwig Ritter von Bruck to close the Reichstag and release a constitution by decree on January 6, 1849. Kletečka, ÖMR, 1: Nr. 12 (January 6, 1849), 77–78. See also Kletečka, "Einleitung (ÖMR II/1)," xix–xx.

49. Kletečka, "Einleitung," ÖMR II/1: xix–xxi.

50. MR January 20, 1849, in Kletečka, ÖMR I/1: Nr. 16, 101.

51. Stadion apparently prepared the first draft of the constitution in a matter of days— a fact that speaks to his knowledge and preformed ideas concerning a constitution and administrative reorganization of Austria. See Helfert, *Geschichte Oesterreichs*, 4/2: 465. For the Council of Minister's discussions of Stadion's March Constitution, see MR, February 11, 12, 20, 21, 23, and 24, 1849, and March 4, 1849, in Kletečka, ÖMR, I/1: 102–34. Redlich reprints much of the discussion in Josef Redlich, *Das österreichische Staats- und Reichsproblem: Geschichtliche Darstellung der inneren Politik der Habsburgischen Monarchie von 1848 bis zum Untergang des Reiches*, 2 vols. (Leipzig: P. Reinhold, 1920-26), 1/2 (Anhang), 84–100.

52. *Kaiserliches Manifest vom 4. März 1849, RGBl* 149/1849.

53. Most recently Gerald Stourzh called Kremsier the "most meaningful constitutional work in old-Austria's constitutional history." See Stourzh, "Länderautonomie und Gesamtstaat in Österreich 1848–1918," in *Der Umfang der österreichische Geschichte*, Studien zu Politik und Verwaltung 99 (Vienna: Böhlau, 2011), 46. An historian from a generation earlier, Robert A. Kann, praised the Kremsier Constitution—despite its weaknesses—because it "was based on complete and publicly unreserved agreement among all the nationalities and parties." See Robert A Kann, *The Multinational Empire: Nationalism and National Reform in the Habsburg Monarchy, 1848–1918*, 2 vols., expanded ed. (New York: Octagon Books, 1964), 2: 38. Here, Kann is following the lead of Josef Redlich, who in his two following history of Austria between 1848 and 1867 praised the cooperation of the representatives of Austria's nationalities in the Reichstag at Kremsier as the "only great reform plan which has been accomplished before the end of the Habsburg Monarchy." This is quoted in Kann, *Multinational Empire*, 2: 21 (Kann's translation). For the original, see Redlich, *Staats- und Reichsproblem*, 1/1: 92–93.

54. For a discussion of the importance of Kremsier for renewed debates concerning Austria's constitution and the national question, see Stefan Malfèr, "Kremsier in der österreichischen Verfassungsdiskussion um 1900," in *Kroměřížský Sněm 1848–1849 a tradice palamentarismu ve střední Evropě*, ed. Eva Danihelová (Kojetín: Rudolf Kalovský—KATOS, 1998), 65–76.

55. See the classic narratives of the period, Friedjung, *Österreich*; and Redlich, *Staats- und Reichsproblem*.

56. Malfèr, "Kremsier."

57. The Kremsier Constitution would not have applied to the provinces which were not represented in the assembly; i.e., the lands of the Hungarian crown as well as the Kingdom of Lombardo-Venetia, which both rebelled against Vienna in 1848. The need to release a constitution for the entire monarchy that included these reincorporated provinces was one of the main pretexts that Schwarzenberg's government gave for the rejection of the Kremsier Constitution. See MR (January 20, 1849) in Kletečka, ÖMR, I/1: Nr. 16, 100–101.

58. The decree closing the Kremsier parliament appeared as *RGBl* 149/1849. The Octroyed March Constitution appeared as *RGBl* 150/1849 on the same day. The municipalities law appeared as Provisorisches Gemeindegesetz vom 17. März 1849, RGBl Nr. 170/1849. See also Bernatzik, *Verfassungsgesetze*, chap. 5, for a discussion of the constitution, complete with an annotated text.

59. The literature on Stadion's constitution is nowhere near as large as that of Kremsier. For the debates surrounding the drafting of the constitution, see Hanns Schlitter, *Versäumte Gelegenheiten: Die oktroyierte Verfassung vom 4. März 1849; Ein Beitrag zu ihrer Geschichte*, Amalthea-Bücherei 9 (Zurich: Amalthea-Verlag, 1920), passim; *ÖZV*, III/1: 304–33; Brauneder, "Verfassungsentwicklung," 120–35.

60. Kenneth W. Rock, "Rejuvenation by Edict: Schwarzenberg, Stadion, and Bach in 1848–1849," *Consortium on Revolutionary Europe, 1750–1850; Selected Papers* (1995): 657.

61. *Doppelgeleisigkeit* has typically not been treated within the rich tradition of Austrian public law as a system in itself. Rather, it is normally written and understood in how various levels of government held their autonomy vis-à-vis the central state. For crownland autonomy, see the articles in Mischler and Ulbrich's encyclopedia of the state: Ludwig Spiegel, "Autonomie und Selbstverwaltung in der Gegenwart. I. Landesordnungen (Gelt. Recht)," in *Österreichisches Staatswörterbuch*, ed. Ernst Mischler and Josef Ulbrich, 2nd ed., 4 vols. (Vienna: Alfred Hölder, 1905-1909), 3: 395–430; Oskar Gluth, "Länder: Autonomie und Selbstverwaltung in der Gegenwart. III. Landesverwaltung," in *Österreichisches Staatswörterbuch*, ed. Mischler and Ulbrich, 3: 430–34. The workings of municipal autonomy and its function within the Habsburg monarchy have generated more interest of late. On developments in municipal autonomy after 1848, see Jeremy King, "The Municipal and the National in the Bohemian Lands, 1848–1914," *Austrian History Yearbook* 42 (2011): 92–95.

62. Jiří Klabouch, "Die Lokalverwaltung in Cisleithanien," in *Verwaltung und Rechtswesen*, vol. 2 of *Die Habsburgermonarchie, 1848–1918*, ed. Adam Wandruszka and Peter Urbanitsch [hereafter *HM* 2] (Vienna: VÖAW, 1975), 275.

63. See also Arnold Luschin von Ebengreuth, *Grundriss der österreichischen reichsgeschichte*, 2nd ed. (Bamberg: C. C. Buchner, 1918), 374–76. The crownland constitutions were proclaimed by imperial decree between late 1849 and September 1850. See Gerhard Putschögl, "Zur Geschichte der autonomen Landesverwaltung in den zisleithanischen Ländern der Habsburgermonarchie," *Mitteilungen des Oberösterreichischen Landesarchivs* 13 (1981): 304–8.

64. Redlich, *Staats- und Reichsproblem*, 1/1, 355.

65. Section 1. *RGBl* 170/1849.

66. Joseph Redlich, "The Municipality.—I. Austria: The Commune System," *Journal of the Society of Comparative Legislation* 8, no. 1 (1907): 18–19.

67. *RGBl* 150/1849.

68. Melville, "Der böhmische Adel," 141.

69. Kann, *Multinational Empire*, 2: 60.

70. For a general history of the district as an administrative unit see Franz Stunder, "Zwanzig Jahre Verwaltungsaufbau—Die Entstehung der Bezirkshauptmannschaften (1848–1858)," in *100 Jahre Bezirkshauptmannschaften in Österreich*, ed. Johannes Gründler (Vienna: Selbstverlag der österreichischen Bundesländer, 1970), esp. 18–19.

71. See Oskar Gluth, "Bezirke: Bezirksverbände," *Österreichisches Staatswörterbuch* 1 (1905): passim. See also Franz Rapprich, "Politische Behörden," *Österreichisches Staatswörterbuch* 3 (1907): 925–27.

72. Ralph Melville, *Adel und Revolution in Böhmen: Strukturwandel von Herrschaft und Gesellschaft in Österreich um die Mitte des 19. Jahrhunderts*, Veröffentlichungen des Instituts für Europäische Geschichte Mainz. Abteilung Universalgeschichte 95 (Mainz: Philipp von Zabern, 1998), 245.

73. Melville, *Adel und Revolution*, 248.

74. See the third part of Stadion's Provisional Municipalities Law, §§159–77, for the articles regarding the county (*Kreis*). *RGBl* 170/1849, 221–22. For historical discussions of the *Kreis* as an administrative unit, see the following articles, Bohuslav von Rieger, "Kreisverfassung in Böhmen," in *Österreichisches Staatswörterbuch*, 3 (1907): 250–71; Franz Stunder, "Die Kreisämter als Vorläufer der politischen Behörden I. Instanz (1748–1868)," in *100 Jahre Bezirkshauptmannschaften in Österreich*, ed. Gründler, 9–17.

75. Rieger, "Kreisverfassung," 265–66.

76. *RGBl* 150/1850, §84.

77. Redlich, *Staats- und Reichsproblem*, 1/1, 360.

78. Putschögl, "Geschichte der autonomen Landesverwaltung," 304–8.

79. Kann, *Multinational Empire*, 2: 60–62.

80. The literature for the diverse group of figures who sought federalist solutions to Austria's "state-problem" is immense. Kann, *Multinational Empire*, is the best place to start. Also, one must not forget the figure of Prince Alfred Windischgrätz, whose position as the leader of antirevolutionary forces gave his politics a heavy weight indeed. For his political position vis-à-vis the revolution and centralism, see Gottsmann, *Der Reichstag*, 22–28; Lippert, *Felix Fürst zu Schwarzenberg*, 161–65; Redlich, *Staats- und Reichsproblem*, 1/1, 328–29; *ÖZV*, III/1: 218–59, esp. 249–52.

81. Alexis de Tocqueville, *The Old Regime and the Revolution*, ed. Furet Furet and Francoise Mélonio, trans. Alan S. Kahan (Chicago: University of Chicago Press, 1998), 105; Waltraud Heindl makes a similar argument concerning Tocqueville's thesis and the Austrian Empire after the revolution of 1848. Waltraud Heindl, "Bürokratie und Verwaltung im österreichischen Neoabsolutismus," *Österreichische Osthefte* 22, no. 3 (1980): 231–32.

82. Helmut Reinalter, *Joseph II: Reformer auf dem Kaiserthron*, Beck´sche Reihe 2735 (Munich: C. H. Beck, 2011), 23–25.

83. Evans, "From Confederation to Compromise," 268–72.

## Chapter 3: The Reforging of the Habsburg State

1. Diary entry from May 22, 1850 (22. květina 1850) in Egbert Belcredi, *Z deníků moravského politika v éře Bachově: Egbert Belcredi, 1850–1859*, ed. Jaromír Boček, Vlastivedná Knihovna Moravská 24 (Brno: Musejní Spolek, 1976), 19.

2. Diary entry from March 13, 1850 (13. března 1850), Belcredi, *Z deníků Egberta Belcrediho*, 14.

3. Diary entry from March 18, 1851 (18. března 1851), Belcredi, *Z deníků Egberta Belcrediho*, 26.

4. Diary entry from April 23, 1851 (23. června 1851), Belcredi, *Z deníků Egberta Belcrediho*, 28.

5. See the entry from May 22, 1859 (22. května 1850), Belcredi, *Z deníků Egberta Belcrediho*, 19.

6. Georg Franz, *Liberalismus: Die deutschliberale Bewegung in der Habsburgischen Monarchie* (Munich: Georg D. W. Callwey, 1955), 87.

7. Hans Lentze, *Die Universitätsreform des Ministers Graf Leo Thun-Hohenstein* (Vienna: Hermann Böhlaus Nachfolger, 1962).

8. Gerő combines this older narrative with a newer one that recognizes some of neo-absolutism's progressive legal developments in Hungary: András Gerő, *Emperor Francis Joseph: King of the Hungarians*, ed. P. Pastor and I. Sanders, vol. 1 (Boulder, Colo.: Social Science Monographs, 2001), chap. 6. For a more balanced, but underdeveloped account from Hungarian history see, Éva Somogyi, "The Age of Neoabsolutism, 1849–1867," in *A History of Hungary*, ed. Peter F. Sugar, Péter Hanák, and Tibor Frank (Bloomington: University of Indiana Press, 1990), 235–41.

9. Diary entry of November 6, 1852 (6. listopadu 1852), in Belcredi, *Z deníků Egberta Belcrediho*, 43.

10. See Josef Mayr's introduction to the diaries of Police Minister Kempen: Johann Franz Kempen von Fichtenstamm, *Das Tagebuch des Polizeiministers Kempen von 1848 bis 1859*, ed. Josef Karl Mayr (Vienna: Österreichischer Bundesverlag für Unterricht, Wissenschaft und Kunst, 1931), esp. 33–42.

11. One of the best and most recent is Ian Reifowitz, "Francis Joseph's Fatal Mistake: The Consequences of Rejecting Kremsier/Kroměříž," *Nationalities Papers* 37, no. 2 (2009): 133–57.

12. Robert A. Kann, *A History of the Habsburg Empire, 1526–1918* (Berkeley: University of California Press, 1974), 260–70.

13. Franz, *Liberalismus*, 61–85; R. J. W. Evans, "From Confederation to Compromise: The Austrian Experiment, 1849–1867," in *Austria, Hungary, and the Habsburgs: Essays on Central Europe, c. 1683–1867* (Oxford: Oxford University Press, 2006), 277.

14. Czoernig exhaustively covers the building of canals and railways in Karl Czoernig, *Oesterreichs Neugestaltung, 1848–1858* (Stuttgart: Cotta, 1858), 307–446.

15. Ibid., 447–53 (telegraph), 471–72 (Post).

16. See the diary entry for November 21, 1850, in Karl Friedrich Kübeck von Kübau, *Tagebücher des Carl Friedrich freiherrn Kübeck von Kübau*, ed. Max Kübeck von Kübau, 2 vols. (Vienna: Gerold, 1909), 2: 53.

17. See the diary entry for November 19, 1850, in Karl Friedrich Kübeck von Kübau, *Aus dem Nachlass des Freiherrn Carl Friedrich Kübeck von Kübau: Tagebücher, Briefe, Aktenstücke (1841–1855)*, ed. Friedrich Walter, Veröffentlichungen der Kommission für Neuere Geschichte Österreichs 45 (Graz: Hermann Böhlaus Nachfolger, 1960), 54.

18. C. A. Macartney, *The Habsburg Empire, 1790–1918* (New York: Macmillan, 1969), 453; See also Walter's long account of Kübeck's proposals for governmental organization at the top and the relationship between the Reichsrat and the Cabinet in *ÖZV* III/1: 441–508.

19. The memoranda were published as three imperial laws in the main imperial law registry under the numbers 194, 196, and 197. For a good overview of these three legal memoranda, see Wilhelm Brauneder, "Die Verfassungsentwicklung in Österreich 1848 bis 1918," in Verfassung und Parlamentarismus, vol. 7, pt. 1 of *Die Habsburgermonarchie, 1848–1918*, ed. Helmut Rumpler and Peter Urbanitsch,(Vienna: Österreichische Akademie der Wissenschaften, 2000), 135–37.

20. Diary entry on August 30, 1851, in Victor Franz von Andrian-Werburg, *"Österreich wird meine Stimme erkennen lernen wie die Stimme Gottes in der Wüste": Tagebücher 1839–1858*, 3 vols., ed. Franz Adlgasser, Veröffentlichungen der Kommission für Neuere Geschichte Österreichs 98 (Vienna: Böhlau, 2011), 2: 488.

21. HHStA KA MR-Protokolle K 14, MRZ 2961/1851 (August 28, 1851) and MRZ 3083/1851 (September 7, 1851). See also *ÖZV*, III/1: 513–14.

22. Edmund Bernatzik, *Die österreichischen Verfassungsgesetze*, Studienaufgabe österreichische Gesetze 3 (Vienna: Manzsche k.u.k. Hof-, Verlags- und Universitätsbuchhandlung, 1911), 208–10.

23. *Grundsätze für organische Einrichtungen in den Kronländern des österreichischen Kaiserstaates. RGBl* 4/1852 with supplement. The edict is reprinted in both Bernatzik, *Verfassungsgesetze*, 210–16; and *ÖZV*, III/2: Nr. 26, 188–93.

24. See Walter's discussion of the *Grundsätze*, *ÖZV*, III/1: 545–47.

25. Alexander Bach (1813–93) did not suffer the same neglect as his colleague Stadion, although new research on the architect of the postrevolutionary Austrian state has not been the subject of new research for three decades. For a useful summary of the secondary literature on Bach and a narrative of his life and career, see Eva Macho, *Alexander Freiherr von Bach: Stationen einer umstrittenen Karriere*, Beiträge zur neueren Geschichte Österreichs 24 (Frankfurt am Main: Peter Lang, 2008). Also useful is Reinhold Lorenz, "Anton Ritter von Schmerling und Alexander Freiherr von Bach," in *Gestalter der Geschicke Österreichs*, ed. Hugo Hantsch, Studien der Wiener Katholischen Akademie 2 (Innsbruck: Tyrolia-Verlag, 1962), 407–30.

26. Wilhelm Brauneder, *Leseverein und Rechtskultur: Der Juridisch-politische Leseverein zu Wien 1840 bis 1990* (Vienna: F. Manz, 1992), 65.

27. Schwarzenberg to Windischgrätz, November 3, 1848. Quoted in Stefan Lippert, *Felix Fürst zu Schwarzenberg: Eine politische Biographie*, Historische Mitteilungen 21 (Stuttgart: F. Steiner, 1998), 173.

28. Macho, *Alexander Freiherr von Bach*, 89–90.

29. Kenneth W. Rock, "Rejuvenation by Edict: Schwarzenberg, Stadion, and Bach in 1848–1849," *Consortium on Revolutionary Europe, 1750–1850; Selected Papers* (1995): 649–64.

30. Plato, *The Republic of Plato*, trans. Allan David Bloom, 2nd ed. (New York: Basic Books, 1991), 53.

31. HHStA, MR. 2820/1849. Printed in *ÖZV* III/2, Nr. 19. Quote on page 106. See also Walter's discussion of the same document in *ÖZV* III/1: 371–73.

32. Victor Franz von Andrian-Werburg, *Denkschrift über die Verfassungs- und Verwaltungsfrage in Oesterreich* (Leipzig: H. Haessel, 1859), 5, 11, 16. Though this pamphlet was published after Andrian's death in 1859, it was written in mid-1851.

33. Victor Franz von Andrian-Werburg, *Centralisation und Decentralisation in Oesterreich* (Vienna: Jasper Hügel & Manz, 1850).

34. Ibid., 1.

35. Christoph Stölzl, *Die Ära Bach in Böhmen: Sozialgeschichtliche Studien zum Neoabsolutismus 1849–1859*, Veröffentlichungen des Collegium Carolinum 26 (Munich: R. Oldenbourg, 1971), 25–40, is useful for the social transformations that took place after the 1848 revolutions.

36. Andrian-Werburg, *Centralisation*, 2.

37. Confer Stefan-Ludwig Hoffmann, *Civil Society, 1750–1914* (Basingstoke: Palgrave Macmillan, 2006).

38. Confer Andrian's ideas with those of his contemporary, Alexis de Tocqueville, in France: Lucien Jaume, *Tocqueville: The Aristocratic Sources of Liberty*, trans. Arthur Goldhammer (Princeton, N.J.: Princeton University Press, 2013).

39. For Bach's ambivalent role in the abolition of Stadion's constitution and the writing of the Sylvester Patent, see Macho, *Alexander Freiherr von Bach*, 143–46; Heinrich Friedjung, *Österreich von 1848 bis 1860*, 2nd ed. (Stuttgart: J. G. Cotta, 1912), 439–86.

40. Kübeck was referring to Bach's work on the Constitutional Revision Commission, which he chaired and of which Bach also served. This commission wrote the text of the Sylvester Patent. See Kübeck's diary entries for December 1851 (quote from December 30, 1851), in Kübeck von Kübau, *Aus dem Nachlass des Freiherrn Carl Friedrich Kübeck von Kübau*, 85.

41. *ÖZV*, III/1: 549.

42. The following account of Bach's reform of Austria's domestic administration draws on the following works: Waltraud Heindl, "Bürokratie und Verwaltung im österreichischen Neoabsolutismus," *Österreichische Osthefte* 22, no. 3 (1980): 235–39; Ernst C. Hellbling, "Die Landesverwaltung in Cisleithanien," in HM, 2: 195–208; Gerhard Putschögl, "Zur Geschichte der autonomen Landesverwaltung in den zisleithanischen Ländern der Habsburgermonarchie," *Mitteilungen des Oberösterreichischen Landesarchivs* 13 (1981): 308–11.

43. Jiří Klabouch, *Die Gemeindeselbstverwaltung in Österreich, 1848–1918* (Munich: R. Oldenbourg, 1968), 45–51.

44. Macho, *Alexander Freiherr von Bach*, 156.

45. See Bach's proposals for establishing district councils, *Ideen zur Bildung von Bezirks-Versammlungen aus Mitgliedern der Landesbewohner* (dated April 2, 1852), in ÖSTA AVA, NL Bach, K 41. The purpose of these councils would not be to legislate, but to advise the government, via the imperially appointed district prefect on matters of education, health issues, conscription, and other local functions of the state.

46. *RGBl* 10/1853.

47. Heindl, "Bürokratie und Verwaltung," 236–37.

48. *Grundzüge für die Organisation der politischen Verwaltungsbehörden*, in *ÖZV*, III/2: 51–59. Franz Stunder, "Zwanzig Jahre Verwaltungsaufbau—Die Entstehung der Bezirks-hauptmannschaften (1848–1858)," in *100 Jahre Bezirkshauptmannschaften in Österreich*, ed. Johannes Gründler (Vienna: Selbstverlag der österreichischen Bundesländer, 1970), 20–21.

49. *Grundzüge für die Organisation der politischen Verwaltungs-Behörden*, released as *RGBl* 295/1849. Bach's proposals for this law discussed in the Austrian Cabinet of Ministers on June 21, 1849. See Thomas Kletečka, ed., ÖMR II/1, Nr. 102 (June 21, 1849), MRZ. 2058.

50. See the August 17, 1849, announcement detailing the administrative divisions of Upper Austria in OÖLA StP Sch. 718, Nr. 1/P.O.

51. Harry Slapnicka, *Oberösterreich unter Kaiser Franz Joseph (1861 bis 1918)*, Beiträge zur Zeitgeschichte Oberösterreichs 8 (Linz: OLV-Buchverlag, 1982), 11.

52. Letter from minister of interior Alexander Bach to Statthalter Dr. Alois Fischer (October 3, 1849), in OÖLA StP Sch. 781, Z. 257/P.O.

53. The administrative plan for Upper Austria in 1849 consisted of a *Statthalterei* with a governor, a *Statthaltereirath* (provincial councilor), three county councilors, one *Sektretär* (an entry-level position for a university-educated official), two clerks (*Konzipisten*), a porter, and a doorman.

54. See the official announcement on the personnel schema for Upper Austria and Salzburg in OÖLA StP Sch. 781, Nr. 2 P.O./1849.

55. For Fischer's list of suggested appointments for district prefects and county council-ors, see Nr. 388/P.O. 1849 in OÖLA StP Sch. 781.

56. Stunder, "Zwanzig Jahre," 20–21.

57. *Allerhöchstes Cabinetsschreiben Seiener Majestät des Kaisers vom 31. December 1851*, *RGBl* 4/1851. The district office had different names in different parts of the monarchy: *Bezirksamt* in the Bohemian and hereditary lands, *Prätur* in Dalmatia, *Stuhlrichter* in Hungarian, and *Distriktkommissariat* in Lombardy-Venetia.

58. Statistics on the numbers of district offices taken from Czoernig, *Oesterreichs Neu-gestaltung*, 41.

59. *Acht Jahre Amtsleben in Ungarn von einem k.k. Stuhlrichter in Disponibilität* (Leipzig: Gustav Dehme, 1861). See also Oszkár Sashegyi, *Ungarns politische Verwaltung in der Ära Bach, 1849–1860*, Zur Kunde Südosteuropäische Geschichte 7 (Graz: Institut für Geschichte der Universität Graz, 1979), 96–99.

60. *Acht Jahre Amtsleben*, 13–20.

61. Ibid., 21–23.

62. The title of *Landeschef* is a general one which encompasses all the imperially ap-pointed governors. The governors of larger crownlands held the title of *Statthalter*. The governors of other provinces held the title of *Landespräsident*. *Statthalter* and *Landes-präsident* were different names for the same position, the head of the central administration and representative of the monarch and his ministries in the crownland. Their offices were respectively known as *Statthalterei* and *Landesregierung*. See Ernst Mayrhofer and Anton Graf Pace, *Handbuch für den politischen Verwaltungsdienst in den im Reichsrathe vertretenen*

*Königreichen und Ländern, mit besonderer Berücksichtigung der diesen Ländern gemeinsamen Gesetze und Verordnungen,* 5th ed., 7 vols. (Vienna: F. Manz, 1895), 1: 366.

63. Decree by the ministers of interior, justice, and finance, January 19, 1853 (*RGBl* 10/1853). See also, Hellbling, "Landesverwaltung," 195–208.

64. Decree by the minister of the interior, April 30, 1854 (*RGBl* 12/1854). See also Hellbling, "Landesverwaltung," 208.

65. The counties were dismantled by 1868, but their specter would remain an important focus of reform proposals until the end of the monarchy. See for instance Bohuslav von Rieger, "Kreisverfassung in Böhmen," in *Österreichisches Staatswörterbuch,* ed. Ernst Mischler and Josef Ulbrich, 2nd ed., 4 vols. (Vienna: Alfred Hölder, 1905-1909), 3 (1907): 250–71.

66. Harm-Hinrich Brandt, *Der österreichische Neoabsolutismus: Staatsfinanzen und Politik, 1848–1860,* Schriftenreihe der Historischen Kommission bei der Bayerischen Akademie der Wissenschafte 15–16 (Göttingen: Vandenhoeck & Ruprecht, 1978), 2: 590–603, 1092–101. Of course, given the differentiation of administrative penetration and the development of administration before 1848 among the various crownlands, the actual increase in expenditures varied widely between the provinces. But everywhere they increased.

67. Brandt, *Neoabsolutismus,* 2: 596 n. 11.

68. See the table of districts in Czoernig, *Oesterreichs Neugestaltung,* 41. Curiously, unlike his other tables, Czoenig does not provide the totals at the bottom of the table, so I have added them together myself.

69. The Upper Austrian governor's office conducted a statistical inquiry of the district and county administrations in 1856. The resulting report—in handwritten draft—can be found in OÖLA StP Sch. 516, Z. 2811 Praes 1856 XV B 1.

70. Altwirth's case is located in OÖLA StP Sch. 526, Z. 1298/1598 Pr. 1852 XV C.

71. For the text of the exam and for an evaluation of Altwirth's answers, see Z. 1298/1598 Pr. 1852 XV C in OÖLA StP Sch. 526.

72. Macartney, *Habsburg Empire,* 460–67.

73. Münk's case: OÖLA StP Sch. 526, Z. ad 932/3698 Pr 1853 XV C.

74. See Salzburg's *Ausschreibung* in OÖLA StP Sch. 517, Z. 5210 Pr 1859 XV B.

75. While we have some statistical basis for calculating the numbers of interns in the pre-1848 period, the data for 1850s is largely absent. For the economics and social scale of the mid- and subaltern officials in the 1850s, see Heindl, "Bürokratie und Verwaltung," esp. 239–58; Karl Megner, *Beamte: Wirtschafts- und sozialgeschichtliche Aspekte des k.k. Beamtentums,* Studien zur Geschichte der Österreichisch-Ungarischen Monarchie 21 (Vienna: VÖAW, 1985), 89–97.

76. The rank and pay schemas were released in January 1853 in separate laws for Hungary and the rest of the crownlands, except Lombardy-Venetia. See *RGBl* 9 and 10/1853.

77. *Verordnung der Minister des Innern und der Justiz vom 17. März 1855 womit die Amtsinstruction für die rein politischen und für die gemischten Bezirks- und Stuhlrichterämter erlassen wird. RGBl* 52/1855. A copy of the office instruction is also available in OÖLA, St. Präs. Sch. 516.

78. The uniform regulations were released as *Erlaß des Ministeriums des Innern vom*

24. *August 1849, womit die mit Allerhöchster Entschließung vom 21. August 1849 genehmigte Uniformierungs-Vorschrift für k.k. Staatsbeamte kundgemacht wird. RGBl 377/1849.*

79. For more on hierarchy and differentiation within bureaucratic organizations as an important step in the developments of modern bureaucracy, see Max Weber, *Economy and Society: An Outline of Interpretive Sociology*, ed. Gerhard Roth and C. Wittich, 2 vols. (Berkeley: University of California Press, 1978), 2: 956–63.

80. *Amtsinstruction, RGBl* Nr. 52/1855, §13.

81. Ignaz Beidtel, *Geschichte der österreichischen Staatsverwaltung 1740–1848*, ed. Alfons Huber, 2 vols. (Innsbruck: Verlag der Wagner'schen Universitäts-Buchhandlung, 1896), 2: 43–44.

82. Helmut Kuzmics and Roland Axtmann, *Autorität, Staat und Nationalcharakter: Der Zivilisationsprozeß in Österreich und England, 1700–1900*, Schriften zur Zivilisations- und Prozesstheorie 2 (Opladen: Leske & Budrich, 2000), chaps. 6 and 8, esp. 281–88.

83. For an evaluation of these evaluations as a source, see Megner, *Beamte*, 42–44.

84. Moritz von Stubenrauch, *Handbuch der österreichischen Verwaltungs-Gesetzkunde nach dem gegenwärtigen Stande der Gesetzgebung* (Vienna: F. Manz, 1852).

85. F. J. Johanus, *Handbuch der Gesetze, Verordnungen und Vorschriften für k.k. österreichische Staatsbeamte* (Vienna: Braumüller, 1857).

86. Carl Mally, *Die neuen Behörden und ihr Wirkungskreis, oder der Wegweiser, wohin und an welche Ämter wir uns in unsern Angelegenheiten wenden sollen*, 1st ed. (Vienna: A. Pichler's Witwe, 1851); Carl Mally, *Die neuen Behörden und ihr Wirkugnskreis, oder der Wegweiser, wohin und an welche Ämter wir uns in unsern Angelegenheiten wenden sollen: Nach dem neuesten Organisations-Statute bearbeitet*, 2nd ed. (Vienna: A. Pichler's Witwe & Sohn, 1853).

87. Mally, *Die neuen Behörden* (1851 edition), 92–96.

88. See Harm-Hinrich Brandt's exhaustive work on the finances of neoabsolutism: Brandt, *Neoabsolutismus*, 551–603, and table 55 on 1092.

89. Carl Czoernig's compendium of "Austria's Renaissance," published in 1858, provides a wealth of information on how much the state in the 1850s invested heavily in its transportation, communication, and commercial infrastructure.

90. Jo Guldi, *Roads to Power: Britain Invents the Infrastructure State* (Cambridge, Mass.: Harvard University Press, 2012).

91. *Grundsätze für jeden diener des staats*, reprinted in *ÖZV*, II/4: 125–26.

92. See, for instance, the many new jobs for the local state administrators in the volume Czoernig, *Oesterreichs Neugestaltung*.

93. Eduard Bach to Alexander Bach, May 26, 1853. Quoted in Heindl, "Bürokratie und Verwaltung," 238.

94. *RGBl* 10/1853. See also, Hellbling, "Landesverwaltung," 195–208.

95. See for instance the arguments in Brandt, *Neoabsolutismus*, 1: 246–69.

96. Waltraud Heindl, "Probleme der Edition: Aktenkundliche Studien zur Regierungspraxis des Neoabsolutismus," in *ÖZV*, III/1: xlvi–xlviii. See also John W. Boyer, *Political Radicalism in Late Imperial Vienna: Origins of the Christian Social Movement, 1848–1897* (Chicago: University of Chicago Press, 1981), 17–19.

97. See Brandt's compilation of statistics Brandt, *Neoabsolutismus*, 2: 747 n. 97. After a

monetary convention in Vienna, an Austrian gulden (Fl.) in 1855 equaled about forty-seven US cents or one-fifth of a British pound. See *Vienna: A Faithful Sketch of the Austrian Metropolis* (Vienna: Gerold, 1869), 118–19.

98. Brandt, *Neoabsolutismus*, 315–26; 704–12; Waltraud Heindl, "Einleitung," in *Die Protokolle des Österreichischen Ministerrates, 1848–1867. III. Abteilung: Das Ministerium Buol-Schauenstein. Band 4, 23. Dezember 1854–12.April 1856* (Vienna: ÖBV, 1987), xvi–xxii.

99. Diary entry from December 26, 1859 (26. Prosince), in Belcredi, *Z deníků Egberta Belcrediho*, 95.

100. Stefan Malfèr, "Zwischen Machtpolitik und Sozialpolitik: Zur Versorgung der 'Bachschen Beamten' in Ungarn in den 1860er Jahren," *Österreichische Osthefte* 36, no. 2 (1994): 231–44.

## Chapter 4: State Building on a New Track

1. *WZ*, Nr. 167, July 16, 1859.

2. Niall Ferguson, *The House of Rothschild* (New York: Penguin Books, 2000), 2: 98.

3. C. A. Macartney, *The Habsburg Empire, 1790–1918* (New York: Macmillan, 1969), 500–502.

4. Harm-Hinrich Brandt, *Der österreichische Neoabsolutismus: Staatsfinanzen und Politik, 1848–1860*, 2 vols., Schriftenreihe der Historischen Kommission bei der Bayerischen Akademie der Wissenschaften 15–16 (Göttingen: Vandenhoeck & Ruprecht, 1978), 2: 871–73.

5. Pieter M. Judson, *Exclusive Revolutionaries: Liberal Politics, Social Experience, and National Identity in the Austrian Empire, 1848–1914*, Social History, Popular Culture, and Politics in Germany (Ann Arbor: University of Michigan Press, 1996), 75.

6. For further reading on the Austrian finances in late 1859 and Bruck's suggestion to give the Reichsrat financial oversight of the state budget, see Brandt, *Neoabsolutismus*, 2: 868–86.

7. *RGBl* Nr. 56. See Edmund Bernatzik, *Die österreichischen Verfassungsgesetze*, Studienaufgabe österreichische Gesetze 3 (Vienna: Manzsche k.u.k. Hof-, Verlags- und Universitätsbuchhandlung, 1911), 217–20; Andreas Gottsmann, "Der Reichstag 1848/49 und der Reichsrat 1861 bis 1865," in Verfassung und Parlamentarismus, vol. 7, pt. 1 of *Die Habsburgermonarchie, 1848–1918*, ed. Helmut Rumpler and Peter Urbanitsch,(Vienna: Österreichische Akademie der Wissenschaften, 2000), 609–11.

8. The reinforced Reichsrat in May 1860 thus consisted of twelve ordinary members, ten imperial appointees (two bishops, six high nobles, one high official and the Ban of Croatia), and the thirty-eight delegates from the crownlands. For further a breakdown of the reinforced Reichsrat according to nationality and social status see Gottsmann, "Reichstag und Reichsrat," 611–12.

9. Wilhelm Brauneder, "Die Verfassungsentwicklung in Österreich 1848 bis 1918," in *Die Habsburgermonarchie, 1848–1918*, ed. Rumpler and Urbanitsch, vol. 7/1, 147.

10. The coalition between bureaucrats and liberal politicians was not without its fissures, however, as Pieter Judson points out. Judson, *Exclusive Revolutionaries*, 70–74.

11. Eötvös's political writings appeared throughout the 1850s and were written or translated by Eötvös himself into German: József Eötvös, *Über die Gleichberechtigung der Nation-*

*alitäten in Österreich* (Pest: C. A. Hartleben, 1850); *Der Einfluss der herrschenden Ideen des 19. Jahrhunderts auf den Staat,* vol. 1 (Vienna: F. Manz, 1851) (vol. 2 was published in Leipzig in 1854); *Die Garantien der Macht und Einheit Oesterreichs* (Leipzig: F. A. Brockhaus, 1859).

12. For a summary of Eötvös's political thought, see especially Gerald Stourzh, "Die politischen Ideen Josef von Eötvös' und das österreichische Staatsproblem," in *Wege zur Grundrechtsdemokratie: Studien zur Begriffs- und Institutionengeschichte des liberalen Verfassungsstaates,* ed. Gerald Stourzh, Studien zu Politik und Verwaltung 29 (Vienna: Böhlau, 1989), 217–37; Robert A Kann, *The Multinational Empire: Nationalism and National Reform in the Habsburg Monarchy, 1848–1918,* 2 vols., expanded ed. (New York: Octagon Books, 1964), 2: 93–99. See also D. Mervyn Jones's preface to József Eötvös, *The Dominant Ideas of the Nineteenth Century and Their Impact on the State,* ed. D. Mervyn Jones (Boulder, Colo.: Social Science Monographs, 1996), 1: 13–56.

13. The calls for the recognition of Bohemian "state" or "constitutional" rights (*Böhmischer Staatsrecht*) made by the conservative nobility demanded what was more or less a substate consisting of the lands of the Bohemian crown—which encompassed the crownlands of Bohemia, Moravia, and Austrian Silesia. Eötvös specifically mentioned the desirability to return these three crownlands into one unit. See Eötvös, *Garantien der Macht,* 9. See also Jan Křen, *Die Konfliktgemeinschaft: Tschechen und Deutsche 1780–1918,* Veröffentlichungen des Collegium Carolinum 71 (Munich: R. Oldenbourg, 1996), 113–15.

14. See Macartney, *Habsburg Empire,* 505.

15. Gottsmann, "Reichstag und Reichsrat," 149.

16. My discussion of the two sides in the Reinforced Reichsrat is informed by a number of studies. Josef Redlich, *Das österreichische Staats- und Reichsproblem: Geschichtliche Darstellung der inneren Politik der Habsburgischen Monarchie von 1848 bis zum Untergang des Reiches,* 2 vols. (Leipzig: P. Reinhold, 1920), 1/1: 460–553; Brandt, *Neoabsolutismus,* 2: 923–65; Gottsmann, "Reichstag und Reichsrat," 613–22.

17. See the initial text of the minority report and its subsquent debate in Gerhard Silvestri, ed., *Verhandlungen des österreichischen Verstärkten Reichsrathes 1860: Nach den stenographischen Berichten* (Vienna: H. Geyer, 1972), 2 vols. 2: 41–44 (report), 44–292 (debate).

18. See the debate from the sixteenth session of the Reinforced Reichsrat, reprinted in ibid., 40.

19. Judson, *Exclusive Revolutionaries,* 76–77; Redlich, *Staats- und Reichsproblem,* 1/1: 607–8.

20. For the biographical details of Plener's early life and career, see Mechtild Wolf, *Ignaz von Plener: Vom Schicksal eines Ministers unter Kaiser Franz Joseph,* Wissenschaftliche Materialien und Beiträge zur Geschichte und Landeskunde der böhmischen Länder 20 (Munich: R. Lerche, 1975), 9–19.

21. *Ministerkonferenz* (hereafter MK), Nr. 215, October 2, 1860, in Stefan Malfèr, ed., *Die Protokolle des Österreichischen Ministerrates, 1848–1867: IV. Abteilung: Das Ministerium Rechberg, Die Protokolle des Österreichischen Ministerrates, 1848–1867,* Die Ministerratsprotokolle Österreichs und der Österreichisch-Ungarischen Monarchie 1848–1918. 1. Serie [hereafter ÖMR IV] (Vienna: VÖAW, 2003–9), 2: 432–33. See also Redlich's discussion of this session of the *Ministerkonferenz,* which debated the form and workings of

municipal and crownland autonomy in the monarchy; Redlich, *Staats- und Reichsprob-lem*, 1/1: 597–612.

22. Fritz Fellner, "Das 'Februarpatent' von 1861: Entstehung und Bedeutung," *Mit-teilungen des Instituts für österreichische Geschichtsforschung* 63 (1955): 549–50.

23. The October Diploma, *RGBl* 226/1860 was accompanied by an imperial proclama-tion, *RGBl* 225/ 1860, two memoranda to prime minister Count Rechberg, one memoran-dum to Count Gołuchowski, who became Austria's foreign minister (*Staatskanzler*), six memoranda to the new court-chancellor of Hungary, Baron Fay, and another memo to Ban of Croatia. In addition, the emperor released four crownland statutes with the October Diploma for Styria (*RGBl* Nr. 227), Carinthia (*RGBl* Nr. 232), Salzburg (*RGBl* Nr. 238), and Tyrol (*RGBl* Nr. 254). See Bernatzik, *Verfassungsgesetze*, 221–49.

24. For overviews of the October Diploma, see Brauneder, "Verfassungsentwicklung," 149–51; Josef Ulbrich, *Das österreichische Staatsrecht*, 4th ed., Öffentliche Recht der Gegen-wart 10 (Tübingen: Mohr Siebeck, 1909), 47–49; Friedrich Walter, *Österreichische Verfassungs-und Verwaltungsgeschichte von 1500–1955*, ed. Adam Wandruszka, Veröffentlichungen der Kommission für Neuere Geschichte Österreichs 59 (Vienna: Böhlau, 1972), 191–97; Redlich, *Staats- und Reichsproblem*, 1/1, 624–71.

25. *Ah. Handschreiben vom 20. Oktober 1860 an den zum Staatsminister ernannten Grafen v. Gołuchowski*, in Bernatzik, *Verfassungsgesetze*, Nr. 59, 229–30. See also Ludwig Spiegel, "Autonomie und Selbstverwaltung in der Gegenwart. I. Landesordnungen (Gelt. Recht)," in *Österreichisches Staatswörterbuch*, ed. Ernst Mischler and Josef Ulbrich, 2nd ed., 4 vols. (Vienna: Alfred Hölder, 1905–9), 3 (1907): 404.

26. Four of these crownland statutes were released simultaneously with the other proc-lamations of the October Diploma on October 20, 1860. These were for Styria (*RGBl* Nr. 227), Carinthia (*RGBl* Nr. 232), Salzburg (*RGBl* Nr. 238), and Tyrol (*RGBl* Nr. 254).

27. Helmut Rumpler, *Österreichische Geschichte, 1804–1914: Eine Chance für Mittel-europa; Bürgerliche Emanzipation und Staatsverfall in der Habsburgermonarchie*, Öster-reichische Geschichte (Vienna: Ueberreuter, 1997), 375.

28. *RGBl* Nr. 226/1860 (Oktober-Diplom), section 3.

29. For the general financial situation in late 1860 see Brandt, *Neoabsolutismus*, 2: 964–67; For information on the 1861 loan, see Macartney, *Habsburg Empire*, 510.

30. Brandt, *Neoabsolutismus*, 2: 968. For the Rothchilds banking politics in this period, see Ferguson, *Rothschild*, 2: 90–119.

31. Redlich, *Staats- und Reichsproblem*, 1/1: 673–88.

32. This was, in essence, the recognition of the historic bond between the crownlands of Bohemia, Moravia, and Silesia—a bond that deserved the status of a "Bohemian sub-state" in the political and administrative framework of the monarchy. Peter Urbanitsch, "Zwischen Zentralismus und Föderalismus: Das 'Problem der Konstruktiven Reichsge-staltung,'" in *Das Zeitalter Kaiser Franz Josephs: 1. Teil: Von der Revolution zur Gründerzeit, 1848–1880*, ed. Harry Kühnel, Elisabeth Vavra, and Gottfried Stangler, Katalog des NÖ Landesmuseums, 147, n.s. (Vienna: NÖ Landesmuseum, 1984), 236.

33. Béla K. Király, *Ferenc Deák*, ed. Hans L. Trefousse, Twaynes's World Leaders (Bos-ton: Twayne Publishers, 1975), 151–72.

34. Redlich, *Staats- und Reichsproblem*, 1/1: 608.

35. Ibid., 684–85. For Austria's increasingly bleak financial situation in 1860 and Plener's activities as finance minister, see Brandt, *Neoabsolutismus*, 2: 968–79.

36. Redlich, *Staats- und Reichsproblem*, 1/1: 672–3, 681–82; Judson, *Exclusive Revolutionaries*, 77–79; Macartney, *Habsburg Empire*, 508–12.

37. My biographical sketch of Schmerling is taken from the following sources: Judson, *Exclusive Revolutionaries*, 79–81; Reinhold Lorenz, "Anton Ritter von Schmerling und Alexander Freiherr von Bach," in *Gestalter der Geschicke Österreichs*, ed. Hugo Hantsch, Studien der Wiener Katholischen Akademie 2 (Innsbruck: Tyrolia-Verlag, 1962), 407–30; Paul Molisch, "Anton von Schmerling und der Liberalismus in Österreich," *Archiv für österreichische Geschichte* 116 (1944): 1–59; Lothar Höbelt, ed., *Österreichs Weg zur konstitutionellen Monarchie: Aus der Sicht des Staatsministers Anton von Schmerling*, Rechts- und sozialwissenschaftliche Reihe 9 (Frankfurt am Main: Peter Lang, 1994), 13–21; Joseph Redlich, "Lasser und Schmerling," *Österreichische Rundschau* 19, no. 2 (1909): 79–93; Heinrich Ritter von Srbik, *Deutsche Einheit: Idee und wirklichkeit vom Heiligen Reich bis Königgrätz* (Munich: F. Bruckmann, 1935), 4 vols. 3: 90–94.

38. Schmerling's legacy has typically been seen as a political one, one in which the generation of 1848 either held true to the principles of the revolutionary year or, like Alexander Bach, abandoned them. Much has been written on Schmerling's complex relationship to Austrian liberalism. In the nineteenth century, Walter Rogge, in *Oesterreich von Világos bis zur Gegenwart*, criticized the still-living Schmerling (Schmerling died at the age of eighty-seven in 1893) as hardly a liberal at all. This and later criticisms of Schmerling's betrayal of liberalism and his pseudo-constitutional regime are often based on the very real disappointment of contemporary liberals in Austria who thought of Schmerling as the state's savior in late 1860 only to find out that many of his policies were not too far to the left of Alexander Bach's at the beginning of the 1850s. See Molisch, "Anton von Schmerling," 3–5, for a survey of views on Schmerling.

39. Molisch, "Anton von Schmerling," 39–43.

40. Stefan Malfèr, "Einleitung," in *ÖMR* IV, 3: ix–xiv, for the lack of domestic support; Brandt, *Neoabsolutismus*, 2: 968–79, on state finances and securing new credit.

41. MK Protokoll Nr. 608 (October 21, 1860), in Malfèr, ÖMR IV, 3: 3. See also, Fellner, "Februarpatent," 549–50; Gerhard Putschögl, "Zur Geschichte der autonomen Landesverwaltung in den zisleithanischen Ländern der Habsburgermonarchie," *Mitteilungen des Oberösterreichischen Landesarchivs* 13 (1981): 312–17.

42. For this process, see above all Malfèr, "Einleitung (ÖMR IV/3)"; Fellner, "Februarpatent."

43. Article 3, *RGBl* 20/ 1861. For the text of the February Patent, along with commentary, see Bernatzik, *Verfassungsgesetze*, Nr. 71–73, 255–69.

44. For analysis of the February Patent, see, above all, Fellner, "Februarpatent"; Gottsmann, "Reichstag und Reichsrat," 622–24. See also Judson, *Exclusive Revolutionaries*; Macartney, *Habsburg Empire*, 511–16.

45. Hungary led the number of delegates with eighty-five; Salzburg had the least number of delegates with only three. These delegates were not elected by general vote

(except in Galicia) but by curiae: the great landed nobility, the cities and market towns, chambers of commerce, and the rural townships. For an overview of the composition of the Reichsrat according to the February Patent, see Gottsmann, "Reichstag und Reichsrat," 622–24.

46. The February Patent differentiated between the lands which comprised the Kingdom of Hungary and the rest of the monarchy. When matters were to be discussed that did not involve Hungary, a "narrower Reichsrat" was to convene. This distinction was an important recognition of Hungarian historic rights. Politically, however, this distinction mattered little, as the Hungarians refused to participate in a parliament for the *Gesamtmonarchie* and thus boycotted the Reichsrat.

47. The end of Francis Joseph's neoabsolutist government also brought to an end the idea that Francis Joseph served as his own prime minister. In 1861 the Ministerial Conference under prime minister Archduke Rainer became the "Ministerial Council" (Ministerrat). See Horst Brettner-Messler, "Probleme der Edition," in *ÖMR, V. Abteilung. Die Ministerien Erzherzog Rainer und Mensdorff*, vol. 1 (Vienna: Österreichischer Bundesverlag, 1977), xliv. For a critical assessment of the February Patent see Eugene N. Anderson and Pauline R. Anderson, *Political Institutions and Social Change in Continental Europe in the Nineteenth Century* (Berkeley: University of California Press, 1967), 72–74.

48. The *Reichsgemeindegesetz* appeared on March 5, 1862, as *RGBl* Nr. 18. The literature on this all-important law and the subsequent development of both autonomous townships and charter cities continues to grow. For general studies of the development of municipal self-government in Austria, see, above all, Carl Brockhausen, *Die österreichische Gemeindeordnung: Grundgedanken und Reformideen* (Vienna: F. Manz, 1905); Jiří Klabouch, *Die Gemeindeselbstverwaltung in Österreich, 1848–1918* (Munich: R. Oldenbourg, 1968); Joseph Redlich, "The Municipality.—I. Austria: The Commune System," *Journal of the Society of Comparative Legislation* 8, no. 1 (1907): 12–40; Joseph Redlich, *Das Wesen der österreichischen Kommunal-verfassung* (Leipzig: Duncker & Humblot, 1910).

49. Regulations regarding the size of the town councils differed across the monarchy, according to the laws of the individual crownlands. Typically, town councils had at least nine members and the number of members was determined by the size of the population of eligible voters. There were individual exceptions to this, however: townships in Lower Austria determined the number of councilmen according to total population of the township, not just the number of eligible voters and town councils in Dalmatia had to have at least twelve members. See Oskar Gluth, "Gemeinden: Staatsrechtliche Stellung und Organisation," in *Österreichisches Staatswörterbuch*, ed. Mischler and Ulbrich, 2 (1906): 320.

50. Ibid.

51. The executive boards could consist of up to one-third of the town council. In cities and market towns, the chairmen of the executive board held the title of "mayor" (*Bürgermeister*). In rural townships, he was simply the chairmen of the board (*Gemeindevorsteher*). See ibid., 324; Jiří Klabouch, "Die Lokalverwaltung in Cisleithanien," in *HM* 2, 284.

52. The town council was entrusted with the hiring and placement of officials; they could, however, turn over this responsibility to the chairman. Gluth, "Gemeinden," 2: 325.

53. Klabouch, "Lokalverwaltung," 280.

54. In Bohemia, Galicia, and Styria, the autonomous district councils acted as the immediate supervisor. For an extended analysis of the supervision of the supervision of higher autonomous administration over the *Gemeinde*, see Brockhausen, *Gemeindeordnung*, 191–224.

55. *RGBl* 18/1862, §4.

56. Ibid., §5.

57. Jeremy King, "The Municipal and the National in the Bohemian Lands, 1848–1914," *Austrian History Yearbook* 42 (2011): 97–98.

58. For a more exhaustive list of "assigned" duties, see Gluth, "Gemeindeverwaltung," 2: 329–31. See also Ernst Mayrhofer and Anton Graf Pace, *Handbuch für den politischen Verwaltungsdienst in den im Reichsrathe vertretenen Königreichen und Ländern, mit besonderer Berücksichtigung der diesen Ländern gemeinsamen Gesetze und Verordnungen*, 7 vols., 5th ed. (Vienna: F. Manz, 1895), 2: 511–70.

59. Bohemia, with eight, had the largest number of committee members. Galicia, Moravia, Lower Austria, Styria, the Tyrol, and Upper Austria each had six. The remaining eight crownlands (Salzburg, Vorarlberg, Carinthia, Carniola, the Littoral, Dalmatia, Silesia, and Bukovina) had four each. See Vasilij Melik, "Zusammensetzung und Wahlrecht der Cisleithanischen Landtage," in *Die Habsburgermonarchie, 1848–1918*, ed. Rumpler and Urbanitsch, vol. 7/2: 1349–52, for a detailed analysis of the construction of the executive committees. Members of the committee were elected to represent their curia in the diet and elected at large.

60. See Redlich, *Staats- und Reichsproblem*, 1/1: 689–701, and especially 697, for a detailed description of Schmerling's origins and the complex interaction between belonging to caste of the Josephine bureaucracy and the Lower Austrian estates.

61. Urbanitsch, "Zwischen Zentralismus und Föderalismus," 237–39.

62. See Wilhelm Brauneder, *Österreichische Verfassungsgeschichte*, 10th ed. (Vienna: F. Manz, 2005), 150–51. The three-class curial system grouped the taxpayers into thirds. The group constituting the first third of the tax base fell into the first curia. The second curia paid the "middle third" of the taxes; this group consisted of the middle-class burgher. Finally the mass of lower middle-class burgher paid the bottom third of the tax base and constituted the third curia. A good English-language explanation of the three-class voting system in Austria's cities and towns can also be found in Anderson and Anderson, *Political Institutions*, 117–21.

63. In some provinces, the law allowed the highest-paying taxpayers to take an automatic seat on the councils, if the amount of their taxes exceeded a certain percentage of the entire direct tax base of a given township. For instance, in Bohemia, a taxpayer who paid over one-sixth of a township's taxes could take an automatic seat. Similar laws existed in Silesia, Lower Austria, and Carinthia. This of course, provided for an even deeper reliance on the wealthiest citizens to hold the reins of local politics in Cisleithania. See Gluth, "Gemeinden," 321; Ulbrich, *Das österreichische Staatsrecht*, 170–71.

64. According to the Imperial Municipalities Law of 1862 (*RGBl* 18/1862), as well as Stadion's Provisional Municipalities Law (*RGBl* 170/1849), township elections constituted

public participation in the administration of assets and property—it was technically not a political act. This worked to effectively exclude the working class and poor from the rosters of voters and preserved the liberal idea of democracy in which only the wealthy citizens who had a financial stake in society should exercise the right to vote. See Klabouch, "Lokalverwaltung," 283–84.

65. Anderson and Anderson, *Political Institutions*, 54.

66. By 1906, for instance, Bohemia's diet contained only six *Virilisten* out of a total of 242 representatives, or around 2.5 percent; while Upper Austria had only one *Virilist* among fifty members of the diet. Galicia, conversely, had the largest number of automatic seat-holding *Virilists* (twelve) which encompassed 7 percent of the mandates in its *Landtag*. Compare the statistics in Spiegel, "Autonomie und Selbstverwaltung," 3: 414.

67. The sum depended on the particular laws of the crownland. For a general discussion of the electoral curiae, see Bernatzik, *Verfassungsgesetze*, 266–69; Melik, "Zusammensetzung," 1314–16; Spiegel, "Autonomie und Selbstverwaltung," 413–18.

68. Stefan Malfèr, "Zwischen Machtpolitik und Sozialpolitik: Zur Versorgung der 'Bachschen Beamten' in Ungarn in den 1860er Jahren," *Österreichische Osthefte* 36, no. 2 (1994): 231–44.

69. *Acht Jahre Amtsleben in Ungarn von einem k.k. Stuhlrichter in Disponibilität* (Leipzig: Gustav Dehme, 1861), 40.

70. Malfèr, "Zwischen Machtpolitik," 234–35.

71. See Z. 3140 1860/4816 Praes. 1861 XV B in OÖLA StP Sch. 518, for charts and information on *disponsibel* officials in Hungary.

72. Ibid.

73. Ibid.

74. For examples of these statistical surveys, which included information on the size of staff and the number of case files each district office processed in each preceding year see Z. 2811 Praes 1856 XV B1 in OÖLA StP Sch. 516.

75. *RGBl* Nr. 237/1859. "Erlaß des Ministers der Innern vom 28. December 1859, betreffend die Auflassung der vier Kreisbehörden im Erzherzogthum Oesterreich ob der Enns."

76. See the Ministry of the Interior's decree on the dissolution of the county in Upper Austria, Nr. 70/ M.I. (March 24, 1860) in Z. 7412–1859/1564 Praes. 1860 XV B, OÖLA StP Sch. 517.

77. See *RGBl* Nr. 142/1860 (June 5, 1860) for Moravia; *RGBl* 73/1862 (October 23, 1862) for Bohemia; and *RGBl* 92/1865 (September 23, 1865) for Galicia. Additionally, see the historical sketch of Austria's administrative changes in Mayrhofer and Pace, *Handbuch*, 1: 22–23.

78. Karl Urban, *Die Finanzen der territorialen Selbstverwaltungskörper in Oesterreich mit besonderer Berücksichtigung Böhmens* (Vienna: Alexander Dorn, 1904), 7–9.

79. R. Meyer, "Finanzwesen," *Österreichisches Staatswörterbuch* 2 (1906): 98–101.

80. The establishment of the district prefectures and the elimination of district offices is usually credited to the Burgher Ministry of 1868, but it was actually planned under Schmerling and especially his "administrative minister" Josef Lasser von Zollheim, in 1864. See Z. 2930/Praes. 1864 in OÖLA StP Sch. 522.

81. See the charts and reforms outlining the cost savings of implementing district pre-fectures: Z. 4931 (November 1864) and Z. 2930/5003 Praes 1864 XV B1 (November 1864–January 1865) both in OÖLA StP Sch. 522.

82. Letter from *Staatsminister* Friedrich Ferdinand von Beust to *Statthalter* Count Edu-ard von Taaffe (January 25, 1867), Z. 414 Praes 1867 [org Z. 6300 StM], in OÖLA StP Sch 522.

83. Karl Megner, *Beamte: Wirtschafts- und sozialgeschichtliche Aspekte des k.k. Beamten-tums*, Studien zur Geschichte der Österreichisch-Ungarischen Monarchie 21 (Vienna: VÖAW, 1985), 344, table 41; See also Waltraud Heindl's excellent discussion of the numbers of bureau-crats, and their inherent sketchiness, in Waltraud Heindl, *Josephinische Mandarine: Bürokratie und Beamte in Österreich, 1848–1914* (Vienna: Böhlau, 2013), 26–34.

84. For the problems plaguing the Reichsrat during Schmerling's administration, see Gottsmann, "Reichstag und Reichsrat," 655–59.

85. Gustav Kolmer, *Parlament und Verfassung in Österreich* (Vienna: C. Fromme, 1902), 8 vols. 1: 59–201, for the general problems affecting parliament from 1861–65; more specifi-cally see, Judson, *Exclusive Revolutionaries*, 102–3; and Macartney, *Habsburg Empire*, 522–23.

86. Judson, *Exclusive Revolutionaries*, 103.

87. See András Gerő, *Emperor Francis Joseph: King of the Hungarians*, ed. Peter Pastor and Ivan Sanders, vol. 1 (Boulder, Colo.: Social Science Monographs, 2001), 121–22; Rob-ert A. Kann, *A History of the Habsburg Empire, 1526–1918* (Berkeley: University of California Press, 1974), 331.

88. Jean-Paul Bled, *Franz Joseph*, trans. Teresa Bridgeman (Oxford: Blackwell, 1992), 147–49.

89. Kann, *Habsburg Empire*, 333.

90. Macartney, *Habsburg Empire*, 554.

91. For more on the *Ausgleich* and its political reception in Cisleithania, see Judson, *Exclusive Revolutionaries*, 109–13; Kann, *Multinational Empire*, 1: 133–38.

92. The Hungarians demanded as part of their negotiations that Cisleithania's constitu-tion be revised so that it, too, like Hungary, would be a constitutional monarchy. This was to ensure that adequate checks on the monarch's power be put in place to prevent another dissolution of parliament and a return to absolutism. See Brauneder, "Verfassungsentwick-lung," 170.

93. For the work of the constitutional committee and the minutes of its sessions, see Barbara Haider, *Die Protokolle des Verfassungsausschusses des Reichsrates vom Jahre 1867*, Fontes Rerum Austriacarum, Zweite Abteilung, Diplomataria et Acta 88 (Vienna: VÖAW, 1997).

94. *RGBl* Nr. 141/1867. Gesetz vom 21. Dezember 1867, wodurch das Grundgesetz über die Reichsvertretung vom 26. Februar abgeändert wird.

95. *RGBl* Nr. 142/1867. Staatsgrundgesetz vom 21. Dezember 1867, über die allgemeinen Rechte der Staatsbürger für die im Reichsrate vertretenen Königreiche und Länder.

96. *RGBl* Nr. 143/1867. Staatsgrundgesetz vom 21. Dezember 1867, über das Reichs-gericht.

97. *RGBl* Nr. 144/1867. Staatsgrundgesetz vom 21. Dezember 1867, über die richterliche Gewalt.

98. *RGBl* Nr. 145/1867. Staatsgrundgeesetz vom 21. Dezember 1867, über die Regierungs- und Vollzugsgewalt.

99. For a critical look at modernity from the perspective of German history—one that fuels my own skepticism of an "Austrian modernity," see Geoff Eley, "German History and the Contradictions of Modernity: The Bourgeoisie, the State, and the Mastery of Reform," in *Society, Culture, and the State in Germany, 1870–1930*, ed. Geoff Eley, Social History, Popular Culture, and Politics in Germany (Ann Arbor: University of Michigan Press, 1996), esp. 73–80.

100. For the particulars of this argument, see Brauneder, "Verfassungsentwicklung," 175–76.

101. Urbanitsch, "Zwischen Zentralismus und Föderalismus," 239–41, quote on 240. Jeremy King makes a similar point, though from the perspective of analyzing how "ethnicism" emerged as the dominant way of understanding the Bohemian history. Jeremy King, "The Nationalization of East Central Europe: Ethnicism, Ethnicity, and Beyond," in *Staging the Past: The Politics of Commemoration in Habsburg Central Europe, 1848 to the Present*, ed. Maria Bucur and Nancy M. Wingfield, Central European Studies (West Lafayette, Ind.: Purdue University Press, 2001), especially 134–35.

102. Gesetz vom 19. Mai 1868, *RGBl* Nr. 44, über die Einrichtung der politischen Verwaltungsbehörden. For the text of this law, see Bernatzik, *Verfassungsgesetze*, Nr. 143, 469–73.

103. *Gesetz über die Einrichtung der politischen Verwaltungsbehörden*, §10. The "existing districts" to which the law refers were first created by Alexander Bach through a special decree on January 19, 1853. See Bach's *Verordnung der Minister des Innern, der Justiz und der Finanzen vom 19. Jänner 1853*, section A: Allerhöchste Bestimmungen über die Einrichtung und Amtswirksamkeit der Bezirksämter, *RGBl* 10/1853, 68–81.

104. These numbers were arrived at by comparing the statistics in Friedrich Schmitt, *Statistik des österreichischen Kaiserstaates*, 2nd ed. (Vienna: Tendler, 1860), 27; and Friedrich Schmitt, *Statistik des österreichisch-ungarischen Kaiserstaates*, ed. Gustav A. Schimmer, 4th ed. (Vienna: Gerold, 1872), 211–12. In addition to the 886 district offices in Cisleithania in 1860, there were a further 83 in the Venetian province (lost to Italy in 1866), and 584 in what would become the Hungarian half of the monarchy.

105. *SPAR*, 4/80 (March 16, 1868), 2224.

106. Ibid.

## Chapter 5: The Years of Procedure

1. The position of *Ministerialrat* was situated just below the *Sektionschef*—or department head. It was classified in the fifth rank in the table of ranks. For the pay scales and ranks of the imperial civil service, see the *Gesetz vom 15. April 1873, betreffend die Regelung der Bezüge der active Staatsbeamten*, *RGBl* 47/1873. See also Karl Megner, *Beamte: Wirtschafts- und sozialgeschichtliche Aspekte des k.k. Beamtentums*, Studien zur Geschichte der Österreichisch-Ungarischen Monarchie 21 (Vienna: VÖAW, 1985), 39–41.

2. Ministerial Erlass Z. 2968/ MI-1881 (March 7, 1881). See the correspondence between Maczak von Ottenburg and the Ministry of the Interior, in Z. 1539, ÖSTA AVA Inneres MdI Präsidium A28.

3. The ministry's response (dated March 29, 1881) is partially burnt, but likewise in Z. 1539, ÖSTA AVA Inneres MdI Präsidium A28.

4. Jacques Derrida, *Archive Fever: A Freudian Impression* (Chicago: University of Chicago Press, 1996), 2–3; Carolyn Steedman, *Dust: The Archive and Cultural History*, Encounters (New Brunswick, N.J.: Rutgers University Press, 2002), 1–3.

5. Compare my treatment with Ben Kafka, *The Demon of Writing: Powers and Failures of Paperwork* (New York: Zone Books, 2012), 30–44. Kafka sees the creation of paperwork as a product of state accountability to its citizens.

6. See the essays in Peter Becker and William Clark, *Little Tools of Knowledge: Historical Essays on Academic and Bureaucratic Practices* (Ann Arbor: University of Michigan Press, 2001).

7. Politically this period covers the years of liberal parliamentary dominance in the 1870s and the rise of the conservative "Iron Ring" of Count Eduard Taaffe's government, which took the reins in 1879 and persisted until 1893. For political histories of the 1870s see above all, Pieter M. Judson, *Exclusive Revolutionaries: Liberal Politics, Social Experience, and National Identity in the Austrian Empire, 1848–1914*, Social History, Popular Culture, and Politics in Germany (Ann Arbor: University of Michigan Press, 1996), chaps. 5–6; Diethild Harrington-Müller, *Der Fortschrittsklub im Abgeordnetenhaus des österreichischen Reichsrats, 1873–1910*, Studien zur Geschichte der Österreichisch-Ungarischen Monarchie 11 (Vienna: Böhlau, 1972). The 1880s will be covered in the second half of this chapter.

8. Peter Urbanitsch, "Zwischen Zentralismus und Föderalismus: Das 'Problem der Konstruktiven Reichsgestaltung,'" in *Das Zeitalter Kaiser Franz Josephs: 1. Teil: Von der Revolution zur Gründerzeit, 1848–1880*, ed. Harry Kühnel, Elisabeth Vavra, and Gottfried Stangler, Katalog des NÖ Landesmuseums, 147, n.s. (Vienna: NÖ Landesmuseum, 1984), 241.

9. For Steed's biography see Peter Schuster, *Henry Wickham Steed und die Habsburgermonarchie*, Veröffentlichungen der Kommission für neuere Geschichte Österreichs 53 (Vienna: Hermann Böhlaus Nachfolger, 1970).

10. Henry Wickham Steed, *The Hapsburg Monarchy* (New York: Scribner's, 1913), 74.

11. Ibid., xxviii–xxx.

12. See, for instance, Emmette Shelburn Redford, *Democracy in the Administrative State* (New York: Oxford University Press, 1969).

13. Kenneth J. Meier and Laurence J. O'Toole, *Bureaucracy in a Democratic State: A Governance Perspective* (Baltimore: Johns Hopkins University Press, 2006), 1. Ezra N. Suleiman, *Dismantling Democratic States* (Princeton, N.J.: Princeton University Press, 2003); Kenneth J. Meier, "Bureaucracy and Democracy: The Case for More Bureaucracy and Less Democracy," *Public Administration Review* 57, no. 3 (1997): 193–99.

14. Meier and O'Toole, *Bureaucracy in a Democratic State*; Meier, "Bureaucracy and Democracy."

15. The phrase is the pithy summary by Nancy and Harold Gordon of the much lengthier analysis by Redlich in Josef Redlich, *Das österreichische Staats- und Reichsproblem: Geschichtliche Darstellung der inneren Politik der Habsburgischen Monarchie von 1848 bis zum Untergang des Reiches*, 2 vols. (Leipzig: P. Reinhold, 1920-26); Harold J. Gordon and Nancy M. Gordon, *The Austrian Empire, Abortive Federation?* Problems in European Civilization (Lexington, Mass.: D.C. Heath, 1974), 76.

318  Notes to Chapter 5

16. Richard L. Rudolph, *Banking and Industrialization in Austria-Hungary: The Role of Banks in the Industrialization of the Czech Crownlands, 1873–1914* (Cambridge: Cambridge University Press, 1976); David F. Good, *The Economic Rise of the Habsburg Empire, 1750–1914* (Berkeley: University of California Press, 1984).

17. For a highly enlightening and critical survey of European state building, see James J. Sheehan, "Presidential Address: The Problem of Sovereignty in European History," *American Historical Review* 111, no. 1 (2005): 1–15.

18. Waltraud Heindl, "Bureaucracy, Officials, and the State in the Austrian Monarchy: Stages of Change since the Eighteenth Century," *Austrian History Yearbook* 37 (2006): 47–48.

19. Gustav Kolmer, *Parlament und Verfassung in Österreich*, 8 vols. (Vienna: C. Fromme, 1902), 1: 232. See also the reply of the lower house to the emperor, "The reform of the entire legislative process [Gesetzgebung] and the administration in the spirit of freedom and progress is an urgent necessity." *SPAR*, 4/8 (June 5, 1867), 178.

20. On the Burgher Ministry, see above all the short and informative article by Lothar Höbelt, "Das Bürgerministerium," *Études Danubiennes* 14, no. 2 (1998): 1–11. Thereafter, all the ministries which governed the Cisleithanian *Reichshälfte* between 1870 and 1918 were *Beamtenministerien*–led by bureaucrats selected by Francis Joseph.

21. Heindl, "Bureaucracy, Officials, and the State," 47.

22. For the accomplishments of the Reichsrat in the drafting of the December Constitution, see above all, Gerald Stourzh, "Die österreichische Dezemberverfassung von 1867," in *Wege zur Grundrechtsdemokratie: Studien zur Begriffs- und Institutionengeschichte des liberalen Verfassungsstaates*, ed. Gerald Stourzh, Studien zu Politik und Verwaltung 29 (Vienna: Böhlau, 1989), 256–58.

23. *SPAR*, 4/80 (March 16, 1868), 2222.

24. *SPAR*, 4/36 (October 14, 1867), 886. Reprinted in Kolmer, *Parlament*, 1: 283.

25. Brauneder describes the "tedious hammering out" (*weitschweifige Ausführungen*), with "aspects of federalism," that accompanied many of the debates on the individual laws. Wilhelm Brauneder, "Die Verfassungsentwicklung in Österreich 1848 bis 1918," in *Verfassung und Parlamentarismus*, vol. 7, pt. 1 of *Die Habsburgermonarchie, 1848–1918* [hereafter HM 7/1], ed. Helmut Rumpler and Peter Urbanitsch (Vienna: Österreichische Akademie der Wissenschaften, 2000), 182.

26. For instance, the laws of the December Constitution failed to explicate the relationship between imperial and crownland legislation. It was impossible for parliamentarians favoring centralization to put in place an explicit sentence that stated that "imperial law trumps crownland law." Stourzh writes, "So it came to leaving open these matters and doing without clear regulation not on account of forgetfulness, but out of political reasons." Stourzh, "Dezemberverfassung," 248.

27. Count Karl Hohenwart was a high-ranking civil servant. He made his career in the provinces as an official in the Ministry of the Interior, eventually rising to the Lord-Lieutenancy of several provinces. For biographical information on Hohenwart, see Emilie Schenk-Sudhof, "Karl Graf Hohenwart" (Ph.D. diss., University of Vienna, 1950); "Hohenwart, Karl Sigmund Gf. von," text, *Österreichisches Biographisches Lexikon und biographische Dokumenta-*

*tion*, 2003, www.biographien.ac.at/oebl/oebl_H/Hohenwart_Karl-Sigmund_1824_1899.xml (accessed March 11, 2015); Helmut Rumpler, *Österreichische Geschichte, 1804–1914: Eine Chance für Mitteleuropa; Bürgerliche Emanzipation und Staatsverfall in der Habsburgermonarchie*, Österreichische Geschichte (Vienna: Ueberreuter, 1997), 433.

28. Elisabeth-Charlotte Büchsel, *Die Fundamentalartikel des Ministeriums Hohenwart-Schäffle von 1871: Ein Beitrag zum Problem des Trialismus im Habsburgerreich*, Breslauer historische Forschungen 17 (Aalen: Scientia Verlag, 1982); Otto Urban, *Die tschechische Gesellschaft, 1848 bis 1918*, 2 vols. trans. Henning Schlegel (Vienna: Böhlau, 1994), 1: 361–75; Alois Czedik, *Zur Geschichte der k.k. österreichischen Ministerien, 1861–1916*, 4 vols. (Teschen: Karl Prochaska, 1917), 1: 200–219.

29. The first curia contained the great landowning class who held estates based on noble right. This was a fairly constant and unchanging curia, which held a good deal of power and eight-five parliamentary mandates. The third curia was relatively small, with twenty-one mandates, and represented the membership of the chambers of commerce and industry. The second and fourth curiae, conversely, would be the subject of repeated expansion in the years following the first suffrage reform of 1873. These contained the votes of the male inhabitants of the cities (second curia) and the rural townships (fourth curia), who paid direct taxes. In 1873, adult male citizens in Austria over the age of twenty-four were given the right to vote in the fourth or second curia if they paid more than ten florins in direct tax. These two curiae were by far the largest block: the second curia of city voters controlled 118 mandates and the fourth curia of rural voters controlled 129 mandates. The total number of mandates elected to the Reichsrat in 1873 was 353. For the electoral reform of 1873, see Stanisław Starzyński, "Reichsratswahlen," in *Österreichisches Staatswörterbuch*, ed. Ernst Mischler and Josef Ulbrich, 4 vols., 2nd ed. (Vienna: Alfred Hölder, 1905–9), 4: 874–76.

30. Oswald Knauer, *Das österreichische Parlament von 1848–1966*, Österreich-Reihe 358–61 (Vienna: Bergland Verlag, 1969); Leopold Kammerhofer, ed., *Studien zum Deutschliberalismus in Zisleithanien, 1873–1879: Herrschaftsfundierung und Organisationsformen des politischen Liberalismus*, Studien zur Geschichte der Österreichisch-Ungarischen Monarchie 25 (Vienna: VÖAW, 1992).

31. Göllerich was a prominent person in Wels between 1860 and his death in 1883, but he remains an obscure figure in the larger world of imperial Austria. For biographical information on Göllerich, see Harry Slapnicka, *Oberösterreich, die politische Führungsschicht: 1861 bis 1918*, Beiträge zur Zeitgeschichte Oberösterreichs 9 (Linz: OLV-Buchverlag, 1983), 91–92; Herbert Lukas, "Wels in der liberalen Ära: Die Stadt unter den Bürgermeistern Dr. Franz Groß und Leopold Bauer (1861–1886)" (Ph.D. diss., University of Salzburg, 1984), 50–59.

32. A short political biography of Göllerich is available in Slapnicka, *Oberösterreich, die politische Führungsschicht*, 91–92. For Göllerich's political activity in the Upper Austrian *liberal-politische Verein*, see Kurt Wimmer, *Liberalismus in Oberösterreich: Am Beispiel des liberal-politischen Vereins für Oberösterreich in Linz (1869–1909)*, ed. Oberösterreichischen Landesarchiv, vol. 6, Beiträge zur Zeitgeschichte Oberösterreichs 6 (Linz: Oberösterreichischer Landesverlag, 1979), 30–41, 95–152.

33. Lukas, "Wels in der liberalen Ära," 77; Gilbert Trathnigg, "Beiträge zur Verwaltungs- und Wirtschaftsgeschichte von Wels im 19. und 20. Jahrhundert," in *Wels von der Urzeit bis zur Gegenwart*, Jahrbuch des Musealvereines Wels 7 (1960): 117–18.

34. Lukas, "Wels in der liberalen Ära," 90–92.

35. See my analysis of Schmerling's Imperial Municipalities Law in the previous chapter. See also Oskar Gluth, "Gemeinden: Die Gemeindeverwaltung," in *Österreichisches Staatswörterbuch*, ed. Mischler and Ulbrich, 2 (1906): 329–31.

36. John A. Fairlie, *Essays in Municipal Administration* (New York: Macmillan, 1908), 320–29.

37. Peter Csendes and Ferdinand Opll, *Wien: Geschichte einer Stadt*, 3 vols. (Vienna: Böhlau, 2001); Franz Baltzarek, Alfred Hoffmann, and Hannes Stekl, *Wirtschaft und Gesellschaft der Wiener Stadterweiterung*, Die Wiener Ringstrasse. Bild einer Epoche 5 (Wiesbaden: F. Steiner, 1975).

38. By the end of the century, Vienna's rapid growth, its well-developed municipal public works and expansion, had become well known and much admired outside Austria, such that the American scholar of city government, John A. Fairlie could write: "Municipal autonomy has been more fully established [in Austria] than in any other country of continental Europe; an indeed—except for the police . . . —more fully than in England or the United States." Fairlie, *Essays*, 316.

39. For economic development in Wels after 1848, see Erich Eigner, "Die städtebauliche Entwicklung von Wels," in *Wels von der Urzeit bis zur Gegenwart*, Jahrbuch des Musealvereines Wels 7 (1960): 109–13; Trathnigg, "Verwaltungs- und Wirtschaftsgeschichte," 115–31; Lukas, "Wels in der liberalen Ära."

40. *SPAR*, 8/71 (November 7, 1874), 220 der Beilagen. The term *political administration* in Austrian governmental language meant the imperial bureaucracy.

41. *SPAR*, 8/75 (November 17, 1874), 2710.

42. Ibid.

43. *SPAR*, 8. Session, 220 der Beilagen.

44. The "German" parties generally supported the government, led by Adolf Wilhelm Prince von Auersperg and his interior minister, Josef Lasser von Zollheim. They consisted of the Progressive Club (fifty-seven members), the Leftists (eighty-eight members), Constitutional Magnates (fifty-four members), and the Ruthenian Party (fourteen). To these could be added the Vienna Democrats (five) and the Polish Club (forty-nine). See Helmut Rumpler, "Parlament und Regierung Cisleithaniens 1867 bis 1914,, in *Die Habsburgermonarchie, 1848–1918*, ed. Rumpler and Urbanitsch, vol. 7/1: 720–22; Kolmer, *Parlament*, 2: 280–83.

45. Göllerich's motion was supported by thirty-four of the consutionally loyal Magnate Party; three liberals (Leftists) including Göllerich and his colleague from Wels, Dr. Gross; five Ruthenians; one German Progressive; one Viennese Democrat; and two Poles. Confer Göllerich's motion, *SPAR*, 8/71 (November 7, 1874) and supplement Nr. 220, with Knauer, *Das österreichische Parlament von 1848–1966*.

46. *NFP*, Nr. 4388, November 11, 1876 (Abendblatt), 2.

47. Parliament voted on November 24, 1874, to establish the committee, *SPAR*, 8/78. For a list of committee members, consult *SPAR*, 8. Session, Anhang. Ausschüsse, 517.

48. The committee's minutes are located in the Parliamentary Archive of the Austrian Parliament, hereafter ÖPA, II Carton 21 z. 21–2–0–93 (1876). I am grateful to Dr. Christoph Konrath, Mr. Johann Achter, and Ms. Silvia Stöckel for their assistance in locating this report. The report, entitled *Bericht des Ausschusses zur Vorbereitung des Antrages des Abgeordneten Göllerich und Genossen, betreffend die Reform der politischen Verwaltung*, can be found as *Beilage* Nr. 331, *SPAR*, 8. Session.

49. *Gesetz vom 19. Mai 1868, RGBl Nr. 44, über die Einrichtung der politischen Verwaltungsbehörden.* A copy of this law is available in Edmund Bernatzik, *Die österreichischen Verfassungsgesetze*, Studienaufgabe österreichische Gesetze 3 (Vienna: Manzsche k.u.k. Hof-, Verlags- und Universitätsbuchhandlung, 1911), Nr. 143, 469–73.

50. Confer *Bericht . . .* , supplement Nr. 331, *SPAR*, 8. Session.

51. *NFP*, November 24, 1876, evening edition, Nr. 4401, 1 and 3.

52. Bernatzik, *Verfassungsgesetze*, Nr. 133, 390–412; Gertrud Sakrawa, "Ferdinand Kronawetter: Ein Wiener Demokrat" (Ph.D. diss., University of Vienna, 1947), 12–14.

53. *SPAR*, 8/205, 7012.

54. Ibid.

55. Vienna, had chartered city status, meaning that its municipal officials had much more responsibility for local government and policy making than their municipal counterparts in cities like Wels. Chartered cities subsumed the administration of the districts; they appointed and directed the local branch of state government instead of the governors. Joseph Redlich, "The Municipality.—I. Austria: The Commune System," *Journal of the Society of Comparative Legislation* 8, no. 1 (1907): 12–40; Karl Brockhausen, "Statuargemeinden," in *Österreichisches Staatswörterbuch* 4 (1909): 450–61; Karl Brockhausen and Richard Weiskirchner, *Oesterreichische Städteordnungen: Die Gemeindeordnungen und Gemeindewahlordnungen der mit eigenen Statuten versehenen Städte der im Reichsrathe vertretenen Königreiche und Länder . . .* , Taschenausgabe der österreichischen gesetze 9/2 (Vienna: F. Manz, 1895).

56. *SPAR*, 8/204 (November 11, 1876), 6982.

57. Ibid., 6990.

58. *SPAR*, 8/205 (November 14, 1876), 7020.

59. Ibid., 7019.

60. For the text of this law with commentary, see Bernatzik, *Verfassungsgesetze*, 390–422.

61. In 1868, Polish politicians had won numerous concessions from the government that codified Galicia's special status among the crownlands. These included concessions for the use of Polish as the language of instruction in all public schools and, just as important, Polish domination of the state bureaucracy in Galicia. By July 1869, the Poles were able to press the government into the declaration that Polish would be the "inner language" of the state service in Galicia. This effectively Polonized the state bureaucracy there. Macartney reports that between four thousand and five thousand German-speaking bureaucrats were dismissed in favor of Polish ones. See C. A. Macartney, *The Habsburg Empire, 1790–1918* (New York: Macmillan, 1969), 576–77; Jean-Paul Himka, *Galicia and Bukovina: A Research Handbook About Western Ukraine, Late 19th and 20th Centuries* (Alberta: Alberta Culture and Multiculturalism Historical Resources Division, 1990), 41–52.

62. *SPAR*, 8/206 (November 17, 1876), 7042.

63. Ibid., 7043.

64. *SPAR*, 8/207 (November 21, 1876), 7085–86.

65. For an analysis of Polish delegates in the Reichsrat and their defense of Galician autonomy, see Harald Binder, *Galizien in Wien: Parteien, Wahlen, Fraktionen und Abgeordnete im Übergang zur Massenpolitik*, Studien zur Geschichte der Österreichisch-Ungarischen Monarchie 29 (Vienna: VÖAW, 2005), 320–36.

66. *NFP*, Nr. 4402 (November 25, 1876) moring edition, 1.

67. For a political history of this period in English see, above all, William Alexander Jenks, *Austria Under the Iron Ring, 1879–1893* (Charlottesville: University Press of Virginia, 1965).

68. Taaffe had been a childhood playmate of Francis Joseph when they both were very young, and, like Francis Joseph, had devoted his life in the service of the monarchy. Taaffe had risen through the ranks of the civil service and had been serving as the governor of Tyrol when he had been recalled by the emperor to Vienna, to take a ministerial position once again. Previously, Taaffe had served as minister of the interior under Count Friedrich von Beust (February–December 1867), Karl Auersperg (1867–70), and Alfred Potocki (1870–71). For a good overview of Taaffe's career, see Bruno Schimetschek, *Der österreichische Beamte: Geschichte und Tradition* (Munich: R. Oldenbourg, 1984), 202–4.

69. The papers of the Taaffe family have recently been donated to the Haus-, Hof- und Staatsarchiv in Vienna, Austria. For papers relating to Taaffe's career in the imperial Austrian administration, see ÖStA/HHStA Sonderbestände, Familienarchiv Taaffe, K 16, 18–23.

70. The central records of the 1880s were heavily destroyed and damaged by the 1927 riot in Vienna. Especially hard hit by this destruction are documents dating from the 1870s through the 1890s, Taaffe's minister-presidency and the period of his tenure as minister of the interior. Many of the documents that survive are charred, fragile, water-damaged, and only partially legible. Moreover, as we will see, officials had a penchant for burning or pulping documents they no longer needed, including mundane information like tax records, reports from local district chiefs, reports about veterinary medicine—all the day-to-day workings that showed how the state-building process worked.

71. See the letter from the governor (*Statthalter*) in Bohemia to the Ministry of the Interior (February 4, 1881), Pr. No. 720/MI in ÖSTA AVA Inneres MdI Präsidium A 41.

72. See the correspondence between the Ministry of Justice, Ministry of Finance, and Ministry of the Interior with the Lord-Lieutenancy of the Littoral in Trieste, Pr. Nr. 675/ MI-1885, ÖSTA AVA Inneres MdI Präsidium A 52.

73. Pr. Nr. 1178 /MdI (February–March 1881) in ÖSTA AVA Inneres MdI Präsidium A 41.

74. The ministry denied the request after consulting the Ministry of Finance. The building was too expensive. See the letters between the governor in Prague to the minister of the interior (March 14 and April 17, 1887), Pr. Nr. 1163, ÖSTA AVA Inneres MdI Präsidium A 42.

75. Correspondence between the governor in Prague and the Ministry of the Interior (January–February 1888) in Pr. Nr. 620/MI, ÖSTA AVA Inneres MdI Präsidium A 42. See also the report, with five attachments, by the archivist of the Bohemian Lord-Lieutenancy in Prague, Karl Köpl, dated November 27, 1887, contained in the same file.

76. See the report on library use, Pr. Nr. 2240/MI in ÖSTA AVA Inneres MdI Präsidium, A 29.

77. Mayrhofer's *Handbuch* is still indispensible and went through several editions. The full record of this multivolume work is Ernst Mayrhofer, *Handbuch für den politischen Verwaltungsdienst in den im Reichsrathe vertretenen Königreichen und Ländern.* The most readily available (and thus the one consulted here) is the fifth edition, which is available on Google Books: Ernst Mayrhofer and Anton Graf Pace, *Handbuch für den politischen Verwaltungsdienst in den im Reichsrathe vertretenen Königreichen und Ländern, mit besonderer Berücksichtigung der diesen Ländern gemeinsamen Gesetze und Verordnungen,* 5th ed., 7 vols. (Vienna: F. Manz, 1895).

78. Joseph Roth, *The Radetzky March*, trans. Michael Hofmann, new ed. (Granta Books, 2003), 26, 29–30.

79. Josef Redlich, "Aus dem alten Österreich. Erinnerungen und Einsichten," in *Schicksalsjahre Österreichs: Die Erinnerungen und Tagebücher Josef Redlichs, 1869–1936,* ed. Fritz Fellner and Doris Corradini, 2nd ed., 3 vols., Veröffentlichen der Kommission für Neuere Geschichte Österreichs 105 (Vienna: Böhlau, 2011), 1: 64–66. Redlich began this essay as a fifty-nine-year-old man in 1928.

80. My analysis of the ordinances relies on Judson, *Exclusive Revolutionaries,* 193–99. The language ordinances are reprinted in Berthold Sutter, *Die Badenischen Sprachenverordnungen von 1897: Ihre Genesis und ihre Auswirkungen vornehmlich auf die innerösterreichischen Alpenländer,* 2 vols., Veröffentlichungen der Kommission für Neuere Geschichte Österreichs 46 (Graz: Hermann Böhlaus Nachfolger, 1960), 1: 273–74. See also the classic treatment in Alfred Fischel, *Materialien zur Sprachenfrage in Österreich* (Brünn: Friedrich Irrgang, 1902); Alfred Fischel, *Das österreichische Sprachenrecht,* 2nd ed. (Brünn: Friedrich Irrgang, 1910).

81. As article 1 of the language ordinances stated, "The legal and administrative authorities in the crownland are obligated to issue decisions, orally or in writing, in whichever of the two official languages the oral or written petition originally is presented." Moreover, any supplementary documentation to be used as supporting evidence could be submitted in either language without the need for translation. Alfred Fischel, *Das österreichische Sprachenrecht: Eine Quellensammlung,* 1st ed. (Brünn: Friedrich Irrgang, 1901), 185–86.

82. For Czech and German national politics relating to the Stremayr Ordinances, see Jan Křen, *Die Konfliktgemeinschaft: Tschechen und Deutsche, 1780–1918,* Veröffentlichungen des Collegium Carolinum 71 (Munich: R. Oldenbourg, 1996), 169–70.

83. This Czech-German struggle over cultural recognition had long-term implications for the way historians have characterized the disruptive nature of nationality politics in the Habsburg monarchy. But the nature of our historiography is changing rapidly from a focus on Habsburg political pathology to a more critical examination of conflict and compromise between national parties. For the state of the scholarship, see Gary B. Cohen, "Neither Absolutism nor Anarchy: New Narratives on Society and Government in Late Imperial Austria," *Austrian History Yearbook* 29, no. 1 (1998): 37–61; Gary B. Cohen, "Nationalist Politics and the Dynamics of State and Civil Society in the Habsburg Monarchy, 1867–1914," *Central European History* 40, no. 2 (2007): 241–78; Jonathan Kwan, "Nationalism

and All That: Reassessing the Habsburg Monarchy and Its Legacy," review article, *European History Quarterly* 41, no. 1 (2011): 88–108.

84. The following paragraphs are reconstructed from appointment files, qualification tables, and letters between the governor of Bohemia and the minister of the interior (Taaffe himself), as well as official petitions regarding high-level provincial appointments to the emperor. These files: Pr. 1779/MI, Pr. 1987/MI, Pr. 2116/ MI, and Pr. 2591/MI, are located in ÖSTA AVA Inneres MdI Präsidium A 129.

85. Alfred Kraus to MdI, March 20, 1883, original Z. 2360 in Pr. Nr. 1987/MI, ÖSTA AVA Inneres MdI Präsidium A 129.

86. See Taaffe's petition to the emperor, April 4, 1883, in Pr. 1779, ÖSTA AVA Inneres MdI Präsidium A 129.

87. See the file to replace the district prefect of the industrial town Gablonz/Jablonec, which was overwhelmingly German speaking until the end of the empire: Pr. 2051 in ÖSTA AVA Inneres MdI Präsidium A 129. Even the governor's suggestion for the post, Maximilian Edler von Matl, had "some familiarity with the Bohemian language."

88. *SPAR*, 11/241 (October 28, 1893), 11497.

89. Letter from governor Franz von Thun und Hohenstein to the Ministry of the Interior (November 29, 1893), in Pr. Nr. 3895, ÖSTA AVA Inneres MdI Präsidium A 43.

90. See Statthalter Kraus's letter to Taaffe as minister of the interior (August 23, 1883, org. Z. 7222), in Pr. 4418, ÖSTA AVA Inneres MdI Präsidium A 129.

91. See, for instance, the edited memoirs of the technical officials Jan Baše and Karel Fasse in Pavla Vošahlíková, ed., *Von Amts wegen: K.k. Beamte erzählen*, vol. 37, *Damit es nicht verlorengeht . . .* (Vienna: Böhlau, 1998), 179–243 and 44–63.

92. Friedrich F. G. Kleinwaechter, *Der fröhliche Präsidialist* (Vienna: Amandus, 1947), 49.

93. See, for instance, the governor of Bohemia, Alfred Ritter von Kraus's commentary on what qualities the district prefect of Pilsen/Plžeň must possess, in his letter to Minister of the Interior Taaffe (March 20, 1883, org. Z. 2360), Pr. 1987, ÖSTA AVA Inneres MdI Präsidium A 129.

94. For contemporary analysis on the cooperation between autonomous units and the imperial government, see two articles by Georg Habermann: Georg Habermann, "Stadt und Land in Gesetzgebung und Verwaltung," *Zeitschrift für Volkswirtschaft, Sozialpolitik und Verwaltung* 9 (1900): 172–81; Georg Habermann, "Das Zusammenwirken lokaler Faktoren mit Stadt und Land bei Lösung von Verwaltungsaufgaben," *Zeitschrift für Volkswirtschaft, Sozialpolitik und Verwaltung* 14 (1905): 148–59.

95. Gary B Cohen, *Education and Middle-Class Society in Imperial Austria, 1848–1918* (West Lafayette, Ind: Purdue University Press, 1996) demonstrates the expanding access to and use of institutions of secondary and higher education during this period.

96. On many occasions the Austrian imperial bureaucracy suppressed data of its own numbers. Even in 1910, when a census was undertaken, members of ministerial bureaucracy rued the possibility that the number of civil servants would be discussed in public or be misused in political debate. See information on the administrative census in See Pr. Nr. 4187/1911 in ÖSTA AVA Inneres MdI Präsidium A 2215. For information the political sensi-

tivity of the issue, see a draft of a letter from the Ministry of the Interior to the Ministry of Finance (June 11, 1910), Pr. Nr. 43557 in ÖSTA AVA Inneres MdI Präsidium A 2215.

97. Compare the state budgets presented to the parliament for the years 1870 and 1889. For 1870, see *SPAR*, 5. Session, supplement Nr. 91. For 1889, see *SPAR*, 10. Session, supplement Nr. 660.

98. The budget allocations for the imperial bureaucracy in the crownlands increased from 4,617,773 gulden in 1870 to 5,625,524 gulden in 1889. This marks an increase of only 21.8 percent (N = 1870) over this twenty-year period.

99. See the letter from governor Alfred von Kraus to Eduard Taaffe (March 8, 1888), in Pr. Nr. 3434, ÖSTA AVA Inneres MdI Präsidium A 87.

100. The governor in Dalamatia reported that his staff was absolutely incapable of keeping up with the insufficient numbers of policy-making civil servants and the "immeasurably increasing workload." He submitted a table of case logs that demonstrated a trebling in the amount of work since 1868. See the letter from the governor in Dalmatia to the Ministry of the Interior (November 2, 1887), likewise filed under Pr. Nr. 3434, in ÖSTA AVA Inneres MdI Präsidium A 87.

101. Letter from the governor in Tyrol to the Ministry of the Interior (May 8, 1888), likewise filed under ibid.

102. See Ibid.

103. Letter from Kielmansegg to the Ministry of the Interior (April 21, 1891, orginial Z. 3180 Praes.) in ÖSTA AVA Inneres MdI Präsidium A 59.

104. For more on the Austrian meaning of *Skartieren*, see the short piece by Maureen Healy, "Dictator in a Dumpster: Thoughts on History and Garbage," *Rethinking History* 3, no. 1 (1999): 81–83.

105. NÖLA, Statthalterei Präsidium Allg. K 741, FA 15, Z. 2096, "Überlassung von Archivalien an das k.u.k. Haus, Hof, und Staatsarchiv."

## Chapter 6: Bureaucracy and Democracy

1. An interpellation is a procedure in parliament, whereby members of parliament formally question the government to justify or explain their actions. The government must then respond to the questions. Robert Ehrhart recalls this episode in *Im Dienste des alten Österreich* (Vienna: Bergland Verlag, 1958), 144–45.

2. Gary B. Cohen, "Nationalist Politics and the Dynamics of State and Civil Society in the Habsburg Monarchy, 1867–1914," *Central European History* 40, no. 2 (2007): 268–70.

3. The trope of "bureaucratic absolutism" in the late imperial period has resembled a strain of highly resistant bacteria: it has been impossible to kill. Above all, see Gary B. Cohen, "Neither Absolutism nor Anarchy: New Narratives on Society and Government in Late Imperial Austria," *Austrian History Yearbook* 29, no. 1 (1998): 37–61; Lothar Höbelt, *Parliamentary Politics in a Multinational Setting: Late Imperial Austria*, Working Paper 92–96 (Minneapolis: University of Minnesota, Center for Austrian Studies, 1992).

4. Bruno Schimetschek, *Der österreichische Beamte: Geschichte und Tradition* (Munich: R. Oldenbourg, 1984), 212–14. On the influence of *Beamtendynastien*, see Waltraud Heindl, *Gehorsame Rebellen: Bürokratie und Beamte in Österreich 1780 bis 1848*, ed. Christian Brün-

ner, Wolfgang Mantl, and Manfried Welan, Studien zu Politik und Verwaltung 36 (Vienna: Böhlau, 1991), 120; Karl Megner, *Beamte: Wirtschafts- und sozialgeschichtliche Aspekte des k.k. Beamtentums*, Studien zur Geschichte der Österreichisch-Ungarischen Monarchie 21 (Vienna: VÖAW, 1985), 78–81.

5. For contemporary criticism of this practice, see Rudolf Springer [Karl Renner], *Der Kampf der oesterreichischen Nationen um den Staat* (Leipzig: Franz Deuticke, 1902); Karl Renner, *Der nationale Streit um die Aemter und die Sozialdemokratie* (Vienna: Vorwärts, 1908). The Young Czech politician Karel Kramář put a great emphasis on infiltrating the Austrian bureaucracy with Czech speakers to help fulfill the "national interests" of Czechs: Karel Kramář, *Annmerkungen zur böhmischen Politik*, trans. Josef Penížek (Vienna: Carl Konegen, 1906), 30–32.

6. See Alfred Ableitinger, "Rudolf Sieghart 1966–1934 und seine Tätigkeit im Ministerratspräsidium: Ein Beitrag zur Geschichte der österreichischen Innenpolitik in ersten Jahrzehnt unseres Jahrhunderte" (Ph.D. diss., University of Graz, 1964), 41–42.

7. Josef Redlich, *Austrian War Government*, Economic and Social History of the World War 6 (New Haven, Conn.: Yale University Press, 1929), 33.

8. Schmidt apparently had become involved in the German nationalist movement "Los von Rom," and, while intoxicated and among his fellow officials in Salzburg, had uttered German nationalist sentiments and insulted the Austrian emperor. The local prosecutor had declined to try Schmidt for *lèse majesté*, instead referring the matter as an internal disciplinary affair to Schmidt's superiors in the Salzburg main customs office. The punishment decided upon was an unremunerated transfer to Spitzmüller's Lower Austrian finance office in Vienna. Alexander Spitzmüller recounts in his memoirs this case as "especially illustrative of the spirit of objectivity, clemency and tolerance" in the Austrian administration. Alexander Spitzmüller, *Memoirs of Alexander Spitzmüller, Freiherr von Harmersbach (1862–1953)*, ed. and trans. Carvel de Bussy, East European Monographs 228 (Boulder, Colo.: East European Monographs, 1987), 34–36.

9. Ibid., 35.

10. Ibid.

11. For thorough discussions of the emergence of these occupational interest groups, see H. Naderer, "Geschichte der österreichischen Beamtenbewegung unter besonderer Berücksichtigung der Entwicklung der Besoldungsverhältnisse von den ersten Anfängen bis zum Jahre 1914," *Jahrbuch der österreichischen Beamtenschaft* 1 (1927): 17–43; John W. Boyer, "Die Grossstadt Wien, die Radikalisierung der Beamten und die Wahlen von 1891," *Jahrbuch des Vereins für Geschichte der Stadt Wien* 36 (1980): 95–176; John W. Boyer, *Political Radicalism in Late Imperial Vienna: Origins of the Christian Social Movement, 1848–1897* (Chicago: University of Chicago Press, 1981), chap. 5. See also, Megner, *Beamte*, 197–209.

12. The first groups, such as the *Erste Wiener Consumverein für Beamte* (established 1861), the *Vorschußverein für Südbahnbedienstete* (established 1862), or the *Erste allgemeine Kranken- und Leichenverein für k. k. Beamte in Wien* were established as mutual aid or insurance organizations. In 1865, the *Erster allgemeiner Beamten-Verein* formed and became an organ for the expression of the material interests of white-collar officials across the entire monarchy.

13. The *Beamten-Verein*'s purpose, for instance, was "to preserve and promote the material, social, and intellectual [geistig] interests of the bureaucratic class [Beamtenstand] and to present a modern and effective representation of its occupational interests." Quoted in Naderer, "Geschichte . . . bis zum Jahre 1914," 20.

14. Ibid., 25.

15. Ibid., 25–26.

16. Boyer, *Political Radicalism*, 262.

17. Ibid., 261.

18. Ibid.

19. See ÖStA AVA Inneres MR-Präsidium ÖMRP A 35 (Separat-Protokolle, 1895), MRZ 50 (June 20, 1895).

20. Erich Graf Kielmansegg, *Kaiserhaus, Staatsmänner und Politiker: Aufzeichnungen des k.k. Statthalters Erich Graf Kielmansegg* (Vienna: Verlag für Geschichte und Politik, 1966), 43–48. Kielmansegg in his memoirs stated the emperor found that "the lack of discipline among officials has reached terrifying levels." Ibid., 47.

21. See the discussions on the Council of Ministers on July 11 (MRZ 56), July 18 (MRZ 58), July 26 (MRZ 60), and August 8, 1895 (MRZ 61), in ÖSTA AVA MR-Protokolle A 35.

22. Officially, this edict took the title "Directives regarding the guarantee of official secrets and the exercise of general rights of citizens of state officials." See ÖSTA AVA Inneres Ministerratspräsidium A 25 c, Z. 762/M-1895 and Z. 788/M-1895. The edict was printed in *WZ*, August 11, 1895, Nr. 186, 1–2.

23. Joseph II's pastoral letter—*Grundsätze für jeden diener des staats*—reprinted in ÖMR II/4: nr. 94, 126.

24. This suffrage reform was indeed similar to the suffrage reform proposal over which Taaffe's government fell in 1893. It left the four existing voting curiae alone, which consisted of the great magnate curia, and curiae for the chambers of commerce, cities, and rural townships. The only change was that for these second two curiae, persons had to meet a lower tax threshold in order to vote—from five to four guldens. To these four curiae, Badeni added a fifth, which was to vote by general manhood suffrage and which was to elected seventy-two additional members of parliament. See C. A. Macartney, *The Habsburg Empire, 1790–1918* (New York: Macmillan, 1969), 662; Höbelt, "Parliamentary Politics," 5–7.

25. For an analysis of the party politics surrounding suffrage and the Badeni crisis, see Lothar Höbelt, "Parteien und Fraktionen im Cisleithanischen Reichsrat," *Verfassung und Parlamentarismus*, vol. 7, pt. 1 of *Die Habsburgermonarchie, 1848–1918*, ed. Helmut Rumpler and Peter Urbanitsch,(Vienna: VÖAW, 2000), 942–57.

26. The ordinances were released separately in order not to give any credence to the idea of greater Bohemian state right, thus emphasizing the separateness of Bohemia and Moravia. The texts of the two ordinances were same. The ordinance for Bohemia is reprinted in *WZ*, April 6, 1897, (Nr. 78). See also Berthold Sutter, *Die Badenischen Sprachenverordnungen von 1897: Ihre Genesis und ihre Auswirkungen vornehmlich auf die innerösterreichischen Alpenländer*, 2 vols., Veröffentlichungen der Kommission für Neuere Geschichte Österreichs 46 (Graz: Hermann Böhlaus Nachfolger, 1960).

27. For an excellent and brief summary of the Badeni Language Ordinances, see

Catherine Albrecht, "The Bohemian Question," in *The Last Years of Austria-Hungary: A Multi-National Experiment in Early Twentieth-Century Europe*, ed. Mark Cornwall (Exeter, England: University of Exeter Press, 2002), 79–81.

28. The debate on the status of Czech in Bohemia and Moravia's administrations was predicated on a rather specific classification of the administrative process. There were three classifications of language: (1) the external service language (*äußere Amtssprache*), (2) the inner service language (*innere Amtssprache*), and (3) the innermost service language (*innerste Amtssprache*). The "outer" service language applied to all communication of an office with the public (this included spoken conversation, public notices, and written communication). The inner service language was defined as all intraoffice communication concerning internal administrative matters as well as interoffice communication in a single branch of the administration. The innermost service language was German. This language would be used in all interoffice communication in separate branches of the administration (for instance, between an office in the Ministry of the Interior and the Ministry of Justice) and all communication between a branch office and the central offices in Vienna. Gerald Stourzh, *Die Gleichberechtigung der Nationalitäten in der Verfassung und Verwaltung Österreichs, 1848–1918* (Vienna: VÖAW, 1985), 100–101.

29. Hans Mommsen, "1897: Die Badeni-Krise als Wendepunkt in den deutsch-tschechischen Beziehungen," in *Wendepunkte in den Beziehungen zwischen Deutschen, Tschechen und Slowaken 1848–1989*, ed. Detlef Brandes, Dušan Kováč, and Jiří Pešek, Veröffentlichungen der Deutsch-Tschechischen und Deutsch-Slowakischen Historikerkommission 14 (Essen: Klartext, 2007), 112.

30. Bilingualism still existed, to be sure, but nationalist political activism sought to limit it as much as possible. Tara Zahra and Pieter Judson have each brought attention to "national indifference" in the Bohemian lands. One particular practice, "trading children" (*Kindertausch*), involved families that spoke Czech and German at home exchanging children with one another, so that the children would easily learn both languages. See Tara Zahra, *Kidnapped Souls: National Indifference and the Battle for Children in the Bohemian Lands, 1900–1948* (Ithaca, N.Y.: Cornell University Press, 2008), esp. 1–3; also, more generally, see Pieter M. Judson, *Guardians of the Nation: Activists on the Language Frontiers of Imperial Austria* (Cambridge, Mass.: Harvard University Press, 2006).

31. Badeni handled these ordinances with less care than he should have. The compromise he tried to reach had to be done both through the crownland diets on the one hand and administrative fiat on the other. Badeni could grant the Czechs' concessions (on the use of Czech within the imperial administration) by fiat, while local autonomy for Germans within Bohemia and Moravia had to be granted by the individual diets in those two provinces. Rather than sorting out such constitutional problems by bringing both sides to the negotiating table once again, Badeni decided to grant the Czechs their language concessions without properly consulting with the German politicians.

32. Helmut Rumpler, *Österreichische Geschichte, 1804–1914: Eine Chance für Mitteleuropa; Bürgerliche Emanzipation und Staatsverfall in der Habsburgermonarchie*, Österreichische Geschichte (Vienna: Ueberreuter, 1997), 110.

33. Höbelt, "Parliamentary Politics," 6.

34. For a colorful, contemporary description of obstruction in action, see the classic article Mark Twain, "Stirring Times in Austria," *Harper's New Monthly Magazine* 96 (March 1898), 530–40.

35. Albrecht, "Bohemian Question," 82. For a lengthy analysis of Article 14, see Gernot D. Hasiba, *Das Notverordnungsrecht in Österreich (1848–1917): Notwendigkeit und Missbrauch eines "Staatserhaltenden Instrumentes,"* Studien zur Geschichte der Österreichisch-Ungarischen Monarchie 22 (Vienna: VÖAW, 1985); for the use of article 14 during the Badeni crisis, 97–104.

36. Adam Wandruszka, "Die Krisen des Parlamentarismus 1897 und 1933: Gedanken zum Demokratieverständnis in Österreich," in *Beiträge zur Zeitgeschichte: Festschrift Ludwig Jedlicka zum 60. Geburtstag,* ed. Rudolf Neck and Adam Wandruszka (St. Pölten: Niederösterreichisches Pressehaus, 1976), 77.

37. Höbelt, "Parliamentary Politics."

38. For a recent study on the reform ideas of Josef Samuel Bloch and the idea of building an "Austrian nation," see Ian Reifowitz, *Imagining an Austrian Nation: Joseph Samuel Bloch and the Search for a Multiethnic Austrian Identity, 1845–1919,* East European Monographs 631 (Boulder, Colo.: East European Monographs, 2003).

39. Wandruszka, "Krisen des Parlamentarismus," 76.

40. See Z. 109/PR 16/ (February 19, 1908), in OÖLA Bezirkshauptmannschaft Wels, Sch. 10, for information relating to the emperor's visit.

41. Gilbert Trathnigg reports that the number of cases in Wels increased between 1870 and 1888 from 2,872 files to 12,650! Kurt Holter and Gilbert Trathnigg, *Wels von der Urzeit bis zur Gegenwart,* Jahrbuch des Musealvereines Wels 10 (Wels: Kommissionsverlag by Eugen Friedhuber, 1964), 170.

42. See Chapter 5. These trends are analyzed in a broad, pan-European fashion in Raymond Grew, "The Nineteenth-Century European State," in *State Making and Social Movements,* ed. Charles Bright and Susan Harding (Ann Arbor: University of Michigan Press, 1984), 83–120; Michael Mann, *The Sources of Social Power,* vol. 2, *The Rise of Classes and Nation-States, 1760–1914* (New York: Cambridge University Press, 1986), esp. chaps. 11, 13–14.

43. Holter and Trathnigg, *Wels,* 170–74.

44. Moravia's bleak budget outlook was increasingly gaining attention. See the official crownland publication released in 1901 in Czech and German: Albert Bervid, *Die Landes-Finanzen der Markgrafschaft Mähren,* ed. Landes-Ausschuss der Markgrafschaft Mähren (Brünn: C. Winkler, 1901), 68–88; Albert Bervid, *Zemské finance markrabství Moravského* (Brno: J. Barviče, 1901), 52–75.

45. For a list of the many different funds and foundations created by the different crownlands, see Josef Freiherr von Friedenfels, "Der Landeshaushalt in Oesterreich, insbesondere im Jahre 1893," *Statistische Monatschrift* 2, n.s. (1897): 635–43.

46. Ibid., 633.

47. Graf St. H. Badeni, "Die Landesfinanzen Galiziens," *Statistische Monatschrift* 6, n.s. (1901): 16.

48. By law, the crownlands could levy surcharges of up to 10 percent of Cisleithanian direct taxes. If the crownlands sought surcharges at a higher rate than this, they had to receive the emperor's express approval. For further information on the sources of income avail-

able to the crownlands, see Ernst Mischler, "Selbstverwaltung, finanzrechtlich," in *Öster-reichisches Staatswörterbuch*, ed. Ernst Mischler and Josef Ulbrich, 2nd ed., 4 vols. (Vienna: Alfred Hölder, 1905–9), 4 (1909): 231–37. For contemporary analysis of the taxation prob-lem, see Friedrich F. G. Kleinwaechter, "Die österreichische Enquête über die Landesfinan-zen," *Jahrbücher für Nationalökonomie und Statistik* 38, 3rd series, no. 1 (1909): 44–46.

49.   Other crownlands which levied a surcharge over the average of 55 percent included Silesia (84 percent), Salzburg (74 percent), Carinthia (71.6 percent), Bohemia (65.3 per-cent), Moravia (68.6 percent), Styria (59.7 percent), and Dalmatia (57.7 percent). See Ernst Mischler, "Der Haushalt der österreichischen Landschaften," *Jahrbuch des öffentlichen Rechts der Gegenwart* 3 (1909): 589; Mischler, "Selbstverwaltung, finanzrechtlich," 236–37.

50.   See the 1899 budget and income figures for Moravia in Bervid, *Landes-Finanzen der Markgrafschaft Mähren*, 75–89; or, see the same version in Czech in Bervid, *Zemské finance Moravského*.

51.   Ferdinand Schmid, "Betrachtungen über die Reform der inneren Verwaltung Öster-reichs," *Zeitschrift für Volkswirtschaft, Socialpolitik und Verwaltung* 14 (1905): 350.

52.   Total expenditures by the crownlands in 1862 equaled 14.8 million kronen; by 1905 this total reached over 279.5 million kronen. Mischler, "Haushalt," 586–87.

53.   For the forms in which the crownlands borrowed to cover their expanding budgets, see Mischler, "Selbstverwaltung, finanzrechtlich," 235–37.

54.   Walter Loewenfeld, "Die Finanzen der österreichischen Kronländer," *Finanzarchiv* 25, no. 2 (1908): 178. Loewenfeld takes his statistics from the *Stenographisches Protokoll der Enquête über die Landesfinanzen. 7. bis 12. März 1908* (Vienna: k.k. Hof- und Staatsdruckerei, 1908).

55.   Mischler, "Haushalt," 586. For an overview of crownland officials, see Robert Fuhrmann, "Einleitung," *Statistisches Jahrbuch der autonomen Landesverwaltung in den im Reichsrate vertretenen Königreichen und Ländern* 1 (1900): xlv–lxxiii.

56.   Hans Rizzi, "Die Landeshaushalte und die Landeshaushaltsstatistik der österreich-ischen Länder," *Statistisches Jahrbuch der autonomen Landesverwaltung in den im Reichsrate vertretenen Königreichen und Ländern* 12 (1914): 31–32.

57.   Mischler, "Haushalt," 586.

58.   Schmid, "Betrachtungen," 352.

59.   For a classic article on the meanings and significance of the Corpus Christi proces-sion in Vienna, see James Shedel, "Emperor, Church, and People: Religion and Dynastic Loyalty During the Golden Jubilee of Franz Joseph," *Catholic Historical Review* 76, no. 1 (1990): 71–92. See also the more recent work Daniel L. Unowsky, *The Pomp and Politics of Patriotism: Imperial Celebrations in Habsburg Austria, 1848–1916*, Central European Studies (West Lafayette, Ind.: Purdue University Press, 2005), esp. 26–32.

60.   For example, see the complaints of the municipal government of Gmunden, Pr. Nr. 7665 /MI (1907) in ÖSTA AVA Inneres MdI Präsidium A 1272.

61.   There have been a good many biographic articles published on Koerber, but only a few studies of his political career. The most notable recent studies have been by the Swedish historian Fredrik Lindström: *Empire and Identity: Biographies of the Austrian State Problem in the Late Habsburg Empire*, Central European Studies (West Lafayette, Ind.: Purdue Uni-

versity Press, 2008), pt. 1; Fredrik Lindström, "Ernest von Koerber and the Austrian State Idea: A Reinterpretation of the Koerber Plan (1900–1904)," *Austrian History Yearbook* 35 (2004): 143–84.

62. Adam Wandruszka, "Die 'Zweite Gesellschaft' der Donaumonarchie," in *Adel in Österreich*, ed. Heinz Siegert (Vienna: Kremayr & Scheriau, 1971), 56–67.

63. For an analysis of the Theresianum, see Gernot Stimmer, "Zur Herkunft der höchsten österreichischen Beamtenschaft: Die Bedeutung des Theresianums und der Konsularakademie," in *Student und Hochschule im 19. Jahrhundert: Studien und Materialien*, ed. Christian Helfer and Mohammed Rassem, Studien zum Wandel von Gesellschaft und Bildung im Neunzehnten Jahrhundert 12 (Göttingen: Vandenhoeck & Ruprecht, 1975), 303–45; Gernot Stimmer, *Eliten in Österreich, 1848–1970*, 2 vols., Studien zu Politik und Verwaltung 57 (Vienna: Böhlau, 1997), 1: 96–98.

64. Parliament had been deadlocked since Badeni released his language ordinances in 1897. The ordinances had been rescinded by prime minister Count Clary-Aldringen in October 1899, the Czech parties responded by their own obstruction of parliament. The literature on this moment in Austrian history is immense. One can content oneself with the masterful study by Lothar Höbelt, *Kornblume und Kaiseradler: Die deutschfreiheitlichen Parteien Altösterreichs, 1882–1918* (Vienna: Verlag für Geschichte und Politik, 1993), 150–86. For a detailed narrative of parliament and obstruction, one should consult Gustav Kolmer, *Parlament und Verfassung in Österreich*, 8 vols. (Vienna: C. Fromme, 1902), vols. 6 and 7.

65. The literature on Koerber as a policy maker and prime minister is limited to a few studies. Alexander Gerschenkron evaluates much of Koerber's projects within his theoretical framework of "economic spurts" and of modernization theory. See Alexander Gerschenkron, *An Economic Spurt That Failed: Four Lectures in Austrian History* (Princeton, N.J.: Princeton University Press, 1977). Alfred Ableitinger's 1973 study, Alfred Ableitinger, *Ernest von Koerber und das Verfassungsproblem im Jahre 1900*, Studien zur Geschichte der Österreichisch-Ungarischen Monarchie 12 (Vienna: Böhlau, 1973), focuses largely on Koerber's politics and his relationship to parliament, especially his plan for a constitutional coup d'état in the summer of 1900. This constitutional restructuring has been republished in Ernst Rutkowski, *Briefe und Dokumente zur Geschichte der österreichisch-ungarischen Monarchie: Unter besonderer Berücksichtigung des böhmischmährischen Raumes*, 3 vols., Veröffentlichungen des Collegium Carolinum 51 (Munich: R. Oldenbourg, 1983–2011), 2: 371–442.

66. *NFP*, January 6, 1900, morning ed., 1.

67. Alois Czedik, *Zur Geschichte der k.k. österreichischen Ministerien, 1861–1916*, 4 vols. (Teschen: Karl Prochaska, 1917), 2: 310–11. Piętak was a "Landesmannsminister," meaning that he was given a cabinet position without portfolio to represent "Polish" interests.

68. Quoted in *NFP*, January 18, 1900, Morgenblatt, 1.

69. This revision of the monarchy is currently well underway. However, the political crises of the post-1897 period still lend themselves to the older picture of imperial decline, which is still widely circulated in wider European history.

70. *Administrative reform* is a term widely used, both in the context of early twentieth-century Austria and in twenty-first-century political science. For our purposes, it is best to

take a most basic and capacious definition: The restructuring or altering of lines of communication and command, jurisdictional boundaries, and, most obviously, personnel in a bureaucratic administration.

71. Rutkowski, *Briefe und Dokumente*, 2: 371–442; See Alfred Ableitinger's 1973 monograph, which analyses this document Ableitinger, *Ernest von Koerber*, passim.

72. Here Koerber was careful to disentangle "nationalist ring-leaders" with doctor titles from a body "which is raised into an intelligentsia by a cosmopolitanism saturated, ameliorated, and rendered more conciliatory through education." Despite the lofty tones, his actual proposal for a suffrage law would put all those with a university degree or certificate from a technical school in this curia. See Rutkowski, *Briefe und Dokumente*, 2: 377–78; 400–401.

73. There were many different oaths according to branch of service, providing variations on the central theme of loyalty to the state and ethical conduct in the execution of office. Rutkowski, *Briefe und Dokumente*, 2: 393–94. For more information on the *Diensteid*, see Josef Ulbrich, *Das österreichische Staatsrecht*, 4th ed., Öffentliche Recht der Gegenwart 10 (Tübingen: Mohr Siebeck, 1909), 90.

74. Alexander Gerschenkron positively evaluates Koerber's infrastructure building program. Gerschenkron, *Economic Spurt*; Höbelt, "Parliamentary Politics," 7–8; See also, David F. Good, *The Economic Rise of the Habsburg Empire, 1750–1914* (Berkeley: University of California Press, 1984), 182–83, which likewise sees Koerber's investment bill as a means to "cool off" hot political tempers.

75. Lothar Höbelt astutely points out that the more concretely Koerber's investment plans unfolded, the less political weight they carried. German or Czech nationalist politicians were less likely to support a bill once it was determined that its benefits were not as great as they had hoped. Subsequent budgets after 1902 were pushed through using Austria's emergency legislation law, the infamous article 14 of the Law on Imperial Representation (*RGBl* 141/1867), one of the five laws which constituted the December Constitution. Höbelt, "Parliamentary Politics," 8.

76. For Koerber's wrangling with parliament after 1902, see Kolmer, *Parlament*, 8: 397–413; 443–57; 508–38.

77. *SPAR*, 12/255 (March 8, 1904), 23353–56 (quote on 23355).

78. *Studien des Ministerpräsidenten Dr. Ernest von Koerber über die Reform der inneren Verwaltung* (Vienna: K. k. Hof- und Staatsdruckerei, 1904). Koerber's *Studien*, as it came to be known, was subsequently republished in Czedik, *Österreichische Ministerien*, 2: 419–52. All subsequent page numbers refer to the original.

79. Koerber, *Studien*, 8.

80. Karl Brockhausen, *Österreichische Verwaltungsreformen: Sechs Vorträge in der Wiener freien staatswissenschaftlichen Vereinigung* (Vienna: F. Deuticke, 1911), 12.

81. Other high-ranking officials who were members of the "first society" had also engaged in debates on how to save the monarchy—often calling into question some aspect of the empire's organization and proposing radical changes to its structure. But their assumptions were much more pessimistic than Koerber's. See, for instance, the exchange between Austria's foreign minister, Count Agenor Gołuchowski, and the then-ambassador to Russia

(and later foreign minister), Baron Alois Lexa von Aehrenthal; in Solomon Wank, "Varieties of Cultural Despair: Three Exchanges between Aehrenthal and Gołuchowski," in *Intellectual and Social Developments in the Habsburg Empire from Maria Theresa to World War I: Essays Dedicated to Robert A. Kann*, ed. Stanley B. Winters and Joseph Held, East European Monographs (New York: Columbia University Press, 1975), 203–39.

82. Schmid, "Betrachtungen," 349–51. See also Jiří Klabouch, *Die Gemeindeselbstverwaltung in Österreich, 1848–1918* (Munich: R. Oldenbourg, 1968), 116–23.

83. Koerber, *Studien*, 23.

84. See, for instance, Koerber's memorandum to all his provincial governors the day after taking office, reprinted in *NFP*, evening edition, January 30, 1900, 2.

85. See the collection of newspaper clippings criticizing the Koerber *Studien* in ÖSTA AVA MdI NL Davy K 2, in a folder entitled "Kritiken der Körberschen Studie." A subfolder containing newspaper clippings from Bohemia contains over fifty separate articles, the overwhelming majority written by protesting Czechs. See also Lindström, "Koerber and the Austrian State Idea," 177–78.

86. John W. Boyer, *Culture and Political Crisis in Vienna: Christian Socialism in Power, 1897–1918* (Chicago: University of Chicago Press, 1995), 41–42.

87. For Koerber's fall and the last months of his first term as prime minister (the second came in 1916), see Kolmer, *Parlament*, 8: 606–17; Czedik, *Österreichische Ministerien*, 2: 346–48.

88. For example Otto Bauer, *Die Nationalitätenfrage und die Sozialdemokratie* (Vienna: I. Brand, 1907); Schmid, "Betrachtungen"; Ludwig Crenneville, *Zur Reform der politischen Verwaltung. Autonomie, staatliche Verwaltung, Staatsbeamte* (Vienna: Verlag der St. Norbertus Druckerei, 1905); Rudolf von Herrnritt, "Zur Reform der inneren Verwaltung in Österreich," *Österreichische Rundschau* 1, no. November 1904–January 1905 (1905): 645–49; Otto Lang, *Das österreichische Staatsproblem und seine Lösung* (Vienna: C. W. Stern, 1905); Georg Michalski, "Über die Reform der inneren Verwaltung in Österreich," *Verwaltungsarchiv* 15 (1906): 235–67; Rudolf Springer [Karl Renner], *Grundlagen und Entwicklungsziele der österreichisch-ungarischen Monarchie: Politische Studie uber den Zusammenbruch der Privilegenparlamente und die Wahlreform in beiden Staaten, über die Reichsidee und ihre Zukunft von Rudolf Springer* (Vienna: F. Deuticke, 1906).

89. Joseph II's "pastoral letter," in *ÖZV*, II/4: 127.

90. Recent work on these crownland-centered national compromises has drawn our attention to the changing nature of citizenship and political rights in the Habsburg monarchy. See Stourzh, *Gleichberechtigung*; Gerald Stourzh, "The National Compromise in the Bukovina," in *From Vienna to Chicago and Back: Essays on Intellectual History and Political Thought in Europe and America* (Chicago: University Of Chicago Press, 2007), 177–89; T. M. Kelly, "Last Best Chance or Last Gasp? The Compromise of 1905 and Czech Politics in Moravia," *Austrian History Yearbook* 34 (2003): 279–301.

91. For a recent treatment of Franz Ferdinand's military chancellery, see Jean-Paul Bled, *Franz Ferdinand: Der eigensinnige Thronfolger*, trans. Susanna Grabmayr and Marie-Therese Pitner (Vienna: Böhlau, 2013), 131–34.

92. For some of the major reform plans that Franz Ferdinand entertained over the

course of this period, see John W. Boyer, "The End of an Old Regime: Visions of Political Reform in Late Imperial Austria," *Journal of Modern History* 58, no. 1 (March 1986): 183–89; Rudolf Kiszling, "Erzherzog Franz Ferdinands Pläne für den Umbau der Donaumonarchie," *Neues Abendland* 11, no. 4 (1956): 362–69; Wilhelm Böhm, *Konservative Umbaupläne im alten Österreich; Gestaltungsprobleme des Völkerreiches*, Österreichprofile (Vienna: Europa-Verlag, 1967).

93. The lectures were later published as Wiener-Juristische-Gesellschaft, ed., *Diskussion über die Denkschrift der Regierung: Studien zur Reform der inneren Verwaltung. (25. Jänner bis 22. Februar 1905)* (Vienna: Verlag der Manzschen k.u.k. Hof- Verlags- und Universitäts-Buchhandlung, 1905).

94. For instance, see the articles by Schmid, "Betrachtungen"; Rudolf von Herrnritt, "Die geplante Reform der inneren Verwaltung Österreichs und die Voraussetzungen ihrer Verwirklichung," *Österreichisches Verwaltungsarchiv* 4 (1907): 289–336.

95. See Max Schuster-Bonnot, "Anregung zur Frage der Verwaltungsreform in Österreich," *Österreichische Rundschau* 1 (November 1904–January 1905): 264–68.

96. For instance, one book advocated a form of Karl Renner's advocacy of national autonomy. Compare Rudolf Springer [Karl Renner], *Der Kampf*; Rudolf Springer [Karl Renner], *Staat und Parlament: Kritische Studie über die Oesterreichische Frage und das System der Interessenvertretung* (Vienna: Ignaz Brand, 1901); to the advocacy of Volksräte in the place of crownlands in Lang, *Das österreichische Staatsproblem*.

97. This is most clearly represented in Crenneville, *Zur Reform*.

98. Ibid., 102.

99. For a history of the expansion of the suffrage in Austria, see above all William Alexander Jenks, *The Austrian Electoral Reform of 1907*, Studies in History, Economics and Public Law 559 (repr., New York: Octagon Books, 1974), 11–27. For more detail, see Ludwig Spiegel, "Wahlen," in *Österreichisches Staatswörterbuch*, 4 (1909): 871–80.

100. For a summary of the composition of the thirteenth session of the House of Deputies, see above all Jenks, *Austrian Electoral Reform*, 177–98; Karl Ucakar, *Demokratie und Wahlrecht in Österreich: Zur Entwicklung von politischer Partizipation und staatlicher Legitimationspolitik*, Österreichische Texte zur Gesellschaftskritik 24 (Vienna: Verlag für Gesellschaftskritik, 1985), 353–57.

101. *SPAR*, 18. Session, "Thronrede Seiner k. und k. Apostolischen Majestät des Kaisers Franz Joseph I." (June 19, 1907), 1/7–1/10. Quotes on 1/8.

102. *SPAR*, 18/4 (June 27, 1907), 130.

103. Ibid., 131.

104. Ibid., 127.

105. Ibid.

106. Ibid., 129.

107. See *SPAR*, 19. Session, 1909, 723 der Beilagen for a copy of Redlich's bill. This initial bill was automatically tabled when the eighteenth session of the Reichsrat closed on July 7, 1909. Redlich would resubmit the bill, with exactly the same wording, in October of the same year. For the second bill, see *SPAR*, 20. Session, 1909, 377 der Beilagen.

108. See Fritz Fellner's biographical essay on Redlich, Fritz Fellner, "Josef Redlich:

Leben und Werk," in *Schicksalsjahre Österreichs: Die Erinnerungen und Tagebücher Josef Redlichs, 1869–1936*, ed. Fritz Fellner and Doris Corradini, 2nd ed., 3 vols., Veröffentlichen der Kommission für Neuere Geschichte Österreichs 105 (Vienna: Böhlau, 2011), 3: 11–12.

109. Josef Redlich, *Englische Lokalverwaltung: Darstellung der inneren Verwaltung Englands in ihrer geschichtlichen entwicklung und in ihrer gegenwärtigen Gestalt* (Leipzig: Duncker & Humblot, 1901); published in English as Josef Redlich, *Local Government in England*, trans. F. W. Hirst, 2 vols. (London: Macmillan, 1903).

110. Fellner, "Leben und Werk," 12–14.

111. Josef Redlich, *Recht und Technik des englischen Parlamentarismus: Die Geschäftsordnung des House of Commons in ihrer geschichtlichen Entwicklung und gegenwärtigen Gestalt* (Lepizig: Duncker & Humblot, 1905); Josef Redlich, *The Procedure of the House of Commons: A Study of Its History and Present Form*, ed. Alfred E. Steinthal, trans. Sir Couurtenay Peregrin Ilbert, 3 vols. (London: A. Constable, 1908).

112. This work produced the following: Josef Redlich, "Einleitung," in *Verfassung und Verwaltungsorganisation der Städte: Österreich*, vol. 6, Schriften des Vereins für Socialpolitik 122 (Leipzig: Dunker und Humblot, 1907), 1–5; Josef Redlich, "Geschichte der österreichischen Gemeindegesetzung und die Entstehung des Reichsgemeindegesetzes von 1862," in *Verfassung und Verwaltungsorganisation*, 51–88; Josef Redlich, "Grundzüge des geltenden österreichischen Gemeinderechtes," in *Verfassung und Verwaltungsorganisation der Städte*, 6: 89–142.

113. Haerdtl had become minister of the interior nine days earlier with the entry of a new government under Count Richard Bienerth, on November 16, 1909.

114. Redlich, *Schicksalsjahre Österreichs*, 2nd ed., 1: 272 (entry for November 27, 1909).

115. See Haerdtl's appointment letter to the minister of the interior: ÖSTA AVA MdI Präsidium A 1362, Pr. Nr. 11261/1908.

116. The *"Allerhöchste Handschreiben"* was subsequently published in *WZ*, Nr. 120 (May 25, 1911), 1–2.

117. Waltraud Heindl, "Was ist Reform? Überlegungen zum Verhältnis von Bürokratie, Staat, und Gesellschaft in Österreich," in *Innere Staatsbildung und gesellschaftliche Modernisierung in Österreich und Deutschland, 1867/71 bis 1914*, ed. Helmut Rumpler (Munich: R. Oldenbourg, 1991), 166–75.

118. Letter from Statthalter in Trieste to the minister of the interior (July 15, 1914), No. 8238/MI-14 (filed with No. 9713/MI-14) in ÖStA AVA Inneres MdI Präsidium, A 1352.

119. The nearly complete meeting minutes and official correspondence of the *Kommission zur Förderung der Verwaltungsreform* are housed in the Austrian State Archives: ÖSTA AVA Inneres MR-Präsidium Verwaltungsreformkommission (16 cartons). See also the brief overview of the commission's work Gernot D. Hasiba, "Die Kommission zur Föderung der Verwaltungsreform (1911–1914)," in *Recht und Geschichte: Festschrift Hermann Baltl zum 70. Geburtstag*, ed. Helfried Valentinitsch (Graz: Leykam-Verlag, 1988), 237–63.

120. Koerber promoted Schwarzenau out of the Ministry of the Interior to the *Statthalterei* of Tyrol in December 1901. By 1911, Schwarzenau was a member of Austria's Supreme Administrative Court. By 1916, he had become its chief justice. I am grateful for Dr. Cle-

mens Jabloner, president of the Supreme Administrative Court of Austria, and Ms. Irene Förster, librarian at the VwGH, for their assistance in accessing files and information relating to Erwin von Schwarzenau and Guido von Haerdtl.

121. Steneographic minutes of the first plenary session of the *Kommission zur Förderung der Verwaltungsreform* (June 28, 1911), in ÖSTA AVA Inneres, MR-Präsidium VRK A 4, Bd. 1.

122. Nr. 266/ M. in ÖSTA AVA Inneres MR-Präsidium VRK A 2.

123. The meetings consisted of Redlich and other commission members conducting interviews in groups. The interviews were conducted on the basis of a questionnaire, consisting of forty-three questions, which had been sent to the participants beforehand. The *Enquête* was published as *Enquête der Kommission zur Förderung der Verwaltungsreform, veranstaltet in der Zeit vom 21. Oktober bis 9. November 1912 zur Feststellung der Wünsche der beteiligten Kreise der Bevölkerung in Bezug auf die Reform der Inneren und Finanzverwaltung* (Vienna: k.k. Hof- und Staatsdruckerei, 1913). For a contemporary discussion of the *Enquête* and its results, see Stephan Licht, *Die Ergebnisse der Enquête über die Verwaltungsreform. Referat erstattet am 14. September 1913 am XXVI. Verbandstag des Zentralverbandes der Industriellen Österreichs in Aussig* (Vienna: Vernay, 1913).

124. Redlich would subsequently call the work of the commission a failure, because of the "silent opposition of the bureaucracy itself." But his views are colored by his own work on the commission and slanted by his postwar perspective. Redlich, *Austrian War Government*, 53–54.

125. *Bericht der Kommission zur Förderung der Verwaltungsreform über die Steigerung der Kosten der staatlichen inneren Verwaltung in der Periode von 1890 bis 1911 und ihrer Vorschläge auf vorläufige Reformen hinsichtlich der Zentralstellen und der politischen Landesbehörden* (Vienna: k.k. Hof- und Staatsdruckerei, 1913).

126. For example, Haerdtl noticed that multiple ministries had separate departments that regulated electricity. In many cases, these separate overlapping offices had two or three university-trained officials—and thus were rather costly—while handling less than one hundred cases per year. See Haerdtl's speech in the third meeting of the combined subcommittees 1 and 3, which summarizes much of his findings, ÖSTA AVA Inneres MR-Präsidium VRK A 11, vol. 28, 11.

127. See also John Boyer's analysis of Haerdtl's report and suggestions for reform: Boyer, *Culture and Political Crisis*, 358–59.

128. ÖSTA AVA Inneres MR-Präsidium VRK A 11, vol. 28, 19–37.

129. Josef Redlich, *Bericht des Mitgliedes der Kommission zur Förderung der Verwaltungsreform über die Entwicklung und den gegenwärtigen Stand der österreichischen Finanzverwaltung sowie Vorschläge der Kommission zur Reform diser Verwaltung* (Vienna: k.k. Hof- und Staatsdruckerei, 1913).

130. Boyer, "End of an Old Regime," 178–81.

131. Other provinces were able to collect more than they spent, but they still did not provide a great return on their investment. The Bukowina spent 1 crown to collect 1.17, when Bohemia, the poster child of complexity, collected nearly four crowns for every one they spent on salaries and incidentals for finance and treasury officials. For a comparison

between cost of collection (in the form of salaries, rents, per diems, and other overhead and incidental costs) and the actual sums raised in direct taxes, see the figures in table 15 in Redlich, *Bericht*, 87.

132. Boyer, "End of an Old Regime," 180.

133. Merveldt's and Rauchberg's study was subsequently published as *Anträge der Kommission zur Förderung der Verwaltungsreform betreffend die Vorbereitung und Prüfung für den Konzeptsdienst der politischen und der Finanzverwaltung* (Vienna: F. Tempsky, 1913).

134. Wittek's study was discussed in the seventh (March 13, 1913) and eighth (May 29, 1913) plenary sessions of the commission. It was subsequently published as *Anträge der Kommission zur Förderung der Verwaltungsrform, betreffend die Vorbildung, Ausbildung und Fortbildung der Staatsbeamten der besonderen fachlichen Dienstzweige der politischen Verwaltung (Techniker, Land- und Forstwirte, Ärzte, Veterinäre)* (Vienna: k.k. Hof- und Staatsdruckerei, 1913).

135. This report also contained a report by Kielmansegg on a reform of office management. *Anträge der Kommission zur Förderung der Verwaltungsreform betreffend die Erlassung einer Geschäftsordnung der k.k. Bezirkshauptmannschaften und die Feststellung von Grundsätzen für das Verfahren von dem politischen Behörden samt Erläuterungen und einem Bericht über die Kanzleireform bei den politischen Behörden* (Vienna: k.k. Hof- und Staatsdruckerei, 1913).

136. Excerpts from the ninth plenary session can be found in ÖSTA AVA Inneres MR-Präsidium VRK A 1 (no number). Redlich has a diary entry on this session: see Redlich, *Schicksalsjahre Österreichs*, 2nd ed., 1: 550–51 (July 3, 1913). See also Hasiba, "Kommission," 237.

137. Redlich noted in his diary that "Haerdtl and Bernatzik fought against Schwarzenau's proposals, somewhat viciously [gehässig]. . . . By 1 A.M. was Schwarzenau's work accomplished [our discussion over]." Redlich, *Schicksalsjahre Österreichs*, 1: 550 (July 3, 1913).

138. Bernatzik's reservations were attached to Schwarzenau's proposals via a *Separatsvotum*. See the "Auszug aus dem Protokoll über die 9. Plenarsitzung der Kommission zur Förderung der Verwaltungsreform am 1. und 2. Juli 1913," 27, in ÖSTA AVA Inneres MR-Präsidium VRK A 1. See also Haerdtl and Bernatzik's minority report in the same material, 33.

139. See summaries of Schwarzenau's *Anträge* in Hasiba, "Kommission," 254–57; Lindström, *Empire and Identity*, 226–27.

140. Koerber, *Studien*, 28.

141. *RGBl* Nr. 52/1855: "Vorordnung der Minister des Innern und der Justiz vom 17. März 1855, womit die Amtsinstruction für die rein politischen und für die gemischten Bezirks- und Stuhlrichterämter erlassen wird."

142. See Schwarzenau's "Erläuterungen" to his *Anträge . . . betreffend die Erlassung einer Geschäftsordnung der k.k. Bezirkshauptmannschaften*, 2: 17.

143. Ibid., 19.

144. Redlich letter to Josef Maria Baernreither (July 3, 1913), ÖStA HHStA, Nachlass Baernreither A 49, quoted in Lindström, *Empire and Identity*, 227.

145. See the letter of the minister of the interior to the imperial governors, Z. 13781/

MI ex 1913 (February 12, 1914), in ÖSTA AVA Inneres MdI Präsidium A 1286. This letter received favorable responses from the governors themselves. See the letter from the imperial governor in Brno/Brünn from July 1914: Z. Nr. 7341/ M.I. in the same carton.

146. *Grundzüge einer Reform der Organisation der inneren Verwaltung* was published as part of the third yearly report of the commission: *Dritter Jahresbericht der Kommission zur Förderung der Verwaltungsreform* (Vienna: k.k. Hof- und Staatsdruckerei, 1914). It also located in ÖSTA AVA Inneres MR-Präsidium VRK A 12.

147. Subcommittees 1 and 4 in a joint meeting held on March 5–6, 1914, discussed Haerdtl's proposals at length. The minutes from these meetings were subsequently published in *Dritter Jahresbericht*, Protokolle Nr. 3. The original is housed in ÖSTA AVA Inneres MR-Präsidium VRK A 12, Band 31, Sitzung der vereinigten Ausschüsse I und IV, vom 5. und 6. March 1914, Referate, Pr. Nr. 2.

148. Federalists like Count Adalbert Schönborn or Dr. Franz Fiedler resented the county as an attack on crownland autonomy. They wanted more administrative authority to revert to the crownlands. See the meeting minutes for the tenth plenary meeting of the commission, (March, 27–28, 1914), printed in *Dritter Jahresbericht*. These minutes are not available in the archives of the VRK.

149. The minutes of subcommittees 1 and 4 were subsequently published as an appendix to as *Dritter Jahresbericht*, sec. Nr. 6. *Stenographisches Protokoll über die am 27. Juni 1914 abgehaltene Beratung der vereinigten Ausschüsse I und IV der kommission zur Förderung der Verwaltungsreform*. Quote on 2.

150. Lindström, *Empire and Identity*, 230.

151. Haerdtl's proposals, *Anträge zur Reform der Organisation der inneren Verwaltung*, are appended to the stenographic minutes of the meeting. See note 149.

152. *Dritter Jahresbericht*. This third report contained reform proposals on the "Reform of the Domestic (State and Autonomous) Administration as Well as a Reform of the Administrative Judicature" (*Verwaltungsrechtspflege*); as well as studies and proposals on the establishment of an archive for the legislature; the education and training of candidates for the service in the court of audit (*Rechnungsdienst*); and a resolution for the financial responsibility of the state for its officials and employees for damages rendered in the exercise of public authority.

153. See Redlich's entry on Haerdtl, the day after Franz Ferdinand's assassination: Redlich, *Schicksalsjahre Österreichs*, 1: 610 (June 29, 1914). Redlich's subsequent diary entries on Haerdtl refer often to his deep pessimism during the war.

154. Stenographic minutes of the twelfth plenary session (December 15, 1914) in ÖSTA AVA Inneres MR-Präsidium VRK A 6, vol. 9, 3–5.

155. Stenographic minutes of the twelfth plenary session (December 15, 1914), in ÖSTA AVA Inneres MR-Präsidium VRK A 6, vol. 9, 52. This phrase would be removed from the report following the commission members' objections. See also Hasiba, "Kommission," 262; Lindström, *Empire and Identity*, 230. See the announcement in *WZ*, Nr. 23 (January 29, 1915), 1.

156. Stenographic minutes of the twelfth plenary session (December 15, 1914), in ÖSTA AVA Inneres MR-Präsidium VRK A 6, vol. 9, 87–88.

## Epilogue

1. See Potiorek's "Persönlichen Vormerkungen" Nr. 30 (dated November 27, 1912) to the Military Chancellery of Francis Joseph in ÖStA KA MKSM SR A 71.

2. Ibid.

3. There is no shortage of narratives on the Sarajevo assassination. See, above all, Christopher Clark, *The Sleepwalkers: How Europe Went to War in 1914* (London: Allen Lane, 2012), 367–91; the classic account is Vladimir Dedijer, *The Road to Sarajevo* (New York: Simon and Schuster, 1966); for an account that focuses on Potiorek, see Rudolf Jeřábek, *Potiorek: General im Schatten von Sarajevo* (Graz: Styria, 1991), 82–96.

4. Potiorek's recount of a letter from minister Leon Biliński, in Res. Nr. 4600, Persönliche Vormerkungen 13 (dated July 1914) to the Military Chancellery of Francis Joseph in ÖStA KA MKSM SR A 71.

5. Gernot D. Hasiba, "Inter arma silent leges? Ein Beitrag über die rechtlichen Grundlagen der österreichischen Verwaltungs im 1. Weltkrieg," in *Modell einer neuen Wirtschaftsordnung: Wirtschaftsverwaltung in Österreich 1914–1918*, ed. Wilhelm Brauneder and Franz Baltzarek, Rechtshistorische Reihe 74 (Frankfurt am Main: Peter Lang, 1991), 17–18. The fundamental law of December 21, 1867, *RGBl* 142, on the "general rights of citizens" provided that the "suspension of rights" temporarily or in specific regions would be determined by an additional law at a later date. This law would be *RGBl* Nr. 66, the law of May 5, 1869, on the "authority of the executive to enact temporary or geographically determined exceptions to existing laws." For a prewar account of the passage of these laws, see Gustav Kolmer, *Parlament und Verfassung in Österreich* (Vienna: C. Fromme, 1902), 1: 350.

6. Most informative on the series of emergency laws is Martin Moll, "Erster Weltkrieg und Ausnahmezustand, Zivilverwaltung und Armee: Eine Fallstudie zum innerstaatlichen Machtkampf 1914–1918 im steirischen Kontext," in *Focus Austria: Vom Vielvölkerreich zum EU-Staat; Festschrift für Alfred Ableitinger zum 65. Geburtstag*, ed. Sigfried Beer et al., Schriftenreihe des Instituts für Geschichte 15 (Graz: Selbstverlag des Instituts für Geschichte der Karl-Franzens-Universität Graz, 2003), 383–407.

7. Gernot D. Hasiba, "Inter arma silent leges?" 24–25. Official discussions of the economic emergency legislation, with a compilation of the laws themselves, can be found in *Denkschrift über die von der k. k. Regierung aus Anlass des Krieges getroffenen Massnahmen*, 4 vols. (Vienna: k.k. Hof- und Staatsdruckerei, 1915–1917).

8. For the planning and establishment of the War Surveillance Office (KÜA), see the recent publication Tamara Scheer, *Die Ringstraßenfront: Österreich-Ungarn, das Kriegsüberwachungsamt und der Ausnahmezustand während des Ersten Weltkrieges*, Schriftens des Heeresgeschlichten Museums 15 (Vienna: Republik Österreich, Bundesministerium für Landesverteidigung und Sport—BMLVS, 2010), 12–28.

9. Z. 991/Brief in Z. 8716/M.I. ex 1914, ÖSTA AVA Inneres MdI Präsidium A 1254. A copy of this letter is also in Ludwig Brügel, *Geschichte der österreichischen Sozialdemokratie*, 5 vols. (Vienna: Wiener Volksbuchhandlung, 1922), 5: 209–10. Brügel provides the commentary that the letter shows Stürgkh's brutal use of executive power and disregard for constitutional law; but Stürgkh would also come to regret the way in which the political administration would have submit to military authority.

10. See for instance, a note from the *Militärkommando* in Vienna to the *Statthalter* in Lower Austria, dated August 10, 1914, which points to the "disagreeable delays" in the handling of affairs by the political administration, which apparently had been communicating with the Ministry of the Interior instead of directly with the Ministry of War. This, the letter indicates, has nothing to do with the bureaucracy's tendency to produce "unnecessary office work"—a nice dig at the administration's inefficiency. Z. 6744/ 2929 L K in Z. 2292, in NÖLA *Statthalterei* Präsidium K 175.

11. Martin Moll, "Hochverrat und 'serbophile Umtriebe': Der Kriminalfall Maria-Rast als Beispiel der Verfolgung slowenischer Steirer zu Beginn des Ersten Weltkrieges," *Blätter für Heimatkunde* 74, no. 1–2 (2000): 40. Martin Moll has done much good recent work on arrest, internment, and denunciations involving Slovene speakers during the weeks of mobilization. See also, Martin Moll, "Österreichische Militärgerichtsbarkeit im Ersten Weltkrieg—'Schwert des Regimes'? Überlegungen am Beispiel des Landwehrdivisionsgerichtes Graz im Jahre 1914," *Mitteilungen des Steiermärkischen Landesarchivs* 50 (2001): 301–55.

12. See the numerous reports from the governor in Carinthia Fries-Skene to the Ministry of the Interior, in ÖSTA AVA Inneres MdI Präsidium A 2120.

13. Präsidium Z. 1782/2 in Pr. Nr. 12069 in ÖSTA AVA Inneres MdI Präsidium A 2137.

14. See the letter of September 28, 1914, from Clary-Aldringen to the Ministry of the Interior, Pr. 13255 in ÖSTA AVA Inneres MdI Präsidium A 2137.

15. See Clary-Aldringen's letter of September 22, 1914 (org. Z. 1929/4), in Z. 12754, ÖSTA AVA Inneres MdI Präsidium A 2137.

16. See ÖStA KA MKSM HR, 1914, Z. 69–11/2.

17. For the letter from the k.k. Ministry for Defense and the k.u.k. War Ministry, see ÖStA KA MKSM HR, 1914, Z. 69–11/2.

18. "Von Miramar bis St. Germain," (unpublished manuscript), in ÖStA KA NL Eichhoff, NL 874/B.

19. Ibid.

20. Ibid.

21. Nachlass Eichhoff, in KA, NL 874/B.

22. Letter (July 26, 1914) from Bezirkshauptmann Holluber to k.k. *Statthalterei*, z. 135/ G in NÖLA, Statthalterei Präsidium K. 174.

23. Letter (August 5, 1914), from Alexander Bosizio Ritter von Thurnberg und Jungenegg to *Statthalter* Richard von Biernerth (original Z. 204/3 Res.) in Pr. 2082/ 1914, NÖLA, Statthalterei Präsidium K 174, I/4 a 16.

24. Unnumberd letter (August 5, 1914) from Alexander Bosizio Ritter von Thurnberg und Jegenegg to Präsidialvorstand Grafen Castell, in I/4 a 16, NÖLA, Statthalterei Präsidium, K 174.

25. See the telegram from the AOK/EOK to the k.k. Ministry of the Interior (August 4, 1914), Res. Nr. 105, requesting the names of qualified officials who will be able to serve as administrators in "newly occupied regions" that the army could expect to overrun in the war. The ministry collected names of bureaucrats who could speak Polish, Russian, and Serbo-Croatian. ÖSTA AVA Inneres MdI Präsidium A 1352, Z. 4278.

26. Aspects of the administrative chaos in Galicia and Bukovina in 1914–15 can be found in ÖSTA AVA Inneres MdI Präsidium A 1407 (Galicia) and ÖSTA AVA Inneres MdI Präsidium A 1393 (Bukowina).

27. A fascinating recent working paper in sociology, for instance, cited the lower levels of bureaucratic corruption and greater levels of trust in officials in east European regions once belonging to the Habsburg monarchy. See Sascha O. Becker et al., "The Empire Is Dead, Long Live the Empire! Long-Run Persistence of Trust and Corruption in the Bureaucracy," *Forschungsinstitut zur Zukunft der Arbeit*, no. 5584, Discussion Paper Series (March 2011).

28. The k.u.k. military fought a standing war against Austria and Hungary's politicians for additional military expenditures as Austria-Hungary fell behind the other great powers in military expenditure. By 1912, Austria-Hungary was spending less per citizen than Germany, France, or Italy. See Günther Kronenbitter, *"Krieg im Frieden": Die Führung der k.u.k. Armee und die Grossmachtpolitik Österreich-Ungarns 1906–1914*, Studien zur internationalen Geschichte 13 (Munich: R. Oldenbourg, 2003), 145–49; David Stevenson, *Armaments and the Coming of War: Europe, 1904–1914* (Oxford: Clarendon Press, 1996), 136–40.

29. Hew Strachan, *The First World War*, vol. 1, *To Arms* (New York: Oxford University Press, 2001), 347–57; Manfried Rauchensteiner, *Der Tod des Doppeladlers: Österreich-Ungarn und der Erste Weltkrieg* (Graz: Styria Verlag, 1993), 135–36.

30. Tellingly, there are very few accounts of the fall of the Habsburg monarchy. These events are most often recounted separately in nationally-focused narratives. For instance, Arthur James May, *The Passing of the Hapsburg Monarchy, 1914–1918*, 2 vols. (Philadelphia: University of Pennsylvania Press, 1966), 2: 760–826; Z. A. B. Zeman, *The Break-up of the Habsburg Empire, 1914–1918* (London: Oxford University Press, 1961), 234–45.

# Index

administration and, 155–57; education
and, 23, 34, 57, 123, 241; equality under,
16, 26, 76, 108, 117, 171; First World War
and, 264–65, 267; Franz Stadion and, 66,
68–69, 78, 83–84, 90, 93, 186; Hungarian,
201; imperial vs. provincial, 143–44, 146;
martial, 67, 263; natural, 15, 45; nobility
and, 12, 32, 45, 47, 96, 99; parliament
and, 85, 91, 171, 179–81, 190; Prussian,
201; public, 2, 32–33, 47, 93, 239, 243;
revolutions of 1848 and, 106, 107; rule
of, 5, 16, 84, 170, 181, 192; suffrage, 236,
245, 247; tax, 212. *See also* Basic Laws;
December Constitution; February Patent;
Imperial Municipalities Law; October
Diploma; Provisional Municipalities Law;
Sylvester Patent
Law on the Organization of the Political
Authorities, 172–73
Law on the Establishment of Political
Administrative Offices, 190
Laxenburg Manifesto, 139, 140
Leitha River, 148, 169
Leitomischl, 200
Lemberg, 56, 182, 242
Leopold II (emperor), 19, 30, 45, 60
liberalism, 90, 101, 103, 144, 149–50, 157–59,
173, 179–88
Linz, 10, 117, 122–23
Lisbon, 75
Líšeň/Lösch, 99
Littoral, 66, 130, 250
"living" constitution, 177–78, 179–80, 196,
198, 202, 212
loans, 31, 137–40, 143, 147, 186, 228, 230
*Lokalität*, 201
Lombardy, 32, 50, 130, 134, 137
Lombardy-Venetia, 37, 72, 88, 94
London, 75, 77, 178, 274
Lorraine, 1
Lower Austria, 47, 51, 118, 130, 150, 158,
161–63, 213, 219–20, 269, 271. *See also*
Upper Austria

Macartney, C. A., 104
Mally, Carl, 129–30
March Constitution (of Stadion), 65, 68–69,

81, 83–96, 100, 101–2, 103–6, 109–11, 115,
138, 149, 154–55
Maria Theresia: Anton Wenzel Kaunitz
and, 14–15, 40, 44; cameralism and, 22;
county offices and, 13–14, 48–49, 82, 85,
99, 163; Francis Joseph and, 1–2, 137;
Friedrich Wilhelm von Haugwitz and,
12–15, 21, 82, 92, 206; Joseph II and,
10–11, 15–16, 21–23, 26, 28–29, 31, 40–41,
45–46, 48–49, 62, 99, 143, 172, 182, 191,
207, 273–74; nobility and, 45–46, 57, 99,
191; provincial diets and, 45, 157; reign
of, 9–17; Theresianum, 23, 232; War of
Austrian Succession and, 9–12
mass politics, 216, 217–23, 226, 238
Maximilian I (emperor), 213
Mayr, Josef Karl, 52
Mayrhofer, Ernst, 201
Megner, Karl, 165
Merveldt, Franz, 254–55
Metternich, Klemens von, 30, 32, 37, 39–40,
45, 66–68, 70–72, 133, 206
Mies/Stříbro, 207
Milan, 37, 67
Ministerial Commission, 112
Ministerial Conference, 140, 145, 148–49,
151, 154. *See also* Council of Ministers
(*Ministerrat*)
Ministerial Council. *See* Council of Ministers
(*Ministerrat*)
ministerial responsibility, 72, 79, 104, 148, 172
ministerial system, 72, 77, 79, 107
Ministry of Agriculture, 43, 233
Ministry of Education and Religious Affairs,
71, 103
Ministry of Finance, 66, 71, 101, 133, 140, 143,
145, 198, 200, 208, 211, 218–19, 233, 254,
261–63
Ministry of Foreign Affairs, 14, 66, 71, 102,
125, 167, 169, 181, 238
Ministry of Home Defense, 267
Ministry of the Interior: Alexander von Bach
and, 95, 99, 107, 109, 113, 115–16, 118,
150; bureaucrats and, 121, 124–25, 160,
162–65, 175–77, 185, 198–201, 203, 205,
210–11, 232; Carl Giskra and, 172, 181;
Ernest von Koerber and, 232–33, 240–41,